I've Got to Make My Livin'

HISTORICAL STUDIES OF URBAN AMERICA

Edited by Timothy J. Gilfoyle, James R. Grossman, and Becky M. Nicolaides

I've Got to Make My Livin'

Black Women's Sex Work in
Turn-of-the-Century Chicago

CYNTHIA M. BLAIR

The University of Chicago Press   Chicago and London

The University of Chicago Press, Chicago 60637
The University of Chicago Press, Ltd., London
Published 2010
Paperback edition 2018

27 26 25 24 23 22 21 20 19 18   1 2 3 4 5

ISBN-13: 978-0-226-05598-5 (cloth)
ISBN-13: 978-0-226-59758-4 (paper)
ISBN-13: 978-0-226-05600-5 (e-book)
DOI: https://doi.org/10.7208/chicago/9780226056005.001.0001

Library of Congress Cataloging-in-Publication Data
Blair, Cynthia M.
  I've got to make my livin': black women's sex work in turn-of-the-
century Chicago / Cynthia M. Blair.
     p. cm. — (Historical studies of urban America)
  Includes bibliographical references and index.
  ISBN-13: 978-0-226-05598-5 (cloth: alk. paper)
  ISBN-10: 0-226-05598-1 (cloth: alk. paper) 1. Prostitution—
Illinois—Chicago—History. 2. African American women—Sexual
behavior—Illinois—Chicago. I. Title. II. Series: Historical studies
of urban America.
  HQ146.C4B53 2010
  306.74'209773'1109041—dc22   2009050080

Contents

Illustrations and Tables

Figures

Maps

Tables

Acknowledgments

This book has accompanied me through many stages of my life. I am so very glad to let it go off on its own and to acknowledge the many people whose intellectual, emotional, financial, and myriad other forms of support have made this journey possible and rewarding. As a young student charting my own intellectual course in the Graduate Program in the History of American Civilization at Harvard University, I received encouragement and support from several people. The late Nathan Huggins taught a clueless graduate student how to think like a historian. The early and enthusiastic guidance of Patricia Yaeger and Werner Sollors helped me to feel comfortable with my own curiosity and prodded me to take intellectual risks. Allan Brandt provided illuminating readings of my dissertation chapters. Evelyn Brooks Higginbotham, my dissertation adviser, helped me in numerous ways. Though we never lived in the same city, I was always aware of her support for my work and her belief in the importance of the project. Her exacting readings of the dissertation and her later engagement with various parts of the manuscript have made the book a stronger piece of historical writing. I am indebted to her for her exemplary scholarship and her generous spirit.

I could not have written this book without the support of several institutions. Harvard University provided research support at the early stages of the project. The Smithsonian Institution Graduate Student and Predoctoral Fellowships at the National Museum of American History and the Carter G. Woodson Predoctoral Fellowship at the University of Virginia gave me the freedom to fully pursue my research and gave me the gift of an expanded and sustaining intellectual community. The Ford Foundation Dissertation Fellowship afforded me the time to write the dissertation. At the University of Illinois at Chicago, the Institute for Research on Race and Public Policy and the Great Cities Institute gave me much needed time away from teaching to rethink and rework the dissertation. Both institutes introduced me to an exciting and deeply engaged community of scholars at my new academic home.

Many research librarians and archivists offered invaluable guidance, and their enthusiasm for the project led me to new sources, new questions, and new energy. Special thanks to the staffs at the National Archives and Records Administration, the Chicago Historical Society (now the Chicago History Museum), University of Illinois at Chicago Special Collections, and the Circuit Court of Cook County Archives. The extensive knowledge and enthusiastic guidance of the late Archie Motley of the Chicago Historical Society proved crucial at the outset of my research. At the Carter G. Woodson Regional Library, Michael Flug provided a novice researcher with important leads at the early stages.

Many people generously gave of their time and read chapters along the way. At pivotal points their warm encouragement and demanding comments expanded my understanding of my own work: Eric Arnesen, Michelle Boyd, John D'Emilio, Lewis Erenberg, Tyrone Forman, Laurie Green, Leslie Harris, Darlene Clark Hine, Jerma Jackson, Amanda Lewis, Bryant Marks, Alexis McCrossen, Deborah McDowell, Barbara Ransby, Beth Richie, the late Armstead Robinson, Hannah Rosen, Daryl Michael Scott, and Peg Strobel. I especially would like to acknowledge the members of the writing group MFTW. I am deeply indebted to our weekly strategy sessions. The creative advice and gentle strong-arming of Michelle Boyd, Helen Jun, Amanda Lewis, Kerry Ann Rockquemore, and David Stovall propelled me forward and over the hump. I would also like to thank the Department of African American Studies and the Department of History at the University of Illinois at Chicago for their flexibility as I completed this project. In particular, I would like to thank Lansiné Kaba and Beth Richie in African American Studies. Mildred McGinnis deserves especially warm thanks for her thoughtfulness and her perpetual optimism. I am also grateful for the diligent work of my research assistants at UIC: Gareth Canaan, Nyshana Summers, and Theresa Pfister.

The insights and support of many people at the University of Chicago Press have contributed immeasurably to this book. Jim Grossman and Tim Gilfoyle provided enthusiastic support from the beginning, and their guidance has been invaluable. I thank them, as well as the anonymous readers for the press, for their exhaustive readings of the manuscript and for their deep engagement with my ideas. Robert Devens has been a wonderful editor. His understanding of the project and his patience have made the path to publication almost smooth— almost. Pamela Bruton's skillful copyediting has strengthened the book in innumerable ways.

Writing is an act of faith, and without my friends and family providing perspective and cheering me on toward the unseen, I would not have been able to complete this book. The sheer force of Robin Magee's belief in me and in the importance of this book kept me focused. Regular check-ins with Jackie Scott and her unwavering insistence that I had every right to complain, complain, complain put me back on course at pivotal moments. Through her gentle pushing and pulling and through her engagement with my at-times murky ideas, Hannah Rosen provided emotional and intellectual sustenance. These women nurtured me and my book through days of deep doubt, and for their friendship I am eternally grateful. Over the years the expansive generosity and caring of Joan Davis, Anita Breitung, and Arnold Breitung reminded me that I have places of retreat in Miller, Indiana, and Aurora, Illinois. Gosia Halota (my daughter's *ciocia*) has blessed my family with her energy, creativity, and love and made it possible for this working mother of a small toddler to rest easy while away from home. Two loved ones passed while I was writing this book. My aunt Esme McKreith was and remains a vigorous supporter, and even if she would shrug her shoulders at the topic of this book, she would love that I wrote it. And my dear friend Pam Watkins continues to provide an example of living faith to the fullest. I hope I can write in the spirit of faith that made her such a vibrant fount of energy and example of grace.

My parents, Gloria and Cecil Blair, have given me much more than I can acknowledge here. I am humbled by your love and fortified by your trust in my instincts. Barry Breitung, my husband and friend, has been with me since the beginning of this project. Your gentle pushing, irreverent humor, and constant companionship have contributed to this book in ways I cannot begin to calculate. I thank you for your love and your at times maddening certainty that the end was just around the corner. And then there is Ava. You are a gift whose beauty and wacky brilliance remind me daily why I write.

"A Class We Have Barely Mentioned"

Vina Fields was a brothel madam whose career in prostitution in Chicago began in the late 1870s and ended in the second decade of the twentieth century. For more than thirty years, Fields ran a succession of brothels that specialized in the sale of black women's sexual services. Through this trade—which, for most of her career, catered to white men only—Fields became one of the most prosperous and best-known brothel madams in Chicago at the turn of the century and one of Chicago's wealthiest African Americans. A 1929 survey of black Chicago's "educational, athletic, civic, and commercial life from 1779 to 1929" described Fields as "a character of the red light district" who had "much wealth in [her] coffers" when she died. Set against the backdrop of the prosperous and respectable men also featured in this survey—restaurant owners, lawyers, caterers, doctors, hotel owners—hers was a curious, if telling, example of black women's economic success.[1]

In 1926 blues singer Bertha "Chippie" Hill recorded "Street Walker Blues" in Chicago. One of many prostitution-themed blues songs recorded from the 1920s through the 1940s, "Street Walker Blues" bluntly depicts the desperate circumstances that drove women to sell sex on the streets:

Got the street walker blues,
Wanna walk the streets all night.
Got the street walker blues,
Walk the streets all night and day.

I'm gonna walk I mean walk,
I'm gonna walk these blues away.

Stood on the corner 'til my feets are soakin' wet.
Stood on the corner 'til my feets are soakin' wet.
Singing the street walker blues to each and everyone I met.

If you ain't got a dollar give me just one lousy dime.
If you ain't got a dollar give me just one lousy dime.
'Cause the landlord's singing the blues because my rent's behind.

Got the streetwalkin' blues,
Ain't gon' walk the streets no more.
Got the streetwalkin' blues,
Ain't gon' walk the streets no more.
'Cause the cops is getting bad and the dough it comes and goes.

Through this frank and harsh portrayal, Chippie Hill offered public recognition of the women whom she saw working on the streets of
the Black Belt in the 1920s.[2] Hill's streetwalker speaks of a vastly different experience within prostitution from that of Vina Fields: the round-
the-clock search for trade, exposure to the elements, incessant police
harassment, and grinding poverty. Hill's streetwalker was no symbol
of individual achievement or racial progress, and unlike Madam Vina
Fields, this nameless streetwalker did not prosper from her sexual labors. Instead, in her struggle with the street, this prostitute represents
the brutal economic realities that countless black women faced in the
early-twentieth-century city.[3]

These contrasting images of madam and streetwalker reflect the different financial positions occupied by a brothel owner and an individual sex worker. Yet this comparison also illuminates the ways that the
experiences of black women working in the sex industry of the 1880s
and 1890s diverged from the prospects of those laboring in the 1920s
trade. Sexual commerce underwent a profound shift between 1870 and
1930: from a late-nineteenth-century economy in which the majority of
black prostitutes worked in brothels located in racially diverse—though
frequently racially divided—sex districts to a trade in which most struggled to earn "just one lousy dime" on the streets, in the apartments,
and in the nightclubs of Chicago's Black Belt neighborhood. African
American migration from the South to northern cities, the increasingly
rigid residential segregation of African Americans, repeated shifts in

2

the location of urban red-light districts, and the growth of commercialized leisure industries together reconfigured the geographical, racial, and economic landscape of black women's sex work. At the same time, these transformations shaped the meanings that both black and white Chicagoans ascribed to black sex work and the women who labored in the sex economy.

In *I've Got to Make My Livin'*, I examine African American women's sex work in Chicago between 1870 and 1930. Black prostitutes actively participated in the transformations that shaped the racial and sexual landscape in cities like Chicago in this period. By establishing and working in the institutions that constituted the city's constantly changing sex economy, these public women both illuminated and transgressed emerging moral, sexual, social, and spatial divides that shaped turn-of-the-century racial politics in Chicago. Black prostitutes working in the city's red-light districts regularly breached the divide that white Chicagoans were in the process of erecting to delimit interracial social and sexual contact. Black sex workers also resisted the exhortations by leaders within the emerging African American community to conform to expectations of public propriety and sexual purity. As they publicly labored to earn money in the sex industry, black sex workers challenged the discourse of respectability, implicitly questioning its relevance to their experiences in Chicago's industrial economy. Furthermore, as they conducted their work, they boldly traversed spatial borders that white and black Chicagoans hoped would protect the "moral geography" of the city.

Prostitution was, and remains, a deeply symbolic issue. Therefore, I examine the struggles that emerged among and between white and black urbanites in response to black women's increasing visibility in the city's sex economy. African American sex workers elicited a complex array of responses from respectable and disreputable urbanites, black and white, that reveal the centrality of race to both widespread ideals of sexual morality and emerging practices of sexual modernity. Indeed, black prostitutes negotiated their economic lives on the shifting terrain of turn-of-the-century sexual ideologies.

Yet the prostitute was much more than a contested symbol; she was a worker.[4] For some black women arriving in the city during this period, sex work was a strategy for economic survival. Thus, this book is equally about black women's attempts to negotiate both independence and a form of self-respect in an urban economy and social environment inhospitable to the financial and social aspirations of urbanizing black women.[5] Black sex workers emerge as conscious actors and historical agents—victims in some cases but very often savvy strategists who daily navigated the economic, racial, and spatial terrain that defined turn-of-the-century sex work. In addition to traversing the moral and spatial barriers erected by respectable black and white Chicagoans, black prostitutes transformed each sexual exchange into a stepping-stone toward their own financial independence.

African American prostitutes were a subset of the black women who struggled to make their way in cities and towns after emancipation and in the early decades of the twentieth century. Though the majority of working black women toiled as servants in the homes of white middle- and upper-class families and in downtown restaurants, office buildings, and hotels, black sex workers labored in the red-light districts that sequestered sexual "vice" away from dignified commerce and respectable residential districts. In southern cities like New Orleans, Richmond, and Atlanta, in old cities of the Northeast such as New York and Philadelphia, and in growing midwestern towns like Detroit, Cleveland, and Chicago, black women in increasing numbers took part in a burgeoning and, for some of them, profitable illicit economy.[6] Though separated by region, these women shared many experiences. Most earned their money through onerous and at times demeaning sexual labor and worked in areas of the city left by city officials to decay and wither as urban development bypassed their haunts. All labored in a society that assumed black women's immorality, scoffed at their aspirations, and mocked their straightforward desire for economic independence. Like other working-class black women, they toiled in a society that held only contempt for the poor, urbanizing African American women who strained in myriad ways to give substance to their freedom.

Most of the women whose hopeful journey to economic independence led them to engage in prostitution in cities and towns across the country were nameless members of an urban underworld. The outlines of the world that black prostitutes inhabited remain largely hidden to us today. Their daily paths are difficult to retrace. And although some particulars of their work environments can be reconstructed, it is a challenge for even the most tenacious and creative investigator to capture the texture of their day-to-day lives as workers, as sexual commodities, and as members of an urban subculture. The elusive nature of these historical subjects highlights the profound social and economic marginality of black prostitutes in turn-of-the-century cities. Yet writing about this group of working women has not been an exercise in futility. Vital traces of their lives and the cultural and economic reverberations of their activities survive in a rich array of sources. Reconstructing the lives and labors of these most marginal of marginal women brings to light their significance in the changing cities in which they dwelled and the sexual subcultures and black communities to which they belonged. As this study shows, African American women prostitutes were an integral part of the story of black urbanization and modernizing sexuality in the North at the turn of the twentieth century.

Chicago is a fitting setting for studying African American women's sex work. Auspiciously located on Lake Michigan and at the mouth of the Chicago River, in the late nineteenth century Chicago grew to be a leader in the manufacturing, trading, and transporting of grain, lumber, steel, and meat in the region and, eventually, throughout the nation. Chicago's precipitous rise to become one of the nation's industrial and commercial centers stimulated phenomenal population growth: between 1870 and 1930 the city grew from 300,000 to 3,400,000. African Americans arrived in Chicago drawn by the promise of prosperity that lured so many others in the decades following the Great Fire of 1871. But they also migrated to Chicago because it promised refuge from the economic stagnation and severe social limitations of rural and small-town life in the South and the Midwest. In 1870, 3,700 blacks lived in the city; by 1930, blacks numbered 234,000. These profound demographic shifts make Chicago an optimal location to examine the convergence of the economic, social, and cultural changes that were transforming city spaces and urban racial and sexual relations at the turn of the century. In addition, for many invested in its future prosperity and expansion, Chicago was a city that had deep symbolic significance. Celebrated nationally and internationally, Chicago pointed the way to America's future—industrially, technologically, and as an example of modern urban living. The experiences of black women working in Chicago's sex marketplace illuminate the contradictions at the heart of the modern urban economy and the racial and sexual anxieties wrought by the modernity that boosters so enthusiastically embraced. This study of African American sex work in Chicago offers a unique vantage point for examining the intersection of industrial expansion, urban development, African American migration, racial segregation, and sexual modernization.

Chicago is an important city for the study of black women's prostitution not only because of its prominence in the national economy and the history of the growth of its black community but equally because of its place in the history of urban prostitution and anti-prostitution reform. Between 1870 and 1912 Chicago boasted two well-known sex districts on the South Side, each in succession bearing the name "the Levee." While smaller sex districts existed on the North and Near West

Sides, the conditions on the South Side—flagrant, entrenched, and seemingly expanding—unsettled the nerves of anti-vice reformers in the city and beyond. Indeed, in the early twentieth century, Chicago was at the forefront of an increasingly frenzied national debate about the spread of the "social evil." What happened in Chicago was pivotal to the national social purity campaign to end "white slavery" and to close down red-light districts across the country.[7] The Vice Commission of Chicago's 1911 publication *The Social Evil in Chicago*—a lengthy social scientific investigation of the causes, nature, and extent of prostitution in the city—spurred other cities across the country to undertake their own investigations.[8] And the closing of the Levee in 1912 secured the city's prominence in the national crusade against prostitution.

Yet, as important as the activities of Progressive Era reformers were to the transformation of the early-twentieth-century sex trade, an exploration of black women's prostitution should not be limited to a focus on reformers. Concentrating on the decades between 1870 and 1930, this study looks beyond Progressive reform and the temporal boundaries frequently used to frame studies of prostitution in turn-of-the-century America.[9] Rather than charting the rise and fall of Progressive anti-vice zeal, this study links the story of urban prostitution to the formation of the Black Belt and the sexualization and policing of racial boundaries in the city. These processes both predated and outlived Progressive reformers' preoccupation with urban prostitution. This book, then, deliberately shifts the attention away from an exclusive focus on white reformers and the red-light district. Not only do black prostitutes become visible by shifting the focus in this way, but it becomes clear that the growth of sexual commerce within the Black Belt and the ensuing anti-prostitution struggles waged within Chicago's black community are a central part of the story of urban prostitution.

Silences

The figure of the black prostitute has long been an important symbol in ongoing battles over black women's sexuality and the place of African Americans in modernizing American society. In the late nineteenth century, the prostitute image was so powerful that it served as a call to arms among middle-class black women. In 1896, in an inflammatory (and infamous) letter, the white president of the Missouri Press Association described all black women as prostitutes.[10] African American women across the country joined forces in a concerted response to this slander and established the National Association of Colored Women's Clubs. Although the image of the black prostitute sparked organized activity among middle-class women, it rarely fostered organized activity on behalf of the women who, for various reasons, actually resorted to sex work. Though the equation of black womanhood with prostitution could generate defensive activity on behalf of respectable black women, black prostitutes themselves remained in the shadows of public discourse.

In *The Philadelphia Negro* W. E. B. DuBois acknowledged his own silence on the subject of black prostitutes. In this monumental 1899 investigation into the causes of black social marginality in Philadelphia, DuBois described four classes, or "grades," of black residents living in the city's Seventh Ward. In descending order DuBois lists the respectable middle-class, the respectable working-class, and the honest poor. Among the lowest class, a group he refers to as "the submerged tenth," DuBois includes criminals, the shiftless poor, and prostitutes. Of the latter he writes that although they make up "one large element of these slums," prostitutes are "a class we have barely mentioned."[11] Referring to his own oversight, DuBois's words reflect the difficulty that many blacks had at the turn of the century in publicly acknowledging the existence among them of women who exchanged their sexual services for financial gain.

These silences about black prostitution pervaded turn-of-the-century discussions among middle-class blacks about African American migration to cities, the virtues and trials of black womanhood, and the centrality of sexual propriety to racial uplift. More generally, as Evelyn Brooks Higginbotham, Deborah Gray White, and others have shown, silence on issues of sexuality was a strategic component of early-twentieth-century discourses of racial advancement. Silence was central to the politics of respectability through which black women refuted charges of their sexual impropriety and moral laxity and through which urbanizing blacks asserted their claim to political and economic equality in the nation's cities.[12] Yet this strategic silence stymied frank discussion of sexual matters in the black community.[13] Because of this politics of respectability, most urbanizing blacks were reluctant to talk straightforwardly about the prostitutes—the fallen women and girls—in their midst. Turn-of-the-century discourses of black uplift pivoted as much on the unuttered and unutterable as on explicitly stated ideals.

Silence has also shaped our own inquiries into the past experiences of African American men and women. Until recently, black prostitution has rarely been the subject of sustained historical examination. While seminal studies by Ruth Rosen, Christine Stansell, Kathy Peiss, and Timothy Gilfoyle have elaborated the complex connections between working women's lives, emerging patterns of urban sexuality, and the "commercialization of sex," they have given only passing attention to African American women's participation in the turn-of-the-century urban sex trade. The insufficient treatment of black women's experiences in histories of the sex trade has been shaped in part by the limited sources that historians have used to explore prostitution in turn-of-the-century cities. Pathbreaking studies such as Rosen's *Lost Sisterhood* have inventively used white anti-vice reform treatises and investigations, the surveys of early social scientists, and journalistic accounts of the "social evil" to explore the social and economic landscape of this socially proscribed economic endeavor.[14] Historians have also used these sources to examine the symbolic role that prostitution played in the ideological struggles over urban sexuality that riveted white civic leaders and social reformers.[15] Although these sources have allowed historians to piece together both the experiences of white native-born and immigrant women in the sex trade and the changing responses of white middle-class urbanites to white women's sex work, they are frequently silent on the subject of black women working in the trade.

Furthermore, the explanatory narratives of prostitution that emerge from turn-of-the-century accounts of prostitution—in particular beliefs about the vulnerability of innocent white women and girls in the city—have averted the gaze of historians from the varied roles that black women played in urban sex economies. The omission of black women sex workers has not only led to the analytical neglect of the peculiar experiences of African American women (who, in many cities, made up a sizable proportion of prostitutes) but also contributed to a lack of attention to the complex role that race played in shaping the turn-of-the-century urban sex economy.

This study simultaneously builds upon the conceptual groundwork laid by Gilfoyle, Rosen, and Stansell and addresses the virtual invisibility of race within these and other historical studies of prostitution's history in America. In doing so, I extend the analysis of Kevin Mumford, whose study of "interzones," or interracial sex zones, reveals the importance of race not only to prostitution economies but to urban sexual cultures at the turn of the century. Yet even this important study fails to place black prostitutes at the center of their own story, overlooking the ways that they used sex work to maneuver through New York City's and Chicago's sex economies. Furthermore, in focusing exclusively on interracial sexual exchange, Mumford narrows the geographical, social, cultural, and economic scope of black women's prostitution and ignores the complexity of the spatial and commercial dimensions of the urban sex economy. A fuller examination of race's role in defining the economic, social, and cultural contours of turn-of-the-century prostitution can be accomplished only by bringing into view the full range of black women's sex work. Therefore, when sources permit, I examine the geography and commercialization of both interracial and intraracial sexual exchanges.[16]

I also examine the multiple responses that black prostitutes generated among black and white urbanites. Progressive reformers have appeared as privileged subjects in studies of urban prostitution, and they appear in this book as well. Yet they were not the only city dwellers who interpreted black women's bodies in the sex trade. Migrating black men and women exhibited an array of reactions to black prostitutes as well. The politics of black women's sex work can be understood only when their voices are incorporated into the story. In addressing this silence, I draw on Hazel Carby's examination of middle-class reaction to prostitution and black women's bodies in cities.[17] I also draw on the work of Judith Walkowitz and Gail Hershatter, whose influential studies of prostitution in late-nineteenth-century London and early-twentieth-century Shanghai, respectively, reconstruct the evolving layers of meaning that a diverse assortment of urbanites attached to women's sex work in modernizing cities. During the era of migration, black women's bodies elicited a range of responses that revealed their centrality to evolving struggles over race and sexuality in the modernizing city.[18]

The neglect of prostitution within the field of African American women's history is somewhat more complicated. Two central projects have guided the writing of black women's history in the past thirty years: unmasking the intersecting structures of power—gender, racial, class, political, economic, and sexual—that have limited black women's lives and reclaiming black women's struggles against these intersecting oppressions. Toward this end, many historians have focused on the strategies employed by working- and middle-class black women who, against so many odds, acted on their own behalf. As workers, as family members, as activists and community leaders, African American women have struggled nobly to define their own place within their communities and within American society. Prostitution does not easily fit into this framework. The subject of prostitution appears to offer few opportunities for chronicling black women's agency or for tracing their economic, political, and cultural activities "in defense of themselves."[19] In fact, rather than providing evidence of black women's ability to withstand and perhaps transform the context of their multiple oppressions, sex work would seem to signify black women's utter defeat.

Along these lines, some writers have suggested that, conceptually, black women's involvement in the sex economy was a post-emancipation continuation of the sexual exploitation that their ancestors endured during slavery.[20] Works by such historians as Deborah Gray White and Darlene Clark Hine reveal not only how painful experiences of physical violation were to individual black women at the turn of the century but also how deeply embedded such experiences were, and continue to be, in African American historical memory. These works show that any discussion of black women's sexuality must take into account both the communal memory of sexual abuse and the continuing centrality of acts of sexual violation to the structure of racial inequality well into the twentieth century. However, while this framework helps us to see continuities in black women's sexual exploitation, it does not adequately account for black women's understanding of their own participation in Chicago's turn-of-the-century sex economy. Exactly how the weight of historical memory shaped black prostitutes' interpretation of their work is difficult to determine. But this historical memory did have a powerful impact on the ways that black community leaders fought against the sex trade in Chicago's growing South Side Black Belt.[21]

Bolstering the representation of black prostitutes as total victims, others have argued that black prostitutes were psychologically or physically coerced into prostitution by male exploiters, usually black male pimps.[22] In this scenario, men's often violent control of black women's bodies and finances explains black women's turn to prostitution. The psychological and physical brutalities that often define the pimp-prostitute relationship have been well documented and provide disturbing testimony to black women's continued economic vulnerability in the nation's cities throughout the twentieth century.[23] However, although nineteenth-century commentaries on prostitution often noted the presence of pimps, men's control of women's work pace, earnings, and bodies did not emerge as an endemic feature of urban prostitution until after 1920.[24]

Underlying each of these perspectives is a reluctance to view prostitution as anything other than a forced choice for black women. However, not all historians have viewed it as such. Some have argued that, rather than being purely victims, black women involved in the sex trade exhibited a willingness to challenge middle-class notions of sexual and economic respectability and claim their bodies as sites for both pleasure and profit. In her study of working-class women in post-emancipation

Atlanta, Tera Hunter situates black prostitutes within a burgeoning leisure economy. As participants in Atlanta's leisure industry, black prostitutes were among the women who "helped to reconfigure gender conventions in public amusements" in late-nineteenth-century Atlanta. In her study of black women in Detroit, Victoria Wolcott takes this approach one step further, finding in prostitution a means by which black women not only participated in new leisure culture but, as "leisure workers," promoted definitions of working-class respectability that were in stark opposition to middle-class ideas of respectability.[25]

I situate black women prostitutes in leisure culture, but I find the concept of "leisure worker" too removed from the economic and social tensions that surrounded black women's sex work. Moreover, the term masks the fact that women provided men with leisure through their *sexual* labor. This work was qualitatively different from the work performed by others in the leisure economy, such as waitresses, blues singers, dancers, and stage performers. And although money earned from prostitution permitted women's access to new leisure pursuits, they were on the job in search of their next dollar when they worked in Chicago's saloons, nightclubs, or after-hours clubs. Similarly, although I agree that black prostitutes did assert new ideas about economic respectability for women, this mode of defining respectability did not necessarily mean that black prostitutes did not also encounter and perhaps even share more traditional ideas about working-class respectability. As Hunter and Wolcott suggest, engaging in prostitution may have been inherently a rejection of middle-class sexual norms, but black prostitutes rarely transcended working-class sexual mores. Even as black prostitutes carved out new cultural territory within the leisure economy and offered up new definitions of respectability, they were neither totally isolated from the values of the families out of which they sprang nor entirely removed from the nearby black community to which many had some familial or social connection.

Rather than asserting that African American prostitutes at the turn of the century embarked on new cultural explorations in the morally unfettered space of commercialized leisure, and rather than asserting that prostitution provided a form of respectability detached from the challenges to that respectability that women daily faced in the course of their work, I demonstrate that black women's sex work was a constant negotiation of working-class notions of respectability, individual self-respect, and economic self-reliance. This negotiation was inseparable from the ongoing struggles over the meaning of prostitution taking place in American cities and within urbanizing black communities. Furthermore, black women's efforts to claim self-reliance through sexual labor were inseparable from *other* urbanites' struggles over the meaning and, indeed, the valuation of black women's bodies in the modern city. These struggles took place within emerging black neighborhoods, between black community leaders and white city officials, and, of greatest consequence for black prostitutes, within the sex economy itself.

I do not approach sex work as an arena of black women's total sexual exploitation; nor do I look at it as evidence of their resistance to middle-class sexual and economic norms. Prostitution was an odd and uneven blend of these, offering black women opportunities to avoid strictures of family and community at the same time that it allowed some to meet family obligations and individual goals. Prostitution also exposed women to sexual abuse, violence, venereal disease, and social disapprobation. Black women's prostitution embodied the tensions in turn-of-the-century society—tensions between sexual pleasure and sexual danger, between emerging women's freedoms and persistent gender exploitation, and between economic and social opportunities in the city and the failure of the modernizing urban economy to fully incorporate black men and women.

Voices

The voices of African American prostitutes are difficult to recover from available sources. The dearth of voices presents problems for the historian striving to bring to light the motivations and record the reflections of black prostitutes. Few profiles exist of individual black women who worked in the trade. In only a few cases am I able to present anything resembling a biography of a prostitute or madam. Yet if their voices are lost to us, their activities are abundantly evident in extant sources. To retrieve black women's lives in prostitution, I have used black and white newspapers, black church records, the federal manuscript censuses, city guidebooks, city directories, police reports, municipal court records, papers of reform organizations, Sanborn Fire Insurance Maps, and the accounts of early-twentieth-century jazz and blues performers. Through this rich array of sources, I have been able to identify many women who worked in Chicago's sex trade between 1880 and 1930, and I have re-created the ways that black prostitutes participated in the economic, institutional, and geographical shifts that transformed the trade over these years.[26]

White Chicagoans generated many of the sources used here. In part to track the outlines of black women's movement in the economy, I have consulted documents that have been used in most studies of turn-of-the-century prostitution. Yet these sources reveal even more about the racial context in which black and white prostitutes conducted their trade. White journalists, reformers, and travel writers may have noted the presence of African American women within the city's red-light districts, but they never rendered in-depth investigations into the experiences of black prostitutes. An overarching concern with the safety of white women guided their attention to black prostitutes and the places where these women worked. Yet how and when white observers focused their various gazes on "fallen" black women constitute an important part of the story of black women's sex work and reveal white city leaders' mounting concern about Chicago's growing African American population, as well as their fears about the collapse of racial boundaries. How white Chicagoans saw black prostitutes and how they acted upon their fears of racial disorder were pivotal to the changing contexts of all women's sex work in the city.

The figure of the black prostitute shaped public debates among urbanizing African Americans at the turn of the century and was equally important in establishing the landscape of black women's sex work. As members of a small but growing community, middle-class black men and women employed silence as a political strategy as they daily faced challenges to their citizenship. Nevertheless, emerging middle-class discourses about black respectability indicated an awareness of the all-too-visible activities of African American prostitutes in their midst. These discourses also revealed African Americans' awareness of their inability to combat an increasingly rigid system of racial segregation that interlocked the fates of the respectable middle and working class and the "submerged tenth." Public reticence, however, was not the only strategy that respectable blacks used to distance themselves from black sex workers. Through daily navigation of contested neighborhood territory, many black Chicagoans forged maps of respectability, crisscrossing pathways that connected home life, churches, community institutions, and "proper" leisure activities. Tracing these maps reveals the deliberate ways that they combated charges of immorality and racial inferiority. In this book, working- and middle-class African Americans are important actors in the drama of turn-of-the-century prostitution.

The drama of prostitution that unfolds in the following pages is quite different from the story typically told about turn-of-the-century sex work. Exploring the ways that black women used the sex trade and the ways that they contended with their sexual commodification reveals that race defined the economic and institutional ordering of the urban sex trade. The responses of black and white Chicagoans to black women's sex work were maneuvers within an escalating struggle in which city leaders worked to assert social and racial order and African Americans fought to claim their right to equality and respect in the modernizing city. Through an analysis of prostitution, this book highlights the ways that, in the period of urbanization before and during the Great Migration, sexuality was a racial battleground—as it was during slavery and in the post-emancipation South.[27]

This book begins with a demographic analysis of African American women who worked in Chicago's late-nineteenth-century sex economy. Between 1870 and 1900, black women were disproportionately represented among Chicago's sex workers. Chapter 1 plots women's paths to Chicago's sex industry. Peripheral to an industrial economy structured by race and gender and restricted to low-paying domestic employment, black working women frequently looked beyond wage work to make ends meet. The sex economy was one of the largest sectors (and perhaps the most visible) of the illicit urban informal economy. However, unlike the formal economy and illicit underground activities like gambling, prostitution offered a steady stream of jobs to young urbanizing black women. This chapter demonstrates that the sex economy occupied a place along a continuum of informal pursuits to which black men and women turned in the late-nineteenth-century city.

Chapter 2 delineates the racial structure of the late-nineteenth-century sex economy. As in the wage economy, from which many women sought refuge, dominant racial ideas influenced the organization of the sex trade. Black women sold their sexual services in a variety of institutions within the Levee, the late-nineteenth-century sex district that thrived from roughly 1880 to 1904. This chapter portrays black women sex workers as active participants in the life of the Levee and explores their often creative efforts to circumvent the limits on their earnings posed by the racial structure of the sex economy and by the meager earnings of their largely working-class clientele.

Chapter 3 argues that as Chicago's black population grew between 1870 and 1900, the visibility of African American prostitutes generated complex reactions among uneasy white residents and respectable urbanizing blacks. Many whites linked the image of the black prostitute to a general discomfort with the increasing number of African Americans settling in the city. The black prostitute body, whether lurking in dark recesses of the Levee or boldly moving about its streets, embodied the potential collapse of racial boundaries in and beyond the sex trade.

For African Americans, black women's involvement in the sex market-place also engendered fears of miscegenation. But for African American leaders in particular, the image of the black prostitute and the specter of racial intermixture were ultimately tied to their concerns about the race's prospects for economic opportunity, political equality, and social freedom in the industrial city. This chapter highlights the ways that working- and middle-class African Americans strove to imprint a moral geography on black city spaces. Black prostitutes struggling to stand their own ground within the sex economy repeatedly frustrated these efforts.

Chapter 4 examines the pivotal role that race played in the forma-tion and eventual demise of the early-twentieth-century sex district, the Twenty-Second Street Levee. Although this second South Side red-light district had been forming as early as the 1880s, it became significant only after 1900. The new Levee was a vibrant leisure district located south of its predecessor and bordering the growing Black Belt. However, unlike in the old Levee, where black brothel keepers and street workers were very much a part of the sex marketplace, by 1910 white male lei-sure entrepreneurs, with the help of city officials, had all but excluded black women and men from the business of selling and buying sex in this new district. This chapter charts the expulsion of black sex entre-preneurs and their clients from the economic and social landscape of the municipally tolerated red-light district. On the eve of the Great Mi-gration, the consequences of these shifts in the sex economy were vis-ible: the criminalization of black prostitutes and the relocation of black sex institutions into nearby black neighborhoods.

Chapter 5 explores the geographical and institutional transformation of black women's work in the sex economy after the turn of the century. Two intertwined developments contributed to this transformation: the expansion of the urban leisure economy within Chicago's Black Belt and the rise of black male leisure entrepreneurs. By 1900 a vibrant lei-sure economy was expanding to meet the needs of Chicago's growing black community. A new class of black male entrepreneurs eagerly took advantage of opportunities to sell black women's sexual services to black and white men beyond the Levee. Cafés, cabarets, and nightclubs mul-tiplied in the Black Belt under their leadership. Black prostitutes were not passive victims of the shift in the sex economy. Many chose to work as employees in male-owned saloons, nightclubs, and cabarets; others managed to operate small brothels and engage in independent prostitu-tion well into the 1920s. Still others created new sex institutions, such as buffet flats and after-hours clubs, that competed successfully with highly visible male enterprises. Nonetheless, black women's independence within the sex marketplace declined after 1910.

Chapter 6 extends the examination of the symbolic potency of the African American prostitute into the twentieth century. Increasingly attached to the central institutions of Black Belt nightlife, black prostitutes sparked divergent responses from black and white Chicagoans. For their part, many middle-class whites were attracted to the new nighttime resorts that offered exposure to black musical talent and access to a new world of sexual experimentation. Others were horrified at the flouting of racial boundaries within the Black Belt. In their encounters with black prostitution, white middle-class Chicagoans engaged in two practices that transformed the racial outlines of modern urban sexuality: slumming and the policing of black prostitution. These practices not only helped to define the black prostitute as a titillating if dangerous commodity but also turned the Black Belt into a sexualized and criminalized territory. Furthermore, they turned interracial sexual exchange into an act of crossing both racial and well-policed spatial boundaries.

For respectable blacks, the presence of black prostitutes within an increasing array of Black Belt amusements continued to generate anxiety about white constructions of the race's sexual morality. But it also sparked a critique of white men and women who crossed neighborhood boundaries and nightly arrived at the doors of morally questionable resorts. Among black church and political leaders, a focus on the moral depredations of white urbanites became part of an emerging attack on white hypocrisy and immorality.

In mapping the range of white and black responses to Chicago's racialized sex economy, chapter 6 places black prostitution at the center of what historians of sexuality have identified as the emergence of modern sexuality in early-twentieth-century America. Examinations of modernizing sexuality have focused primarily on the separation of sexuality from the strictures of family surveillance and the dictates of procreative heterosexuality. This chapter shows, however, that ideas of racial difference were at the core of modern sexual identities and practices for both white and black Chicagoans.

The epilogue returns African American sex workers to the center of the story. It begins by examining the criminalization of African American prostitutes, a process that intensified after the 1912 closing of the Twenty-Second Street Levee. This shift in policing registered several simultaneous changes that transformed the Black Belt prostitution economy: black men's entrepreneurial inroads into the neighborhood sex trade, white men's and women's increasing patronage of Black Belt leisure resorts, and white reformers' discomfort with the growth of interracial sexual commerce. In the ever-shifting sex marketplace and in the context of black women's intense criminalization, establishing control over their work lives remained a complicated and constantly challenging proposition for black sex workers. This final part of the book analyzes the intersection of black women's sex work, the criminalization of black prostitutes, and modern urban sexuality.

Writing about black prostitution has been challenging intellectual work. I have had to overcome my preconceptions about the causes and consequences of paid sexual labor and about the lives of women who have turned to this form of work. The stories of the countless unnamed black women who have worked in the urban sex economy are more complex than can be conveyed here. Nevertheless, in giving visibility and voice to these marginalized black women, I throw into bold relief the centrality of prostitution to a more complete understanding of the myriad oppressions and modest triumphs that working black women experienced in a modernizing city at the turn of the twentieth century. This story does not end in 1930. The harsh economic, racial, and sexual landscapes in which turn-of-the-century black prostitutes labored should call our attention to the too often invisible battles that working-class and working-poor black women continue to wage in their own defense.

ONE

"The Sources of Courtesanship": African American Women's Wage Work, the Informal Economy, and the Search for Independence

In 1870 a *Chicago Times* reporter accompanied a group of investigators who ventured into Chicago's sex district to discover the thoughts of madams and prostitutes on a matter of great public concern. The Common Council was in the throes of a debate to determine whether or not Chicago should institute a system of registering and inspecting its houses of prostitution. While the unidentified interviewers sought to elicit the opinions of brothel keepers regarding the proposed system of regulating their businesses, the reporter's concerns were elsewhere. He seemed utterly fascinated with the group of women he encountered—largely white madams in charge of Chicago's most prosperous houses of prostitution. Well-dressed and gracious to their curious visitors, these women were thoughtful and unrestrained in expressing their ideas about regulation and prostitution more generally. To the question "What induces a girl to turn out?" one prostitute answered, "Love of dress, and a desire to go more; [and a] love of liberty." The committee leadingly asked one brothel keeper, "Don't

99 in 100 women turn out for love of money and good clothes?" to which she succinctly responded, "Yes." It is not clear whether these women sincerely believed these statements or if they were echoing popular explanations for the growth of the sex trade in cities like Chicago. Nevertheless, the reporter culled through the numerous responses of prostitutes and madams to the investigators' questions and promised to reveal "Some Startling Facts" about "The Sources of Courtesanship."

Yet to the *Times* reporter the scope of the interviewers' examination of prostitution in Chicago proved incomplete. After the team of investigators concluded their task, the reporter went out on his own into what he described as a "dark and dank" area of the red-light district. "Winding in and out, stumbling up and down, splashing in mud, and staggering over broken steps and nameless obstacles, there were visited haunts whose character would never be conceived by the wildest and most prurient imagination." Crowded together in this dirty and ominous terrain were the houses of prostitution in which black and white women worked side by side. "Obese wenches in the arms of sodden white men; fair young girls nestling close to the side of sooty negroes— such were the aspects of the social problem as it presented itself in the lower haunts of this fair city." He eventually approached one black prostitute and asked, "Well aunty . . . What shall we do with you women, eh?" Apparently unruffled by the disdain lurking behind his question, she responded frankly, "Well, boss, we must live anyhow."[1]

With her brief and matter-of-fact reply, this nameless black woman encapsulated the predicament that led many women to choose employment in Chicago's sex economy. Some prostitutes may have regarded prostitution as a means of attaining a degree of freedom from the strictures of family and marriage; others may have chosen sex work as a way to earn enough money to allow them to participate in the city's bustling consumer economy, an arena open mostly to middle-class wives and daughters. Yet for many women laboring "in the lower haunts" of Chicago's sex economy, especially poor African American women, prostitution provided something more basic—it was a means of survival.

African American Women's Wage Work

In the last decades of the nineteenth century, black women appear to have been disproportionately represented among Chicago's prostitutes. In 1890 African Americans made up a meager 1 percent of the city's population, and 2 percent of "gainfully" employed women were black.

Yet black houses of prostitution accounted for 12 percent of all broth-els listed in the *Sporting and Club House Directory*, an 1889 guidebook directed at white men looking for safe and discreet sexual pleasure in the city.[2] Black women's disproportionate representation among Chica-go's prostitutes may in part be attributable to the racial attitudes of the directory's compiler. When it came to determining the occupations of African American women, he may very well have been like most white Americans at the end of the nineteenth century, who consumed and believed the varied portrayals of black women's innate sexual deprav-ity. These portrayals may have contributed to the frequency with which this investigator branded black women with the label of "prostitute." In fact, at the end of the century the commonplace usage of this char-acterization of black women by white politicians and political writers, journalists, and historians, North and South, helped galvanize African American women to organize a club movement that would eventually form the basis of the National Association of Colored Women.[3]

The data culled from the *Sporting and Club House Directory*, however imprecise, shed critical light on the workings of race in prostitution and the limits of black women's wage work in the nineteenth-century city. First, even assuming that some overcounting occurred in the brothel directory, the numbers nevertheless point to the inordinate presence of black women among Chicago's sex workers and entrepreneurs. Second, African American women were highly visible inhabitants of the city's sex terrain. Whether they occupied the "dark and dank" recesses of the city (as characterized by the *Times* reporter) or shared the bright and boisterous streets at the center of the sex district (as reflected in the sporting directory), black women were noticeably active participants in Chicago's sex trade. Finally, for untold and perhaps unknowable num-bers of African American women, sex work provided a viable, often necessary, means of earning money in an industrializing and rapidly expanding urban economy.

Some black women who became sex workers were likely longtime residents of the city; most, however, were among the growing number of African Americans who migrated to Chicago after 1880. In 1880 and 1900, the vast majority of black brothel workers were born outside Illi-nois. Like thousands of other migrant women and men, they had come to the city hoping to find the makings of a life better than what they had left behind. They sought economic opportunity for themselves and very often for their families back home, and they hoped to experience the social freedoms that life in a northern city promised. Once in Chi-cago they each confronted the often overwhelming financial demands of city living. Black men seeking opportunities in the city's industrial economy also faced a limited job horizon. White employers relegated most black men to work as unskilled laborers in the city's factories or as porters, waiters, and janitors in the bustling enterprises of this fast-growing marketplace. Yet navigating a job market rigidly structured by both race and gender, black women faced an even narrower range of job opportunities. Most found employment as low-wage servants in down-town businesses or in the homes of Chicago's growing white middle class.[4]

In the late nineteenth century, virtually all of Chicago's working black women toiled as service workers. In 1890 black women made up 4.3 percent of all female servants, roughly four times their proportion of the city's women. Despite black women's overrepresentation among servants, white housewives, restaurateurs, and hotel managers were more likely to hire immigrant women to fill openings for cooks, wait-resses, charwomen, laundresses, and general help. Foreign-born white women—the largest proportion of whom came from Germany, Ireland, Sweden, and Norway—made up 66 percent of all women so employed. Native-born white women made up the balance of women in domestic and personal service.[5] In such northeastern cities as Boston and Philadel-phia, as well as in southern cities and towns, with older black commu-nities and with a longer tradition of hiring black women as household workers, opportunities for domestic employment abounded. Compared with women working in these cities, black women who moved to Chi-cago in search of employment faced a particularly constricted job mar-ket. These limited prospects may have checked the rate at which black women moved to Chicago. Until 1900 black women lagged behind black men as migrants to the city.[6]

By 1900 employment opportunities gradually widened, both within and beyond household service. In 1890, 77 percent of working black women in Chicago held jobs as service workers, and 16 percent worked as semiskilled laborers. By 1900, when 71 percent of working black women labored in household or other personal service, their propor-tion of the city's service workforce had nearly doubled, reaching over 8 percent. In addition to gains in the service sector, 20 percent of black women held jobs as semiskilled workers. Yet even semiskilled workers were unable to escape black women's traditional work entirely. They ei-ther found jobs in the expanding fields of mechanized domestic labor—such as in commercial laundries—or they secured positions in domestic fields previously closed to them. Of the 998 African American women classified as semiskilled in 1900, 55 percent were seamstresses and dressmakers, and 26 percent were housekeepers in hotels, commercial rooming houses, or boardinghouses.[7] Few held factory jobs. Unlike white women, who after 1880 enjoyed a broadening array of commercial and industrial occupations, black women found few paths into the diversifying economies of the city.[8]

African American women came to Chicago in the last decades of the nineteenth century aware that they would more than likely be employed as domestic servants, although many might have hoped otherwise. They arrived with the belief that, unlike in the towns or rural districts of the South and Midwest, once in the city they could make the restricted field of service suitable to their needs. Their concentration in domestic work, however, was rarely a comfortable fit. Whether employed as household domestics, as cooks or waitresses in restaurants, or as charwomen in downtown office buildings and hotels, black female service workers labored under adverse conditions. In the homes of middle-class and wealthy white families, black women endured long, grueling hours, limited free and family time, and, too often, the sexual advances of male employers. As cooks in downtown restaurants, their employers gave them the least desirable and most strenuous tasks. As cleaning women in office buildings and hotels, black women worked under physical conditions more onerous than those suffered by their white female coworkers. And, more than any other group of service workers, black women consistently toiled at the lowest rung of the earnings ladder.

With considerable ingenuity and often with some sacrifice, black women struggled to mold the low wages and limited occupations of service work to suit their personal aspirations, economic needs, and family obligations. This struggle eventually transformed urban domestic labor relations. After the turn of the century, black women domestic workers across the country asserted their preferences for work that afforded them the most flexibility. Like their counterparts elsewhere, black women in Chicago increasingly preferred day work, living out (i.e., not living in the homes of their employers), and the relative independence of laundry work.[9]

In the late nineteenth century, however, the obstacles African American women faced in their efforts to find employment, make a living, and at the same time defend their independence and dignity within the urban wage system pushed some to look elsewhere for their money. Peripheral to a thriving industrial economy and restricted to onerous and low-paying domestic employment, many black working women struggling to make ends meet moved beyond wage work and ventured into the city's underground economy. For many women, work in this alternative urban economy entailed selling sexual favors in Chicago's thriving sex trade.

The Informal Economy

In addition to those categories of labor that census takers recognized as "gainful employment," there were numerous other ways of earning money within Chicago's South Side economy. Only the shadows of this world of work appear in government statistics of gainful employment. Nonetheless, the informal, or underground, economy has historically been a vital arena of economic activity, encompassing an array of endeavors. In turn-of-the-century Chicago, it was a dynamic arena of commerce, sustaining individuals and neighborhoods and affording black women opportunities unavailable to them in the legal wage economy.

The concept of the "informal," "underground," or "shadow" economy was formulated in the 1970s and has since undergone a great deal of theorization. Economists, anthropologists, and sociologists developed the term as a way to bring into analytical view areas of labor and modes of income generation existing outside formal wage relations.[10] In the late nineteenth century, as in the late twentieth, the informal economy was a network of economic endeavors and community relations that supported both the generation of income and the exchange of goods and services outside officially sanctioned or regulated networks of exchange.[11] Black women and men who worked in the informal sector of the urban economy took advantage of the needs of both black community members and whites living beyond community borders for a variety of goods and services. Hot foods peddled on busy street corners, medicinal tinctures prepared at home and advertised through neighborhood information networks, "policy" shops concealed in kitchens, basements, and cigar shops,[12] gambling dens tucked away in the back rooms of barbershops and saloons—each of these economic undertakings represents a strategy by which black city dwellers earned money outside the wage economy. Prostitution was situated along a continuum of economic enterprises, legal and illegal, that women and men developed to earn money in turn-of-the-century Chicago.

As the prominence of prostitution suggests, much of the urban informal economy was linked to men's leisure. In the late nineteenth century, numerous commercial leisure establishments emerged to cater to the recreational needs of working black men who had a bit of discretionary income. Saloons were the most plentiful of such places. These resorts offered a variety of diversions and services in exclusively male social environments. While many saloon proprietors aspired to respectability, others flouted such standards. Several black saloon owners profitably blurred the line separating reputable businessman and purveyor of illicit entertainment. Savvy saloon owners hoping to earn more than the legitimate sale of alcohol could bring opened up back rooms to such activities as billiards, pool, card games, and craps. In 1890 John "Mushmouth" Johnson and a partner opened one of the most popular gambling saloons among Chicago's black sporting men. Robert Motts ran his own saloon and gambling den in the 2700 block of State Street. Both Johnson and Motts gained considerable notoriety and wealth as proprietors of both legitimate and illegal recreational enterprises. Establishments such as these provided jobs for black men who, like women, sought alternatives to low-paying, menial employment. For the black working men who frequented their back rooms, these and other gambling saloons held out the remote possibility of multiplying—and the less remote possibility of losing—the slim pay earned in the wage economy.[13]

Prostitution, like gambling, catered to the recreational needs of men. It rivaled gambling as one of the largest and perhaps the most visible sector of the urban informal economy. Unlike gambling, however, the sex trade offered a steady stream of jobs to women. Yet it was not the only informal avenue open to black women. A wide range of women pursued income-generating opportunities along the spectrum of activities that composed Chicago's underground economy. Some black women who migrated to Chicago at the turn of the century came with skills—such as sewing, teaching, and nursing—that were not immediately transferable to Chicago's racially segmented economy.[14] For these women, involvement in informal activity represented an inviting alternative as they struggled within and beyond the limited world of paid domestic work. Some turned their homes into neighborhood businesses. Women skilled in sewing engaged in home-based needlework, capitalizing on fashion trends disseminated through magazines and in downtown stores.[15] Others turned their homes into places for black women's hair grooming. Hairdressing, perhaps more than other services exchanged within the black community, exposes the hidden nature of black women's income-generating activity and their small-scale entrepreneurship. In the late nineteenth century, black women's hair care was a private affair conducted in the homes of mothers, sisters, friends, and neighbors. Unlike the more formalized barbershops, home-based hair care may not initially have been defined by cash exchanges. Rather, hairdressing was most likely woven into an informal system of barter or of reciprocal courtesies and services between women.[16] Newspaper advertisements for elocutionists, music teachers, and herbalists reveal other ways that black women carved out niches for themselves in the South Side's market economy. While not exclusively the preserve of middle-class women, these informal occupations were most often available to women who possessed some education beyond elementary school and who usually had middle-class aspirations. These employments reveal how widespread informal economic activity was within Chicago's black community.

Most black women who engaged in informal work did not have specialized training, however. The majority of black women who migrated to Chicago in the last decades of the nineteenth century came from farming communities and small towns. If they had work experience before arriving in the city, it was most likely in agricultural or low-wage domestic employment. But few of the respectable skills learned as household help, cooks, washerwomen, or agricultural workers promised to enlarge the potential for earning money outside Chicago's low-paying formal marketplace. With limited choices even in the informal economy, many women participated in illegal methods of acquiring needed cash. They found such opportunities easily enough, especially as successive waves of black newcomers pursued recreation that could be found only in the city. Running kitchen distilleries or operating policy shops were just two of the ways that women capitalized on their neighbors' growing need for diversion and entertainment. For many black women, though, sex work represented the most important moneymaking enterprise within Chicago's underground economy.

In her study of black women domestic workers in post-emancipation Atlanta, Tera Hunter has argued that women's "incessant effort to try to find better terms for their work" could lead them to "move in and out of the labor market."[17] For many women, Chicago's sex economy was an important part of their mobility "out of the labor market." Yet black women involved in sex work did not actually leave the labor market. Rather, they moved into a shadow market in which they could not only replace low-wage work but often far exceed any earnings they could expect in the formal economy. Faced with the pressure of paying for food and rent with insufficient wages earned in the legitimate economy, many black women turned to the sex industry. Sex work was the only occupation that promised to pay a living wage. Some black women found in prostitution a remunerative hiatus from the financial challenges of self-support; others sought a reprieve from the impossible demands of maintaining a family on a domestic's wages.[18]

Turning to Prostitution

For African American women hoping to evade the patriarchal and racial structure of the legitimate wage economy, the sex trade offered a certain degree of financial independence. And though the trade ostensibly peddled a single commodity—women's sexual services—it nonetheless provided black women with a number of different ways to pursue economic security. Women working as prostitutes labored in a variety of settings. Like their counterparts in many other nineteenth-century cities, the majority of Chicago's prostitutes worked in brothels.[19] The brothels where many were employed could be large or small, cheap or fancy. Prostitutes who did not work in houses of prostitution sold their services out of saloons or hotels or in boardinghouses. Others used the streets to secure trade. In addition to prostitutes, women labored in the trade as madams, businesswomen whose entrepreneurial skills helped them to provide the institutional cornerstone for the city's sex trade. Still others combined the roles of sex entrepreneur and sex worker, usually working on their own out of their apartments or private rooms in rooming houses. The varied organization of the urban sex trade allowed black women to find a form of sex work that suited their financial needs, planned length of stay in the trade, familial obligations, or temperament.

If it is easy to fathom the economic motivations that led some black women to seek employment in the various branches of Chicago's underground sex economy, determining who the women were who made this choice is a much more challenging undertaking. Few archival sources exist that deal specifically and at any length with black women in the sex trade. Unlike white prostitutes, about whom turn-of-the-century moral and Progressive Era reformers showed unwavering concern, black sex workers were never the object of sustained investigation. Aside from offhand comments regarding black women's extreme moral degradation (as in the description penned by the Chicago *Times* reporter), reformers and investigators regularly overlooked the experiences of African American women laboring in Chicago's sex economy.[20] Yet if local keepers of moral and civic order showed no interest in probing the causes of and remedies for black prostitution, federal officials seeking to enumerate the occupations of the city's men and women left illuminating clues to some of the characteristics of black women who worked within Chicago's largest and most concentrated sex terrain, the Levee. In fact, federal census data collected in 1880 and 1900 provide some of the most detailed information about this most hidden group of economically and socially marginal urbanites.[21]

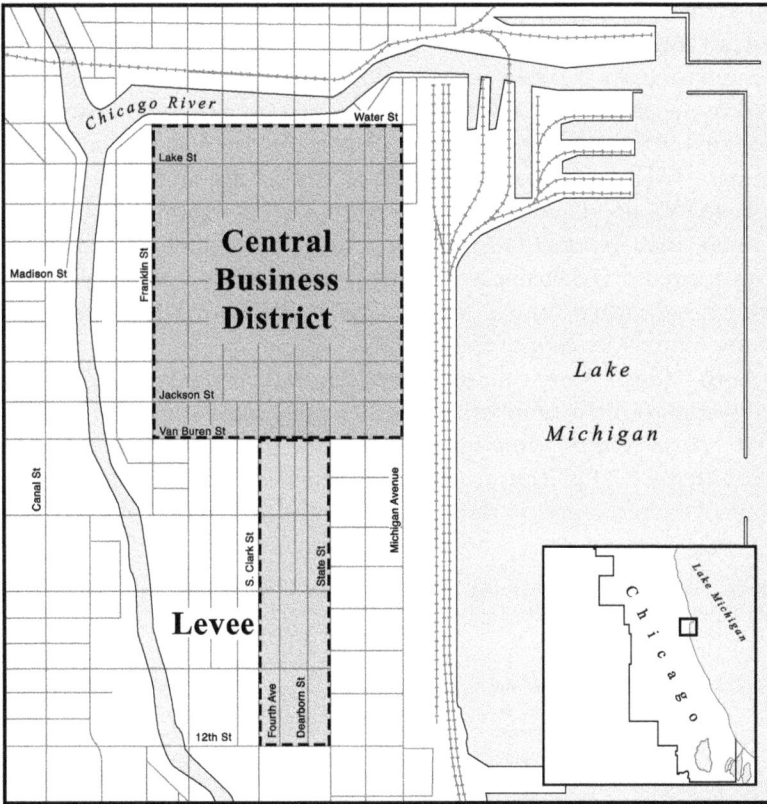

Map 1.1   The Nineteenth-Century Levee District. *Source*: Rand McNally and Co., *Street Guide Map of Chicago* (Chicago: Rand McNally and Co., between 1897 and 1899), http://www.lib.uchicago.edu/e/su/maps/chi1890/G4104-C6-1897-R3.html.

In existence between 1874 and 1904, the Levee—the first of two sex districts to bear this name—was located just south of downtown, framed by Van Buren Street on the north and Twelfth Street on the south, State Street on the east and Clark Street on the west (see map 1.1). Walking through the late-nineteenth-century Levee, where brothels operated openly and with little interference from the police, some federal census enumerators explicitly recorded the occupation of numerous black and white women as "prostitute" and "keeper of house of ill-fame." More discreet enumerators listed women who worked in known brothels as "boarders" and "housekeepers."[22] However census takers designated them, in both census years (as well as in 1889, when the *Sporting and Club House Directory* appeared) black women were over-

27

represented among Chicago's brothel workers (table 1.1). In 1880, when African Americans composed 1 percent of the city's population, black women accounted for 15 percent of the 207 Levee prostitutes enumerated by federal census takers. Nineteen percent were white women of foreign birth, and the majority, 66 percent, were native-born white women. Twenty years later, when black women accounted for 2 percent of the city's population and for 3 percent of all "gainfully" employed women, their representation among Levee prostitutes remained high. They made up 17 percent of 287 sex workers, while foreign-born white women accounted for 25 percent and native-born white women accounted for 57 percent of the total.[23]

Both African American and American-born white women made up a disproportionate number of brothel prostitutes (tables 1.2–1.5). In 1880, 78 percent of white sex workers were native born. In 1900, they accounted for 70 percent of white prostitutes. Some immigrant groups were overrepresented within brothels. Canadian-born women made

Table 1.1. Race and nativity of Chicago brothel prostitutes, 1880 and 1900

	1880		1900	
	Percentage of brothel prostitutes (207 total)	Race and nativity of general population[a] (%)	Percentage of brothel prostitutes (287 total)	Race and nativity of female population (%)
African American	15	1	17	2
White native born	66	58	57	65
White foreign born	19	41	25	33
TOTAL	100	100	99	100

Sources: U.S. Bureau of the Census, Tenth Census (1880), Chicago Manuscript Schedules (microfilm), Enumeration Districts 5, 8, and 9; U.S. Bureau of the Census, Twelfth Census (1900), Chicago Manuscript Schedules (microfilm), Enumeration Districts 12, 21, 24, 30, 38, 42, 43, and 161.
Note: Figures do not include madams.
[a]Figures for female population of Chicago are not available for 1880.

Table 1.2. Nativity of white brothel prostitutes, 1880

	Number of white brothel prostitutes	Percentage of white brothel prostitutes
Native born	136	78
Foreign born	39	22
TOTAL	175	100

Source: U.S. Bureau of the Census, Tenth Census (1880), Chicago Manuscript Schedules (microfilm), Enumeration Districts 5, 8, and 9.

Table 1.3. Place of birth of white foreign-born prostitutes, 1880

Country of origin	Number	Percentage of all white prostitutes	Percentage of all foreign-born prostitutes
Canada	26	15	67
Ireland	5	3	13
Sweden	3	2	8
Austria	1	< 1	2.5
England	1	< 1	2.5
Baden-Baden (Germany)	1	< 1	2.5
Scotland	1	< 1	2.5
South America	1	< 1	2.5
TOTAL	39	22	100.5[a]

Source: U.S. Bureau of the Census, Tenth Census (1880), Chicago Manuscript Schedules (microfilm), Enumeration Districts 5, 8, and 9.
[a]Rounding of figures has caused the total to exceed 100%.

Table 1.4. Nativity of white brothel prostitutes, 1900

	Number	Percentage of white brothel prostitutes
Native born	165	70
Foreign born	71	30
TOTAL	236	100

Source: U.S. Bureau of the Census, Twelfth Census (1900), Chicago Manuscript Schedules (microfilm), Enumeration Districts 12, 21, 24, 30, 38, 42, 43, and 161.

Table 1.5. Place of birth of white foreign-born prostitutes, 1900

Country of origin	Number	Percentage of all white prostitutes	Percentage of all foreign-born prostitutes
Canada	33	14	46
France	15	6	21
Germany	7	3	10
England	5	2	7
Sweden	4	2	6
Poland	2	1	3
Denmark	2	1	3
Ireland	1	0.5	1
Norway	1	0.5	1
At sea	1	0.5	1
TOTAL	71	30.5[a]	99[a]

Source: U.S. Bureau of the Census, Twelfth Census (1900), Chicago Manuscript Schedules (microfilm), Enumeration Districts 12, 21, 24, 30, 38, 42, 43, and 161.
[a]Some percentages result from rounding of figures.

up 15 percent of white brothel workers and fully two-thirds (67 percent) of foreign-born brothel workers in 1880. In that year Canadians made up only 6.5 percent of the city's foreign born. In 1900 they accounted for 14 percent of white and 46 percent of foreign-born sex workers. Few young women from the largest immigrant communities in Chicago—Germans, Irish, and English—worked as prostitutes. At a time when immigrant women from Europe made up 40 percent of Chicago's women (in 1890), their underrepresentation among brothel employees is notable.[24]

The relative dearth of immigrant women among Chicago's brothel prostitutes can shed light on why native-born women in general, black and white, entered the city's brothels. In the late nineteenth century, many immigrants sought to transplant to the context of American cities traditional familial and community controls over the sexual morality of daughters. Many of these controls were economic. Young immigrant women were more likely to contribute their earnings to the parental family economy, receiving in return the protections of a close-knit family while experiencing restrictions on their personal spending and their ability to explore the city on their own. Many African American and native white women enjoyed a greater degree of freedom within the city. Often sent to the city to earn money to help support families remaining in the rural areas of the upper South or in the farming communities and small towns of the Midwest or Northeast, they lived away from relatives more often than foreign-born women, who usually arrived in Chicago with their families.[25]

Indeed, black and American-born white women accounted for the largest proportion of Chicago's "women adrift"—that is, single, self-supporting women who lived on their own in the city.[26] The inadequacy of available census figures for 1880 makes it difficult to draw direct comparisons; however, they do illustrate the overrepresentation of native-born women among women adrift. In 1880, when the native born accounted for 44 percent of all of Chicago's working men and women, native-born women accounted for 55 percent of the city's self-supporting women. African American women made up 4 percent of women living on their own, though blacks accounted for 1 percent of Chicago's overall population.[27] Though many American-born women were themselves recent migrants to the city, they could more easily navigate the city as independent workers and as participants in the alluring world of urban entertainment. Parental controls over employment and sexual behavior, while still powerful in the minds of many young urban women, were increasingly distant and could not compete with the freedoms and temptations that the city had to offer.[28] Furthermore, parental urgings of respectability could not always counterbalance the pressing need for money. Native-born women's greater degree of mobility made it easier for them to explore alternative means of employment in their quest for financial security.

Indeed, native-born women who worked in Chicago's brothels were largely urban transplants, drawing from, though not necessarily mirroring, the diversity of migrants who arrived in the city from states across the country. In 1880 and 1900 one-quarter of native-born white prostitutes were born in Illinois; the rest came to Chicago from towns in the Northeast or the farming communities of the Midwest. Among black brothel workers in 1880, only 6 percent were born in Illinois (table 1.6). Like Chicago's black population, the largest group of prostitutes, 41 percent, came from Tennessee, Kentucky, and other states of

Table 1.6. Region of birth of black prostitutes, 1880

State of birth	Number per state	Percentage by region
Illinois	2	6
Midwest (not including Illinois)		
Ohio	4	
Wisconsin	2	
Indiana	2	
Michigan	1	
Total	9	28
Northeast		
New York	1	
New Jersey	1	
Total	2	6
Upper South		
Tennessee	4	
Kentucky	4	
Virginia	2	
Maryland	2	
Missouri	1	
Total	13	41
Lower South		
Louisiana	3	
Alabama	2	
Georgia	1	
Total	6	19
TOTAL	32	100

Source: U.S. Bureau of the Census, Tenth Census (1880), Chicago Manuscript Schedules (microfilm), Enumeration Districts 5, 8, and 9.
Note: Statistics for the states and regions of birth for blacks, not just black prostitutes, living in Chicago are not available for 1880.

the upper South. Twenty-eight percent of black prostitutes came from midwestern states, in particular Ohio, Wisconsin, and Indiana; and 19 percent came from the Deep South states of Alabama, Georgia, and Louisiana. Twenty years later, a much larger proportion of black brothel workers, 31 percent, had been born in Illinois, exceeding the 20 percent of Chicago's black residents born in the state (table 1.7). Twenty-one percent of black prostitutes had come from other midwestern states, compared to 15 percent of black Chicagoans from the Midwest; and 24 percent were born in the border states of the upper South. Forty-three percent of Chicago's blacks were born in this region.[29]

Although a large number of black prostitutes were born in Illinois at the turn of the century, most were born outside Chicago. Like other

Table 1.7. Region of birth of black prostitutes and of black population in Chicago, 1900

State of birth black prostitutes	Number per state	Region of birth of black prostitutes (%)	Region of birth of black population of Chicago (%)
Illinois	9	31	20
Midwest (not including Illinois)			
Ohio	4		
Indiana	2		
Total	6	21	15
Northeast			
New York	2		
Pennsylvania	1		
Massachusetts	1		
Total	4	14	4
Upper South			
Kentucky	4		
Tennessee	2		
North Carolina	1		
Total	7	24	43
Lower South			
Mississippi	2		
Georgia	1		
Total	3	10	17
TOTAL	29[a]	100	99

Sources: U.S. Bureau of the Census, Twelfth Census (1900), Chicago Manuscript Schedules (microfilm), Enumeration Districts 12, 21, 24, 30, 38, 42, 43, and 161. State-of-birth figures for native-born nonwhites are derived from Allan H. Spear, Black Chicago: The Making of a Negro Ghetto, 1890–1920 (Chicago: University of Chicago Press, 1967), 13.

Note: Figures for blacks in Chicago were folded into the category "native non-white" in the Twelfth Census population tables, from which these overall regional statistics are derived. The overwhelming majority of native nonwhites were black.

[a]In 1900 census enumerators recorded the state of birth for twenty-nine of forty-eight black brothel prostitutes. For the remaining nineteen, place of origin was listed merely as "U.S.

African American migrants to Chicago, many no doubt had been born and raised in small towns in southern Illinois. As black men and women fled the border states of Kentucky and Tennessee in the 1880s and 1890s, some families established themselves in such towns as Cairo and East St. Louis, Illinois. Thus, the in-state migrants who came to Chicago at the turn of the century were most likely establishing new roots in the city rather than following in the footsteps of relatives or family friends who had made their way there before them. This contrasts with the era of the Great Migration, when migrating black women relied on the support of family contacts to ease their transition to urban life. Rather than entering a growing black community to which they were drawn by kin or family acquaintance, black women (and men) arriving in Chicago in the last decades of the nineteenth century—including those working in the sex trade—were at the head of the stream of migrants that would later foster the chain migrations of the 1910s and 1920s.[30]

If familial controls were important in keeping immigrant women—and, to be sure, many American-born women—on the straight and narrow, physical distance from such influence could make the choice of prostitution easier for some women. Yet distance from relatives only partly explains why black women were so numerous among Chicago's sex workers. Perhaps African American women who chose sex work had an ability to block out the moral urgings of members of their new community that set them apart from other black women struggling in the city. Such musings about the psychological motivations behind prostitution are speculative at best. They overlook the financial motivations so deeply intertwined with other factors, such as an individual's temperament and family circumstances. The most powerful incentive for black women's forays into the sex economy remains their status as the lowest paid of urban workers. Prostitution offered migrant women a practicable strategy for achieving economic independence.

While the sex trade drew heavily from those women who, once in the city, confronted the limits of urban employment, it also drew from another group of women: those whose economic marginality had led them to the sex trade even before they arrived in Chicago and who had no intention of seeking out wage work in the new city. Women already experienced in sex work may have been attracted to Chicago because of the notoriety of its late-nineteenth-century sex district. Information about Chicago's red-light district traveled through the sex districts and other informal economic networks that provided employment to white and black women in other Illinois and midwestern towns. While the Levee's reputation may not have lured black women who resided in far-away southern towns to Chicago, it could entice black and white sex workers living in towns and cities in nearby states.

Chicago was especially attractive in the early 1890s when news of the upcoming Chicago World's Columbian Exposition aggressively drew black and white women into the city's Levee district. Anticipating the influx of potential customers, institutions within Chicago's Levee district expanded considerably. Prior to the fair's opening in the summer of 1893, laboring men flooded into the city to build the great fairgrounds.[31] During the summer of the world's fair, millions of people arrived in the city from the Illinois countryside, across the country, and even Europe. While most tourists came to see the fair and to enjoy the wonders of the city, many male visitors also hoped to enjoy the illicit pleasures for which Chicago was famed. Along with the steady flow of new customers, the influx of sex workers made the expansion of Chicago's Levee trade possible. As white prostitute May Churchill recalled, "The World's Fair was a gold mine for me and my friends during the years 1892 and 1893. . . . The first of those years we nicked the builders, the second the visitors."[32] After the fair shut down, Churchill and her friends left the city, perhaps hoping to find equally lucrative gigs elsewhere. Black women also took advantage of the fair-time surge in Levee patrons. During the fair, Madam Vina Fields's house reportedly grew to over sixty black women, making it the largest brothel in the city at the time. No doubt many of these women were themselves visitors to Chicago hoping to capitalize on the fair-time sex economy.[33]

Knowledge of the Levee or, for that matter, other midwestern sex districts could be crucial for black women who, for whatever reason, found it desirable or necessary to trade one place of residence for another. The case of black prostitute Eliza Dennis points to the kind of mobility that some sex workers exercised as they sought to maximize their economic opportunities as self-supporting urbanites. Moreover, Dennis's movements illuminate the links that existed among red-light districts across the Midwest. In 1881 Dennis was arrested for shooting a patron in her house of prostitution in Chicago. Upon her release on bail, she immediately skipped town. Chicago police authorities tracked her movements first to Milwaukee, then to Detroit, and eventually to Cleveland, where they finally apprehended her.[34] The extent of her mobility may have been uncommon, but the pattern of her movements suggests a similarity with the movements of black women who engaged in sexual commerce before they arrived in Chicago. Like Dennis, many made their way to cities that had robust, if small, sex districts. Black women experienced in sex work gravitated to cities that, in addition to having thriving sex trades, also had growing black populations. Though Dennis's escapades made her highly visible, in such cities as Chicago, Detroit, Cleveland, and Milwaukee more cautious black women established links with other black women and men engaged in informal work and practiced their trades in relative obscurity.[35]

Most women working in the sex trade not only lived away from family but also lived on their own. In both 1880 and 1900 over 90 percent of black and white prostitutes were without husbands. This did not necessarily mean that they lacked consorts, however. Eliza Dennis was the mistress of Bill Hall, "a colored pick-pocket, said by the people to be the most famous in this country."[36] Together, they fled Chicago to dodge Dennis's impending assault case. If prostitutes entered long-term relationships with men, they rarely legalized such bonds while they remained in the trade.

Most women worked in the sex trade as young adults. Prostitution in Chicago, as elsewhere, was a profession defined by its reliance on the sexual labors of young women (table 1.8). In 1880 the overwhelming majority of prostitutes fell between the ages of nineteen and twenty-four: 78 percent of black sex workers and 65 percent of white workers were in this age group. While these figures suggest that men preferred the sexual services of young women, they disclose something more telling about prostitution in the 1880s. Neither black nor white workers

Table 1.8. Ages of brothel prostitutes, 1880 and 1900

Age	Black prostitutes (%)	White prostitutes (native and foreign born) (%)
1800		
15–18	13	16
19–21	25	37
22–24	53	28
25–29	6	13
30+	3	6
TOTAL	100	100
1900		
15–18	4	2
19–21	35	26
22–24	27	33
25–29	23	28
30+	10	11
TOTAL	99	100

Sources: U.S. Bureau of the Census, Tenth Census (1880), Chicago Manuscript Schedules (microfilm), Enumeration Districts 5, 8, and 9; U.S. Bureau of the Census, Twelfth Census (1900), Chicago Manuscript Schedules (microfilm), Enumeration Districts 12, 21, 24, 30, 38, 42, 43, and 161.

used prostitution as a long-term means of accumulating income. Rather, they considered it a short-term strategy for coping with economic crises or avoiding undesirable employment. The ability to move out of the sex trade flew in the face of anti-vice reformers' grave portrayals of prostitution as a profession that inevitably took girls and women on a downward spiral to impoverishment, degradation, and death.[37] As powerful an indictment of the "social evil" as this scenario appeared, it did not accurately represent the fate of women working in the trade, at least not those in brothels. Late-nineteenth-century sex workers, black and white, experienced a surprising degree of mobility in and out of the sex economy.[38]

In 1880 black sex workers in particular took advantage of the permeable boundaries that separated sexual labor and domestic work, usually turning to sex work in their early twenties and returning to the legitimate economy after a short stint in the informal sphere. More than half of black prostitutes—53 percent—were between twenty-two and twenty-four, while only 27.5 percent of white prostitutes were in this age group. In addition, fewer black women than white women worked as prostitutes before the age of twenty-two: 38 percent of black prostitutes and 53 percent of white prostitutes entered the trade as teenagers or very young women. Furthermore, black women were less than half as likely as white women to work in brothels after the age of twenty-five: at a time when 19 percent of white brothel workers were at least twenty-five years old, only 9 percent of black brothel workers were this age. The ages of the seven women working in Elizabeth Moore's Levee house—all between twenty-two and twenty-four—reflect the tendency of black women in the 1880s to find temporary, at times brief, employment in Chicago's sex industry.[39]

The age differences between black and white sex workers suggest distinct patterns of participation in the late-nineteenth-century sex economy. If many African American women saw sex work as an alternative to domestic employment, they were less likely than white women to do so over the course of their working lives. Black women entered brothels at a later age and left earlier than their white counterparts. Of course, exceptions existed. At the age of forty-five, Marie Morris, a worker in Georgia Styles's four-prostitute house, was almost twice the age of the next-oldest prostitute working for Styles, twenty-three-year-old Della Denice.[40] Morris was an anomaly. Few black women approaching forty worked in the trade in the 1880s.

By 1900, however, black women worked in the sex industry at a later age than their counterparts had twenty years earlier. Indeed, as both black and white women migrated to Chicago in increasing numbers at the end of the nineteenth century, women from a wider age spectrum sought and found employment in the sex trade. At the turn of the century, black women resorted to sex work at virtually all ages before forty. The prime years for brothel employment remained between nineteen and twenty-four. Yet women between twenty-two and twenty-four made up only 27 percent of all black sex workers. Moreover, fully one-third of black prostitutes were twenty-five and above, more than three times the proportion of women in this category twenty years earlier.[41] (A maturing had taken place among white brothel workers as well by the turn of the century, 39 percent of whom were twenty-five or older.)[42]

The brothel run by Madam Vina Fields illustrates this trend. In 1880 Fields employed eight women, not one of whom was older than twenty-three. In 1900 her house had nineteen workers, and five of these women were over twenty-five. The aging of black sex workers revealed itself in other brothels as well. In 1900 brothel keeper Annie Jones employed three women: Irene Parker, who was twenty; Nettie Miller, who was twenty-five; and Myrtle Timmel, who was forty. In the same year in Sadie Clemons's resort, three of her six boarders were older than twenty-five: Georgia Moran was twenty-six, Lottie Smith was twenty-seven, and Carrie Taylor was thirty-eight.[43]

Several factors contributed to this important shift among Chicago's African American sex workers. First, some older women may have been among the veteran prostitutes who, like other purveyors of amusements, turned up in Chicago during and after the 1893 world's fair. In the years after the fair, Chicago maintained its reputation as an open town, hospitable to gamblers, con artists, saloon keepers, and prostitutes. African American men and women on the social and economic margins joined those drawn to Chicago's Levee in search of their own chance to amass quick and, they hoped, easy cash. Indeed, the illegitimate economy was especially important after 1893, when a depression that gripped the nation descended on Chicago with full force. Thousands of Chicagoans found themselves unemployed and without prospects. Out-of-work men and women used various strategies to survive the tough economic times. Hoping to find work, some men and women used dwindling resources to pay unscrupulous employment agencies to secure jobs that turned out to be nonexistent. Some pawned valuable items to get cash from equally unscrupulous pawnbrokers. Discouraged, some men and women left Chicago altogether.[44]

For the majority who remained in the city, especially the working poor, staying afloat proved an arduous task. They crowded into shelters and relied on neighborhood churches and soup kitchens. Even saloon and brothel owners did what they could to meet the needs of struggling men and women. Unemployed men received free lunches in the saloons that survived the depression. Many men went to brothels whose madams, in an effort to keep their own doors open, distributed free meals. One reformer noted that, throughout the first harsh winter of the depression, Madam Vina Fields daily "fed a hungry, ragged regiment of the out-of-works."[45] Although madams directed their generosity at laboring-poor men, such charitable acts provided only temporary relief from want. When scrounging for jobs proved futile and when neighborhood welfare was not enough, many men and women entered the informal economy.

The economic crisis hit domestic workers and personal servants particularly hard. Middle-class families who could no longer afford the luxury of live-in help quickly let their servants go.[46] African American women lost their jobs at an alarming rate during the 1890s depression. Of the women who became prostitutes in the 1890s, some may have worked as prostitutes when they were younger; others may never have considered sex work before but, pushed by their extreme circumstances, now sought refuge in the Levee's sex trade.

After the economy rebounded, a wide range of African American women continued to engage in prostitution. The most significant experiences that led women to sex work occurred in Chicago's formal sector. By 1900 black women were slowly making their way out of private households and into new areas of work.[47] Yet whether they found jobs as "semiskilled" workers laboring in hotels, laundries, and rooming houses or labored in the homes of middle-class families, virtually all black women remained service workers. Black women's continuing efforts to avoid servitude coupled with the difficulty of finding alternative legitimate employment probably led more older women to seek earnings in the prostitution economy than had been the case among an earlier generation of black working women.

Paradoxically, when the barriers to black women's work outside domestic employment in private homes began to weaken at the turn of the century, a broader range of black women sought financial refuge within the sex economy. Thus, the ages of turn-of-the-century black prostitutes suggest a deeper contradiction within the wage economy. While Chicago's employment landscape was inviting to some black women, offering them expanded opportunities within the service sector, it was precisely the constraints of service work that pushed a wider range of black women to seek temporary or recurring stints in the sex economy.

White women also relied on the sex economy in new ways, suggesting that they, too, were affected by the depression and that working-class and working-poor white women were equally frustrated by the inadequate offerings of the wage economy.

Finally, the rise in the average age of prostitutes also suggests a gradual change in patterns of women's mobility in and out of the sex trade. Toward the end of the nineteenth century, civic and religious organizations in Chicago (and across the country) pressured public officials to cleanse the city of prostitution. The increased involvement of civil authorities in the policing of prostitution contributed to the stigmatization of sex workers and eventually made it difficult for some to move out of the social world of the sex trade.[48] Limitations on women's mobility were not complete, however. For most black and white women, prostitution was still not a full-time or long-term means of accumulating money; yet it increasingly functioned as a safety net across a broader span of many women's working years.

Black Madams

If the sex economy offered economic opportunities for women struggling to survive in an urban economy, it promised a different order of financial security for women who ran the sex enterprises of the late-nineteenth-century Levee. Women who operated houses of prostitution gained access to the considerable sums of money flowing through Chicago's sex economy. Their labors as businesswomen were central to the development of the turn-of-the-century sex economy. They provided the places—houses or apartments—where women worked and sex-seeking men pursued their desires. The best of them smoothed over relationships with local police officers and thus secured protection for both prostitutes and their customers. Indeed, brothel keepers bore a great amount of responsibility in the sex economy. All madams daily invested time, effort, and money in the operation of their brothels. Their work included advertising their establishments; making sure that the premises were presentable, inviting, and clean; and providing food, drink, and, sometimes, nonsexual entertainment for clients. They also established work discipline among their employees, navigated the needs and personalities of several different young women, and oversaw financial transactions between workers and visiting men. Because brothel work was the most common form of prostitution in the late nineteenth century, madams' role as employers influenced prostitutes' earnings throughout the sex industry. And the financial rewards for enterprising women could be significant. Extracting a generous percentage from the sexual exchanges of several working women, they regularly took home more than any one prostitute could earn on her own. If madams worked at a remove from actual sexual transactions, they nonetheless defined the late-nineteenth-century sex marketplace.

Like sex workers, many madams sought to conceal the nature of their businesses from census authorities. In both 1880 and 1900 many brothel keepers were listed simply as "house keeper" or "boarding house keeper" in the census. Black and white brothel keepers were equally disinclined to announce their profession, fearing the repercussions if authorities discovered their illegal businesses. While prostitution itself was not a crime at this time in Chicago, a woman could be fined or imprisoned for operating a house of ill fame. I identified seven African American and fourteen white madams in 1880, and six black and twenty-one white madams in 1900.

In some ways, black madams were like the women who boarded with them. They were among the successive groups of African American women who migrated to the city in hopes of economic opportunity and social freedoms. In both 1880 and 1900 almost all hailed from the Midwest and the upper South. Only one woman in each census year was born in Illinois. In age, however, black madams diverged from their workers: they tended to be older than the population of prostitutes. Brothel keepers, like their workers, tended to conceal their ages—many undoubtedly lied to census takers. For example, Carrie Watson, a white keeper of an elite brothel, reported her age as thirty-nine in 1880, but in 1900 she listed herself as only forty.[49] In 1880 black madam Vina Fields stated that she was thirty years old. Thirty years later she had shaved three years and reported that she was fifty-seven.[50] However much black and white madams may have undercounted their years, they were at least ten years older than their boarders. In 1880 four out of seven keepers were age thirty or above, with the average age being thirty-two. In 1900 black madams were slightly older, averaging thirty-six years of age. With the exception of one twenty-nine-year-old, all were thirty years of age or older. The average age of white madams for both years was thirty-four and a half.

As proprietors black brothel keepers worked in an area of the sex trade that did not require youth. Largely exempt from the fickle tastes of clients, they could enter the economy at a later age. For the same reason they could remain in the informal economy longer than most prostitutes. The experience that an older woman accumulated in the prostitution economy, whether as prostitute or as madam, helped her to navigate a competitive sex marketplace. A keeper's maturity could also set the tone for her establishment. In fact, age worked to her ben-efit in dealings with prostitutes and brothel visitors. At age thirty-eight, Elizabeth Morris was twice the age of her two young employees, Minnie and Jennie. Rachel Gibson, thirty-three years old, had more than ten years on the three women who boarded with her.[51] This age difference might reassure younger women as to the soundness of the enterprise they had entered. It could also work to the older women's advantage in their financial dealings with inexperienced prostitutes. By the turn of the century, when the average age of black prostitutes was higher, age offered less of an advantage, though younger women might still be intimidated by an assertive, older employer. Equally important, a mad-am's age shaped interactions with clients. An older woman could affect an authoritative style that served to discipline not only her workers but her customers as well.

Because they were older women, one might expect that African American brothel keepers were more likely than their employees to have been married at some point. This was not the case in 1880. In that year one of the seven keepers claimed experience with marriage—she reported that she was a widow. The remaining six were single. Though a small sample, marital patterns among these black madams are sugges-tive and distinctly differ from the self-reported marital status among women in the 1900 sample. In that year only two of six madams were single; two were widows, and two were married (though no husbands were listed among brothel residents). By comparison, of the twenty-one white madams identified in 1900, ten were married, two were widowed, two were divorced, and seven were single.

Just as keepers could misstate their ages, so some also lied about their marital status. Indeed, a woman could shift her marital designation whenever she felt the need to do so. Vina Fields, whose brothel in the Levee was one of the most prominent in the late-nineteenth-century sex industry, alternately identified herself to city directory compilers as Miss and Mrs. Fields. In one 1894 exposé of political corruption in Chicago, she is identified as Mrs. Vina Fields, but in both the 1880 and 1910 cen-sus she lists herself as single.[52] Most women were less inconsistent about their status. As female heads of households, some women claimed ei-ther an absent or a deceased husband. This could bestow a degree of respectability on those who chose not to declare prostitution as their line of work. For women who did not hide their occupation, brothel keeping appeared to be compatible with the apparent respectability of marriage or widowhood. In fact, in some cases women may have used the earnings of a husband, dead or alive, to start their businesses.

The paths that led black women to the business side of the urban sex trade are the aspect of their lives most shielded from our gaze. Black women took up brothel keeping after encountering the same challenges all black women faced in Chicago's racially structured wage economy. Many keepers undoubtedly worked as prostitutes in other brothels prior to opening their own establishments. In 1888 Lillian Richardson was a boarder in a house of prostitution in an emerging sex district south of the Levee. By the next year she was proprietor of her own brothel a few doors away.[53] Although many keepers had previously worked as prostitutes, Richardson's career trajectory was rare for most sex workers: few prostitutes became madams. The vast majority worked their way out of prostitution entirely rather than into the ranks of brothel keepers.

Some black women turned to the business end of prostitution in the wake of a financial crisis—such as losing a job or losing the economic support provided by a husband or partner. After such losses, black women frequently opened legitimate, though informally organized, boardinghouses to help them cover rents that were beyond their means as single wage-earning women. Yet keeping a boardinghouse was not always profitable, and some women in search of greater and more reliable income turned their boardinghouses into houses of prostitution. Perhaps this was the case for Annie Jones. In 1900 this forty-five-year-old widow ran a small brothel that employed three boarders. In the same year Jennie Carter, a forty-nine-year-old widow, employed seven women in her brothel.[54] Annie and Jennie may well have been women who had spent years in Chicago's sex industry prior to their enumeration in the federal census. They could also have been among the women who belatedly discovered that operating a boardinghouse for prostitutes was more lucrative than keeping a legitimate house.

Whatever path led African American women to the sex economy, madams, like their employees, were self-supporting women who created opportunities for independent living in the city. They did this through informal entrepreneurship: renting out rooms, apartments, or buildings that they fashioned into brothels of varying sizes and degrees of refinement.

As entrepreneurs, black madams (as well as some white keepers) were poised to profit from other black women's marginality in the wage economy. Yet they were frequently as economically vulnerable as their employees or boarders. They faced competition from other houses in the Levee. Because they generally had few resources with which to build and maintain elegant, high-priced brothels, their establishments did not attract elite white men with deep pockets. Perhaps most important, black women did not earn as much as white women working in Chicago's sex marketplace. As was the case in the formal economy, race decisively structured earnings in the sex economy. Still, black sex entrepreneurs stood to earn more money in this informal pursuit than they could as "gainful" employees. In addition, as black women made a way for themselves as brothel keepers, they provided numerous other women with a chance to dodge unemployment or to temporarily escape the drudgery and low pay of domestic work.

Prostitution's Tendrils

The sex economy translated men's urban recreation into women's earnings. It literally transferred men's legitimate (as well as illegal) wages to women's hands and thus helped to support those most marginal in Chicago's industrial economy—poor, self-supporting women. This socially proscribed enterprise was anything but a self-contained economy, however. The profits generated in the sex trade circulated beyond the women who sold or who organized the sale of sexual services. A good portion of the money flowing through the sex economy accrued to men and women who had supporting roles in the production and maintenance of men's pleasure retreats. Many men and women took advantage of the better-than-average wages they could earn as housekeepers, chambermaids, or porters in the Levee's brothels.

Women who may never have considered sex work to be suitable employment for themselves toiled in a variety of positions in Chicago's brothels and boardinghouses for prostitutes. Black women served as chambermaids and general housekeepers in both black and white houses of prostitution. White madams, however, employed the largest number of black women as servants. In 1880 forty-year-old Amelia Cummins worked as a cook in Allie Archer's white house of prostitution. At a neighboring brothel, Mary Lewis, twenty-eight, cooked for seven women in Lizzie Moss's white house of prostitution. Lewis did not work alone. Inez Crary, twenty-five, was the brothel's housekeeper. Employing thirteen prostitutes, Belle Dimick ran her brothel with the help of four black women. Laura Washington, a forty-five-year-old widow from Kentucky, worked alongside Susan Smith, also widowed, thirty-five-year-old Annie, and twenty-two-year-old Laura. One of the Levee's most prominent white madams, Carrie Watson, employed four black women as servants in her posh, seven-woman parlor house. In 1900, when her resort had grown to eleven prostitutes, Watson hired thirty-nine-year-old Sally Phillips and twenty-two-year-old Adams Baker as servants.[55]

Black madams, whose houses tended to be smaller in size and on the whole less elaborate than nearby white brothels, were less likely to employ live-in servants. Black madam Elizabeth Moore had seven boarders and no extra live-in help. By contrast, white madam Mollie Fitch, who employed seven women as prostitutes and whose brothel was two doors away from Moore's, employed a cook, a porter, and a chambermaid, each of whom was black. In an interesting twist, Vina Fields, who in 1880 had eight black prostitutes working for her, employed one white woman as the servant for her resort.[56]

Black men also found work in Chicago's brothels. A thirty-nine-year-old black man named M. F. Geary worked as a porter at Lizzie Moss's resort in 1880. Laura Washington's twenty-four-year-old son worked alongside her at Belle Dimick's place, most likely as a porter. In 1900 Vina Fields employed three men as porters to help with her large nineteen-prostitute brothel. Brothels provided living accommodations for single black men who, like many brothel workers, had dreams of making it big in the city. In 1900 James Proctor and Benny Franklin were actors who resided at Jennie Carter's resort. While they looked for their chance in Chicago's theater scene, or as they waited to leave to tour with a vaudeville show, these and other men found lodging and perhaps stop-gap employment in houses like Carter's.[57]

Chicago's sex economy did more than trade in sex, then. Like other endeavors in the informal economy, it supported black households that had a difficult time making it any other way. John and Hannah Gragham worked together as servants in Annie Clyde's white brothel. Such a position was better than working and living apart, a choice facing many black working couples. If a black woman ran a boardinghouse for prostitutes it was not uncommon for a relative to also board at the house. Georgia Styles provided a place to stay for her younger relative, William Styles, a painter.[58]

In their effort to find employment in Chicago's late-nineteenth-century economy, black men and women frequently crossed the blurred lines that separated legitimate from illegitimate employment. The underground economy, of which the sex trade was so vital a part, touched the lives of the people not directly involved in it. Beyond brothel walls, prostitution often thrived within an intricate network of neighborhood institutions such as boardinghouses, pool halls, and saloons. To the distress of many community leaders, men and women unattached to the sex trade could find themselves within its orbit. Boardinghouse keepers both within and beyond the sex district rented rooms to individual women who worked independently in the trade. By turning a blind eye to the illicit activities of their boarders, keepers, most of whom were women, hoped to secure a stable income. They also facilitated the intermingling of prostitutes and independently living working men and women. In a city in which housing for African Americans was limited, sharing living spaces with prostitutes was often unavoidable. Even when unsought, the money circulated in the sex trade assisted many community residents in their struggle to gain economic stability in the face of their uneven incorporation within the urban wage economy.

Race and the Sex Economy

Black women who traded their sexual services for cash did not escape the devaluation of their labor that plagued their efforts to earn a living wage in the formal economy. Like the wage economy from which they sought refuge, the sex economy was organized in distinctive ways by race. In an industry in which a woman could generate as much as $20 or as little as 25¢ for her sexual services, black women found themselves consistently earning less than their white counterparts.

A complex intermingling of factors depressed black women's earnings in the sex trade. The financial status of a madam had direct consequences for the earning ability of black brothel workers. While some black women worked in interracial houses of prostitution under the leadership of white madams, most worked in houses operated by other black women. The limited access to capital that hampered all black women constrained the ability of black sex entrepreneurs to enter into the most lucrative sector of the late-nineteenth-century sex economy—the parlor house trade. Requiring large outlays of cash for furnishings and decorations, entrance into the elite branch of prostitution eluded most white women as well. Yet many white women were able to generate the needed money, whether through marriage, inheritance, savings from wage work, or earnings in the informal economy. Few black women had access to these resources, and consequently only a handful ranked among Chicago's numerous parlor house madams. Hence, proportionally fewer black prostitutes earned anything close to what the highest-paid white prostitutes could earn.

Despite their low representation among the top-paid madams and prostitutes, black women established a niche within Chicago's sex marketplace. The earnings of black and white laboring men provided the foundation for black women's labors in the sex economy. White women, too, depended on working-class men as customers; yet they generally could draw from a larger pool of clients than black women. While white middle-class men might make their way to small, humble white brothels, many sporting men observed social proscriptions against interracial sex and shunned entering black houses of prostitution. To be sure, there were white men of all classes who eagerly ignored such prohibitions, and black women made the most of white men's sexual curiosity. On the whole, however, black women had only infrequent opportunities to earn more than they could squeeze from the meager wages of working men.

Even when black and white women worked in brothels of equal status, black women routinely earned less for their sexual services than white women. In the late 1880s Lillian Richardson's parlor house charged between $3 and $5 for her employees' sexual services; white parlor house madams regularly charged between $5 and $20.[59] In some instances, this disparity may have reflected black prostitutes' attempts to accommodate the pockets of the low-wage black men who provided a good share of their earnings. However, this was not always the case. The women who worked for Richardson entertained white patrons exclusively.[60] The difference between black and white women's earnings exposes the primary role that race played in the economics of urban prostitution. It also underlines the commodification that was at the heart of prostitution. Black and white women were distinctly different commodities within Chicago's sex marketplace.

When black and white women worked alongside each other, the racial mayhem that ensued was particularly distressing to respectable observers. At the same time, such racial intermingling among brothel workers attracted an equally diverse range of clients. We need only return to the portrait painted by the *Chicago Times* reporter to get a sense of both the horror and the fascination such places generated. "Obese wenches in the arms of sodden white men; fair young girls nestling close to the side of sooty negroes—such were the aspects of the social problem as it presented itself in the lower haunts of this fair city."[61] In mixed houses in the Levee's "lower haunts," both white and black women paid the price—in the form of depressed wages—for black women's (and black men's) presumed sexual debasement.

African American women's comparatively low earnings within the sex trade reveal a crucial component of black women's sex work: to work in Chicago's sex industry, black women regularly endured white men's low estimation of their sexuality and their sexual labor. Even for those black women who rarely entertained white customers, white men's assessment of "value" in the sex marketplace determined what black women could charge any man—irrespective of race or class—for her services. The racial organization of women's legitimate wage work that led a disproportionate number of black women to turn to prostitution was replicated in the sex economy.

Nevertheless, if black women suffered from being devalued commodities in the informal sex economy, they benefited from men's willingness to pay relatively well for their illegal pleasure-providing services. They also benefited from not being imagined by their customers as dependent daughters or "attached" women, financially sheltered by father or husband. Rather, like the white women beside whom they worked in Chicago's sex districts, black prostitutes were paid the comparatively high wages attainable almost exclusively within the underground economy. At the same time, powerful racialized sexual ideologies depressed these earnings. Among sex workers, the commodity that black women sold remained the least valued. As a group, they were the poorest among the city's prostitutes. The intersection of race, sexuality, and the economy must have been frustrating for even the best-paid black prostitutes and madams. Though paid as self-supporting women, black women who worked in Chicago's sex industry suffered the economic consequences of the era's racial-sexual hierarchy.

Conclusion

For African American women, working in the sex industry provided no escape from the severe racial prejudices that weighed so heavily upon them in the formal economy. Indeed, white notions of black women's inferiority dogged them in every financial transaction and in their sexual interactions with customers. Given the widespread image of the black whore, it might be difficult to fathom why black women in turn-of-the-century Chicago would willingly seek employment in the underground sex trade. One might think that the intimate nature of such a racial mythology would lead black women to strenuously avoid association with this degraded and degrading figure; this image could make the idea of prostitution even more distasteful than it might otherwise have been. Indeed, how could a group of women, most of whom arrived in Chicago between 1870 and 1900 in search of the economic opportunity and social freedoms that the urban North was reported to offer, engage in work that so publicly advertised acceptance of their lot as morally debased women?

Though contemporary onlookers, as well as many paying customers, labeled black sex workers as morally depraved and socially dangerous women, such dehumanizing characterizations obscured the reasons that black women turned to prostitution in the late nineteenth century. Participation in the sex trade resulted from black women's profound economic marginalization. Yet black women were not passive victims of economic displacement. Resorting to prostitution exemplified resourcefulness within Chicago's racially and gender-stratified industrial economy. African American women strategically made use of the opportunities available within the late-nineteenth-century sex economy. Their mobility in and out of the trade suggests that they incorporated sex work into a scheme of survival in a hostile economy. This scheme or strategy changed over the course of the late nineteenth century. The fact that by 1900 more older women than before found themselves selling their sexual services highlights the deepening chasm that lay between black working women's goals in the city and the reality of the urban economy. Employment in prostitution, then, represents black women's efforts to adapt to both changing economic times and heightened expectations of urban living.

For all its remunerative potential, prostitution was not an ideal method of earning money. In the practice of their trade, women faced social ostracism from neighbors and religious and social reformers. Many no doubt maintained a distance from relatives, shielding themselves from the disapproval of their own families. Relations with clients bore their own hazards. There was the chance of pregnancy, the looming threat of contracting venereal disease, and the possibility of physical abuse. Even the financial compensations that led women to endure the rigors and abuses of sex work were not always predictable. Police harassment diminished a brothel's earnings. And as workers in the leisure economy, women bore the same vulnerability to economic downturns as their middle- and working-class clients. A sluggish economy quickly shrank the Levee's customer base.

For many black women, sex work could be an assertion of self-respect.[62] Prostitution helped to liberate black women from the meanest of circumstances in the city. In addition, the sex trade offered a con-

crete means of escaping dependence—on parents, other relatives, husbands, or even charitable agencies. A late-nineteenth-century prostitute
relied on her own resources. The sparely worded assertion of the black
prostitute that opened this chapter—"we must live anyhow"—evokes
both the economic hardship and the personal resourcefulness of black
women in the sex industry. Significantly, these words explained not just
this one woman's predicament. This unnamed woman explicitly acknowledged a similarity of experiences and perhaps outlook that linked
her to other black women working in the Levee sex trade. In their struggle to "live anyhow," black prostitutes developed strategies both to cope
with the numerous dangers and indignities of the job and to realize
the promise of financial independence that led them to become sexual
commodities in a racialized marketplace.

TWO

Working the Prostitution Economy, 1870–1900

The majority of black women working in Chicago's sex economy worked in an area popularly known as the Levee (see map 2.1). Located to the immediate south of the central business district, the Levee stood geographically apart from the respectable downtown commercial district and the middle-class residential enclaves in outlying areas. Yet it was within easy reach of middle-class men, who in their travels into and out of the heart of the city frequently passed through Levee district streets. Other pockets of sex trade and gambling existed at this time as well and, like the Levee, were well positioned to take advantage of the traffic of men into and out of the central city. In the 1860s and 1870s a small sex district emerged along a six-block stretch of Clinton Street, a thoroughfare several blocks west of downtown.[1] In addition, in the 1880s another sex district began to grow south of Eighteenth Street. Centered on State Street, it would gradually radiate outward to neighboring streets. This sex district would become the center of Chicago's sexual commerce after the turn of the century. (After 1904 it, too, would bear the name Levee.) In the late nineteenth century, however, the original Levee was the largest and most popular sex district in the city.

Black women were prominent in all sectors of the Levee sex trade. Most, however, worked in the district's humblest brothels and saloons. In these resorts black women entertained the black and white working-class and poor men who dwelled in the Levee. Some black prostitutes worked

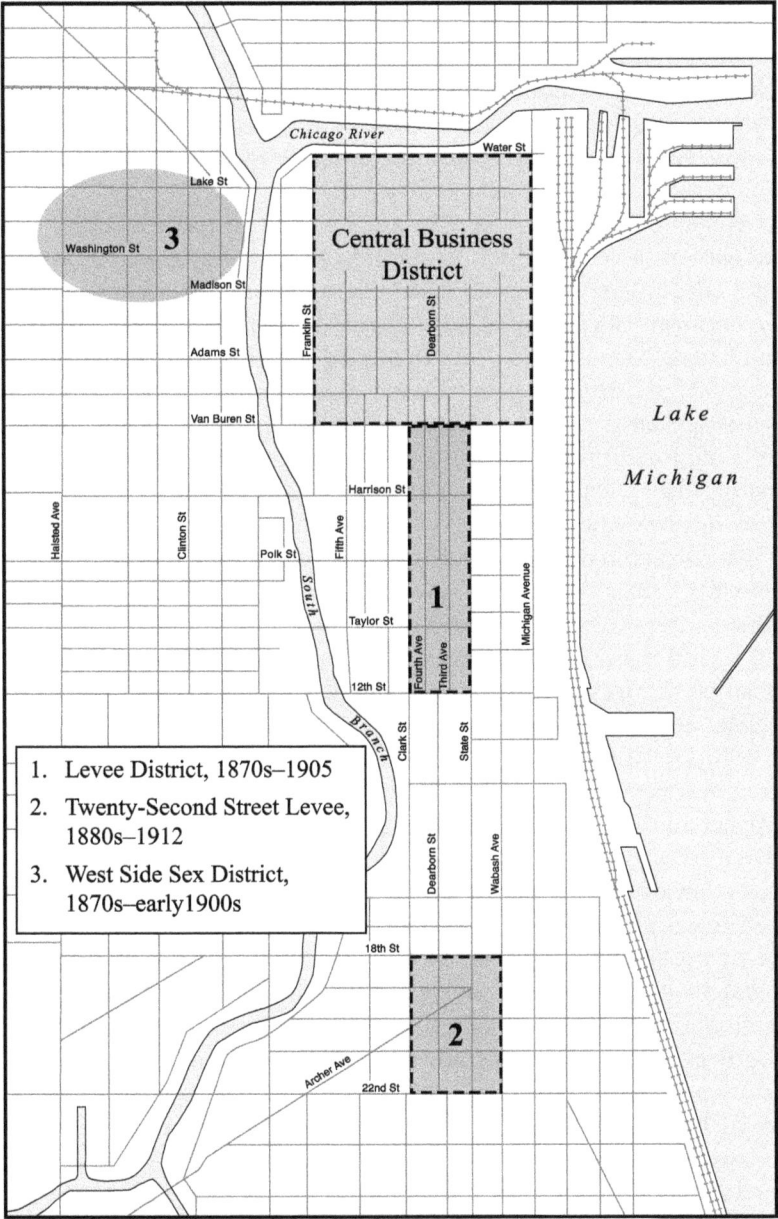

Map 2.1 Chicago's Main Sex Districts, 1870–1900. The boundaries of both the old and the new Levee districts held firm through the turn of the century, though business owners frequently tried to extend the boundaries of the sex trade beyond them. The West Side sex district was much smaller and less concentrated than the other two areas. Most resorts of the West Side sex district were clustered along Madison and Lake streets, with pockets of the trade scattered throughout the area west of the southern branch of the Chicago River to Halsted. *Source:* Rand McNally and Co., *Street Guide Map of Chicago* (Chicago: Rand McNally and Co., between 1897 and 1899), http://www.lib.uchicago.edu/e/su/maps/chi1890/G4104-C6-1897-R3.html.

in parlor houses, the Levee's elite sex institutions, where they provided sexual services to middle- and upper-class white men. However, the working-class and laboring-poor neighborhood that surrounded the sex trade gave character to the industry, and Levee residents provided black women with much of their clientele.

Available sources do not give voice to the attitudes of black women's clients, black or white. In their daily work, however, black prostitutes encountered a range of widely held notions about gender, sexuality, and race. Black clients likely carried beliefs about male dominance and female subordination into their paid sessions with prostitutes. And many white customers held widespread ideas about black women's "deviant" sexuality. Thus, in addition to facing notions of male superiority endemic to all phases of prostitution, black prostitutes also navigated the racialized sexual beliefs and prurient fascination of middle- and working-class white men.

Race structured Chicago's turn-of-the-century sex economy in often rigid ways. Black prostitutes confronted a racial hierarchy that determined where they worked and how much they earned. Though most black (and many white) women sold sexual services to black men, the racial preferences of working- and middle-class white men in many instances meant that black and white women worked in separate resorts. In addition to the racial segregation of Levee sex workers, a racially hierarchical pay system stratified black and white women. Black brothel keepers and prostitutes consistently charged the lowest rates for their sexual services.

As they daily encountered a racial structure that undermined their efforts to earn money in the sex trade, black sex workers and keepers frequently found ways to cross the lines that defined the economy's racial hierarchy. Many even took advantage of the racial boundaries that gave economic and institutional structure to Chicago's sex trade. Though poorly paid workers in a socially proscribed economic arena, black prostitutes possessed a heretofore-unacknowledged degree of agency. Just as young black women determined when to become prostitutes and when to leave the trade, they also shaped the circumstances under which they sold their sexual services. Through often strategic and bold acts in brothels, panel houses (see below), hotels, and furnished rooms and on Levee streets, black sex workers and madams temporarily reconfigured the unfavorable terms of their economic and sexual exploitation within late-nineteenth-century society. In the process some were able to attain economic self-sufficiency.

The Levee

Between 1870 and 1904 Chicago's Levee district, like other "segregated vice districts" in U.S. cities, had clear boundaries: Van Buren on the north, Twelfth Street on the south, State on the east, and Clark on the west (map 2.2). Yet the Levee was not only a geographically isolated sex district but also one of several working-class districts that emerged in Chicago in the last decades of the nineteenth century. Most of the city's workers' districts were characterized by some degree of ethnic diversity; usually, however, one ethnic group predominated in working-class neighborhoods.[2] For example, Irish workers' enclaves had formed close to the light industries located on the north branch of the Chicago River and in the southwest community of Bridgeport at the center of the meatpacking industry. Many German immigrants lived just north of the central business district and on the city's northwest side.[3]

The Levee was different from other working-class communities. Rather than being dominated by any one ethnic group, it contained a wide diversity of residents, reflecting the waves of migration and immigration that swelled the city's population in the last decades of the nineteenth century. Since the 1860s single men and women and, to a lesser extent, families crowded into the humble dwellings of this southern section. While most were unskilled men of Irish and German descent, a large and growing number were recent immigrants from Italy, Poland, and Russia, who made this poor district their initial residence in the city. Like many of the American-born white workers who also lived here, most found employment in downtown warehouses, in nearby freight yards, or in the light industries lining the banks of the southern branch of the Chicago River. Working men predominated in the area, yet employment opportunities drew women to this district as well. Some were married, though a large proportion lived on their own in the area's many boardinghouses. Most white women worked in the needle trades, in private homes, or in downtown service industries.

A large proportion of Chicago's African American men and women lived in the rooming and boardinghouses that accommodated the slim budgets of newcomers to the city. Most African American men and women looking for employment found themselves sequestered in menial and domestic labor. While native-born white and immigrant men worked as laborers in nearby industries or as clerks in downtown businesses, black men most often found jobs as servants in downtown hotels and restaurants or as porters in the homes of white middle-class

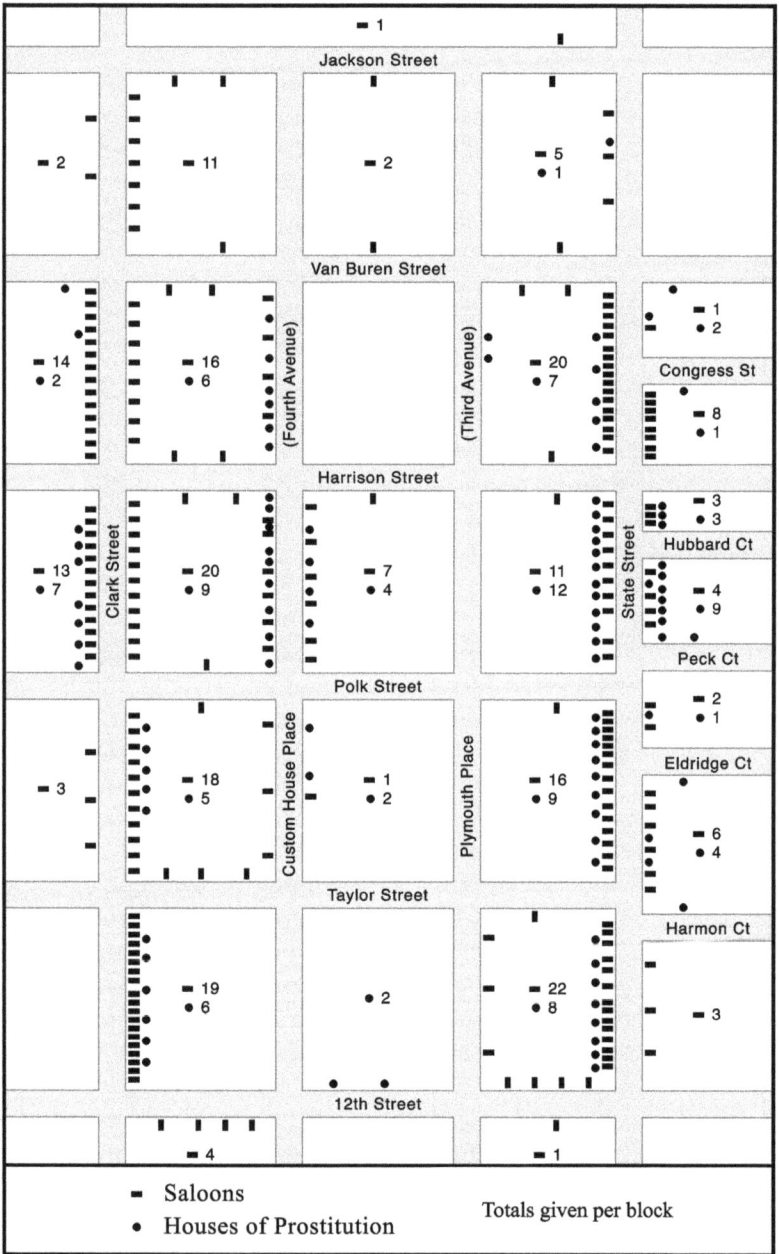

Map 2.2   "The Levee." *Source*: Adapted from *Chicago Tribune*, March 10, 1883, 2.

families on the periphery of the central business district. Black women found employment only as household workers or as servants in downtown hotels, laundries, or restaurants. Like other low-paid workers, many black working men and women made their initial home in the cramped and inexpensive confines of the Near South Side residential district. Many professional and entrepreneurial black men and women opened businesses or rented office space in the Levee as well. Between 1870 and 1900, when blacks composed between 1 and 2 percent of Chicago's population, they accounted for roughly 10 percent of the residents of the wards making up the Levee.[4]

White middle-class and elite men and women frequently expressed discomfort at the spectacle of racial and ethnic intermixture found in the Levee. Newspaper reports of an 1874 fire in the district reveal both the neighborhood's motley character and onlookers' dismay. One reporter described the fire victims as "Polish Jews, Italian, French, colored, and a very light sprinkling of Germans and Americans." One writer described the area as a "thieves', prostitutes', and niggers' paradise." Another report of the Levee's streets depicted the neighborhood as "the abode of colored people, white prostitutes, thieves, pimps, blacklegs, and low-bred and dangerous people of every kind."[5]

Even though outsiders saw the area primarily as a vice district, it was a neighborhood in which men and women found their bearings in the urban economy. The housing in the area—largely boardinghouses, rooming houses, furnished rooms, and hotels—attests to the temporary living arrangements most Levee residents sought. Most inhabitants of the district eventually moved to other neighborhoods to the north, west, and south of the central business district. Many Levee dwellers, however, established roots here, creating businesses that catered to the area's quickly changing population. Intermixed with the rooms and small businesses of the neighborhood were the institutions of the sex economy. Like neighborhood dry goods stores, restaurants, cigar shops, and saloons, the sex resorts of the Levee catered largely to the needs of the pool of unattached men—native-born white, immigrant, and African American—who lived in the district.

Black sex workers had access to a large and unusually concentrated pool of black customers in the South Side sex district. A large proportion of the city's African American men lived in the First and Second wards—the districts containing and bordering the Levee. In the last half of the nineteenth century, black men greatly outnumbered black women as residents of the Levee wards. In 1860 seventy-four out of every hundred black residents of the First Ward were male. Thirty years later, the First Ward's boundaries had been extended, but black men continued to outnumber black women and accounted for 66 percent of the area's black residents.[6] By 1900 that figure had risen again, reaching 72 percent.[7]

These population figures illuminate an important—though rarely discussed—context in which black women sold their sexual favors: they shared the streets of the Levee with a sizable group of young, unattached black men. Few studies of prostitution have acknowledged that black women regularly entertained black men.[8] Integrating black men into an analysis of black women's sexual labor reverses previous studies' silence about this particular form of sexual interchange. Furthermore, interrogating the ways that black men were part of the economic and geographical landscape of black sex workers reveals the important role that black prostitution played in the development of black urban sexuality at the turn of the twentieth century.

Like white working-class men, African American men of the First Ward lived in the furnished rooms, boardinghouses, and residential hotels that shaped working-class residential life in the Near South Side community.[9] While some black men worked in downtown businesses and leisure institutions, others found employment in neighborhood institutions and in the leisure resorts of the Levee. Working as waiters in nearby restaurants or as porters in neighborhood saloons, boardinghouses, hotels, and brothels, black men were woven into the Levee's economy of leisure, transiency, and commercial sex. For black men living and laboring within the Near South Side community, prostitutes, black and white, were a part of the overlapping landscapes of home, work, and leisure. In their daily pursuits black men of the First Ward had regular opportunity to both witness the labors and engage the services of black sex workers. Opportunity did not slip necessarily into patronage, but like their white working-class counterparts, more than a few black men undoubtedly made their way to the rooms of nearby sex workers.

Despite the predominance of black and white working-class men in the Levee, the most profitable sex institutions in the Levee were the resorts that enticed middle-class white men to travel district streets as they searched for sexual entertainment. Whether catering to workers or well-to-do pleasure-seekers, a variety of institutions provided employment for the black and white working-poor women who inhabited the Levee neighborhood.

The Brothel Trade

The brothel represented the most visible sex institution within the Levee. Houses of prostitution came in many forms. Small, inconspicuous places housing two or three women occupied one end of the spectrum. At these modestly priced resorts working women generally attracted little attention as they quietly entertained customers on and off of the Levee's main streets. At the other extreme and overshadowing these small houses were the extravagantly outfitted and expensive parlor houses that catered to white middle-class visitors to the Levee. In pursuit of sexual leisure and other recreation, these men regularly crossed the divide that separated the Levee from the nearby central business district. Most black women worked in the inexpensive brothels that crowded together in pockets on the main thoroughfares of the Levee sex trade—Custom House Place, Plymouth Place, and Clark Street. Black women working in these houses took advantage of what might seem to be a limitation of the trade—that their clientele, the black and white working men who lived in the Levee, had limited money to expend in the leisure economy. Yet in the area's numerous affordably priced houses of prostitution, black and white sex workers took advantage of the traffic of black and white working men who moved daily through Levee streets on their way to and from work and who after work sought out recreation in nearby saloons and pool halls. Levee prostitutes provided affordable outlets for a local trade of laboring men in search of paid sexual entertainment.

African American women staffed 19 percent of the seventy inexpensive houses listed as "dives" in an 1889 brothel directory. Even among these low-priced houses, there was considerable variety. A successful madam might operate a brothel that occupied an entire house or a three-story apartment building. Hattie Briggs ran two such resorts in the 1890s on Clark Street.[10] Resorts of this size employed as many as ten women. Other black brothels were located in small frame houses, apartments, or furnished rooms.[11] These little resorts, such as Effie Hammonds's house of prostitution on Custom House Place, were usually the province of independent sex workers. At the age of twenty-three, Hammonds worked alone in a diminutive house built in the backyard of a larger residential building.[12]

Most black women worked in brothels that employed between two and five women. These brothels occupied multi-roomed flats in apartment buildings or above saloons, restaurants, and other businesses.

Elizabeth Morris operated a small house of prostitution at 116 Custom House Place.[13] Morris, a thirty-eight-year-old woman, kept a "boarding-house" that housed, in addition to herself, two other prostitutes, Minnie Carter and Jennie White. In 1880 Annie Kerr, a twenty-five-year-old woman, ran a small resort at 124 Custom House Place. Kerr's house supported only four black prostitutes. Another African American woman, Georgia Styles, kept an unassuming house of prostitution on South Clark Street that housed four women (map 2.3).[14]

As sites of sexual labor houses such as those run by Elizabeth Morris and Annie Kerr held out certain attractions for late-nineteenth-century prostitutes. At a basic level brothels provided shelter for young, single black women who found it difficult to both work and secure affordable room and board in the city. Brothels were not only places of work but also homes for the women who labored in them. Because many brothels were designed to be attractive and comfortable to prospective customers, they provided homelike comforts to the women who staffed them. Madams frequently provided meals and clothing, and even if they deducted the price of each (at often-exorbitant rates) from a prostitute's earnings, such an arrangement might appeal to women on their own in the city. Furthermore, this arrangement compared favorably to the prospect of live-in domestic work. While employers of live-in servants provided food and shelter, live-in work was unappealing for many black women because of the low pay, isolation in the homes of white families, and severe limitations on a woman's free time. Finally, the social context of the brothel, where women lived with at least two other women, often of the same age, was undoubtedly attractive to some black women, most of whom were young, unattached migrants for whom the city was an economically and socially challenging place.

The main attraction of brothel prostitution for black women was the potential for earning money. The pay could be good, especially for women whose other labor opportunities were so severely restricted. Even in inexpensive houses, a black woman earning $1 per customer and seeing only two men a day could generate $14 per week. It was customary for brothel keepers to take half of their employees' earnings. Even with this significant reduction in pay, a black brothel worker could earn $7 at the end of the week, roughly two times the wages black women earned as domestic workers.[15]

Black women's average earnings from prostitution were comparable to what white women working in similarly modest houses made. Many white prostitutes, and a handful of black prostitutes, however, earned far more than this. These women worked in the ornate and

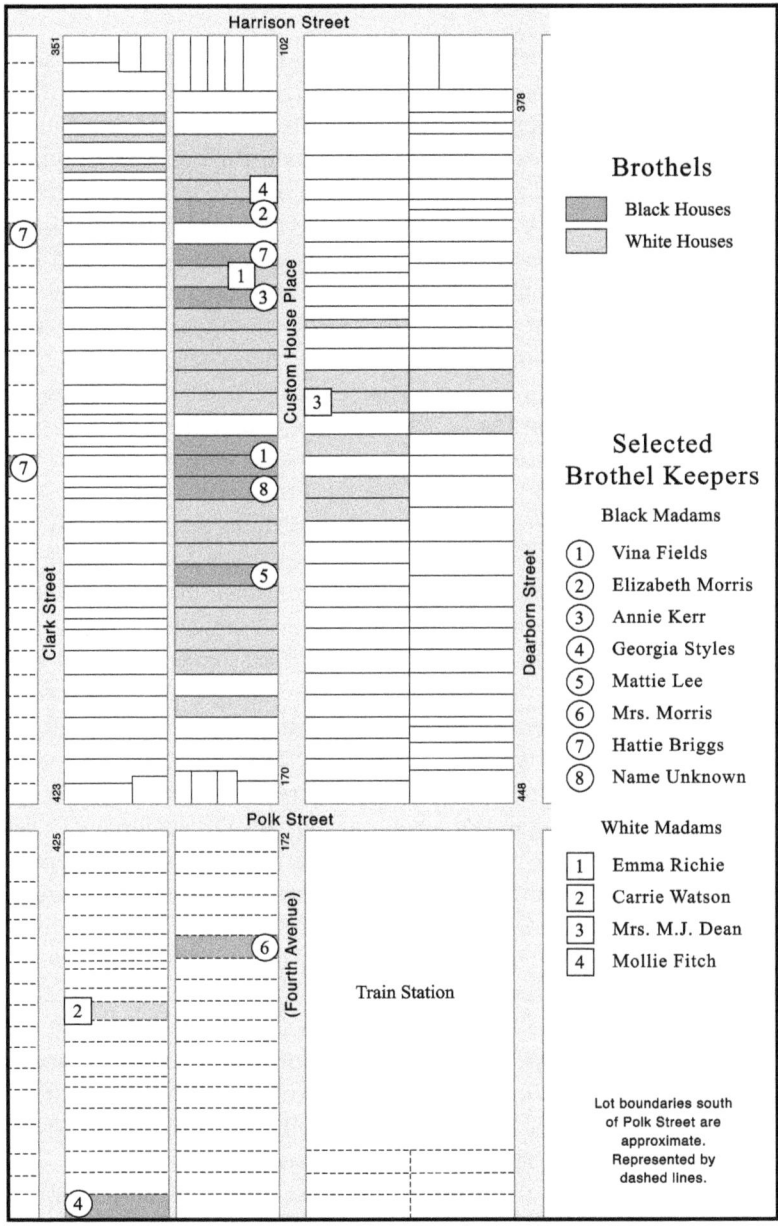

Map 2.3 Brothels and Selected Brothel Keepers in Section of Nineteenth-Century Levee.
Sources: William T. Stead, *If Christ Came to Chicago* (Chicago: Laird and Lee, 1894); Clifton R. Wooldridge, *Hands Up! In the World of Crime* (Chicago: Thompson and Thomas, 1901), 47; U.S. Bureau of the Census, Tenth Census (1880), Chicago Manuscript Schedules (microfilm), Enumeration Districts 5, 8, 9; U.S. Bureau of the Census, Twelfth Census (1900), Chicago Manuscript Schedules (microfilm), Enumeration Districts 12, 21, 24, 30, 38, 42, 43, 161.

expensive houses for which the Levee was best known. Parlor houses catered to an exclusive, white trade, entertaining local men of wealth and pleasure-seeking business travelers. These institutions combined the attractions of the saloon, the billiard hall, the concert saloon, and the brothel, placing all these amenities within the confines of a magnificently decorated home.[16] During the 1880s and 1890s, the majority of Chicago's parlor houses clustered along Custom House Place and Clark Street between Harrison and Taylor streets. Though they entertained a clientele quite different from the customers who visited the area's humble brothels, parlor houses stood alongside their cheaper counterparts. Such palaces of sexual pleasure as Carrie Watson's Clark Street resort or Emma Ritchie's Custom House Place brothel neighbored the workplaces of many black prostitutes. The proximity of elite houses helped to bring inexpensive black resorts into the center of the Levee trade.

Keepers of parlor houses expressly excluded black men from their resorts. Black women, however, were able to establish a niche within this elite, and profitable, trade. Though few in number, black women operated and worked in some of the Levee's most prestigious sex resorts. Out of sixty-seven parlor houses listed in the *Sporting and Club House Directory*, three were "colored houses," accounting for 4 percent of such resorts.[17] Whether run by black or white women, these high-class brothels sold something in addition to sex. They promoted themselves as protected domains of white male pleasure. They did this, ironically, not only by promoting men's sexual play but also by deploying in both their internal structure and their management notions of the house as an idealized male terrain.[18] This idealized space was designed as a retreat for middle-class men seeking refuge from the ravages of daily life in the public world of commerce and industry. As such, parlor houses were in an odd way connected to the ideal of the Victorian home. Unlike the unpretentious brothels that catered to the Levee's working men, elite institutions of prostitution fashioned a brand of domesticity shaped in part by middle-class Victorian ideology. Exploring the parlor house illuminates black women's relation to the domestic ideal sold to wealthy white men in the turn-of-the-century sex trade.

Detailed entries in the *Sporting and Club House Directory* reveal the centrality of the ideal of domestic space to the popularity and prosperity of elite brothels in Chicago. In his description of the houses listed in the guide, the unnamed "investigator" used such terms as "magnificently furnished" or "pervaded with an atmosphere of quiet elegance." Prominent in the guidebook's many descriptions is a preoccupation with ornament. The compiler succinctly described the women with words like "entertaining," "pleasant," and "pretty." By contrast, he gave an inordinate amount of space to descriptions of the interiors of these houses. The house run by Rome Buskirk, for example, had been "recently renovated and remodeled" and was, according to the directory's compiler, "one of the handsomest in the city." In addition, "the interior decorations are costly and in excellent taste, and the general effect is exquisite." Lizzie Moss's house was "one of the best and most handsomely furnished in the city." Not all parlor houses were this extravagant. Madam Frank Elgin ran a house that was described simply as "quiet and pleasant." Through the creation of both lavish and more restrained interiors, parlor house madams aspired to seduce male visitors by appealing to their desire for comfortable and visually alluring locales of sexual exploration. That Mollie Parker of Plymouth Place ran "one of the most home-like establishments in the city" was tremendously important for the profitability of her resort and for the success of parlor houses like hers.[19]

The image of the domestic retreat was only one of the ideals guiding the design of these pleasure reserves. Other nonsexual amenities contributed to the popularity of this branch of sexual commerce. By the end of the nineteenth century, aspects of men's commercialized entertainment found their way into parlor houses. According to the guidebook compiler, white madam Carrie Watson's establishment blended these other features quite exquisitely:

Nothing west of the Alleghaneys [sic] begins to compare with it in brilliance or magnificence. In the basement are billiard and pool rooms, with perfect appointments. On the first floor are five parlors and . . . these parlors defy description. One sees the first and one exclaims "magnificent." One sees the second and one exclaims "more magnificent." One sees the third and one murmurs in an ecstasy of delight, "this is certainly the most magnificent" for the decorations in this parlor are arranged with an ingenuity almost divine.[20]

Like numerous other parlor houses, Watson's catered to the multiple interests of men pursuing urban recreation. Not all parlor houses were large enough to have separate rooms for billiards or for musical entertainment. For these, an adjacent saloon or billiard hall complemented the offerings of the house. Almost all parlor houses sold wine, and many sold beer and whiskey.[21]

Neither the extravagant furnishings nor such supplemental amusements as pool rooms could on their own produce the peculiar attractions of the parlor house. That required the continual labor of madams and their workers. Like the houses that combined home-inspired features and commercialized sexual interactions, the women working in parlor houses could embody seemingly incongruous ideals. Mrs. M. J. Dean, for example, ran a house on Custom House Place that, according to the directory, was among the city's most opulent in ornament and accommodations. Mrs. Dean had established "an atmosphere of *quiet* elegance rarely met with in a sporting house." The demeanor of her fourteen boarders, though, was equally fashioned to appeal to the tastes of traveling men of wealth: "Most of Mrs. Dean's boarders are eastern people, and while they are modest, and ladylike they are still full of fun and music and entertain callers with a grace all their own."[22] Parlor houses such as these crafted a complicated blend of "fun" and feminine "modesty" for male consumption.

The requirement that brothel workers be sexually alluring while simultaneously exhibiting grace and modesty points to the labor involved in the cultivation of a white middle- and upper-class clientele. For her part, the madam, or hostess as she was often called, set the tone of the establishment, maintaining decorum, directing the traffic in men through the many rooms and diversions of her house, guiding them to drink and ultimately to partake of the sexual services offered by her workers.[23] The women continued the labors of their madams by reproducing the ideals of the house in every encounter with a customer and, in a simultaneously restrained and seductive way, catering to men's desire for abandoned recreation set in opulent ladies' boudoirs.

African American women working in the Levee sex trade faced financial challenges that limited their numbers among parlor house madams. The capital needed to rent, decorate, and furnish these multi-use and multi-roomed houses outstripped the means of the vast majority of African American madams and prostitutes working in Chicago's sex economy. Yet a few notable women were able to make these investments and meet the criteria of refinement, domesticity, and exclusivity upheld in the most lavish white houses. The compiler of the *Sporting and Club House Directory* ranked their places among the "better class of colored houses" (fig. 2.1). Vina Fields ran a parlor house that occupied two adjoining houses on Custom House Place. Lillian Richardson operated a brothel away from the Levee, in the small sex district farther south. Ella White's resort was also in this emerging district, only two blocks away from Richardson's brothel.[24]

Of these three brothels, Fields's house enjoyed the most success. In 1889 she was a well-known madam who after ten years in the city had turned the peddling of black women's sexual services into a large, pros-

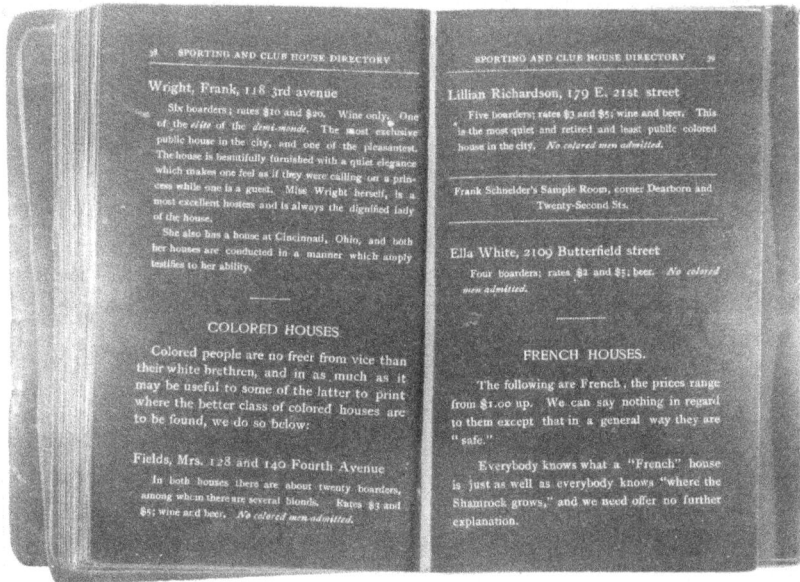

2.1   Colored parlor houses featured in *The Sporting and Club House Directory* (Chicago: Ross and St. Clair Publishing, 1889). Courtesy of Chicago History Museum.

perous, and highly visible enterprise. Though her resort received a scant three-line description in the sporting directory, Fields and her brothels figured prominently in the history of prostitution in turn-of-the-century Chicago. In the 1880s and 1890s, Fields's House of Pleasure[25] was one of the city's largest and most successful brothels, with each house typically lodging fifteen women. When business flourished, as was the case during the world's fair, her parlor house boasted more than sixty women.[26]

Like other parlor house madams, Fields offered her white male clients diverse amusements and some degree of privacy. Her resorts also offered her patrons something akin to the restrained yet seductive homelike leisure environment that white parlor madams sought to manufacture. Fields's own ruminations suggest her deliberate effort to fashion her resort in accordance with ideals of domestic leisure. Investigating the sources of the Levee sex trade, British social reformer William Stead queried several madams in 1893 about the sources of prostitution's success. In response, Fields mused suggestively about the relationship between the idea of the home and the inner workings of the high-status house of ill fame. Her assessment of what she saw to be the crisis facing young men and women at the end of the nineteenth century revealed surprisingly Victorian beliefs about the home and the respective roles of men and women within it:

The only remedy for prostitution will be to educate woman in the value of home life. . . . The great cry of today is the advancement of woman—that means for all to make a grand rush for outside employment, other than home work. . . . While the husbands and sons are walking the streets idle the mother and sisters are earning a living, and by so doing, the homes of necessity are dirty. . . . The husbands, when they have money, naturally seek the house of ill-fame, as wives are too tired from work or devoting their time to society, to give husbands even a pleasant word. Yes, I say, the only way out of this trouble is to teach girls the value of home.[27]

Fields made explicit the relationship between the house of ill fame and the home. She also provided a framework for evaluating the source of her own success.

According to Fields, the home was the proper place for women's work. "Outside employment" (women's work beyond the home) emasculated men, who, presumably because their wives, daughters, and sisters had usurped their role as providers, were now "walking the streets idle." Women had taken men's part in the public sphere, leaving them no proper place to express their manhood. Furthermore, the private realm suffered woefully because of neglect. Just as the upkeep of the home deteriorated, so did the relationship between wives and their husbands. In Fields's estimation, this lamentable situation directly resulted in pushing men away from their gloomy homes and to the doors of houses of prostitution.

In an intriguing omission, Fields did not define the necessity of the brothel in relation to the failure of wives to satisfy their husbands sexually. Rather, she privileged the idea of the home as the place that in its management, design, and embellishments expressed and fostered the relation that should naturally exist between men and women: "When women in mass elevate their homes and make them all that the word implies, that is, clean, home-like and cheerful, their kitchen the cleanest and most cheerful room in the house, and their parlor for use of the family instead of strangers; the houses of ill-fame will have to shut up shop. They will have to close for want of patronage."[28] The home was the seat of a man's comfort, ceaselessly inviting him to the pleasures of domesticity. To Fields, the house of ill fame served as an oasis for men whose home life had been degraded by their poorly trained wives and mothers or destroyed by the misguided notions of female equality. The brothel, then, provided a necessary substitute for the domestic pleasure that in the best of worlds originated from the familial home. The brothel's seduction, Fields proposed, relied on its relation to ideals of middle-class domesticity. The work of the women within the brothel was to carry out the duties of domestic seduction and to do so by producing home spaces—the parlors, the boudoir, and even the kitchen—pleasing to men.

Lillian Richardson and Ella White, like Vina Fields, endeavored to create resorts that appealed to the tastes of white men of leisure. Richardson's and White's resorts were neither as well established nor as large as Fields's House of Pleasure. Each housed four to five women. Furthermore, while Fields's House of Pleasure was located in the heart of the Levee, White and Richardson operated at a distance from this bustling district. Despite differences in size and location, all three resorts offered an array of amusements for their select clientele. They provided wine and beer for their patrons, thus incorporating the festive environment of the saloon. Probably occupying places more modest in decor than the houses of many of their white counterparts, these madams nonetheless endeavored to keep the site of sexual exchange separate from the spaces of manly recreation. Their resorts contained both private boudoirs and parlors for men's socializing and recreational drinking. Vina Fields's resort had four pianos for her guests' entertainment.[29]

One feature that helped to place White's and Richardson's brothels among elite houses was their ability to guarantee privacy for their guests. This was in part due to their location. Although Fields's House of Pleasure was in the heart of the Levee, White's and Richardson's resorts were situated well beyond this bustling red-light district and removed from the heavy traffic of pleasure-seeking men farther north. Twenty of the sixty-seven parlor houses described in the *Sporting and Club House Directory* were "pleasantly located" in this quiet district.[30] By locating their resorts beyond the city's most visible concentration of sexual commerce, Richardson and White secured privacy for white clients who preferred not to publicize their interest in sexual commerce, especially their desire for black women's sexual services. Sensitive to his white readers' preference for discretion, the directory's compiler noted that Richardson's brothel was "the most quiet and retired and least public colored house in the city."[31]

Although discretion was a desirable attribute of black houses of prostitution that catered to white men of means, location outside the sex district was not as important as another feature shared by all three black parlor houses. In the entries for White, Richardson, and Fields, the brothel guide highlighted a criterion essential for admittance to parlor house status: *"No colored men admitted"* (emphasis in original). All parlor houses observed this ban on black customers (though black men frequently worked as porters in parlor houses), yet only the entries for these colored houses explicitly state this prohibition. The requirement that no black men be entertained by black sex workers was a profound testimony to the relationship between white men's illicit sexual desire and constructions of racial and gender supremacy. The prohibition of black male customers assured prosperous white men that they would have exclusive access to black women's sexual favors. Such exclusive access allowed middle-class white men to imagine that they enjoyed unchallenged dominion (albeit temporary) over the black women whose services, or sexual servitude, they purchased. More than any other feature, the ban on black customers determined the status of black sex establishments.

In adopting this style of brothel, Fields, White, and Richardson undertook a challenging negotiation with the Victorian discourse of the home. For white middle-class men, this ideology at its very core excluded black women and men except as servants.[32] Brothels such as those run by Fields, White, and Richardson both expose the racial components of the parlor house's peculiar domestic ideology and raise questions about the kind of work required of black women who catered to a middle-class and elite trade.

Part of the daily labor of black parlor keepers and employees was to navigate the uneasy relationship between parlor house domesticity and black prostitutes' construction as doubly illicit and degraded objects of white men's sexual desire. They accomplished this by creating restrained and tasteful resorts. Richardson ran a "retired" resort, and Fields "prided herself not a little upon the character of her establishment." According to William Stead, Fields ran her house with a firm hand, posting "the rules and regulations of the Fields house" in every room, thereby "enforc[ing] decorum and decency with pains and penalties which could hardly be more strict if they were drawn up for the regulation of a Sunday school."[33] All parlor house madams established rules governing their workers' behavior, and the labor discipline required in their houses was tremendous.[34] Yet the severe restrictions that Fields placed on the behavior of black brothel workers represented one black madam's method of simultaneously navigating and servicing elite white men's racialized desires. While manufacturing domesticity within their brothels, Fields, White, and Richardson and the women working for them also had to sell what their customers in all likelihood experienced as a degraded variant of the domestic relation: degraded, not because these relations so explicitly incorporated monetary exchange, but because of the racial identity of the sex workers. To be sure, relations of commerce threatened to undermine the domestic fantasy performed in the most elaborate of white parlor houses, and the incorporation of a variety of other leisure time activities under the same roof further compromised this fantasy. Yet black women were hard-pressed to reproduce even the attenuated fantasy of home-inspired gender relations that white brothel workers labored to achieve. Indeed, for brothel keepers like Fields, White, and Richardson, the only domestic relation that black sex workers could reproduce for their white clients was not that of husband and dutiful wife but, rather, that of master and obedient servant.

The relations of racial subordination performed in black parlor houses account in large part for the lower price black women's sexual favors commanded in comparison to the prices white men might pay for white women's sexual services. Both Lillian Richardson and Vina Fields charged customers between $3 and $5 for their workers' sexual services. Ella White's prices went as low as $2. White women working in elite brothels, on the other hand, could command from between $5 and $30 for their services. Although affluent white men sought out the particular delights they believed black women could offer, the relatively low prices they paid for these illicit pleasures highlight the contempt with which these men approached the objects of their sexual desire.[35]

Paradoxically, white male constructions of black women's sexuality were as much a financial benefit as a burden to black sex workers. To the extent that elite white men sought out the sexual services of black women based on fantasies of their own sexual dominance or based on contemporary mythology regarding the hypersexual nature of black women, a steady stream of customers arrived at the doors of "colored" parlor houses, and their madams were able to charge higher prices than nearby brothels that indiscriminately entertained working-class men.

By maintaining an exclusively white clientele, these parlor houses serviced and even promoted white men's illicit desires for black women. Keepers like Fields, White, and Richardson endeavored to undermine the degraded circumstances that appeared to define such work. Each attempted to wrestle some respectability for herself and her employees, manufacturing not opulence but decorum and offering it as one of their resorts' distinctive attractions. This feat was difficult—performing propriety within paid sexual relations with white men. In their effort to negotiate a form of respectability, the black women who worked for

Fields and in similar brothels were not unlike other women working in the homes of white families, where conditions of intimacy, or merely sustained proximity, could invite all manner of insult and sexual trespass.[36] Vina Fields's insistence on decorum, then, was perhaps not only a strategy to make black women's sexual services specially appealing to affluent white men; nor was it primarily a strategy to avoid embarrassing police intrusions. Such efforts could serve to subtly discipline white male customers to "respect" the women with whom they spent time. In her "quiet" brothel, Richardson might similarly have sought to set standards for the behavior of both her workers and their white clients.

In tone, price, and clientele, parlor houses differed from the resorts in which most black prostitutes worked. The rigid standards of behavior imposed within elite houses did not govern the work experiences of black women employed in inexpensive brothels. The environments in low-priced houses mirrored the boisterous atmosphere of nearby working-class saloons and pool halls. Nor were women who worked in less exclusive resorts likely to infuse their transactions with domestic rituals. In settings where rapid turnover rather than elaborate performances promised increased earnings, workers stripped sexual encounters of time-consuming artifice and focused mostly on the physical gratification of each customer.

Despite these differences, workers in both inexpensive and elite brothels contended with the racial ideas of their customers. Many white men, elite and working class, refused to engage the services of black prostitutes. Responding to the myth of black women's racial inferiority and sexual depravity with revulsion rather than curiosity, some white men avoided black houses altogether. The unwillingness of white men of means to visit black prostitutes may account in part for the low representation of black resorts among parlor houses; yet demand was enough to allow at least a few establishments to thrive in the Levee sex economy. For black prostitutes in cheaper brothels, the patronage of black customers and white workers who had few qualms about the race of their sexual partners offset middle-class white men's refusal to patronize them.

Navigating the racial terrain of Chicago's late-nineteenth-century sex marketplace presented distinct challenges to black women trying to make it on their own in the city. In addition to enduring the racial and gender inequalities frequently reproduced in interracial sexual encounters, black women working in brothels faced other disadvantages as well. The daily labors that prostitutes had to perform within brothels were demanding: greeting and entertaining men; constantly assuring prospective clients of their desirability or urbanity; the constant self-care required to produce alluring personal effects and reflect well on the establishment. With the exception of Vina Fields's House of Pleasure, few black brothels employed servants to cook or clean; thus, black women's brothel work included the domestic upkeep of the house.[37]

The wages of brothel work may not have compensated for the scrutiny that workers had to endure as brothel representatives. The watchfulness of a brothel madam could constrain a prostitute's activities in both inexpensive and elite houses. It could also limit the amount of money a worker might earn from a customer. The standard procedure of splitting earnings from a night's or a week's labors with a madam meant that brothel prostitutes watched large portions of their hard-earned money drift away from them. Some women might secretly try to get tips from patrons; but a madam's vigilance made it difficult for workers to conceal extra earnings. Some brothel keepers forbade their employees from seeing men outside the brothel, further constraining prostitutes' earning opportunities.[38]

In parlor houses, the domestic discipline under which women performed their sexual labor could chafe those who desired more freedom in the pursuit of their trade and the money it could bring. Such discipline pushed Flossie Moore from Vina Fields's resort shortly after her arrival in the city in 1889. According to a police reminiscence, Moore was "high-strung, restless," and "self-willed" and eventually tired of Fields's rules and regulations. After she "packed up and left" Fields's house, she became one of the "toughest thugs, footpads and pickpockets in Chicago."[39] Moore's career trajectory after leaving Fields's brothel was not typical, but her choice to seek other opportunities within the city's informal economy was common. Although brothels offered some comforts, temporary community, and the possibility of economic security, many black prostitutes echoed Moore's dissatisfaction with brothel work. They created other opportunities for themselves within the Levee sex economy.[40]

Alternatives to the Brothel

Some African American women seeking to avoid the rigors of brothel prostitution found employment in other institutions of the late-nineteenth-century commercial sex landscape. Through work in assignation houses and hotels, black and white prostitutes exploited the Levee's concentrated traffic in male pleasure-seekers and thereby extended the geography of male sexual leisure. The form of sex work that developed around these rented spaces helped prostitutes to escape the surveillance of madams and the economic limitations of brothel work. Black women working in these alternative sex resorts engaged in a form of self-employment. Working on their own in saloons or casually meeting men in other commercial establishments or on Levee streets, prostitutes took their customers to these quiet places for sexual intercourse. Assignation rooms in hotels, boardinghouses, or attached to saloons were successful enterprises because their association with legitimate businesses camouflaged their illicit activities. Assignation hotels preserved the anonymity of their patrons by allowing them to register pseudonymously. Furnished rooming houses that accepted "transient" couples protected themselves and their clients by assuming reputable fronts and by requiring the propriety of all their guests. Saloons that rented upstairs rooms for sex concealed this enterprise by providing side entrances and alley exits for both participants in clandestine exchanges.[41]

As freelance sex workers, women who used assignation houses and hotels worked under minimal constraints. Moreover, perhaps more easily than brothel prostitutes, women working on their own could move in and out of the sex economy. Somewhat protected by the hidden nature of their sexual encounters, black and white women who rented rooms for assignation were not as publicly identified with the sex trade as women working in known houses of prostitution. Most important, they exerted greater control over their income and hours than women working in brothels. Though part of their earnings were turned over to profit-seeking hotel managers or boardinghouse keepers, in private rented rooms prostitutes could negotiate their own terms for sexual exchange.

Black women working in disorderly saloons enjoyed a similar ability to negotiate with their clients. Unlike in brothels, parlor houses, or assignation rooms, sexual commerce was only one diversion among several others offered in bawdy saloons. These institutions appealed to the pockets and leisure habits of working- and middle-class men who sought more boisterous amusement and raucous sociality than they could find in more reserved saloons. Blending the saloon atmosphere with musical entertainment, dancing, and sometimes gambling, disorderly resorts provided an alternative to the minimally outfitted working-class brothel and flouted the restraint and respectability of the parlor house and the assignation house. By allowing prostitutes to openly circulate among patrons, saloon keepers exploited black and white men's attraction to the potent mixture of drinking and sexual adventure. Such bundling of urban leisure pursuits worked to the financial benefit of saloon keepers throughout the Levee.

African American saloon proprietors actively participated in the sex economy. One of the most prosperous African American resort owners was Pony Moore, whose saloon and gambling house was notorious for the interracial exchanges it supported.[42] Other black saloon keepers, like John "Mushmouth" Johnson, were less blatant about fostering interracial sexual exchanges. Black saloon owners who did not draw an interracial clientele nevertheless supplied opportunities for interactions between black men and women of the "sporting set." For black prostitutes, these emerging institutions of male leisure provided an attractive alternative to brothel work. In disorderly saloons, keepers encouraged and profited from sexual commerce but usually did not oversee transactions. Like their counterparts in rooms rented for assignation, black women working in saloons exercised a measure of freedom in setting the terms of each sexual exchange.

Working the Streets

Historians of turn-of-the-century prostitution have frequently associated African American women with the shabbiest confines and most dangerous sectors of the sex industry.[43] Black women's apparent concentration in streets, cribs, and alleyways, some historians have argued, demonstrates their fundamental degradation in the urban sex economy.[44] Furthermore, the sex work that began in the streets and concluded in exposed alleys appears to be both physically isolated and categorically distinct from the other types of sex trade that characterized the red-light districts in which street workers performed. Careful examination of black women's street work in Chicago, however, raises doubts about these commonly held assumptions. First, at the end of the nineteenth century, black women worked neither solely nor even primarily on Levee streets but participated fully in the city's brothel trade as well as in other arenas of sex work. Second, the streets of the Levee and the women who worked on them were not removed from the sex trade conducted in the district's many institutions but were well integrated into all phases of the local sex economy. Finally, even for women who worked primarily outdoors, the streets offered more numerous ways of conducting sex work than historians have assumed. Yet even if street work did not represent black women's isolation within the sex economy, the necessity of street work did demonstrate the economic vulnerability of individual black women and the financial instability of the black brothels, bawdy saloons, and other leisure establishments supporting black street workers. Streetwalking demonstrates the various ways that black women simultaneously exploited opportunities within the sex trade and worked to redefine the limits that they faced within the Levee's sex economy.

All women's street work was made possible by the constant stream of men through the streets of Chicago's sex district. Indeed, the public spaces of the Levee were defined more by the presence of men shopping for sexual adventure than by the activities of black and white sex workers in the streets. One *Chicago Tribune* reporter noted with some distress the "Fourth Avenue [also known as Custom House Place] houses of prostitution ablaze with light, carriages flitting to and fro, and little knots of drunken young bloods walking from place to place." White men from afar daily wound their way through this South Side terrain; and as their days shifted from work to leisure, male Levee dwellers shifted their uses of neighborhood avenues.[45]

The steady flow of men through Levee streets in search of sexual entertainment connected what was happening in the streets with the more concealed world of Levee institutions. Indeed, rather than being detached from the trade taking place in the streets, brothels, saloons, and assignation hotels relied heavily on activities occurring along sex district thoroughfares. Saloon keepers, brothel madams, and brothel prostitutes strategically used sex district streets to gain access to these men's pockets. Black and white women regularly solicited patronage for their establishments from passersby on the streets. William Stead described the practice of window hustling at one white Custom House Place brothel: "The girls sat in couples at windows, each keeping watch in the opposite direction. If a man passed they would rap at the window and beckon him to come in. If a policeman appeared . . . the curtains would be drawn and all trace of hustling would disappear. But before the officer was out of sight the girls would be there again."[46] Police detective Clifton Wooldridge recalled that most Custom House Place brothels in the 1890s aggressively solicited men from the streets:

Here at all hours of the day and night women could be seen at the doors and windows, frequently half-clad, making an exhibition of themselves and using vulgar and obscene language. At almost all of these places there were sliding windows, or windows that were hung on hinges and swung inside. These swinging or sliding windows were used by the women to invite pedestrians on the street to enter these places and also for the purpose of exhibiting themselves. . . . The habitues of this place embraced every nationality, both black and white, their ages ranging from eighteen to fifty.[47]

Black brothel keeper Susan Winslow used similar stratagems to draw men into her resort. Her employees "attracted attention by tapping on the window and hissing with the mouth like a rattle snake" to men strolling by her den at Clark and Twelfth.[48]

On thoroughfares thick with houses of prostitution, brothel keepers faced stiff competition. In an effort to make their resorts stand out, many black brothel owners required their employees to make even more active use of the streets. An illustration that appeared in an 1895 treatise on the poor in Chicago showed a group of black women variously positioned in front of an entranceway, presumably to a house of prostitution, in a section of the Levee known as the "Bad Lands."[49] Prostitutes working in black resorts frequently targeted male passersby for invitations to sexual pleasure. A. Rapp, a white man who lived in a middle-class enclave on South Wentworth, reported being "seized by a negro woman who attempted to force him into her house" of prostitution on Custom House Place.[50] In 1880 Alice Green, Bell Parker, and Ida Snow lured a Wisconsin man as he passed by their Clark Street resort, eventually robbing him of more than $50.[51] Such bold occupation of Levee streets made black women highly visible. For women working in houses that could not compete with the extravagantly attractive fronts and window devices of larger brothels, aggressive self-promotion was a necessity.

Such efforts to secure trade made women visible to policemen, who were under orders to keep the sex traffic from the streets. Officers frequently patrolled Clark Street, State Street, and Custom House Place to clear them of all "sidewalk sylphs" and "black women of bad character."[52] The risk of arrest, however, did not deter sex workers. Street soliciting gave black prostitutes inexpensive and unmediated access to prospective customers. On the streets they could strategically advertise their lower rates and in so doing attempted to stem the traffic flowing to white resorts.

At the same time, on the streets black women directly offered themselves as racialized objects of sexual desire—illicit delights unavailable in their competitors' resorts. Perhaps more than other sex institutions, the panel house relied heavily on women working the streets to manipulate men's—particularly white men's—expectations of black women's sexual availability. Panel houses were putative houses of prostitution where workers unceremoniously fleeced men of whatever cash and valuables they held. They appeared to fit well under the category of brothel—physically, most resembled the sex resorts, large and small, that lined Clark Street and Custom House Place; and women who worked in them ostensibly did exchange sexual services for cash. Yet panel houses were founded on the principle that men's sexual desire could be used against them. Panel workers used both men's expectations of sexual exchange and the form of house-based prostitution to support their main enterprise—robbing unsuspecting men of all they carried.[53]

In a "panel game," a client was usually robbed during the sex act, the money spirited away by an accomplice who hid in a closet, behind a concealed door (a "panel door"), or some secret chamber in the house.[54] Usually, the "thieving prostitute" feigned ignorance of the robbery or, if discovered, escaped through a hidden passageway leading to a street or by taking refuge in a nearby house of prostitution. Such subterfuge required that sex workers work in pairs and in some cases relied on the cooperation of madams of other brothels.

Most area residents and district habitués knew the Levee panel houses. These thieving dens therefore thrived, not on the trade of district denizens, but on the steady traffic of men new to the area's offerings and unfamiliar with its dangers. Detective Wooldridge observed that "a greater part of the victims [of panel houses] are strangers passing through Chicago" or "young men from rural towns who go to great cities with a consuming desire to see the great sights that lurk in the shadows of levee resorts."[55] In identifying their marks, panel house workers shrewdly assessed the flow of money through Levee district streets.

Black women were prominent among Chicago's panel house madams and the "footpads" who worked in them.[56] Detective Wooldridge described one stretch of State Street as an area full of black "thieving dens of prostitution."[57] Yet black women established panel houses throughout the Levee, as well as in other sex districts. In 1880 Eliza Dennis, "a notorious negro wench" who lived and worked in the small West Side sex and gambling district, was reported by the *Tribune* to have "stolen from men whom she enticed into her den more money than has been similarly stolen by any other three cyprians in the city for ten years past." Unlike most panel house operators, Dennis appears to have worked alone. This proved to be no handicap for her, however. She regularly found customers from whom she stole "sums varying from $3,000 to 50 cents."[58] Hattie Briggs, on the other hand, was reputed to operate two thieving resorts on Clark Street, each of which housed several workers.[59] In 1896 another black woman, Mattie Lee, ran an elaborate panel house on Custom House Place that employed at least six "panel house workers and footpads." "It was not an unusual thing," Detective Wooldridge recalled, "for from five to ten men to be robbed in a single night in her house by the panel game."[60] African American keepers of panel houses were particularly astute when it came to cultivating and exploiting black and white—especially white—men's desire for brothel-based excitement and black women's sexual favors.

For panel house workers, street solicitations functioned simultaneously as invitations to sex and as fronts for more remunerative exchanges. Flossie Moore, after leaving Vina Fields's house, took to the streets with considerable gusto (fig. 2.2). According to one source, "her victims were mostly strangers and traveling men found around the vicinity of the Polk street depot,"[61] which emptied travelers directly onto the streets of the Levee. One reporter described Moore as "one of the most daring and successful pickpockets and thieves in the United States." Moore worked mostly along Clark Street and in that thoroughfare's panel houses. According to the *Tribune*, she had stolen as much as $30,000 from traveling men in 1892 and 1893 alone.[62]

Minnie Shouse, a prostitute and a pickpocket, was equally adept at using the streets in this way (fig. 2.3). According to Detective Wooldridge, this "bright-skinned colored woman" had been arrested at least thirty-six times a year for robbing men on the streets of the sex district. Wooldridge may have been given to exaggeration, but in 1893 and 1894 Shouse appeared before the Cook County Criminal Court on at least five occasions. In February 1893 Shouse was tried for larceny. Finding her guilty, a jury recommended that she be sent to prison for one year. The presiding judge suspended this sentence, however, once Shouse assured him that she would change her ways. Shouse did not take his leniency to heart. In April 1893 local police again arrested Shouse and charged her with robbery of $42 and a $3 revolver from twenty-five-year-old Napoleon Barland of Bourbonnais Grove, Illinois. Initially Shouse's victim testified for the prosecution, but Barland eventually dropped the case against her after he accepted a $20 bribe to leave town from an officer friendly to Shouse. The following month Shouse appeared again before criminal court, this time for robbing John Owens of $99. The judge sentenced her to one year in Joliet Correctional Center, though she appears not to have served the entire sentence. In February 1894 Shouse was charged with larceny for stealing $38 from James Bois, a Chicago resident who lived some distance from the Levee, at 355 Ashland Boulevard. Finally, in June 1894 Shouse appeared before the criminal court, along with unnamed accomplices, charged with robbery of $60 from William Rundell. Neither criminal court records nor

2.2 Flossie Moore. From Clifton R. Wooldridge, *Hands Up! In the World of Crime* (Chicago: Police Publishing Co., 1901). Courtesy of Chicago History Museum.

2.3 Minnie Shouse. From Clifton R. Wooldridge, *Hands Up! In the World of Crime* (Chicago: Police Publishing Co., 1901). Courtesy of Chicago History Museum.

newspaper accounts of her exploits document the outcome of these last two cases. Yet Shouse's multiple thieving acts illuminate an important aspect of black women's work within the sex industry. Minnie Shouse and others targeted men of some means—very often visitors to the city who were known to walk the streets with a lot of cash.[63] In choosing their victims so wisely, they not only gained access to large amounts of money but challenged men's—in particular, white men's—expectations of racial and gender dominance.

Although white women regularly robbed unsuspecting men in the panel house game,[64] black women appeared to be particularly astute street workers. Not only did street work broaden women's opportunities for securing paying clients, but the *pretense* of street work gave black women access to men, especially white men, in search of sexual recreation. In 1892 a policeman caught Jennie "Ginger Heel" Paine in the process of "robbing a farmer" on Custom House Place before she made her escape into a black-owned saloon nearby. Similarly, Hattie Smith (aka Hattie Washington), Mary Logan, and Lena Blake were arrested for trying to rob a drunken "old farmer" in front of a Clark Street resort.[65] It appears that in each of these cases no sexual transaction actually occurred. Yet it is likely that Paine, Smith, Logan, and Blake eased their approach to these out-of-town men by presenting themselves as prostitutes.

On its own the activity of women on the streets could not ensure the success of thievery within the sex economy. A network of Levee institutions supported street hustlers. When Lena Blake and Mary Logan robbed their farmer on Clark Street, they were living in Lizzie Davenport's house of prostitution on Custom House Place. Detective Wooldridge described Davenport's resort as "one of the worst dives in the city . . . patronized by some of the cleverest strong-arm women and pickpockets that ever operated in Chicago." When Jennie "Ginger Heel" Paine tried to escape pursuing police officers, she took refuge in one of Hattie Briggs's saloons. When Mamie Levelle, "a colored thief and pickpocket," fled from the police after she stole nearly $500 from a man out for a "stroll" along Custom House Place, she headed toward a house of prostitution run by Grace St. Clair.[66] Whether panel houses such as that run by Mattie Lee, small brothels such as that operated by Eliza Dennis, or saloons such as the ones run by Hattie Briggs, sex resorts lent refuge to thieving street workers and provided bases from which to execute their plans. Rather than working in isolation, street workers were part of an active network of brothel prostitutes, madams, and panel house workers. This network helped street workers to keep their earnings safe and provided protection from angry customers or zealous police officers.

The prevalence of theft within prostitution and black women's prominence among Chicago's thieving prostitutes suggest that black women worked hard to augment or supplant the consistently low wages they earned from sexual labor. In such use of the streets and institutions of the sex district, these black women attempted to circumvent the racialized rate structure of the South Side sex economy. In the process they demonstrated savvy about the economics of men's leisure habits in the city and proved themselves astute readers of signs of men's affluence. Perhaps more than white women, with whom they shared Levee streets and who also set traps for fun-distracted men, black women found in street work the ultimate confidence game. In this game they manipulated white men's desires and perhaps their belief in their own supremacy and invulnerability, temporarily reversing the relations of power that defined both street solicitation and illicit interracial sexual relations.

Most black street workers did not engage in panel house work or other thieving ploys. Rather, they worked the streets to attract more clients. For black women street work was a necessary means of drawing attention to their wares in a marketplace that at each level was crowded with competing attractions. Black women struggled to enhance their visibility precisely because of the lower earnings that they could net from any sex act.

Although for some black women street work proved an advantageous way of working the sex economy, it had several drawbacks. The constant pursuit of clients no doubt exhausted the most energetic worker. They had to approach white men who might respond hostilely to their solicitations. They also experienced theft and physical assault by customers and street thieves, who could easily make a getaway. Furthermore, those who engaged solely in street work could not rely on a regular clientele. Events that slowed the traffic of men to the sex district posed one of the greatest challenges to their ability to earn a steady income. Women and resorts that relied on street-generated trade suffered, for example, when the police sweeps of district thoroughfares scared away potential clients.

Black street workers' visibility to police officers imposed added costs. When arrested, they often faced harsh penalties for their public transgressions. In 1876 police officials arrested Dora Perry, described in the *Daily News* as "a black wench," and charged her in police court with vagrancy. A judge found Perry guilty of being "a prostitute of the worst kind" and fined her a substantial $20. White women were rarely given such exorbitant fines. A month earlier police officers had raided a small sex district on the city's West Side and arrested 137 male and female "inmates" in several "dens of infamy." The same judge imposed fines ranging from $1 to $10. Reflecting an interpretation of the women's activities quite different from that guiding Perry's punishment, the judge warned the women that their arrest and fines were designed "to keep them from the doors [of their houses], and to let them know that they were law-breakers." Perry's $20 fine carried no gentle warning. Rather, the judge also threatened to confine her to the Bridewell (the city's prison) if she was unable to pay.[67] Many black women assumed similarly heavy burdens for their visibility on the streets.

The difficulties of working on Levee streets notwithstanding, black sex workers at almost all levels of the trade incorporated street work into their labors. Whether they entertained white and black working men or white men of means, black prostitutes used the streets to enlarge their earnings in the trade. Black brothels, bawdy saloons, and other leisure establishments supporting black sex workers also relied on street work. Working the streets indicated the economic disadvantage at which most black women and most black sex institutions operated in the Levee marketplace. Black women who creatively used the streets not only ameliorated their own circumstances but bolstered the fragile economies of the sex resorts with which they were connected.

Black Women and Sex Entrepreneurship

Though street work aimed to make African American women's sexual favors competitive with other sexual commodities sold in the Levee, it could not overcome the economic instability endemic to running a prostitution business. Whether housing black or white women or both, most brothels, saloons, and even panel houses teetered on the brink of financial ruin. Indeed, instability defined the Levee sex trade. Although the spatial boundaries of sexual commerce remained relatively fixed between 1870 and 1904, the economy itself constantly changed. Black and white brothel owners battled the vicissitudes of sex entrepreneurship by continually seeking out new business opportunities within the trade. They did so by exploiting the flexible property relations that supported the city's sex economy.

At the industry's height in the late nineteenth century, constant turnover affected all but the most elite resorts. Few houses of prostitution stayed at an address for any length of time. Many houses moved around within the vice district. Several successful brothels relocated to take advantage of leisure markets growing in other parts of the city, such as the Twenty-Second Street sex district. Others—perhaps most—simply failed and faded from the sex economy altogether. Even some parlor houses buckled under the economic pressure of maintaining extravagant pleasure palaces with earnings collected from middle-class men whose entertainment budgets expanded and contracted with the health of the city's economy. The inexpensive resorts where most black women worked were among the most vulnerable.

In any given year a survey of Chicago brothels might find several black houses in one Levee block. A few years later, however, one or all of those houses may have moved on, replaced by white establishments, other black resorts, or the residences of working-class families. For example, the 1889 brothel directory noted eleven "coon dives" concentrated south of Polk Street on Custom House Place. Four years later, in 1893, however, an investigator counted only two houses with black prostitutes south of Polk. In the same year, William Stead found only one black house of ill fame south of Polk and only one in the northern section of Custom House Place.[68]

Perhaps the greatest pressure black brothel keepers faced arose from their status as renters in a district defined by lucrative rental arrangements. The Levee sex trade brought significant profits to landlords who turned a blind eye to the illegal use of their properties. For such "protection," managers of the area's sex resorts paid extremely high monthly rates. In the 1890s black madam Susan Winslow reportedly paid $40 a month for "a dilapidated two-story wooden shanty" at Clark and Twelfth streets. In 1898 Vina Fields paid $175 a month to rent a house adjacent to her Custom House Place resort.[69] A house fitted up for trade and located in the center of sporting traffic could bring owners between $200 and $300 a month.[70] As the abundance of black resorts attests, African American madams hoping for healthy returns on their monthly investments regularly engaged in these rental transactions, though at some risk. Whether occupying entire town houses or small apartments, black madams had to meet high weekly or monthly expenses, even though the women who worked for them earned less than white workers in the trade. The often fleeting life span of individual black houses of prostitution suggests that many could not generate enough money, or not with a necessary degree of regularity, to pay exorbitant leisure district rents.

Black madams Georgia Styles, Annie Kerr, and Elizabeth Morris were casualties of the high turnover endemic to the brothel trade. Each ran resorts in 1880. By 1889 Morris's Custom House Place resort had been replaced by a white "dive," one of several "establishments of such a character that the publishers do not feel justified in vouching for them in any way."[71] Annie Kerr had also relocated by 1889. In her place a white madam, Miss Clara, ran a brothel. For most houses of prostitution, such turnover appears to have been the norm, with brothels under the management of different madams following each other often in rapid succession. Thus, four years after Miss Clara resided at 124 Custom House Place, William Stead found neither Annie Kerr nor Miss Clara but a resort kept by Miss Monroe. In the 1889 sporting guide, the location of Georgia Styles's 1880 resort was now home to a nameless white "dive." Though Styles had moved elsewhere, the Clark Street confines of her old brothel remained within the sex economy, at least for a while. By the mid-1890s Stead identified no prostitutes working there; and in 1894 neighborhood investigators for Hull House found Polish workers residing at this address.[72]

The frequent closings of houses of ill fame were at times necessary responses to unwelcome and insistent police attention. Not surprisingly, panel houses were particularly sensitive to police surveillance. Detective Wooldridge described the turnover in low "dives" and "thieving dens" in the Levee: "One day a colored woman would occupy the house, and the next a white woman would be installed. . . . Almost daily these houses were raided by the police, but when one party was broken up and driven out another was ready to go in, and in a few days things would be as bad and perhaps worse than before."[73] Landlords factored such swift changes into the rental arrangements they made with some brothel keepers. Many charged not by the month but by the day. Perhaps most panel houses were more stable than this rental system suggests, but they seemed to thrive on their ability to relocate with ease and at minimal expense. Black panel house keeper Mattie Lee exemplifies the benefits of such mobility within the vice district. In 1896 her "den of vice" at 150 Custom House Place became the target of a police raid. In the raid officers arrested Lee and several of her workers, charging Lee with keeping a disorderly house. In the process of the raid, officers destroyed the panel doors and tunnels that assisted Lee's employees in their thieving endeavors. Despite this setback, Mattie Lee had reestablished herself two years later in a brothel across the street from her old place.[74]

Mobility typified not only panel houses but other resorts as well. Keepers who operated no-frills establishments could take quick advantage of new rental opportunities within the vice district or try their luck in new areas opening up to institutions of the vice economy. For example, before she was at her Custom House Place address, Annie Kerr had a resort at 1527 Butterfield Street, south of the Levee and perhaps inconveniently far from the district's heavy traffic in men. In 1880 she sought to maximize her earnings and risk the expense of occupying Levee property. That she apparently did not thrive on Custom House Place attests to the competition that defined the late-nineteenth-century sex industry and that constantly imperiled black women's position within it.[75]

The most stable African American madams tended to operate within the Levee, but in the 1880s and 1890s some sought out the quieter surroundings of the emerging entertainment district south of Eighteenth Street. Both Ella White and Lillian Richardson, black parlor house keepers, exemplify this trend. In 1889 the sporting directory found Richardson at 179 Twenty-First Street. She was apparently successful at this address. In 1893 she expanded her business to meet the needs of male visitors to the World's Columbian Exposition, renting out a second address around the corner on State Street. Ella White, whose brothel was located at 2109 Butterfield in 1889, was still in business in 1893, although she had moved her resort next door to number 2107.[76] At a time when a business might close within months of opening, White's and Richardson's ability to remain in business over several years suggests both their success within the brothel trade and the profitability of Chicago's newer sex district.

Amid the strategic relocations and business failures of other brothels, Vina Fields's House of Pleasure was unique in its ability to beat the odds against which all black madams labored. Fields's comparative prosperity—reflected in the size of her establishment—and her rank among the city's best sporting houses set her apart from other black sex entrepreneurs. Her longevity in the trade, and at so visible a level, further distinguished her career. Between 1879 and 1904, Fields remained headquartered at 138–140 Custom House Place. Only a handful of the city's white madams—including Carrie Watson, Emma Ritchie, and Lizzie Allen, whose careers extended from the late 1860s through the turn of the century—enjoyed similar long-term success in the trade.[77] Fields's astute management of a profitable parlor house no doubt contributed to her staying power and wealth. Unlike most sex district madams, however, she also owned property. As owner of at least one house in the Levee, Vina Fields joined madams such as Watson, Ritchie, and Allen, who converted the profits they amassed from the sale of sex into the economic security of real estate.[78]

Evidence of women's property ownership in late-nineteenth-century Chicago is difficult to obtain. In 1894 reformer William Stead compiled a detailed "Black List" of owners of property used for immoral purposes. This list is only partial, covering selected sections of Levee thoroughfares. Nevertheless, in revealing the names of men and women whose real estate holdings along Clark Street, Custom House Place, Plymouth Place, and Dearborn Street harbored the sex trade, Stead's Black List provides a clue to patterns of property ownership and use among Chicago's madams. Of the 164 properties that Stead found to be given over to commercial sex, 39 (or 24 percent) had women as sole owners. Of these 39 women, Stead identified 5 as madams. However, it is likely that a greater proportion of women property owners were madams. Some, like white brothel keeper Lizzie Allen, used an assumed name for work and her actual name, Ellen Williams, for property transactions.[79]

An important feature of ownership emerges from closer examination of Stead's list. Although five keepers were property owners, they did not necessarily work out of the buildings that they owned. Instead, they frequently leased their properties to other madams. For example, white madam Emma Ritchie, who in the 1870s kept one of Chicago's biggest brothels, owned three properties in 1893, one at 122 Custom House Place and two in the twentieth block of South Dearborn Street in the emerging leisure district. Ritchie ran her own resorts at two of these addresses but rented the third to white madam Minnie Ross.[80] Vina Fields also owned property that she rented to other brothel keepers. Although she owned 132 Custom House Place, she rented it to white brothel keeper Madame Cloquette. Fields herself resided at her brothel a few doors away at 138–140 Custom House Place. For owners, leasing property, and at exorbitant rates, promised lucrative returns.

Like white madams, most black keepers did not own vice district property. They nevertheless exploited the rental relations that shaped land use in the Near South Side leisure district. Hattie Briggs made enterprising use of rental properties in the Levee, operating resorts at three different addresses.[81] As brothel managers, renters, and landlords, Vina Fields, Hattie Briggs, and other savvy sex entrepreneurs found multiple ways to utilize sex district property (map 2.3). In 1893, during the world's fair, Fields enlarged her brothel operations by renting the properties on either side of her Custom House Place resort. Although herself a property owner, she used rental opportunities to take advantage of the increased demand for "colored girls" by visitors to the city.[82]

An intricate web of property relations linked madam landlords and renting brothel managers, and this often worked to the benefit of black women seeking accommodations for their own resorts. One black woman about whom little is known beyond her name, Mrs. Morris, operated a house at 182 Custom House Place, a property owned by a white madam, Mary Monroe. Monroe, who resided at 184 Custom House Place, next door to Morris's establishment, owned another house at 178 Custom House Place. She paid rent for the structure that housed her own brothel at 180 Custom House Place. Interestingly, while Monroe's brothel employed white women exclusively, this was not the case of the two neighboring resorts that she rented out. Mrs. Morris ran a "colored" house, and Dora Lyons, at 178 Custom House Place, operated a racially mixed house. Just as Fields profited by renting out her own property to a white brothel, Mary Monroe prospered by allowing black women to operate out of her buildings. While the trade was segregated by race and class of establishment in some places, sex district property relations joined black and white resorts and their owners together in an intricate and intimate economy.[83]

Most of the district's landlords were not women—nor were they men linked directly to the sex trade. Property owners included wealthy or middle-class men, most of whom lived far away from the Levee and the newer sex district to the south; others were successful saloon owners who dwelled and worked in the vicinity.[84] Local and regional railroad companies also owned property in the Levee. Planning to eventually expand their routes into the financial and trading heart of the city, in the 1890s companies such as the Atchison, Topeka, and Santa Fe Railroad Company rapidly bought up property south of the central business district. Owners readily made their holdings available for use by sex vendors, black and white. Sallie White's "house of ill-fame and den of colored thieves" at Clark Street used a building owned by the estate of C. E. Robinson, which had several holdings in the Levee.[85] The Atchison, Topeka, and Santa Fe Railroad Company owned many properties on Plymouth Place (Third Avenue), where many black houses of prostitution were clustered.[86] Despite the obstacles to solvency that faced black sex workers and madams, white property owners understood that renting to black women in the sex trade could generate a healthy profit. If one of these ventures failed, landlords cycled their vacated properties back into the prostitution economy. Thus, though the sex enterprises of individual renters frequently failed, owners of sex district property enjoyed relatively stable incomes from the trade.

Conclusion

The challenges African American madams encountered reflected—and no doubt exacerbated—the hardships black prostitutes faced daily as they worked in a racially organized sex trade. Yet precisely because they were among the poorest-paid prostitutes and the most economically insecure madams, black women in Chicago's sex economy labored in a variety of ways to forge new pathways to financial independence. Surveying the geographical, racial, and economic structure of the Levee sex economy brings into view the too-often-overlooked activities of these black women.

Examining the structure of the Levee sex trade also helps to challenge assumptions that underlay previous analyses of black prostitution. Scholars have argued that black prostitutes labored on the economic, social, and physical fringes of urban sex economies. Yet rather than working on the periphery of a vibrant sex trade, black women's labors helped to shape the institutions of the late-nineteenth-century sex trade. Furthermore, while some writers have suggested that black prostitutes passively endured their construction as degraded sexual commodities, black sex workers' actions belie this reading of their experiences in the trade. In choosing prostitution, black women in the late nineteenth century appear to have conformed to their construction as debased women. Yet black women's assertive and creative actions in defense of their earnings in the industry demonstrate that they understood their role as anything but passive. Through their work in brothels, furnished rooms, panel houses, and hotels and on the streets of the Levee, black women challenged not only their construction as debased merchandise but also their position as the lowest-paid workers in the city.

Economic uncertainty nonetheless plagued the majority of black sex workers. Financial insecurity was only one of the obstacles they faced on the job. African American prostitutes also contended with the reactions of respectable white and black citizens who were repulsed by the visible presence of black women in Chicago's sex trade. The responses of black and white middle-class Chicagoans to what they characterized as the moral poverty of countless black prostitutes constituted a political battleground on which the social meanings of black women's sex work was contested. The battle that ensued was only in part about black prostitutes themselves, however. Rather, the image of the black prostitute became one of the central figures in emerging debates about the place of African Americans in the modernizing city.

THREE

Race and the Spatial Boundaries of Respectability

The motley character of the Levee aroused considerable distress among white city leaders. In the eyes of many middle-class Chicagoans, the racially and ethnically unruly assortment of working-class and poor men and women who dwelled in this thickly settled neighborhood threatened to destabilize an emerging social order based on class and racial boundaries. Outsiders found equally troubling the cross-racial sexual associations that they feared took place regularly among the area's poor workers. Responding to the collapsed racial and ethnic boundaries within the local sex trade, white writers and observers branded this region as a hotbed of iniquity, a "vile locality."[1] At the root of their anxiety was the specter of miscegenation perpetrated by a lawless band of black men and women who, with their white accomplices, gleefully overran the physical borders that surrounded their habitat and threatened to trample the moral boundaries securing racial order in the city. Representations of menacing black prostitutes formed a central image in late-nineteenth-century depictions of urban disorder in the Levee and in the city.

Preoccupation with the movement and activities of black prostitutes intensified as black men and women arrived in Chicago in increasing numbers toward the end of the century. Between 1880 and 1900 Chicago's African American population more than doubled, growing from

14,000 to just over 30,000. With this steady influx, black neighborhoods took firm hold of the stretch of land that extended southward from the central business district. In 1880 nearly half of all black Chicagoans resided close to downtown, between Harrison and Sixteenth streets. Many residents lived beyond this district, however, having established footholds in less congested, largely white neighborhoods farther south. More-prosperous African Americans had begun to rent and buy property in these South Side areas as early as the 1870s.[2] This southward trend accelerated through the remainder of the century, so that by 1890 two-thirds of the city's blacks lived in the neighborhood stretching in a thin band from Harrison Street to Thirty-Third Street. In 1900, 80 percent of the black population lived within these boundaries.[3] Yet even though African Americans increasingly settled in newer neighborhoods on the city's South Side, many remained in the Levee district.

If the idea of black prostitutes roaming the streets of the sex district elicited the fear of middle-class whites, a more diffuse peril worried respectable black men and women who lived in and near the Levee. African Americans who lived along the pathways of the sex trade risked being linked in the minds of white middle-class Chicagoans with the moral degradation that surrounded them. To a wide swath of white northerners, all black men and women embodied social backwardness and sexual immorality. Black Levee dwellers, then, had to contend both with white Chicagoans' disparagement and with the "immoral territory" where many of them lived.

Respectable African Americans daily challenged white assumptions of their moral backwardness. They did so by attempting to forge a virtuous community life in urban spaces frequently seen as odious by outsiders. They carefully navigated city streets that overflowed with the sale of all forms of sex; they established social networks that elevated the character of neighborhood spaces otherwise given over to illicit commerce; and they aggressively defended their right of access to respectable recreational pursuits beyond the Levee. These black Chicagoans claimed the late-nineteenth-century city as a place in which to assert their own modern and moral identity.

The Black Chicagoan in the White Mind

Respectable middle-class whites living beyond the Levee's borders generally looked with disdain upon this neighborhood of working-poor men and women. Their displeasure emerges clearly in newspaper reports following a fire that swept through the district in 1874. The "Little Fire of 1874" caused significant damage to the homes of working-class residents living in its path. It also exposed the Levee's inhabitants to the scrutiny of outsiders. In vivid and harrowing terms, reporters from all the city's newspapers described the scenes of social disorder revealed by the fire:

It was THE PARADISE OF THE RAZOR-MOUNTED DARKIES and the eyesore of the law-abiding and the good. . . . The mere destruction of this vile locality would be a positive blessing to the city. The tenements out of which greedy sharks of landlords so long thrived upon the profits of lechery and miscegenation lay in smoking ruins, and their miserable occupants huddled together, bruised, burned, wretched, and houseless, all but lifeless, upon the street they have so long rendered a curse and a terror.[4]

Razor-wielding blacks, tenement houses abandoned by corrupt landlords to crime, lewdness, prostitution, and miscegenation, smoldering streets crowded with an unseemly horde of displaced men and women—this horrifying spectacle assailed readers of the *Chicago Times* on the morning of July 15, 1874. In this scene, an obviously distressed reporter described the ruins of a landscape devastated by fire. According to most accounts, the fire began late in the afternoon in a wooden shanty on Taylor Street between Clark Street and Fourth Avenue (Custom House Place). Before it was over, the Little Fire of 1874 had swept through nearly fifty acres in the southern region of the central city.[5]

Stories of the fire's origins reveal the preoccupation among writers and their middle-class and well-to-do readers with the racial and ethnic identities of the district's displaced residents. "Among the ruins" along Clark Street, one writer found "the heart of the colored population's colony. . . . Of rag-pickers, Polish Jews and Bohemians, there were also many. It was the haunt of the lowly to say the least." Along Third Avenue, another reporter sorted out fire victims as "Polish Jews, Italian, French, colored, and a very light sprinkling of Germans and Americans." In a more general fashion, the *Chicago Tribune* described a group of people crowded in a vacant lot west of Clark Street as "nondescript fugitives [from the fire] who spoke all the languages of Babel."[6]

Newspaper accounts of the fire's destruction did not limit themselves to cataloging the racial and national origins of the victims. In the days following the fire, writers presented vivid images of the social disarray and moral disorder bred by the South Side's working-class and laboring-poor population. Describing the vicinity of the fire's origin, a *Chicago Times* reporter found premises "occupied for a variety of purposes":

Some of them were third and fourth rate stores with the upper floors occupied by lodgers of Israelitish, Bohemian, and a very decided proportion of African extraction. The rooms were generally greasy and anything but inviting, cleanliness as a rule being in this particular quarter much more honored in the breach than in the observance. Assignation restaurants, kept by vicious Germans and Polish Jews, thrived upon the wages of sin, earned in misery by girls tender in years but old, alas, in sin.[7]

In descriptions such as this, fire journalists placed moral and economic responsibility for the district's sex trade in the hands of an assortment of unclean and reprobate immigrants and lodgers "of African extraction." This and similar renderings of the South Side's social geography reveal that in the minds of Chicago's middle- and upper-class white residents, the intermingled dwelling places of immigrant and African American working poor provided a breeding ground for moral disintegration and posed a particular threat to the morals of the area's young native-born white women.

African Americans' visibility seemed to heighten alarm about the collapse of moral order among the city's poor. In vivid language, journalists described the racial mixture in the near southern district. They paid special attention to the interspersing of the residences of white and black working-class men and women and the immediacy of those homes to institutions of sexual commerce. Most newspaper accounts of the Little Fire of 1874 portrayed black residential space as part of the intricate network of illicit or otherwise-immoral institutions proliferating south of Harrison. One *Chicago Times* writer reported, for example, that Fourth Avenue between Taylor and Polk "was lined with small green grocers' establishments and rookeries, where VICE FLAUNTED ITS INSIGNIA and easy virtue made itself a staple of merchandise. This street, also, was the abode of a large proportion of the colored population of the city." In the ruins of "old tumbledown rookeries," another reporter found "colored people, lewd women, and degraded white trash."[8]

To a few white writers, African Americans' proximity to the institutions of vice revealed their circumscribed economic and social condition within the city. To most, however, the overlap of black residential space with the property and pathways of sexual commerce implicated the black community in the immorality surrounding them. Yet African Americans were associated, not with a generalized immorality, but with a very specific moral transgression. Sexual commerce seemed to thrive wherever black people lived. One paper bluntly described the intersection of Taylor and Fourth as a "thieves', prostitutes', and niggers' paradise."[9] In another report, Taylor Street was depicted as "the abode of colored people, white prostitutes, thieves, pimps, blacklegs, and low-bred and dangerous people of every kind."[10] Other accounts described the streets on which blacks lived—major thoroughfares like State and Clark or small passageways like Eldridge and Hubbard Court—as equally corrupted by the openness and variety of establishments offering women's sexual services. These descriptions linked the moral status of the black community with the degraded condition of the prostitutes and thieves surrounding them. Indeed, they characterized black residents as one of several outlaw groups endangering urban stability.

To reporters filing accounts of the fire, perhaps the most menacing aspect of this immoral locality was the possibility of cross-racial intimacy. Descriptions of interracial resorts or, in the words of one disdainful reporter, "miscegenous" rookeries, surfaced throughout the 1874 fire narratives. In an alleyway between State and Clark streets, one writer found "the lowest classes of saloons and houses of prostitution," where "white and colored . . . mixed up in a manner that would satisfy the most enthusiastic civil rights advocate."[11] While the prospect of miscegenation was enough to torment reporters, it was the coupling of interracial sex with sexual commerce that added stridency to the alarms that these images sounded.

To many middle-class whites, the heart of the problem of "the social evil" was the white prostitute's indiscriminate acceptance of any and all men who arrived at her doorstep able to pay for her services. Commercial interracial sex faced no deterrent save the white woman's belief in her racial superiority and her individual discretion. Within the congested South Side the geographical barriers that protected white women living at a safe distance from downtown were nonexistent.[12] Concerned observers feared that the physical proximity of prostitution to the homes of working-class blacks constituted a clear threat to white prostitutes and poor women, whose exposure to the area's debauched atmosphere left them morally weakened. This proximity foretold the collapse of racial boundaries not only in the sex district but also in the city as a whole. Voicing, and perhaps goading, the fears of white civic and industrial leaders, reporters swiftly linked Levee prostitution to the specter of miscegenation and, ultimately, black urbanization.

The sex trade that occurred in resorts where black and white women catered to all paying men, regardless of race, figured prominently in the statements of white journalists, city leaders, and police officers. One reporter described a scene of "indiscriminate" or "promiscuous mixing" in the following terms: "Obese wenches[13] in the arms of sodden white men; fair young girls nestling close to the side of sooty negroes—such were the aspects of the social problem as it presented itself in the lower haunts of this fair city."[14] Later representations were equally contemptuous of interracial liaisons. Dan Webster, a notorious black bail bondsman, also ran a Pacific Avenue saloon, dance hall, and brothel in the 1870s, where, one account went, "the rottenest, vilest, filthiest strumpets, black and white, reeking with corruption, are bundled together, catering indiscriminately to the lust of all."[15] Charles Mortimer, another black saloon owner, ran the Saratoga at the corner of Polk Street and Custom House Place. In 1880 the police raided his saloon and carried away fifty-two men and women. Both black and white women were included in the haul, but most of the women were white and, according to the *Tribune*, "of the lowest possible type."[16] Not all this commerce took place in saloons. In 1893 Hull House investigators surveying the conditions on the Near South Side found that "in some houses [of prostitution] the whites and blacks are mixed."[17]

Although black women entertained white men, black men also figured in constructions of promiscuous intermingling. Descriptions of interracial sex commerce often expressed greater concern for black men's access to white women than for white men's patronage of black women. The reporter covering the raid of Charles Mortimer's saloon remarked that, of the fifty-two people arrested, "most . . . were gayly-attired young colored men of immoral tendencies."[18] The derisive term "coon dive" illustrates the preoccupation with black men's role in the Levee sex industry. To outsiders as well as to white patrons, both the race of customers visiting area resorts and the race of prostitutes shaped their interpretation of and participation in the sexual marketplace.

In Chicago guidebooks and newspaper accounts of the Levee, writers employed elaborate terminology to describe institutions within the sex economy. They alternately referred to inexpensive resorts of men's sexual leisure as "dives" or "dens of vice." In the minds of late-nineteenth-century observers, "dive" did not refer to a clearly identifiable institution. Rather, as one dictionary of American slang defines it, a nineteenth-century dive was "a disreputable, cheap, low-class establishment or public place." Above all, a dive was "a place of bad repute" where an assortment of base activities took place—prostitution, gambling, excessive drinking, improper dancing, and crude musical entertainment.[19] Such dives included rowdy saloons, dance halls, small assignation apartments, or run-down houses of prostitution. These institutions were identified not only by the activities they supported but also by their lack of amenities—in particular, the absence of middle- or upper-class furnishings and fashion. Unlike in parlor houses or even in some modest brothels, the black or white women who worked in dives were not required to produce a sexualized brand of domesticity for well-paying white clients. While the term "dive" expressed the contempt of respectable urbanites, it also helped direct the flow of pleasure-seeking white men through the Near South Side sex terrain, either warning them away from resorts believed to be dangerous or inviting them to a different brand of entertainment altogether.[20]

Guidebook writers used the repellent term "coon dive" when describing resorts of sexual leisure they considered to be even less inviting to traveling white businessmen or affluent members of the local sporting fraternity. Not only did these resorts lack the refinements and discreet management of reputable sporting houses, but they also teemed with black women.[21] By so designating the double jeopardy to which white men exposed themselves in traveling to cheap black houses, city directories, newspapers, and guidebooks revealed the complicated nature of white men's relation to black women's sex work. As they did with white prostitutes, the efforts of self-appointed guides to the Levee to establish a hierarchy among black sex workers shaped patterns of paid sexual relations across racial lines.

The presence or exclusion of black men further influenced white men's evaluation of Levee sex resorts. The critical feature that separated the "dive" from the "coon dive," and the "coon dive" from other houses of prostitution where black women worked, appears to have been the entertaining of black male customers. These terms warned white pleasure-seekers as well as respectable onlookers about the depths to which Levee sex trade could descend. Neither black nor white women escaped the taint of sex with black men, and writers classified among the most dangerous and wretched institutions those places where women labored indiscriminately for the sexual pleasure of men of all races. Because respectable white Chicagoans considered the resorts where cross-racial socializing and sexual contact took place to be among the Levee's most disorderly, they received inordinate police attention, and the black and white women who served a mixed clientele were more vulnerable to arrest than prostitutes who did not cross racial lines.[22]

Respectable white onlookers, police officers, and men of leisure did not direct their displeasure about interracial sexual commerce only at black men, however. In the last decades of the nineteenth century, equally strenuous warnings expressed the revulsion that many white middle-class Chicagoans felt toward the conspicuous presence of black women within the city's vice landscape. The "unladylike" carriage of black women in Levee streets prompted some writers to designate en-

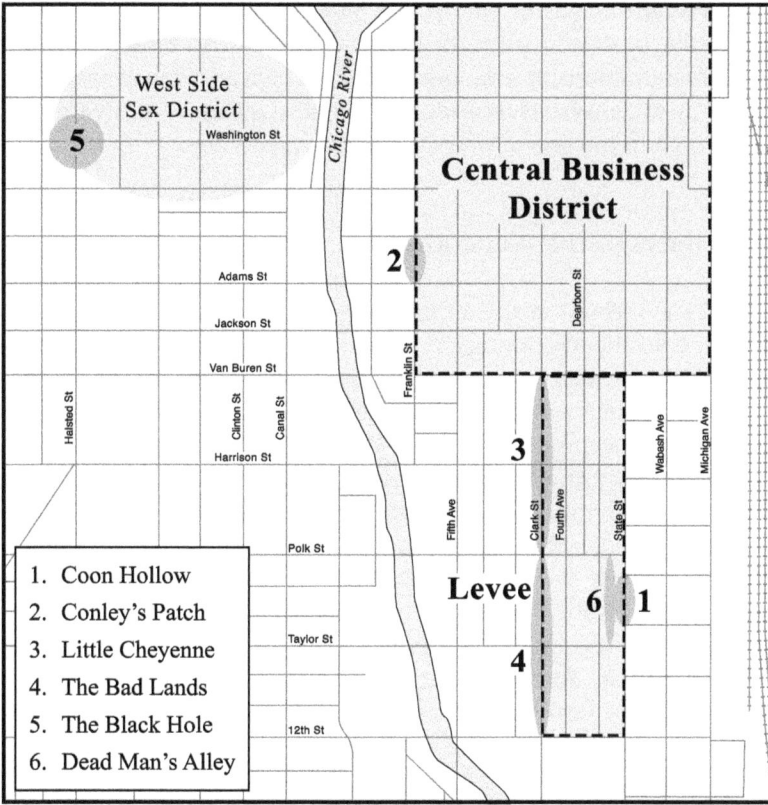

West Side
Sex District

5

Washington St

Chicago River

Central Business District

Adams St

2

Dearborn St

Jackson St

Van Buren St

Franklin St

Halsted St

Clinton St

Canal St

Harrison St

3

Wabash Ave

Michigan Ave

Polk St

Fifth Ave

Clark St

Fourth Ave

State St

Levee **6** **1**

Taylor St

4

1. Coon Hollow
2. Conley's Patch
3. Little Cheyenne
4. The Bad Lands
5. The Black Hole
6. Dead Man's Alley

12th St

Map 3.1   The Territories of "Amazonian" Black Women. From the 1870s through the 1890s, white guidebook writers, police officers, and newspaper reporters described certain streets and alleyways as harboring dangerous "Amazons." *Source:* Rand McNally and Co., *Street Guide Map of Chicago* (Chicago: Rand McNally and Co., between 1897 and 1899), http://www.lib.uchicago.edu/e/su/maps/chi1890/G4104-C6-1897-R3.html.

tire sections of the Levee as ominous territories populated by one or more dangerous black prostitutes. Portraits of unsafe and disorderly black women and their places of work were vividly juxtaposed against descriptions of the gentility and grandeur of the Levee's parlor houses and their white employees. To further separate black prostitutes from white sex workers, white writers mapped spatial divides designed to separate black men's leisure resorts and the landscapes of interracial sexual commerce, on the one hand, from the posh sex retreats of well-to-do white men, on the other. In imagining clear racial boundaries within the Levee, these urban cartographers demonstrated impressive agility. They manufactured tidy divisions where none existed (map 3.1).

The divergent arenas of elite men's and laboring men's sexual leisure frequently coexisted within the same cramped urban terrain. Nevertheless, representations of ominous African American women marked the Levee's most dangerous recesses, warning those fearless white men who endeavored to traverse both spatial and racial divides.

"Prostitutes of the Worst Kind"

In 1892 a guidebook entitled *Chicago by Day and Night* entertained readers with colorful descriptions of the exciting amusements awaiting visitors to Chicago, a city the author proudly called "the Paris of America." Highlighting such wide-ranging attractions as theater houses, dime museums, and concert saloons, Harold Vynne, the guide's author, addressed the book to a brotherhood of pleasure-seeking white men. Vynne provided vivid descriptions of Chicago's titilating pleasure spots, gleefully piloting his readers through Chicago's landscape of sexual commerce.

In the process of outlining the abundant sexual excitements of the city's leisure resorts, Vynne directed a specific warning to white traveling men. Of a section of the Levee known as Little Cheyenne, Vynne wrote, "There are dark forms lurking in alley-ways and doors, eager for prey. They carry razors as well as pistols, and will stop at nothing when booty looms in sight." In the course of guiding his male readers away from dangerous spots in the city's sex district, Vynne offered a specific alarm about the hazards of braving the terrain populated with black prostitutes. The most striking spectacles in Little Cheyenne, Vynne wrote, were "several dusky female characters of whom the police have a wholesome dread. . . . They are Amazonian in physique and being thoroughly abandoned, are ready for any hideous devilment which may or may not turn up." While Vynne described these Amazonian women as typical of Little Cheyenne, he named one of them as the undisputed boss of the area. "Big Mag," according to Vynne, was "the wickedest and most notorious character" of the area. She was "nearly six feet in height, as straight as an arrow and of such marvelous strength that no officer on the force would undertake to arrest her single-handed."[23]

By the 1880s a particularly menacing image of black prostitutes began to appear with some degree of frequency in daily papers, city guidebooks, and popular accounts of city living. A composite sketch of the black prostitute as drawn by the pens of various city writers pulls together a strange bundle of excesses. Extraordinarily large in height and girth and possessing brutish strength and cunning, she was prone to violent rages and harbored an insatiable appetite for criminal activity. In craftiness this figure was not unlike other thieves, prostitutes, highwaymen, and gamblers imagined by sensational writers to lurk in the city streets. Yet in sheer strength and violence of character, she was larger-than-life, out of proportion to the landscape she roamed.

Representations of black Levee prostitutes diverged considerably from the representations of white prostitutes that reporters and travel guide writers generated. Images of white women in the Levee sex economy varied in content and in tone. While some writers depicted refined parlor house workers, others drew images that revealed concerns about the moral dangers awaiting white women exposed to the urban sex trade. At one extreme were young and frail girls, innocent victims of the moral snares that awaited girls and women living in or near the Levee. At the other extreme were seasoned, devious prostitutes, who through trickery or uncommon allure guided unsuspecting white men to their moral and economic downfall. These figures of wasted white virtue tapped into prevailing fears about the threat that the city posed to white womanhood.

Descriptions of black prostitutes articulated a different set of fears. Portraits of monstrous black women were tinged simultaneously with awe and a mean humor. Through 1900, representations of these "prostitutes of the worst kind" expressed a deep concern among some whites about African American women's unconstrained entanglement with the city's sex marketplace.[24] Additionally, depictions of these ill-governed and menacing black women cast a criminal shadow over all black women residing in the district. In popularizing the image of the brutish black prostitute, writers cast a racially tinged shadow over the entire Levee.

An early exemplar of this emerging type was the Bengal Tigress, a woman purported around 1870 to dominate an area of the West Side sex district known as Conley's Patch. A 1936 *Tribune* article, "How Vice Grew Up in Chicago," described the Bengal Tigress as a "gigantic black woman" who "bossed" a group of black prostitutes and who "always was ready to battle with the police when her place was raided." Herbert Asbury, a popular writer in the 1940s, summarized her character in similar fashion: she was a "gigantic" woman whose "avocations were fighting, drinking, and raising hell generally. When she went on a rampage, the denizens of Conley's Patch barricaded their doors and windows and waited in fear and trembling for the worst to happen." As he continued, Asbury provided a level of descriptive detail that had been a staple of late-nineteenth-century sketches of other criminal black women: "The police seldom bothered her, but when they did they came in force; no fewer than four cops were required to drag her to the lockup."[25] In the 1870s newspaper reporters attributed to the Bengal Tigress the explosive violence of a predatory animal, whose heft was matched by her brute strength and her bent for evildoing. The figure of the ferocious Tigress likely generated both fascination and terror among consumers of these images—largely white middle-class men and women living at a safe distance from the central city.

Late-nineteenth-century reports of Chicago's underbelly—in sources as varied as city newspapers, police reminiscences, anti-vice literature, and travel guides—fleshed out the portrait of the ferocious black woman. In these narratives numerous figures vied for the title of the most fierce of the "gigantic Negresses," who, one writer remarked, "seemed to have been so plentiful in Chicago."[26] Dangerous women such as Big Mag, Hattie Briggs, and Black Susan Winslow were rumored to lurk about sections of the sex district that were branded with names like Cheyenne, the Bad Lands, and Coon Hollow. These women were alternately called "Amazons," "African giantesses," or "gigantic Negresses," and representations of them offered late-nineteenth-century Chicagoans and visitors alike a compelling and cautionary symbol of black women working in Chicago's sex marketplace.

The names Little Cheyenne and the Bad Lands drew directly upon images of the lawless West to convey the dangers lurking in Levee streets. Cheyenne, Wyoming, was one of several towns that sprang up in newly settled western territories in the second half of the nineteenth century. Beginning in the 1860s, men seeking their fortunes as cowboys, railroad workers, and lumbermen flooded Wyoming Territory. With its preponderance of young, unattached men (in 1880 and 1890 the male-to-female ratio was 2.5 to 1), Cheyenne quickly gained a reputation as a wide-open cow town where liquor and prostitutes were plentiful and where violence, rather than law enforcement, ruled.[27] Similarly, the name Bad Lands evoked an image of untamed western territory. Originally denoting barren and wild topography (as in the Badlands of South Dakota), when imposed on urban terrain "Bad Lands" referred to "regions where civilization has broken down and licentiousness reigns."[28]

Writers characterized the streets of Chicago's Little Cheyenne as uncivilized and perilous, but the depths of depravity they found in the Bad Lands set it apart from the rest of the Levee. Observers designated it the stomping ground of a black woman known as Big Maud. According to one writer, the large and "ferocious" Big Maud ran the Dark Secret, a small and inexpensive resort near the corner of Clark and Twelfth streets. In 1899 Clifton Wooldridge, a police detective whose reminiscences of his life on the job found many avid readers at the turn of the century, described Big Maud as more massive and brutish than the legendary Bengal Tigress. Men entering her establishment, he recalled, risked both theft and a beating. In his work in the Bad Lands, Detective Wooldridge encountered other grotesque characters occupying resorts equally hazardous to pleasure-seeking white men. He described Hattie Briggs, who owned a saloon and a house of prostitution, as standing "over six feet tall, weigh[ing] about two hundred and twenty pounds, . . . as black as a stick of licorice" and "as ugly as any one could imagine."[29] Wooldridge described Black Susan Winslow, proprietor of a Clark Street brothel, as weighing 449 pounds and "wider in every direction than any door or window in her dive." Like visitors to Big Maud's Dark Secret, men entered Winslow's resort allegedly at their own risk. According to one account, Winslow's workers regularly treated patrons to beatings, stripping them of their cash and jewelry.[30]

Significantly, these ominous black female figures were not tucked away in houses of prostitution passively awaiting their prey. Rather, they roamed the streets and alleys, hid in corners, and hovered in doorways. Among these was Emma Ford, dubbed "the Colossus of the Levee" by Detective Wooldridge. According to Wooldridge, Ford was a seasoned thief who operated through a network of saloons, brothels, and cheap rooming houses throughout the Levee district. "She has muscles of steel, and is as fearless as she is ferocious," the detective wrote. She represented "a remarkable specimen of physical development. Six feet tall, straight as an arrow, weighing two hundred pounds, and as black as a starless midnight, she looks like an African giantess." In the minds of sex district cartographers, the movements of massive and ferocious black women both within and beyond sex district institutions transformed the crisscrossing streets of the Levee into a treacherous web. Coon Hollow, the block of State Street between Polk and Taylor, contained numerous bawdy saloons and "thieving houses of prostitution" where black women stripped unsuspecting men of their money. In Dead Man's Alley, an alleyway between State and Plymouth, black strong-arm women posing as prostitutes lured unwise men to beatings and robberies.[31]

The preposterous outlines of large, criminal black women like Susan Winslow and Big Maud, while perhaps curious to us today, were familiar to white men and women readers of published accounts and newspaper communiqués of European expeditions to Africa. To many late-nineteenth-century white city dwellers, this dark and mysterious continent provided the backdrop against which they viewed the perplexing activities of urbanizing blacks. In the latter half of the nineteenth century, narratives of the exploration of Africa proved tantalizing fare for readers in Europe as well as in North America. Explorers Sir Richard Burton and Henry M. Stanley and missionaries such as David Livingstone wrote best-sellers that exoticized Africa and exaggerated the physical and temperamental attributes of African women.[32]

Of the African lands that appeared throughout the literature of African exploration, travelers repeatedly represented the kingdom of Dahomey (in what is now Benin) as an especially savage and violent society. Tales of cannibalism, human sacrifice, and ritual beheadings gave a savage tinge to accounts of Dahomey's inhabitants, the Fon or, as explorers called them, Dahomeans. Alongside these stories of brutality emerged a remarkable portrait of one group of Dahomean women. In what European travelers described with clear fascination as a bizarre custom, adult virgin women composed the bulk of the kingdom's elite military force. These Amazons, as they came to be called, formed the military backbone of the state and served nobly as the king's protectors. Explorers illustrated tales of Amazon bravery with lavish descriptions of their imposing physical bearing and astonishing strength. By the middle of the nineteenth century, at least seven accounts of Dahomey and the Amazons had been published in English alone (and several others in French), each marveling at the spectacle of virgin female warriors.[33]

Not all travelers were impressed with Fon women. In an 1860s travel memoir, English explorer Richard Burton described the Amazons as an army of "hideous" women, most of whom were "taken in adultery or too shrewish to live with their husbands." The size and "muscular development of the frame" of the women he saw resembled those of the village's men. "Femininity," he charged, "could be detected only by the bosom."[34] Burton's representations provided the framework in which Dahomean women, and Dahomean culture, would be characterized in subsequent accounts of travels through West Africa (fig. 3.1). In the following years, travelers routinely described Dahomean women as hideous embodiments of the barbarism of their kingdom—a barbarism evidenced by the violence that they performed for their king, by the distorted gender relations suggested by their militarism, and by their masculinized bodies. By the 1880s this portrait had hardened into an important stock representation for all African women that regularly circulated in published travel accounts and in communiqués printed in newspapers like the *Chicago Tribune* and the *Chicago Daily News*.[35]

3.1 "An Amazon" (1864). Drawing by Richard Francis Burton, from his *A Mission to Gelele, King of Dahome* (New York: Praeger, 1966). Courtesy of Special Collections, University of Illinois at Chicago Library.

The Bengal Tigress represented an early incarnation of the urban Amazon. Yet not until the 1890s did the Amazon fully capture the imagination of writers and readers fascinated by the inner workings of Chicago's sex district.[36] The 1893 World's Columbian Exposition strengthened the connection many white Chicagoans and visitors to this modern city made between black urban women and the outsize and fierce African woman.

The majestic White City of the world's fair represented the fruits of American industrial achievement and pointed the way to the nation's future. Housing exhibitions of new and diverse technological wonders, the White City presented to fairgoers lessons about the exuberant progress of Western civilization. But situated along the Midway Plaisance that stretched westward away from the stately White City was an equally educational exhibit. Nestled among the refreshment booths, restaurants, and other amusements that provided fairgoers relief from the lofty exhibits of the White City was an elaborate display of human racial diversity—reconstructed villages from around the world. Walking along the Midway a visitor encountered re-creations of Irish, Javanese, Samoan, Sudanese, Egyptian, and Chinese village life. At the far end of the Midway were two Native American villages. And at its farthest reach was the Dahomean village. Conceived of and organized by the exposition's Department of Ethnology, the ethnic villages were designed to both entertain and educate fairgoers.

Between May and September about seventy Fon men, women, and children lived in a village encampment on the Midway. One journalist stated that "sixty-nine of them are here in all their barbaric ugliness, blacker than buried midnight and as degraded as the animals which prowl the jungles of their dark land. . . . Dancing around a pole on which is perched a human skull . . . their incantations make the night hideous."[37] Such "savage amusements"[38] made the Dahomeans an object of derision. But their spectacular performances also offered viewers a lesson in the course of human progress. "There is no doubt," wrote another commentator, "that the Dahomans are more closely allied with the cruel and superstitious practices of savagery than any other country represented in the Midway."[39]

The figure of the Amazon was central to all descriptions of Dahomean barbarity. One account stated: "The women are as fierce if not fiercer than the men and all of them have to be watched day and night for fear they may use their spears for other purposes than a barbaric embellishment of their dances."[40] Another guide to "Midway Types" asserted that "the reputation of these black women is of the most sanguinary character. . . . It is said that they are absolutely ignorant of fear; and they are credited with being educated to the use of warlike weapons and schooled in the tactics of their savage battles from childhood" (fig. 3.2).[41] Taking quite seriously the evolutionary framework that guided the exposition's display of world cultures, a repulsed fair visitor concluded: "It is impossible to conceive of a notch lower in the human scale than the Amazon, or female Dahomey warrior, represents."[42]

Fairgoers eagerly imbibed the evolutionary message conveyed in the exhibit of the world's villages. In particular, Dahomey and the Amazons offered white visitors, as well as consumers of the many journalistic il-

3.2 "Four Amazons." From *Midway Types: A Book of Illustrated Lessons about the People of the Midway Plaisance* (Chicago: Engraving Co., 1893), vol. 12. Courtesy of Special Collections, University of Illinois at Chicago Library.

lustrations of the village, a framework for fitting the American Negro into the triumphant narrative of national, industrial progress. As literary critic Denton Snider mused: "The Africans of Dahomey have a special interest for people of the United States. The negro is there seen in his native element, we can witness what he does for himself when he is left alone." Arriving at a similar conclusion, another spectator wrote: "In these wild people we can easily detect many characteristics of the American negro." Despite such disparaging assessments of African Americans' roots, some spectators believed that exposure to American civilization provided the wedge that could separate American blacks from their benighted cousins. In fact, the American Negro provided further proof of the triumph of American progress. As one observer declared, "the American negro. . . . has learned the language of civilization, and by its teachings has been raised above the deplorable level of his less fortunate kinsman."[43] Even Frederick Douglass found a useful message in the Dahomean village. Initially offended by the inclusion of the exhibit, in a speech delivered on Colored American Day at the fair, Douglass incorporated the village into an argument for racial justice and the expansion of African American political rights. "Look at the progress the Negro has made in thirty years! We have come up out of Dahomey unto this. Measure the Negro. But not by the standard of the splendid civilization of the Caucasian. Bend down and measure him—measure him from the depths out of which he has risen."[44]

To Chicagoans concerned about the city's sex economy and the presence of black women within it, the links between the urban black woman and her "less fortunate kins[wo]man" had not been as irreversibly severed by civilization as some hoped. Black women working within Chicago's sex district seemed to offer proof of an inescapable kinship. The context of black women's "savage amusements" had changed; yet the attributes that set her apart from white women, even those working in the sex trade, remained the same. Bloodthirsty, physically enormous, and by all accounts "hideous" embodiments of distorted gender relations, to respectable white observers black prostitutes and brothel keepers working in the Levee were both biological and conceptual cousins of the barbarous Amazons of Dahomey.

For writers of urban guidebooks and urbanites familiar with narratives of African women's primitive violence, the Amazon seemed out of place in the urban setting. Yet in portrayals of women like Emma Ford and Susan Winslow, readers of newspaper reports and guidebook descriptions of the Levee learned that she had indeed been transplanted to modern city streets. Unlike world's fair spectators who might wait for "the language of civilization" to subdue this savage woman, city officials believed that the excesses of the urban Amazon required the civilizing force of the police. Police efforts to maintain some semblance of law and order in the Levee frequently focused on the bodies of uncivilized and unruly black women.

Hyperbole characterized descriptions of police encounters with black women of the Levee. According to Harold Vynne, the women who populated the Bad Lands and Little Cheyenne were so fierce that "most officers would rather engage in a grapple with half a dozen male desperadoes than with one of those formidable negresses" (fig. 3.3).[45] Another guidebook stated that those areas were so dangerous that no policeman "would dare to enter alone in the day-time, and [it] would have been suicidal for him to enter in the night-time."[46]

Exaggerations of the fierce nature of black women served to justify the use of violence against black women working in the Levee. Such hyperbole infused Detective Wooldridge's description of the chase and struggle that ensued when he and his officers tried to arrest Hattie Smith (aka Hattie Washington) after she accosted an "old farmer" on the street. Attempting to elude the pursuing officers, Smith slipped into

3.3 One of the "gigantic Negresses" described in Harold Vynne's *Chicago by Day and Night: The Pleasure Seeker's Guide to the Paris of America* (Chicago: Thomson and Zimmerman, 1892). Courtesy of Special Collections, University of Illinois at Chicago Library.

a store and hid under a bed in the store's rear room. However, police soon discovered her hiding place and four officers dragged her from under the bed. Wooldridge described the arrest in the third person:

She fought and kicked and it became necessary to put the "come-alongs" on each wrist. When this was done, Wooldridge had one arm and Fitzgerald the other. The wagon was called, but before it reached the place the "come-alongs" caused Hattie to scream with pain, and she promised, if they would take them off, she would behave herself and submit to the arrest peaceably. Fitzgerald released her from his "come-alongs," and as he did so she struck him a stinging blow under the ear which came near upsetting him. She was just in the act of striking Wooldridge, who still had his "come-alongs" on her other wrist, when he took a twist on them which cut down into the flesh and left their marks for months. Hattie was thrown on her knees, and some five or six officers grabbed her and placed her in the wagon.[47]

In the account of his run-in with Smith, Detective Wooldridge incorporated her animal-like cunning and ferocity. A predator, Smith finds her prey in an "old farmer," a rural innocent, out-of-place in the mean Levee streets. Detected by police, she seeks cover in a nearby establishment whose owner is either unaware of her entry, ill-equipped to stop her, or a willing accomplice to her predations. Forcibly removed from her hiding place, she is immediately restrained by two policemen. However, handcuffs are not sufficient to confine Smith, and through trickery, she frees one arm for battle. Her attack on Officer Fitzgerald and her attempted attack on Wooldridge unleash the full force of police powers: officers mercilessly twist handcuffs into her wrist and throw her to the ground; half a dozen men drag her subdued and pained body into the police wagon (fig. 3.4).

Hattie Smith did not stand alone in testing police resolve. Other black female thieves, prostitutes, and brothel keepers received similarly brutal treatment from the pens of writers and, we may assume, at the hands of exasperated policemen. Detective Wooldridge's reminiscences of the apprehension of Black Susan Winslow further illustrate the extraordinary use of police force against savage black women.

In the 1890s Chicago police officers received numerous complaints of robberies at Winslow's house of prostitution. Wooldridge took a special interest in the case. The problem facing Wooldridge was how to extract Winslow from her brothel and transport her to the police station. Winslow's reported 449-pound frame made it impossible to remove her from her home without her consent. And consent she did not. Rather, "she sat down and refused to go one step." Faced with Winslow's resistance, Wooldridge ordered his officers to lay two sixteen-foot-long wooden planks between the doorway of Winslow's house and the back of the police wagon. He next secured one end of a heavy rope to a horse's collar and cinched the other end around Black Susan's waist. Then, as he tells it, he set the horse running, a gambit that dragged Susan's huge body to the doorway of her house. Before being dragged out of her resort and onto the planks, she agreed to walk to the wagon and be taken to the police station.[48]

The grotesque image of a mountainous black woman being dragged by horse from her home was no doubt meant to be both comical and awe inspiring. Yet Wooldridge's boastful description of his own ingenu-

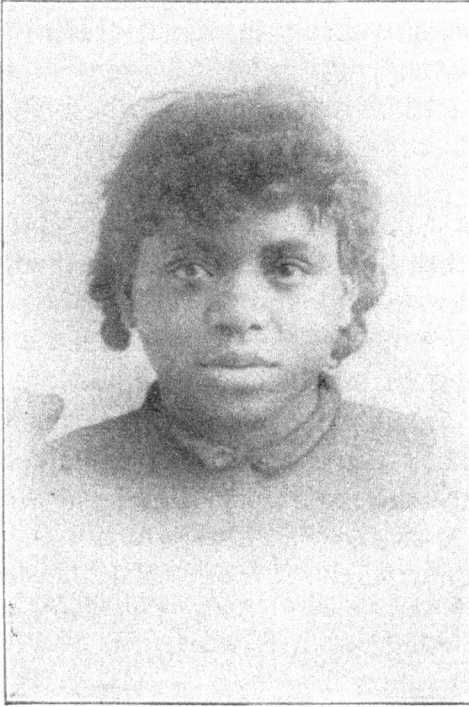

3.4 Hattie Smith. From Clifton R. Wooldridge, *Hands Up! In the World of Crime* (Chicago: Police Publishing Co., 1901). Courtesy of Chicago History Museum.

ity vividly illustrates the subhuman character ascribed to black women working in the South Side sex district.

These images of black women's subdued bodies did more than prop up one police detective's ego. They also popularized the legend of the urban Amazon and in the process validated the use of violence to suppress black women's disruptive activities in the Levee.[49] In accounts such as Wooldridge's, the disruptions that Winslow and Smith caused were specific: accosting defenseless old men on the street or stealing from equally defenseless men within a brothel. Yet the disorder these women wrought went far beyond their thieving. They victimized defenseless white men, the pleasure-seekers to whom Harold Vynne addressed his warnings to stay clear of the Bad Lands and Little Cheyenne. Amazon-like women embodied the racial disorder that loomed ominously in the Levee. Together—and they were always lumped together—they provided a distorted lens through which to view the Levee and the opportunities for paid interracial sex that it offered.

Wooldridge and other chroniclers of Chicago's seedy underside created in the African Giantess an entertaining character that added color to scenes of Chicago street life. Yet the exaggerated portrayals of the Bengal Tigress, Hattie Briggs, Emma Ford, and Susan Winslow served several other purposes as well. The excesses of the Levee "Amazons"—their size, strength, and ferocity—firmly removed them from the realm of femininity. Such fearsome women had no connection to customary gender roles, whether wife, mother, or, as was the case for the majority of working black women, domestic servant.[50] Black women's ferocious nature also distanced them from the brand of female domesticity sold in Levee parlor houses. In caricaturing black sex workers, popular images of the Amazon effectively desexualized black women working in the Levee. In her asexuality the Amazon resembled the Mammy of southern lore. Yet unlike the Mammy figure, whose bodily excesses were framed within a narrative of willing service and affection for her white employers, portrayals of the African Giantess stripped her of any humanizing attributes. Descriptions of her animal-like nature and her masculine qualities highlighted her lack of resemblance to womanhood generally and, specifically, to white women working in the sex district. As an embodiment of distorted gender norms, the figure of the barbarous black woman stood as a warning deterring white men from crossing the boundaries that elsewhere in the city's social life separated black from white.

Although guidebook writers, journalists, and police officers employed a variety of descriptive place-names to delineate the separate geographical territories, in reality areas such as Coon Hollow and Dead Man's Alley were never as isolated from other spaces and networks of the sex trade as the urban cartographers would have had their readers believe. The institutions of black prostitution remained intermingled with white women's resorts through the end of the century. Furthermore, even as some writers expressed revulsion at the idea of white men intermingling with savage black women, many white men continued to make their way to the doors of the brothels run by women like Eliza Dennis, Hattie Briggs, Hattie Smith, Big Maud, and Black Susan Winslow.

Space and Respectability

African American men and women who lived in and near the Levee found the fragile spatial barriers that surrounded the sex trade especially vexing. Respectable African Americans—working- and middle-class men and women who shunned involvement in the area's immoral and illicit enterprises—interpreted the perils of the Levee landscape quite differently from white newspaper reporters and travel writers worried about racial and ethnic mixing. Rather than deploring the ethnic heterogeneity of the district, respectable black Chicagoans objected to the forced intermixture of different moral classes that the race had to endure in the compressed neighborhood. Within this context, where one sought entertainment and chose associates had profound consequences for racial advancement. Ferdinand L. Barnett, an African American lawyer and the publisher and editor of the *Chicago Conservator*, implored his readers to make careful distinctions in their social life. Warning of the threat to race progress posed by the careless intermingling of the disreputable and the respectable, Barnett asked his readers, "Can we afford to lower our social status?"[51] Black men and women did not have the luxury of being inattentive to social decorum. The morally heterogeneous streets of the Levee daily lured the most vulnerable members of the community to their downfall, threatening to besmear the reputation of the most upright representatives of the race.

Facing emerging patterns of segregation that confined a large proportion of the community to the area encompassing the Levee, Chicago's respectable African Americans fiercely battled to define moral spaces for their families and for their community as a whole. Historians of Chicago have most frequently traced the city's nineteenth-century moral geography along the lines charted by municipal authorities, white middle-class residents, and reformers.[52] Such a perspective affords an incomplete rendering of the city's moral topography. A focus primarily on the concerns of white middle-class residents ignores the ways that other communities struggled to both guide their members through morally treacherous areas and impose moral maps on city streets. These maps competed with those drawn by white urbanites. A closer look at the ways blacks used urban space, in particular Levee streets, complicates the view of the cityscape as seen by disdainful white urbanites.

Living within an area believed by middle-class whites to foster immorality, intemperance, sexual dissolution, and promiscuous racial intermingling, many blacks struggled daily to redefine their compressed space. If the Near South Side was known as the Levee to civic leaders, real estate developers, moral reformers, and the municipal police, many black Chicagoans knew it as the home space, principal business district, and playground of their growing community. Members of Chicago's South Side black community plotted a moral geography that was persistently compromised by the presence of immoral institutions competing for the attention of black residents and by the insistence with which the daily press and daily police practices defined the Levee as the seat of urban depravity.

The disregard of black men and women whose everyday pursuit of relaxation and amusement took them into morally suspect places further troubled the moral outline of black urban spaces. The growing range of public amusements—saloons, theaters, dance halls, poolrooms, restaurants, and gambling dens—presented longtime residents and waves of black migrants from the South with inviting recreational opportunities. In seeking out these entertainments, both working- and middle-class blacks traveled through terrain thickly settled with institutions of sexual commerce. The expensive parlor houses, unimposing brothels, bawdy saloons, and assignation hotels that crowded the streets of the South Side Levee were constant reminders of the tenuous boundaries protecting Chicago's black moral geography.

In their active use of South Side thoroughfares, African Americans incorporated contested urban spaces into a grid of respectable community life. Basic needs of personal and family upkeep, as well as the need for social connection, guided their everyday movements through the city. Whether shopping for household provisions, pursuing recreation, forging social bonds with neighbors or family, or seeking spiritual restoration, African American men and women carved out a community landscape that contradicted the negative estimation of whites who characterized the Near South Side as, among other things, a foreboding "nigger's paradise."[53] To be sure, layering respectability over streets that were at times saturated with disreputable activities may not have been uppermost in the minds of black Chicagoans. Rather, their everyday use of the city's streets and public spaces bespoke a more basic desire—to create a safe and welcoming community within a hostile urban environment. Nonetheless, many African Americans superimposed a map of respectability onto streets like Clark and Custom House Place.

Churches stood at the center of black public life. The largest and most prominent of the city's black churches—such as Bethel African Methodist Episcopal Church, Olivet Baptist Church, and Quinn Chapel A.M.E.—dated back to the middle of the century.[54] In the last decades of the nineteenth century, most of these prominent black churches had one by one moved away from the central city and were "pleasantly situated within easy reach" of affluent members, who now formed residential enclaves on the Far South Side. By the end of the century, numerous smaller churches emerged to serve recently arrived African Americans or those of modest means. These churches clustered within and near the Levee (map 3.2).[55]

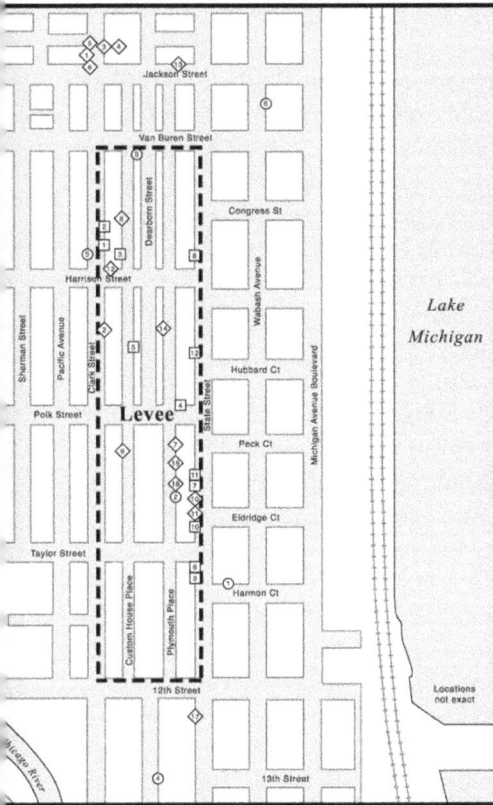

Churches, Lodges, and Benevolent Associations

Churches
① Olivet Baptist Church
② Bethel A.M.E. Church
③ Quinn Chapel A.M.E.
④ St. Thomas' Church

Lodges and Associations
⑤ Masonic Hall
⑥ Odd Fellows Hall

Saloons and Other Leisure Resorts

Saloons and Sample Rooms
1 J. J. Turner's Saloon and European Hotel
2 Johnson, Bryan, and Whiting Sample Room and Billiard Parlor
3 Congress Hall
4 S. A. Gray's Winerooms
5 Scott and Hunter's Sample Room and Billiard Parlor
6 Snowden and Beasley Sample Room
7 George Cross Wine, Cigars, and Billiards
8 H. Jones and Co. Sample Room

Leisure Resorts
9 David Blakemore's Bee Restaurant
10 R. L. Lamar's Restaurant
11 Byrd, Bryan, and Horton, Dining Room and Ice Cream Parlor
12 Mrs. M. L. Smith Restaurant

Other Businesses and Offices

Newspapers
① Chicago Observer
② Chicago Conservator

Law Offices
③ F. L. McGhee
④ Edward Morris
⑤ John G. Jones
⑥ Ferdinand L. Barnett
⑦ J. W. E. Thomas

Barbershops
⑧ T. Buck's Barbershop
⑨ Al Totten
⑩ Autumn Barbershop
⑪ G. W. Young Barbershop
⑫ The Equality Shaving Parlor
⑬ The Palace, Taylor's Shaving and Hair Dressing Parlor

Dressmaking
⑭ Mrs. Hyatt Fashionable Dressmaking
⑮ Mrs. D. W. Brown, Dressmaker
⑯ Mrs. Wm. C. Gunn and Miss Sadie Prichards, Dressmakers
⑰ Miss Emma L. Walls and Mrs. Jessie Compson, Fine Millinery and Dressmaking

Map 3.2   African American Community Institutions and Businesses in and near the Levee.
Source: Rand McNally and Co., *Street Guide Map of Chicago* (Chicago: Rand McNally and Co., between 1897 and 1899), http://www.lib.uchicago.edu/e/su/maps/chi1890/G4104-C6-1897-R3.html.

As social centers African American churches gave moral definition to city spaces otherwise devoted to commerce, leisure, and illicit activity. They sponsored picnics, fairs, dinners, and recitations and provided spaces for political meetings and gatherings of social and literary clubs. Churches multiplied the ways that black men and women could make use of streets in the Levee and in the neighborhood forming farther south.

Active club life also transformed Levee streets, if only temporarily. Lodges, benevolent organizations, and social clubs met in an intricate network of institutions. They utilized meeting halls, schoolhouses, the commodious homes of club members, and the rear rooms of black-

109

owned barbershops and restaurants. Meetings and organized leisure activities encouraged African Americans to traverse morally questionable public spaces. Several clubs and organizations met in buildings in the Levee. The Masonic Hall was located at 326 South Clark Street, in the heart of the Levee, and the Odd Fellows met in a nearby building on Wabash Avenue. The Original Autumn Club, which one black business directory described as "one of the leading social organizations in the city of Chicago," had its headquarters at T. Buck's Barbershop on Fourth Avenue, a street thick with brothels and rowdy saloons.[56] By encouraging community members to travel back and forth through Levee streets, churches and clubs drew thoroughfares brimming with illicit commerce into the legitimate project of community building.

African Americans also took advantage of the opportunities for leisure that lay beyond community institutions and social networks, multiplying the ways that they redefined questionable urban streets. Like white urbanites, black Chicagoans traveled into the central city to partake of an expanding array of urban amusements, including theaters and dime museums. They faced the challenge of wending their way through landscapes filled with morally suspect diversions. White proprietors' practices of racial discrimination made partaking of reputable commercialized leisure all the more difficult for Chicago's blacks.

Going to the theater drew African Americans with discretionary income into the thick of Chicago nightlife. Most of the city's theaters were located in the heart of the central business district and in the section that included the Levee. Some of these venues had admitted blacks as early as the 1870s. The Grand Opera House and McVicker's were well-established houses known for offering attractions that one guidebook author described as "uniformly first class and of a high order of excellence." In 1882 the *Conservator*, at the time Chicago's only black newspaper, alerted its readers to performances running at Haverly's Theatre, the Olympic Theatre, and Hooley's Theatre, centrally located downtown venues that presented professional dramatic and musical performances of national fame.[57]

Although some downtown theaters welcomed blacks, ticket prices were prohibitive for most African Americans (as well as for white working men and women)—averaging between 50¢ and $1.[58] The majority of theatergoing blacks instead frequented the less expensive houses situated on the fringes of the downtown theater district. In the southern and western sections of the central business district, low-priced playhouses and early vaudeville theaters competed for the dimes of working men and, increasingly, women. Several low-priced theaters catered to an exclusively male clientele. As historian David Nasaw points out, many cheap theaters were little more than saloons with makeshift stages or adjacent music halls for live performances. These variety theaters and concert saloons featured less high-minded fare than their more respectable neighbors, with singers and actors often performing sexually suggestive material. The raucous environment of working-class male camaraderie at times allowed for racial intermingling in variety houses. The Adelphi variety theater, at Congress and Wabash, welcomed blacks until it was destroyed by the fire of 1874.[59]

Although some theaters welcomed black patronage, it appears that most of them practiced some form of discrimination. Some establishments might admit blacks, but only to restricted seating; others sought by various means to obstruct African American attendance altogether. Such discriminatory practices became more difficult for white theater owners after the passage of the Illinois Civil Rights Act of 1885. This act provided African Americans equal access to and equal treatment within all public accommodations, amusements, and conveyances.[60] The new law did not put an end to discriminatory practices in Chicago's theaters, however. It nevertheless gave a few bold African Americans an avenue for redressing their grievances against unjust treatment.

Emboldened by the 1885 legislation, black men and women who could afford the accommodations tested the limits of the law in everyday attempts to be treated respectfully in downtown restaurants, hotels, saloons, and theaters. In many of the city's theaters, they still confronted policies that restricted their seating to uninviting balconies. The balcony, or gallery, carried a double mark of shame for African Americans. In the early and mid-nineteenth century, theaters reserved the upper galleries for prostitutes and their rowdy consorts.[61] By the late nineteenth century the prostitutes' perch had disappeared from most newly respectable theaters that hoped to attract white women and families. As blacks moved to northern cities in the last decades of the nineteenth century, however, they replaced prostitutes in the upper tiers of theaters. According to theater owners the relegation of African Americans to the gallery was designed to preserve the decency of an expanding white theatergoing public. Thus, segregation was only one aspect of the insult that blacks faced when directed to the upper tiers of urban theaters. African Americans also suffered being physically and symbolically linked with the most dishonorable elements of the city.[62]

Black men and women continued to resist the blanket presumption of their immorality. In 1888 Reverend Bird Wilkins, pastor of Bethesda Baptist Church, brought suit against the Columbia Theater after being directed to the theater's balcony. Refusing to be so humiliated, he and his guest left the theater.[63] Black women found the practice of associating African Americans with sexual immorality particularly distressing. For women whose free use of public space was already circumscribed both by Victorian restrictions on all women's movement and by sexualized racial ideologies that branded black women as morally suspect, fears that whites would link them with immoral leisure further limited their ability to freely partake of public amusements.

One woman's battle to be seated in a Chicago playhouse illustrates the threats to black women that all too frequently awaited them when they ventured beyond community networks. On a Sunday evening in June 1886, Josephine Curry attempted to purchase tickets to a performance at the People's Theatre for herself, her husband, and two guests. The People's Theatre teetered on the edge of respectability. Like other theaters south of downtown in the early 1880s, this run-of-the-mill variety theater provided raunchy musical entertainment for men of all classes. Yet by 1885, in an attempt to distinguish the venue from neighboring variety theaters and concert halls, the People's owners began to upgrade their shows. A notice in the *Daily News* remarked that "the People's theater has certainly improved the quality of its future attractions. . . . The People's will soon cease to be known as a variety house."[64]

The Currys were members of Chicago's black middle class. Mr. Curry owned a barbershop, and Mrs. Curry made and sold her own line of skin care products. Upon approaching the People's ticket counter, the respectable couple and their two friends were directed instead toward the Park Theatre, a neighboring establishment that operated as a bawdy theater. The Park had a reputation for showcasing "exhibition[s] which would be more in place in Sodom and Gomorrah than in Chicago." One outraged visitor declared that "the moral level of its stage is below that of a decently conducted sporting house." The sporting atmosphere extended to the boxes above the stage and the wine rooms on the upper floors. There, male patrons of the stage shows could purchase liquor from the house and be privately entertained by actresses who agreed to meet with them between acts or after the performance.[65]

Recognizing the class of theater to which she had been directed, Mrs. Curry returned to the People's, where a box office attendant refused to sell her tickets. After an extended dispute, Mrs. Curry and her party finally acquired tickets but, once escorted into the theater, found themselves directed to the balcony. After enduring this humiliation, Josephine Curry brought charges against the People's Theatre under the Illinois Civil Rights Act of 1885.

In their defense the owners of the People's argued that, in a neighborhood where the boundaries separating reputable from disreputable amusement were not always clear, they had to protect their respectable white clientele by any means necessary. This usually meant turning away African American patrons or selling them unnumbered seats so that they could be easily moved if white patrons complained. Black patrons, the owner testified, offended white theatergoers' notions of public respectability.[66] Mrs. Curry herself was well aware of the fragility of the line separating respectable leisure from morally suspect entertainment. This consciousness sparked her outrage at being directed to the neighboring Park Theatre, which, the *Chicago Tribune* recorded, she described as "no place for ladies and gem'men."[67]

In 1888 a judge found the theater owners in violation of the Illinois Civil Rights Act and awarded Josephine Curry $100 in damages. Mrs. Curry's attempt to challenge the racial restrictions at People's Theatre—as well as to avoid the immorality of Park Theatre—illustrates the onslaught of racial insult and moral hazards that black women and men faced in making active use of the city's leisure institutions. Within this unfriendly landscape, members of Chicago's black community, women in particular, tried to observe dictates of public propriety and social respectability. However, as Curry's case shows, white businessmen frequently thwarted these efforts, using their own need to establish respectability to justify the humiliation of African Americans.

Like Josephine Curry, many respectable blacks hoping to escape the morally dangerous environment of the Levee sought to protect their respectability by partaking of entertainment outside the emerging Black Belt. As they moved beyond community boundaries in search of amusement, African American men and women faced white Chicagoans' competing notions of respectability, notions predicated in part on a belief in black inferiority. For blacks forced into theater balconies or denied entrance to "respectable" venues altogether, challenges to their right to move about freely in the city's center were all too reminiscent of white southerners' increasingly harsh methods of racial segregation. While Illinois statute prohibited the use of the "Whites Only" theater entrances that were increasingly prevalent in the South, black Chicagoans nevertheless experienced white attempts to maintain racial separation and establish white superiority. Northern-style segregation in public amusements complicated, and often thwarted, African American attempts to expand their respectable uses of city streets.

Many black Chicagoans took part in leisure activities imbued with even greater moral ambiguity than theater houses. Prominent among these were such institutions of male leisure as saloons, wine rooms, cigar shops, billiard halls, and gambling dens. These amusement spots were located along the pathways that linked black residences, workplaces, and social life. By 1880 barrooms and gambling houses were conspicuous features of the crowded Levee neighborhood. Many were working-class saloons that catered to the social needs of the Levee's single working men. Cigar shops, billiard halls, and saloons nestled among the small immigrant- and black-owned businesses along State, Third, Fourth (Custom House Place), Clark, and Dearborn, catching the flow of men on their way home from work downtown. Saloons and gambling dens also took advantage of the diverse traffic of men on their way to nearby brothels, bawdy theaters, and assignation houses. The majority of these establishments catered to white and immigrant middle-class men and working men. Several resorts, however, catered primarily to black working-class men. Black working men increasingly sought relaxation and entertainment beyond the networks established by churches and respectable secular clubs.

By the late 1880s drinking establishments flourished within Chicago's black community. Because of their physical proximity to boardinghouses and hotels for unattached black men, they occupied a prominent place in the social life of African American men migrating to Chicago in the 1880s and 1890s.[68] They were also profitable business ventures for aspiring entrepreneurs. Together with barbershop and restaurant ownership, owning a saloon was one of the "leading branches of business which the colored people are engaged in." Opening a saloon did not require much capital on the part of prospective proprietors because brewing companies readily extended credit for liquor and fixtures to new saloon owners. Thus, the financial barriers that kept black men (and women) out of other business ventures did not exist for aspiring saloon keepers.[69] One 1886 black business directory listed sixteen purveyors of "wet goods." Advertisements in black newspapers from other cities, such as the *Indianapolis Freeman* and the Minneapolis-based *Western Appeal*, as well as in Chicago's daily papers, suggest that the business directory list was anything but exhaustive. The number of black-owned watering holes continued to increase in the 1890s, so that by the turn of the century, Chicago had more than forty black-owned saloons.[70] Most black drinking establishments occupied the section of the South Side between Harrison and Twelfth streets, and the majority of these were concentrated along State and Clark. One 1893 visitors' guide to the city alerted white visitors that "after passing Polk street one finds a number of expensively fitted up saloons . . . which are owned and patronized exclusively by colored persons."[71]

The liquor business could be the source of both considerable income and racial pride among the city's black middle class. Celebrating the achievements of the most prosperous saloon owners, the *Indianapolis Freeman* proclaimed, "The saloons owned by colored men are for the most part elegantly furnished, being fitted up in the latest fashion, and possessing all modern conveniences." According to I. C. Harris, the compiler of a black business and professional directory, the twenty saloons and sample rooms owned by blacks "were fitted up in grand style, with all the modern improvements calculated to make them compare favorably with the finest in the city."[72]

While black saloon owners' financial success conferred upon them a measure of respectability, many black Chicagoans questioned the propriety of the liquor enterprise. Middle-class saloon proprietors tried by various means to establish the reputations of their resorts as locations of refined leisure. To circumvent accusations of impropriety and sometimes to avoid the licensing fee required of saloon owners after 1885, many black sellers of spirituous drinks opened "sample rooms." Initially a reference to rooms set aside by liquor retailers for customers to taste goods they might eventually purchase in bulk, by the 1880s the name covered a range of enterprises that sold liquor to the public.[73] Saloon owners often used the term to distinguish their establishments as places where discerning men gathered to taste, or sample, fine liquors. The gentlemanly moderation suggested by the term "sample room" opposed images of raucous sociality and unrestrained drinking that respectable middle-class urbanites associated with working-class saloons. Daniel Scott and John Hunter operated Scott and Hunter's Sample Room and Billiard Parlor on Fourth Avenue; S. R. Snowden and William Beasley owned the Snowden and Beasley Sample Room at 480 State Street; H. Jones and Co. Sample Room conducted business at 295 State Street; Constable J. Q. Grant and a partner ran their sample room farther south at 2112 State Street. Other proprietors, such as S. A. Gray on Polk Street near State Street, operated "wine rooms," private rooms in restaurants, saloons, or hotel taverns used for small parties to sample drinks. By 1900 wine rooms would be firmly linked with illicit sexual encounters in the public mind—and very often in practice—but in the 1880s the designation "wine room" distinguished sites of polite social drinking from less refined watering holes. For African Americans, opening sample or wine rooms allowed them to assert male respectability within an area of urban leisure—public drinking—that often inspired charges of immorality.[74]

Many middle-class saloon owners worked hard to keep their saloons the exclusive preserve of men, firmly prohibiting women's patronage. Henry Smith's Clark Street saloon and billiard parlor employed such a policy. Saloons and sample rooms frequently stressed in newspaper advertisements that they were for men only. John F. Benson emphatically promoted his Palace Sample Room as a "Gentlemen's Resort!"[75] The exclusion of women from "gentlemen's resorts" gave black men a homosocial retreat in the city. Of equal importance, it prohibited the introduction of prostitution to this middle-class leisure spot. Furthermore, the prominence that advertisements gave to this show of refinement sprang from the proprietors' desire to protect both black men and black women from accusations of loose living.

Despite the efforts of some saloon owners to project an image of respectable male leisure, these enterprises competed for space, and sometimes for customers, with neighboring saloons that showed little consideration for the niceties required in locales of gentlemanly social drinking. Establishments that flouted such standards presented an attractive array of amusements for male patrons untroubled by the mandates of social decorum. Like classier resorts, some saloons provided rooms separate from the bar for billiards or pool; but in contrast to more respectable establishments, these back rooms often stood as invitations to members of Chicago's gaming fraternity, a disreputable lot engaged in illegal activities. Such was the case with John "Mushmouth" Johnson's saloon at 464 State Street. In 1890 Johnson and a partner named Scott took over George Cross's saloon, and Scott and Johnson's soon became one of the most popular gambling houses among Chicago's black sporting men. Robert Motts ran his own saloon and gambling den in the 2700 block of State Street. Both Motts and Johnson played significant roles as entrepreneurs in Chicago's black leisure industry after the turn of the century.[76] At the end of the nineteenth century, they gained considerable notoriety and wealth as proprietors of illegal enterprises.

Black gambling houses faced regular police pressure, and hauls of gambling men taken to the police station were often quite large. In a raid at a saloon on the city's West Side in May 1893, police arrested forty-two black men for playing craps. At the height of an anti-gambling crusade that seized Chicago after 1890, police kept black saloons under steady surveillance. Municipal authorities demonstrated particular concern about the playing of craps among African Americans. In 1892 police officers zeroed in on "a lively 'crap' game" going on in a saloon at

157 Clark Street and arrested nine men. Soon after this raid the chief of police sought and gained intelligence regarding a questionable saloon at 2634 State Street run by "Dick" Cook, a "colored citizen . . . not satisfied with the sales he derives from the sale of liquor." In the rear of his establishment, police discovered, Cook ran a "gambling layout" where a "crap game attracts a very considerable patronage."[77] Indeed, by 1892 the playing of craps had spread beyond black gaming men, having been "adopted by the white gambler as a new and interesting form of amusement." The popularity of craps among white and black gamblers prompted the Chicago police chief in 1893 to issue an order "specially directed against crap games in saloons." According to the *Tribune*, the order "spread dismay along State Street in the levee district."[78]

African Americans interested in promoting black economic success in Chicago took pains to distinguish the respectable gentlemen's resort from the disreputable saloon, but in fact the boundaries between these realms of economic activity were insecure and often brazenly disregarded. Several cases vividly illustrate the fragility of saloon respectability. While the *Indianapolis Freeman* proudly ranked Scott and Johnson among black businessmen who "seem to be getting rich" in Chicago, their saloon and gambling resort underwent frequent raids. In one January 1894 raid, fifteen "black men and boys" were arrested, it appears for merely "sleeping around the saloon."[79] Such heavy-handed police action was common. While the raid at Scott and Johnson's did not uncover legally questionable activity, happenings at other saloons frequently overstepped the law. At T. S. Rector's saloon on Fourth Avenue, a dispute over a crap game in 1887 ended in a shooting.[80] In 1893 two disputes over craps at one of Daniel Scott's lucrative gambling saloons ended in shootings, one fatal.[81] Such violent altercations drew the attention of city patrolmen to black-owned saloons, undermining the attempts of African American businesses and their supporters to claim urban respectability for saloon ownership. The *Indianapolis Freeman* praised Andrew J. Scott as a Chicago citizen "adept at the art of making money." According to the reporter, he owned "racing stock and a fine saloon, and can sign a check for $60,000." Other observers, however, were less impressed with Scott's accomplishments. In his 1893 exposé of vice and political corruption in Chicago, British reformer William Stead noted that Andrew J. Scott's saloon and gambling house occupied two floors of a Fourth Avenue building. City police knew Scott's saloon not as an upstanding business but as "the most extensive gambling-house for colored men in the city."[82]

White middle-class Chicagoans may have viewed popular portraits of black saloons and gambling houses as evidence of black men's moral debasement. Many black middle-class citizens regarded these businesses with a different kind of distaste. These establishments' regular run-ins with the law embarrassed black residents who hoped to distance themselves from the community's disreputable elements. Ferdinand L. Barnett, lawyer and publisher of the *Conservator* (and husband of leading civil rights and women's suffrage activist Ida B. Wells), expressed a general concern when he reminisced that in the 1880s "the behavior of many of the Negroes was characterized by loose living and lack of proper standards." Barnett witnessed this "loose living" daily as he walked between his Clark Street law office and the offices of the *Conservator* just two blocks south. On this short walk he would pass the H. Jones and Co. Sample Room; the Johnson, Bryan, and Whiting Sample Room and Billiard Parlor; and J. J. Turner's Saloon. Whether or not these drinking establishments attracted police attention, for many of the city's blacks they were nothing less than stops along the road to moral abandon.

Because saloons assumed so many different manifestations, they drew complicated and often-contradictory responses from black residents. Some might cast them as dens of intemperate activity or illicit leisure, while others pointed to them as proof that progressive economic forces were stirring among Chicago's blacks. The tension surfaced in the pages of the *Conservator*. Barnett regularly accepted advertisements for saloons and gentlemen's sample rooms. Yet Barnett and his partners— equally prominent men in the black community—hoped that their paper would act as a counterweight to the "gambling, vice conditions, and saloons [that] were making a swift inroad into the life of the Negro."[83] This contradictory stance was no doubt largely due to the paper's need for money. Yet the discrepancy also betrays the difficult task that black men and women faced as they navigated a leisure economy and an urban terrain strewn with moral hazards.

"Can We Afford to Lower Our Social Status?"

The proximity of houses of prostitution, gambling dens, and disorderly saloons to the homes and meeting places of respectable working- and middle-class residents fueled the press's and the pulpit's condemnation of immoral public behavior. To the frustration of respectable black residents, this proximity too often led outsiders to assume connections that community leaders adamantly disavowed. Such an incident occurred in 1877 when Mayor Monroe Heath concluded that some members of

Olivet Baptist Church were in fact inmates of Dan Webster's house of prostitution. Reverend R. De Baptiste quickly responded to Heath's accusation with a letter to the *Chicago Tribune* editor: "My attention was called to Mayor Heath's statement relative to members of my church being inmates, or rather residents of the Webster rendezvous. I am constrained to deny the allegation, as no person stopping or residing at above house is such, nor have they any connection with the better elements of colored society."[84] In this brief letter, Reverend De Baptiste drew a clear line between the respectable and disreputable elements of Chicago's black community.

If the *Tribune* and other white city papers carelessly repeated accusations of the easy association between disreputable and respectable blacks, the pages of the community's only paper endeavored to tell a different story. In the *Conservator*, the city's blacks saw the best of their community and expressed their own concern over transgressions of social and class standards.[85] Their remarks carried the voice of self-conscious middle-class men and women. One African American reader, "a lady of the first class in our city," wrote a letter to the *Conservator* expressing distress about the lack of discrimination within amusements. Her main concern: social dances arranged for the amusement of young men and women that were too often tarnished by the admission of sporting men and women. She specifically condemned the practices of the organizations that sponsored these dances at public halls and opened their doors to any paying patron. Her strong opinions elicited an equally strong response from another *Conservator* reader. Lewis White acknowledged the "contaminating" influence of "the offensive rabble" who infiltrated otherwise-dignified gatherings, but he also leveled a blistering critique at black "society" folk who would denigrate the young men and women who partook of these all-too-public amusements. "They must have amusement," he argued. "Why censure them for this indulgence, when you and your compeers in your immaculate and exalted sphere of social exclusiveness, make no attempt to supply the deficiency? . . . The responsibility should be placed where it belongs." In their reluctance to offer wholesome outlets for social dancing, members of Chicago's black elite, White opined, engaged in "senseless tirades" that amounted to nothing more than "sanctimonious hypocracy [*sic*]."[86]

White may have been correct in identifying the lack of alternatives for young men and women who sought recreation away from churches. His exchange with the "lady of the first class," however, revealed tensions among a black elite unclear about how to negotiate their own class position and simultaneously engage in public life. The neighborhood south of the central business district was indeed a quarter filled with moral dangers that could not always be guarded against. Most troubling, the younger generation of black Chicagoans seemed unconcerned about these dangers. To the chagrin of their elders, they readily availed themselves of the pleasures of public dancing, even as they rubbed elbows with prostitutes.

The editorial reply to White's letter to the editor underscores the fragility of the social and geographic boundaries protecting respectable amusement among the city's blacks: "Our correspondent says it is captious fault-finding to raise our voice against associating ourselves, our wives, and sisters with the most degenerate inmates of prostitution. Chicago society has so long tolerated this festering evil that it now finds excuse and palliation. What greater proof do we need of its degenerating influence?" Posing the question "When do we ever find the residents of the Avenue mixing with denizens of the gilded hells of infamy?" the editor drew attention to the distinctions in moral geography diligently observed by "residents of the Avenue"—the white men and women residing in elite neighborhoods. Just such vigilance, he suggested, constituted the unimpeachable social status of middle- and upper-class white Chicagoans. In a tellingly worded counterstatement, Barnett, the paper's publisher, pointed out that African Americans of social standing found it difficult to "give entertainments and protect their respectable patrons from the jeers and elbowing of street walkers." The term "street walkers," as Barnett used it, included a range of urban types—loiterers in front of saloons, gamblers, and pickpockets—but it most urgently evoked a contested landscape in which prostitutes figured prominently. Prostitutes not only troubled the flow of respectable traffic on Black Belt streets but were also likely to invade the public gatherings of socially aspiring men and women. Too often, Barnett complained, "white and black prostitutes" crashed gala events hosted by black social organizations, and "the grand entertainment degenerates into a fancy house ball."[87]

More than an uncomfortable physical proximity defined the context for the *Conservator*'s call for vigilance. The editor's reiteration of the fears expressed by the "lady of the first class" reveals what was at stake for black middle-class residents: "Can we afford to lower our social status? What respect will white people have for us, if they know that we mingle freely, good, bad and indifferent all in one motely [sic] mass for the sake of money?"[88] These remarks both called upon Chicago's middle-class blacks to prove their capacity for moral progress and gave voice to their desire for self-preservation and racial advancement.

Of course, Chicago's impoverished and working-class African Americans collided more directly with the traffic of neighborhood prostitutes than did their middle-class counterparts. Unable to pick up and relocate to the more expensive and morally hospitable neighborhoods farther south, working-poor blacks were among the "motley mass" against which Barnett and others inveighed. Each day, they too strove to delineate spheres and pathways of respectability. So despite middle-class blacks' moral exhortations, most black Chicagoans asserted the moral character of black community life in their everyday engagement with the social and physical landscape of Chicago's South Side. As was true for middle-class blacks, competing claims to the use of space in the African American residential district reaching southward from downtown repeatedly frustrated attempts to create separate moral climates.

Conclusion

At the end of the nineteenth century, optimistic industrial leaders of southern cities sought in a limited fashion to incorporate migrating blacks into the vision of urban progress and regional rebirth at the heart of the post–Civil War New South ideal.[89] Most white northerners, however, saw African American men and women as neither desirable nor potentially productive contributors to the economic life of the region's growing cities. African Americans arriving in Chicago after 1870 encountered a white middle-class and civic elite dubious about their preparedness for orderly life in the modern city. Their bodies and their labors recalled the backwardness of the southern slave economy. Furthermore, African American men and women embodied the licentiousness popularly imagined to be at the heart of southern slavery. Antislavery literature and traveling minstrel shows broadcast, albeit with differing aims, the strong undercurrent of sexual dissolution shaping life in the slave South. As they left communities in the South and Midwest, blacks bore the taint of sexual immorality.

An odd and ominous representation of black backwardness and sexual threat emerged in the figure of the urban Amazon. In images of untamed Levee thoroughfares overrun with animalistic black women, African Americans confronted the sexualization of their very presence within the city. The frequent juxtaposition of "lechery and miscegenation" in reports of urban disorder revealed the extreme discomfort middle-class whites experienced when faced with the reality of black bodies within city space. It was not merely an aberrant black sexuality but the wanton disregard for racial boundaries manifest in the streets of the Levee that whites believed threatened to undermine white racial purity and the moral order of the modern city.

African Americans daily challenged ideas of their moral depravity. Segregated in the poorest of Chicago's neighborhoods, they nonetheless forged a community life in urban spaces frequently characterized as moral wastelands. In making moral claims on Levee streets, respectable black residents struggled to forge a moral geography that both undermined the assumptions of disdainful whites and counterbalanced the all-too-real immorality that surrounded them.

Between 1900 and 1915 the geographies of sexual commerce and of African American residence changed dramatically. The new configurations of urban space after the turn of the century did not free black Chicagoans from their physical association with the city's sex industry. Both the vice district and the ethnically and racially diverse community of working men and women would move away from the central city. Yet as immigrants gained the means to move away from the sex industry, practices of residential segregation forced an even larger segment of Chicago's growing black community to live near a new district of sex trade. The new vice district presented African Americans who sought to protect the moral outlines of their community with a fresh set of challenges. It also presented black prostitutes and madams with challenges of their own.

FOUR

Race and the Reconstruction of the Urban Sex Economy, 1900–1915

In 1900 Vina Fields's House of Pleasure on Custom House Place was still a going concern. Since the days of the 1893 World's Columbian Exposition, when Fields's resort employed as many as sixty black women, her house had settled down to a more manageable size. When census enumerators canvassed her "home" in 1900, they counted nineteen boarders, ranging in age from nineteen to thirty-two. To run an establishment of this size—still larger than most other brothels—Fields employed a four-person support staff. Kitty Montgomery, a thirty-eight-year-old black woman, was Fields's housekeeper, and three black men (all in their forties) worked as porters. Fields's business did so well in the 1890s that by 1896 she had purchased a home for herself at 4830 South Wabash in the virtually all-white neighborhood miles south of the Levee and some distance from the areas of black residence to the north. (She remained the owner of the property until 1909, when she sold it for $8,075.) Fields clearly did not limit the use of her money to the sex trade. In her correspondence with reformer William Stead, Fields disclosed that some of her money went to educate a daughter, who, in Stead's words, "knows nothing of the life of her mother in the virginal seclusion of a convent school." She also sent money to her sisters in Missouri. Fields had not only converted her income from the commerce in black women's sexual services into property (both within and beyond the sex district) but also used it to assist family members and to secure for her daughter a future unlike her own.[1]

By 1910 Vina Fields's resort had moved from Custom House Place and now occupied a house at 1834 South Dearborn. As many other brothel keepers did in the 1890s, Fields made the move into what became Chicago's new Levee district. Giving her age as fifty-seven (although according to the 1880 census report she was at least sixty), Fields managed a resort that was half the size of its precursor. Employing ten black women, ages twenty-two to thirty-one, Fields adapted her establishment to the changing landscape and to new demands placed on black sex workers and entrepreneurs in the new South Side Levee. Still, ten women was no small number, and Fields remained among the more prominent keepers in the new sex district.[2]

The shift in the geography of sexual commerce was accompanied by other changes, especially in the institutions of men's urban leisure—the saloons, hotels, dance halls, and nightclubs—that supported black women's sex work. As she had in the late nineteenth century, in the first decade of the twentieth century Fields occupied a unique—and uniquely visible—place within the urban sex economy. Her experience, and apparent financial security, contributed to her longevity and enabled her to weather the storm of changes that reorganized Chicago's sex economy after the turn of the century. Yet her distinction as a prosperous black madam did not set her completely apart from other black madams or, for that matter, from prostitutes. Like most black women working in the early-twentieth-century sex industry, Fields was vulnerable to shifts in the spatial, racial, and institutional landscapes of sexual commerce.

Virtually simultaneous changes in residential, commercial, and industrial geographies brought a gradual end to the Near South Side sex and residential district. By 1910 the old Levee was no longer in existence, replaced by a vibrant and by all accounts more audacious Levee farther south. The reputation of Chicago's new red-light district reached almost-mythic proportions, drawing the disdain of reformers and the curiosity of pleasure-seekers locally and nationally. The Levee's reputation sprang from the continued vitality of one institutional form of sexual commerce—the brothel. But it also hinged on the brothel's geographical and economic association with other increasingly important commercial leisure institutions.[3]

Significantly, at the same time that a new South Side Levee emerged, black sex workers' position within this geographically bounded economy became increasingly tenuous. In the first decade of the twentieth century, the number of African American prostitutes working in the Levee's brothels, saloons, and assignation houses declined considerably. Pushed out by white vice syndicates and local police officials, black women who had earlier been an integral part of the city's illicit economy found it nearly impossible to stay afloat in the restructured Levee trade.

The Rise of the New Levee

Sexual commerce in Chicago underwent significant changes after 1900. The most visible and perhaps most consequential change was the relocation of the city's brothel district from the Near South Side to an area farther south. The new Levee extended from Eighteenth to Twenty-Second streets and from Wabash Avenue on the east to Clark Street on the west (map 4.1). By some accounts the move southward of the city's most prominent institutions of sexual exchange was accomplished swiftly.[4] However, the migration south had been under way since the late 1880s.

Economic forces, coupled with the motivations of the area's inhabitants, set in motion the southward relocation of sexual commerce. Among the impersonal catalysts was a gradual change in the use of land just south of the central business district. By the late nineteenth century not only was this area attractive to prostitutes and the working poor who lived there, but depressed property values eventually also drew manufacturers seeking low rents and easy access to downtown customers. By 1890 the expansion of book printing and light industry south of Van Buren Street along Dearborn Street and Plymouth Place (Third Avenue) challenged the dominance of cheap housing, retailers, saloons, and houses of ill fame in the area. In addition, interstate railroads bought large tracts of land along their routes into the city. In 1887 the Santa Fe Railroad purchased land for freight yards along State Street between Polk and Sixteenth streets. By 1890 the Santa Fe and other railroads had built yards that overshadowed the western edge of the Levee. According to one student of Chicago's central business district, by the late 1880s the area south of downtown "was more than ever in the grip of the terminal properties which surrounded it."[5] As railroads converted Near South Side land to railway terminals and freight yards, they gradually displaced nearby houses of prostitution and the homes of the poor.[6] At the time of the 1893 world's fair, many brothels still operated on Santa Fe property, but after the turn of the century most madams,

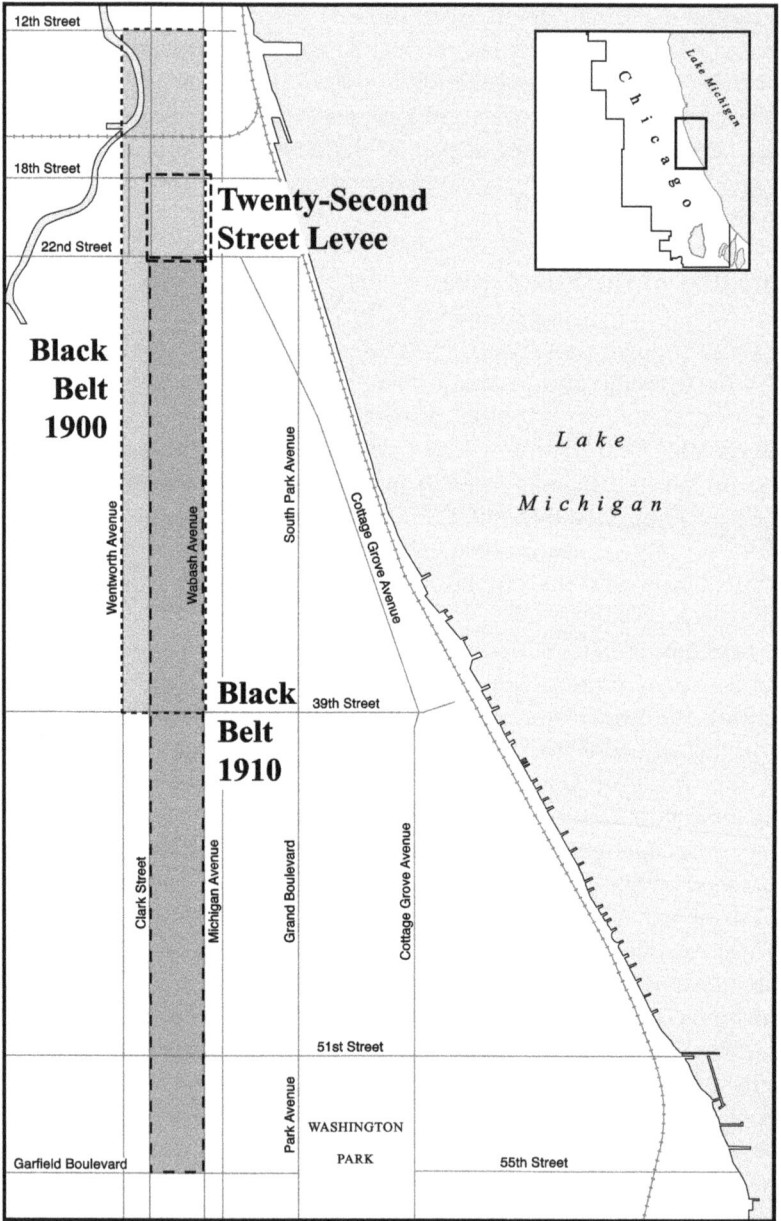

Map 4.1   The Twenty-Second Street Levee and the Growing Black Belt, 1900–1910. *Source*: Rand McNally and Co., *Street Guide Map of Chicago* (Chicago: Rand McNally and Co., between 1897 and 1899), http://www.lib.uchicago.edu/e/su/maps/chi1890/G4104-C6-1897-R3.html.

saloon owners, and working-class men and women would find themselves evicted from their Near South Side residences.[7]

Perhaps hoping to both bolster the southward expansion of downtown business and light industry and push sin and racial mixing out of the central city, Mayor Carter Harrison tried to hurry the transformation of the district's character. In 1897 new electric streetcar tracks were installed on South Clark Street, linking an expanding belt of working- and middle-class neighborhoods on the South Side to the city's center. The laying of electric railway lines for intra-urban travel did not in and of itself necessitate the removal of houses of prostitution, bawdy saloons, and the homes of the black and immigrant poor from this area. However, Harrison found in the coming of the streetcar an incentive to rid the Near South Side of at least some of its illicit institutions and "vicious" elements. Harrison said that he decided to push sex and gambling resorts from Clark "to protect passengers in the Clark Street street-cars, [who were] compelled to use this transportation to get to the down town district from Englewood and the Stockyards." This cleanup drive was not decisive, however. In 1900 Carrie Watson still operated her famous resort at 441 Clark Street. And in 1903 inexpensive brothels occupied Clark Street south of Polk.[8]

Hoping to "give the old levee . . . a thorough cleaning," Mayor Harrison made another move against the area's inhabitants. In 1904 he directed the police to order resort keepers along State Street and Custom House Place south of Van Buren Street to remove to other parts of the city.[9] Although Harrison implied that his order had delivered the critical blow to the flagging Levee district, a 1904 police report suggested that Levee debauches were only "curtailed." Still, the report hopefully pronounced that "an insignificant remnant [was] soon to disappear, where once flourished scenes of lewdness impossible to imagine at present." Police officials claimed final victory in 1906 when they cheered "the entire disappearance of the disorderly houses from Custom House Place" and from a few West Side streets. "Gigantic as the task was," the report continued, "it has been satisfactorily accomplished during the year, to the credit of the police department." With this final push the old Levee faded from view, and the geographical stage was set for the ascendancy of what would become Chicago's infamous red-light district.[10]

Brothel keepers were not the only ones who had to look elsewhere for new homes. Changes in land ownership and Mayor Harrison's cleanup drive gradually pushed working men and women and poor families from the neighborhood's boardinghouses, flats, and modest homes. European immigrants who lived in the First Ward—largely Irish and German settlers who had arrived between 1850 and 1890—moved away from the city's center. Some settled in the working-class communities that formed on the North and West Sides after 1860; others established residence in the new homes built for working men and their families near new industrial developments on the southern and western edges of the city.[11] The exodus of old immigrant settlers and their native-born children from the old South Side Levee community left room for the wave of southern and eastern Europeans who came to the city in increasing numbers after 1890. Like their predecessors, Italian, Polish, Russian, and Czech men and women viewed the cramped and dilapidated housing near downtown as transitional. By the early twentieth century they too would move away from the central city, populating working-class neighborhoods at good distances west, southwest, and north of the central business district.[12]

Just as the Near South Side became inhospitable to both sexual commerce and residential occupancy, concurrent transformations in land use farther south made the area between Sixteenth and Twenty-Second streets attractive to brothel managers and other sex merchants. In the 1880s the area south of Sixteenth Street had been inhabited largely by German, Irish, Czech, and Swedish immigrants. But as industry and rail yards pushed south from the city's center, many residents found the district less suitable for family occupancy. Hoping to profit from the southward movement of warehouses and light industry, real estate speculators bought up considerable property east of the Rock Island Railroad tracks. While they waited for the land to deliver the projected returns, speculators built and rented inexpensive, often-shabby housing; at the same time they invested no extra capital in preserving existing rental properties. As residential property values declined along the railroad tracks, which converged as they headed downtown, middle-class families east of State Street and many working-class residents to the west moved away from the area.[13]

As early as 1889, when the *Sporting and Club House Directory* was published, brothel madams were taking advantage of the slow exodus of middle- and working-class families from the neighborhood south of Sixteenth Street. In the late nineteenth century, pioneer sex entrepreneurs were drawn by the district's low rents and for a while paid less than the women who maintained resorts in the recognized Levee district to the north. Settling here yielded other benefits as well. Distant from the bright lights of the Levee, madams and keepers of disorderly saloons more easily maintained a low profile, a feature that drew clients who required discretion. For a time it seemed that brothel keepers in this district could operate quiet resorts with little risk of costly and embarrassing run-ins with the police.[14]

In the 1890s even more madams established themselves in this second South Side district. No doubt many were encouraged by the success of relocated resorts like those run by old-timers Emma Ritchie and Lizzie Allen south of Twentieth Street. Early news of the coming World's Columbian Exposition encouraged still more madams to cast their eyes southward. Hoping to capitalize on the steady flow of traveling men heading south to the fair from downtown train terminals, astute sex entrepreneurs opened resorts and bawdy saloons in the burgeoning sex entertainment district. By 1893 the area was well served by internal transportation lines—a cable car line on State Street and an elevated railway between State and Wabash. Noting the growth of this district, in 1893 William Stead found more than forty houses of prostitution between Twentieth and Twenty-Second streets on Dearborn Street and Armour Avenue.[15]

By the turn of the century, the area bounded by Eighteenth, Twenty-Second, State, and Armour had become the city's premier red-light district, the Twenty-Second Street Levee. The new Levee came into being in part because of shifting real estate patterns and in part because of the actions of sex entrepreneurs. It was the tolerance of city officials, however—police officers, aldermen, and the mayor—that allowed it to thrive. Although the municipal code prohibited the operation of houses of ill fame, disorderly saloons, and assignation houses, civic authorities enforced these ordinances with only fluctuating vigor in the new vice terrain.[16]

In 1905, making his own bid to "clean up" vice in Chicago, Mayor Harrison's successor Edward Dunne attempted to codify what had until then been a customary practice. Before a special grand jury, Mayor Dunne "suggest[ed] that districts be mapped out on each side of the city wherein to interne vice." With the help of Police Chief Francis O'Neill, Dunne proposed to establish firm geographical boundaries around the areas of Chicago's sexual commerce. This strategy, he believed, would keep "disreputable women within these districts." On the South Side, the "segregated district" was to encompass State and Clark streets from Sixteenth to Twenty-Second and was to stretch southward along Wabash Avenue from Harrison to Thirty-Ninth Street. Smaller districts were also mapped out for the West and North Sides.[17]

The proposal provoked heated debate. Among those protesting the plan were property owners whose holdings were within the mapped areas, pastors of prominent white churches near or within the proposed segregated territories, and organizations of middle-class white women outraged by the city's planned complicity with the degradation of women. "Dealers in real estate, on the other hand," one reporter commented, "generally approved the mayor's suggestions."[18] Despite the complaints of prominent white civic and church leaders, police authorities carried out the policy of tolerating Levee prostitution and of policing border infringements.[19] For more than a decade, the banner of the Levee boldly waved over this new concentrated district catering to men's desire for boisterous recreation and sexual entertainment.

The Brothel Landscape

In her migration south, Vina Fields followed the shifting geography of sexual commerce. She shared this new terrain with numerous other women who, with varying degrees of success, worked to extend the popularity of the brothel into the twentieth century. Among them were sisters Minna and Ada Everleigh, the proprietors of the best-known brothel in early-twentieth-century Chicago—the Everleigh Club.

Beginning in February 1900, Minna and Ada operated the Everleigh Club, which for twelve years flourished at 2131 Dearborn Street. Many considered it the most lavishly appointed sex resort in the United States. In 1902 the sisters purchased a neighboring house at 2133, appropriately called The Annex. The Everleigh Club was unrivaled in splendor and in the status of its clientele and became, in the words of one writer, "the showplace of the Levee." The Everleigh sisters elevated the domestic opulence of late-nineteenth-century parlor houses to new heights of luxury and male comfort. They also expanded the entertainment features of the parlor house by providing dinners and live musical entertainment, as well as serving wines and champagnes in ornately decorated wine rooms.[20] The club dominated the sphere of sexual commerce both as a moneymaking venture and as the embodiment of elite white male urban leisure.

On a smaller scale, other white-owned sex resorts patterned themselves on the Everleigh Club, and several resort keepers who moved from the old district hoped to tap into the high-class white male market that the Everleigh Club courted so successfully. Among the Everleighs' competitors were Victoria "Vic" Shaw on Dearborn Street; Georgia "Georgie" Spencer, whose establishment operated a few doors away from the Everleigh Club; and Aimee Leslie, who with her husband, Ed Weiss, managed a resort next door to the Everleigh Club. Other popular houses of prostitution had fewer extravagant pretensions but nevertheless cultivated a well-paying trade. Bearing such colorful names as the Sappho Club and the House of All Nations, Levee brothels openly advertised the special attractions of their inmates and drew waves of white men into the new sex district.[21]

As prominent as these brothels were, they accounted for only a portion of the houses of prostitution operating openly in the Twenty-Second Street Levee. The 1910 census of Armour Avenue and Dearborn Street between Eighteenth and Twenty-Second streets reveals rows of virtually uninterrupted "houses of ill-fame." Indeed, the Twenty-Second Street red-light district appears to have been dominated by the brothel. Census enumerators designated at least 95 residences—from small apartments to entire buildings—as houses of prostitution. Anti-vice investigators found even more houses openly operating in the area. In 1910 the Vice Commission of Chicago—more deliberate in their search for houses of ill fame than census takers—counted 119 brothels in the South Side Levee and another 73 scattered in other areas of the city (figs. 4.1 and 4.2).[22]

4.1   "Houses in Levee District, 2117 S. Federal Street." *Chicago Daily News*, DN-0063323, no date. Courtesy of Chicago History Museum.

4.2 "Vic Shaw's Resort at 2014 Dearborn" in the Levee. *Chicago Daily News*, DN-0008043, 1910. Courtesy of Chicago History Museum.

A close examination of the census reveals another important feature of the Twenty-Second Street Levee: few black female brothel keepers weathered the geographical shift of the sex economy. In 1900 black houses of prostitution accounted for 18 percent of the brothels found in both the old red-light district and the emerging Levee. By 1910, however, black women keepers were nearly invisible in the brothels of the new Levee. Of the ninety-five houses of ill fame counted in the census, only four (4 percent) were run and staffed by black women. Of the black brothel keepers appearing in the 1900 census, only two could be found in 1910: the venerable Vina Fields and the younger Maggie Douglas, two women whose entrepreneurial choices reveal the kinds of obstacles that black women faced within the Twenty-Second Street Levee.[23]

Drawing the Color Line

The exact date of Vina Fields's arrival in the Twenty-Second Street Levee is uncertain. Most likely, she left Custom House Place sometime between 1904 and 1907. By 1907 she operated a resort at Nineteenth Street and Armour Avenue in the new district. In 1908 she moved to 1834 South Dearborn Street, where she remained for about two years, through 1910. However, in 1911 she operated yet another house, this one located at 1900 South Dearborn. Fields's repeated changes of address are revealing: though her earlier brothel remained at 138–140 Custom House Place for at least twenty-five years beginning in 1879, her later career was characterized by notable mobility.[24]

Financial insecurity characterized the business of running—and working in—a brothel in the late nineteenth century. This instability marked twentieth-century brothels as well. Between 1900 and 1910 the majority of houses—white and black—disappeared from areas of concentrated sexual commerce. Yet some keepers—including old-timers like Japanese madam Minnie Shima and newcomers like the Everleigh sisters—secured for themselves a niche within the sex marketplace that protected them from such instability.[25] Fields's staying power in the old red-light district augured well for her ability to weather the changing winds of Chicago's sex economy. As she moved south, she seemed poised to take advantage of new opportunities within an expanded arena of white men's leisure. However, she too experienced the challenges that undercut the best efforts of many keepers in the new Levee.

Several factors could explain Fields's mobility after 1900. Perhaps her association with several different houses did not represent movement at all: she may have operated brothels at each of these addresses simultaneously. Such an intensified engagement with the brothel economy is plausible. In the late nineteenth century she was financially connected to at least one other brothel in the old Levee besides her own. While Fields resided at her own parlor house at 138–140 Custom House Place, she appears to have owned property that she rented to another brothel keeper. One such house, located at 132 Custom House Place, a few doors away from her House of Pleasure, was occupied for a time by white brothel keeper Madame Cloquette. Fields eventually sold this property in 1908 for the astounding sum of $29,000.[26] Though in her lengthy career Fields profited from the complex and remunerative property relations that shaped the brothel economy,[27] she herself apparently never managed more than one brothel at a time. While it is not improbable that she simultaneously operated several resorts, drawing firm conclusions from available sources is difficult. That her different brothel addresses appear in successive years suggests that Fields moved her resort from one place to another.[28]

Fields's occupancy at three different addresses in five years suggests another important shift in her circumstances—she may have been a renter in the new sex district. Although a property owner in the old Levee, in the late nineteenth century she also rented property with the hopes of expanding her Custom House Place business. In April 1898 she entered into a yearlong rental agreement with Paul Brown, whose building at 142–142½ Custom House Place neighbored her House of Pleasure. Seizing an opportunity that only the illicit use of his holdings could provide, Brown charged Fields $175 per month in rent for property that would normally receive only $40 per month. To be sure, even at the exorbitant rates brothel madams invariably paid, renting had its advantages. For Fields, renting could double the size of her already-large operations.[29] For the average brothel keeper, though, renting offered other benefits. If quarters at one address became unsuitable, if the rental agreement severely undercut profits, or if a certain location became unappealing, a madam could pick up and relocate. Such a motive perhaps explains Fields's 1907 move. In 1907 Fields's Armour Avenue resort received publicity that could only have hurt business. A small-pox scare led the Health Department to quarantine Fields's Armour Avenue house. As the *Chicago Daily News* reported, "At least thirty women inmates of the resort have been exposed" to the virus. As a sanitary measure, said the paper, "a police guard has been put about the house and no one will be allowed to enter or leave."[30] While so public an association with disease may have prompted Fields to leave her Armour Avenue resort, the reasons for her subsequent moves remain obscure. What is clear is that, even as she frequently moved about in search of better accommodations for her business, she remained committed to keeping her brothel within or near a clearly defined brothel district. As a member of an older generation of female sex entrepreneurs, Fields stuck to the phase of the business that she knew best. But her confidence in segregated prostitution may not have stood her in good stead in her later years.

The nature and probable causes of Vina Fields's peregrinations are clearer when we look at competing institutions operated by white madams like the Everleigh sisters, Vic Shaw, and Georgia Spencer. Again, Minna and Ada Everleigh were unique among Levee madams. Few if any could invest even a fraction of the reported $55,000 worth of improvements and furnishing that the Everleighs poured into their club.[31]

Several women, however, found ways to capitalize their resorts and in doing so remained competitive in the new sex landscape.

The Everleigh sisters made their initial investment in Levee property in part with inherited money; other white women established or expanded their brothels with money made by their husbands, most of whom were saloon keepers or proprietors of other district entertainment venues. Vic Shaw, who ran a resort at 2012 Dearborn, was the wife of Roy Jones, the proprietor of the Casino saloon at the southeast corner of Twenty-First and Dearborn. Jones operated his own "disorderly resort on the same premises" as his Casino saloon.[32] Victoria Moresco, another madam, was married to Jim Colosimo, one of the biggest names in Chicago organized crime in the first two decades of the century. After their marriage, Colosimo took over operation of Moresco's resort at Armour and Archer avenues, turning the Victoria into one of the largest sex establishments in the Levee. Colosimo himself ran a saloon and restaurant in the 2100 block of Wabash. Theresa McCafey and husband Bob Gray ran the California, which, according to one source, "was the toughest parlor house in the district."[33] Georgia Spencer, whose resort was located at 2125–2127 Dearborn, was married to John Jordan, an important Levee figure who owned a saloon at Twenty-First and Wabash.[34] Aimee Leslie operated a brothel at 2135 Dearborn, next door to the Everleighs. Her husband, Ed Weiss, was part owner with Fred Buxbaum of the Buxbaum saloon at the corner of Twenty-Second and State. Weiss also owned his own saloon at the northeast corner of Dearborn and Twenty-Second streets.[35] Such mixing of personal and business affairs occurred in other cases as well. When forty women were indicted on charges of keeping disorderly resorts in 1908, police officials found that "in many instances . . . men own the places run by the women."[36]

The incursion of white men into the business end of the sex trade marked a pivotal shift in the economic relations of brothel keeping in particular and Levee prostitution in general. On the one hand, it suggests that white men were finding ways to increase their proportion of the profits circulating within the Levee sex economy. To be sure, male landlords and property owners and their agents who leased their buildings or apartments to women in the trade had long been involved in the prostitution economy. While white men dominated this class of property owners, a few black men took advantage of the trade's property relations as well. In 1893 J. W. E. Thomas, a black lawyer, was arrested and charged with leasing property at 198 Custom House Place to madam Susan Redmond for immoral purposes. In the same year, Chicago police charged saloon and gambling house owner Andrew J. Scott with leasing his property at 86 Custom House Place for immoral purposes.[37] While real estate owners had long passively profited from the illicit activities conducted in their buildings, and many saloon owners had long linked their businesses to houses of prostitution or assignation rooms upstairs, few of these men had actively participated in the sex trade.[38] However, white men now earned money within the economy more directly and exercised significant influence over the operation of these establishments. They did this in many capacities—as saloon keepers whose wives or lovers ran houses of prostitution attached to their saloons, as partners with paramours, as sole managers, and even as employees of houses of prostitution. More men than ever actively connected prostitution to their own business enterprises. Above all, male entrepreneurs wove the prostitution economy into a larger economy of men's urban leisure institutions.

Mounting anti-prostitution activism in large part transformed businessmen's involvement in Chicago's sex trade. At the turn of the twentieth century, religious and civic reformers vociferously voiced distress about the unfettered expansion of prostitution in growing cities like Chicago and the political and moral corruption it bred. Urban red-light districts like the Levee received concentrated attention from church and secular reform organizations. However, fears of "white slavery"—the organized trafficking in young, usually white, women—fueled the most insistent attacks on the urban sex trade. Organized anti-prostitution activism eventually pitted individual madams and sex workers against police officers under pressure to "clean up" their cities, close houses of prostitution, and protect young women from traffickers. In Chicago the police demonstrated their half-hearted commitment to attacking the "social evil" by conducting occasional raids of Levee houses of prostitution. The sporadic anti-prostitution enforcement effectively put economically vulnerable madams out of business. Corrupt officers seized the opportunity occasioned by the white slavery scare to extract protection money from businesswomen, prosperous and vulnerable alike.[39]

While the spread of prostitution outraged reformers, many male leisure entrepreneurs hoped to profit from the expansion of the urban sex trade. They also took advantage of financial opportunities created by the system of police protection. Seeing potential profits in integrating prostitution into a growing male leisure economy and able to access greater resources to actualize this potential, businessmen—frequently saloon owners—helped struggling madams by investing in their enterprises and brokering protection with local police officials. Over time, they took greater shares of business profits and eventually displaced many madams as proprietors of houses of prostitution altogether.[40] They also encouraged prostitution to flourish in other Levee leisure resorts. Thus, an interlocking array of forces chipped away at women's control of Chicago's sex industry: anti-prostitution reformist activism, police graft and political corruption, and male entrepreneurs' access to money. By the turn of the century, white businessmen had made significant inroads into an economy that for decades had been primarily in the control of women.

Certainly madams remained prominent: Frank Wright, French Emma, Madam Leo, Eva Lowry, Minnie Shima, and Black May (Maggie Douglas), to name a few. Men, however, operated equally important leisure resorts: saloons, brothels, hotels, nightclubs, and dance halls. They included "Dago" Frank Lewis's saloon; Mike Monahan's brothel; Maurice Van Bever's two resorts; George Little's adjoining brothels, the Imperial and the House of All Nations; Harry Hopkins's and Jake "Jakie" Adler's Silver Dollar brothel; Ike Bloom's and Solly Friedman's dance hall, Freiberg's; Ed Weiss's dance hall, the Capitol; and Louis Weiss's brothel, the Sappho.[41]

These resorts, along with others, are spotlighted in Herbert Asbury's 1940 exploration of Chicago's criminal underworld. To be sure, the brothels and saloons featured in Asbury's popular and at times sensational history of the Twenty-Second Street Levee constitute only a fraction of the ninety-five houses of prostitution enumerated by census takers in the Levee. Yet Asbury's selective attention to the most prominent and notorious sex resorts and drinking places nonetheless reveals an important trend: between 1900 and 1910, white male leisure entrepreneurs established a secure footing within the sex economy.

As long as the Levee thrived, this changing economic climate proved to be a mixed blessing for white prostitutes and brothel keepers. On the one hand, the financial assistance of these white male entrepreneurs gave many women economic advantages that they might not have achieved on their own. Such help provided security during periods of sluggish trade. It also financed improvements and expansions that could make a flagging business competitive. However, the prominence of white men in the Levee sex economy severely undercut white madams' ability to shape the marketplace as freely as they did decades before.[42]

Asbury's account shows that as individual businessmen, white men took firm hold of institutions that supported the Levee sex trade. But what Asbury's work does not disclose is the increasing organization of the landscape by groups of white males bent on seizing control of the Levee's illegal economies. For white female sex entrepreneurs, such organization had mixed results. For seasoned black madams and for young black women trying to earn money through their sexual labors, the inroads of these white male entrepreneurs had destabilizing consequences. Most influential in this regard were the "vice syndicates" that came to control a large share of the Levee's illegal enterprises.

The history of vice syndicates in early-twentieth-century Chicago has received considerable popular and some scholarly attention.[43] Though the Prohibition era was the heyday of organized criminal networks in the city,[44] the first two decades of the twentieth century witnessed the growing organization of the city's illegal businesses. The Levee was the center of this early syndicate activity. Many Levee saloon and brothel keepers joined together in coalitions that protected their financial interests against rival entrepreneurs. Most importantly these syndicates secured cordial relations between local police officers and individual business owners. In a 1909 investigation of police graft on the city's South Side, State's Attorney John Wayman uncovered "a gigantic system of corruption" that involved police officials and proprietors of "immoral" leisure resorts. Among these establishments were "red-light dives," "shady hotels," "all-night saloons," "immoral theaters," dance halls, and gambling houses. Annual payments to the police reportedly exceeded $200,000.[45] To be sure, police graft had long been a part of the city's underground economy. However, this elaborate "system of corruption" dwarfed the web of graft payments that protected earlier illicit enterprises in Chicago.

While these payments provided protection to individual proprietors, the management of the system of payments gave certain men considerable control over the local sex economy. In 1914 Wayman's successor, State's Attorney Maclay Hoyne, found that three "vice rings" controlled prostitution and gambling in the district. Each "ring" was run by a group of "vice kings," who, according to Hoyne, "have been collecting money from the little fellows and splitting it with the police and the politicians." Before the closing of the South Side district, these syndicates thrived on extorting regular payments from saloon operators and brothel keepers, money that the syndicates funneled to ward politicians and local police officers.[46]

The rise of syndicates simultaneously transformed the economics of urban prostitution and altered the geographical and racial relations of Levee commerce. First, individual saloon keepers, madams, and prostitutes very often worked in territory defined by its association with white male members of one or another syndicate (see map 4.2). In addition to brokering graft payments to police officers, these men paid the fines and legal fees of resort keepers entangled in the municipal court system.

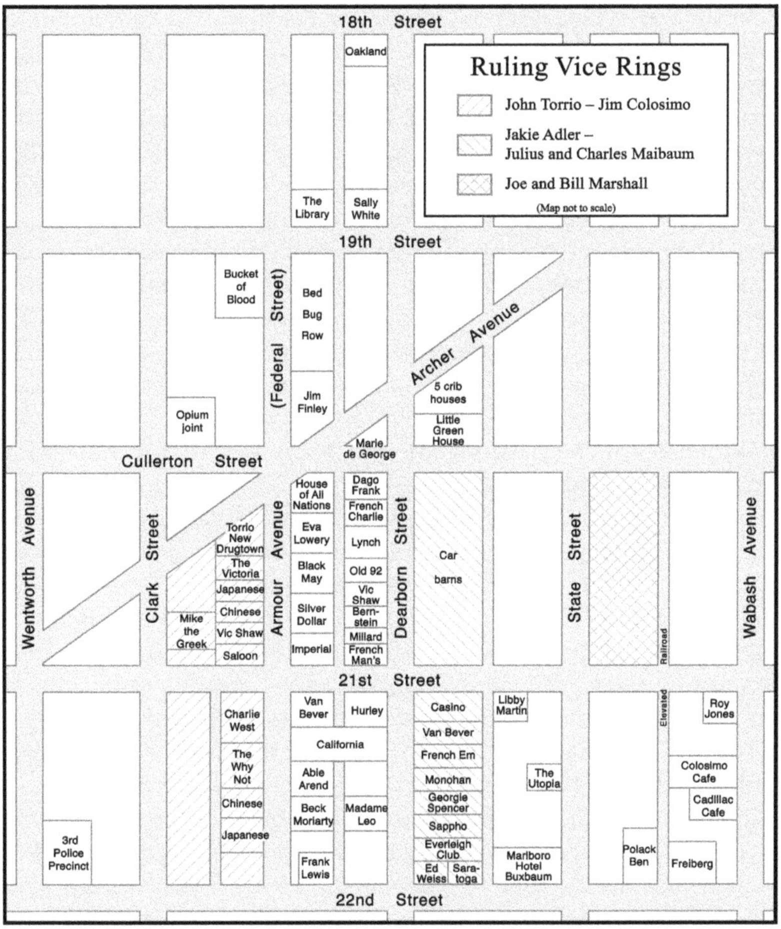

Map 4.2   Institutions and Controlling Vice Syndicates of the Twenty-Second Street Levee, 1900–1912. *Sources*: Original map of Levee resorts from Herbert Asbury, *Gem of the Prairie: An Informal History of the Chicago Underworld* (New York: Alfred A. Knopf, 1940; repr., DeKalb: Northern Illinois University Press, 1986), facing p. 265. Map of vice syndicate control courtesy of Richard C. Lindberg.

Aided by friendly police officers and ward politicians, syndicates established a system of organizing and supervising the illegal activities of the Levee. Such "regulation" supported their own individual investments in Levee businesses. In their dual capacities as entrepreneurs and illegal regulators, syndicate members either directly funded or otherwise exerted considerable influence over the expansion of commercialized amusements within the area.[47]

Second, as syndicates took control of the illegal and entertainment economies in the Levee, they played a pivotal role in shaping the racial organization of sexual commerce within the district. The racial reorganization of the sex trade mirrored in large part the racial exclusivity of these early crime organizations. Black saloon keepers like John "Mushmouth" Johnson and Pony Moore had played a large and visible role in Chicago's late-nineteenth-century gambling and prostitution economies. Their saloons had often hosted a male camaraderie that crossed racial lines. However, within the twentieth-century red-light district, the interracial character of the "sporting fraternity" seems to have diminished.[48] None of the black saloon keepers who were prominent within the old Levee entered the ranks of vice organizations in the new district.

Without some formal association with a syndicate, few black-owned gambling saloons could secure necessary police protection. The case of Pony Moore supports this conclusion. Since the late nineteenth century, Moore had operated the Turf Exchange on Twenty-Second Street, a prominent gambling resort and assignation hotel (the Hotel de Moore). In 1905, however, Moore's place suffered a series of raids, and in November it closed for good. By 1910 virtually no saloon owned or patronized by black men survived in the Levee, greatly diminishing the number of black leisure enterprises within the segregated district.[49]

For black women who kept brothels in the new Levee, syndicate control created its own set of challenges. Regular payments to police officers or to syndicate affiliates were probably more than most could afford. The high premiums for protection[50] no doubt upset the delicate financial balance required to maintain sex resorts whose workers generally earned less than white sex workers. Whether saloons or brothels, black resorts suffered a precarious relation to the structure of protection and consequently were the most vulnerable to police harassment.

The transforming racial face of Levee businesses pointed to an underlying shift in ideas of white male sexual leisure. While the racial intermingling that characterized many late-nineteenth-century resorts was highly orchestrated—organized institutionally around a set of racial bars—this intermingling was a notable, if often disdained, aspect of the old Levee district. For a short while, to the alarm of civic authorities, it was also a feature of the Twenty-Second Street Levee.

Soon, however, Chicago police became increasingly vigilant about clamping down on resorts that fostered interracial intermingling. White fears of miscegenation escalated as African American migration to Chicago accelerated after the turn of the century and as black men and women actively took part in leisure pursuits throughout the city. At the height of the white slavery scare, places that encouraged young, unprotected white women to interact socially, and perhaps even sexually, with black men intensified respectable white Chicagoans' alarm about threats to white women's sexual purity in the city. Responding to this alarm, police regularly surveilled interracial resorts, culminating in a series of raids in September 1905 in which Police Chief Collins and his detectives fanned out in the Levee and delivered an edict "barring . . . white men and women from the saloons conducted by negroes" and prohibiting "the racial admixture that has become common in the saloons of white proprietors." Thereafter, such "promiscuous" cross-racial association appears to have been shunned—by white independent entrepreneurs and by syndicate managers alike. White Levee goers got the message as well. In the wake of Collins's raids, "no white men or women could be seen in the many negro saloons along Dearborn street and Armour avenue." This no doubt led many black saloon owners to seek their fortunes in other parts of the city. Still, despite police attempts to "draw the color line through resorts," a few businesses that provided black women's sexual services for white men endured, such as Black May's brothel. However, as a result of ongoing police pressure, most if not all leisure resorts in the district—saloons, hotels, dance halls, houses of prostitution, and nightclubs—catered to an exclusively white clientele.[51]

Black men and women were totally barred from white leisure institutions, however. Many of these resorts, especially the nightclubs and cabarets that provided live entertainment, hired black musicians, dancers, and singers. Early jazz pianist Jelly Roll Morton was known to play regularly in Levee resorts. Expressing obvious disdain, one newspaper noted that Buxbaum's kept "a band of negro singers busy all night for purposes of 'entertainment.'" The stage singer Ada Smith, better known as "Bricktop," recalled that before World War I she sang in the back room of Roy Jones's saloon at Twenty-First and Wabash streets. Jones's resort "didn't draw a high-class clientele," Bricktop remembered, but white men and women came in large numbers to hear the "first rate" black entertainers, who made Jones's back room "one of the best in Chicago." Blues singer Alberta Hunter spent two years of her early career singing at Dago Frank's, a saloon and brothel located at Archer Avenue and State Street.[52]

Police pressure fueled syndicate control, then, and together they effected the virtual removal of black men from the Levee terrain as entrepreneurs and pleasure-seekers. As the numbers of white women frequenting nighttime leisure institutions grew after the turn of the century,[53] the outcry of reformers and city police against interracial association in institutions of sexual leisure became increasingly shrill.[54] In the eyes of syndicate leaders, the ejection of black men from the Levee served to make the Levee "safe" for white women pleasure-seekers. White entrepreneurs also hoped that, by removing black men from the sexual marketplace, they protected themselves from the scrutiny of reformers and police officials. By 1910 the Twenty-Second Street Levee was the playground of white men and growing numbers of white women, a tolerated district of sexual commerce defined in part by keeping black men out. Perhaps the biggest challenge in this regard for keepers of brothels and proprietors of the increasingly popular dance halls and cabarets that fostered cross-gender mingling was to keep black men away from white women.

This enforcement did not necessarily mean the total exclusion of black women from the Levee, however. As was true in the late nineteenth century, some black sex entrepreneurs utilized white men's expectations of privilege to their own economic advantage.

African American Women in a Changing Levee Economy

An old-timer like Vina Fields remained in the brothel business, yet her competitive advantage diminished as white men reorganized the city's sex industry. Her type of resort became more vulnerable and perhaps less profitable. If the case of Vina Fields highlights the insecurity of black women sex entrepreneurs within the Levee, how do we account for the success of another black brothel keeper who, like Fields, remained in the district until it was closed in 1912? Both Maggie "Black May" Douglas and Vina Fields had long careers in the South Side sex economy. But after the turn of the century, Madam Douglas achieved a notoriety that surpassed that of Vina Fields. The nature of her reputation reflects the new place that black brothels—and black women's sexual labor—occupied within the twentieth-century sex district.

In 1900 Maggie Douglas ran a house of prostitution at 2029 Armour Avenue with five black female boarders and one black male boarder. Listed as a twenty-nine-year-old married woman, Douglas, like her female boarders, had no occupation according to census enumerators. In an area crowded with other houses of prostitution, Douglas's resort appears nondescript. With five workers, she ran an average-size house. Within ten years, however, the size of Douglas's establishment had doubled, and she had collected various new sobriquets—Mary Douglas, Black Mag, and Black May. She now enjoyed a notoriety distinct from the kind Vina Fields experienced in her later years.[55]

According to popular lore, Douglas provided light-skinned black women for the exclusive enjoyment of white men. As in the old Levee district, supplying black women, especially light-skinned women, to white men was one way of establishing a special niche within the sex economy. But Douglas distinguished her resort in another way.[56] Stories of the wild debauches that went on in Douglas's resort were widespread. "Perverted sex behavior"—a term for both same-sex intercourse and oral sex—between black women for the viewing pleasure of white men was the house's main attraction and drew curious customers to the place. White men watching black women engage in "perverted" sex acts for their entertainment resembled the racial dynamics of blackface minstrelsy so popular on the nineteenth- and early-twentieth-century stage. In blackface, white stage actors entertained white audiences by blacking up and performing in a manner they and their audiences believed to be authentically "black." This commodification of "blackness"—black mannerisms and cultural practices—represented whites' efforts to grapple with new patterns of interracial interaction in northern cities and on the western frontier.[57] Live sex shows at Douglas's resort commodified a different aspect of "blackness," highlighting not African American music and dance but sexual practices that white men believed to be widespread among debased black women. The obvious difference between minstrelsy and Douglas's commodification of black women's sexuality was that black women were the performers on the brothel stage. Yet the popularity of Douglas's resort after the turn of the century reveals that black women's sexual performances functioned in a way similar to minstrel acts. By enacting white men's fantasies about black women's sexual depravity, Douglas's resort commodified evidence of black women's difference from white women—even those women working in the Levee. Such commodification reproduced scenes of white men's domination of enslaved black women. It also provided Douglas's white male customers with a means of locating black women (and men) along a social hierarchy that the steady influx of black migrants to the city threatened to unsettle.

Douglas no doubt banked on the interplay of racial contempt and sexual fascination that drew so many white men to her door. Her house's reputation also drew the attention of police and anti-prostitution reformers. In a flurry of anti-vice activity in 1912, State's Attorney Wayman cited Black Mag's notorious dive as "the specific case" for which his office hoped to secure the key to the coded locations of sex resorts described in the Vice Commission of Chicago's 1910 report *The Social Evil in Chicago*. In addition to addresses this key provided detailed information about the proprietorship and ownership of the houses of prostitution and other institutions of sexual commerce discussed in the report. With the evidence provided by the key, Wayman hoped to exert special pressure on the property owner who leased the house to Douglas. Unfortunately for Wayman, the Vice Commission never released the key.[58]

Douglas and Fields conducted their businesses in strikingly different ways. In part these contrasts simply reflect the variety of resorts that dotted the landscape of sexual commerce in the first decade of the twentieth century, whether housing black, white, or, in a few cases, Asian women.[59] But they also suggest the changing nature of black women's role within the sex economy. If at the turn of the century Fields continued to pride herself on the respectable deportment of her establishment, just a decade later Douglas's fame was based on an entirely different packaging of black women's sexual services for sale to white men—a packaging that offered white customers and alarmed onlookers evidence of the unique degeneracy of urbanizing black women.

In addition to Fields and Douglas, two other black women reveal how others operated resorts in and around the Twenty-Second Street Levee. Mollie Vinefield, a widow originally from Kentucky, ran a resort with six boarders at 1900 Dearborn. Like Vina Fields, Vinefield was an older woman in the trade. At sixty she was older than most of the resort keepers working in the district in 1910. If she had been in the business before this date, she had not yet appeared in the sources. Her sudden appearance in 1910, and at such an advanced age, suggests a number of interpretations. First, it reveals the failure of available sources to fully disclose the extent and nature of black women's participation in Chicago's sex economy. Few women entered the field of sexual commerce at such a late age, so it is likely that Vinefield had been in the business for some time. Her invisibility before 1910 suggests that she was like many other women in the late nineteenth century who quietly operated small resorts in the old Levee district. Perhaps this discretion accounted for her apparent longevity in the business. The stability, if not financial success, that Vinefield enjoyed because of her circumspection may also account for the maturity of some of her employees. While four of Vinefield's workers were younger women between the ages of twenty and twenty-seven, one, Anna Jackson, was thirty-nine years old, and another, Anna Bently, was forty-five.[60]

Vinefield's appearance on the scene at age sixty suggests a second, more complicated interpretation. She may have been none other than Vina Fields. In 1911 Fields occupied the same Dearborn Avenue address that Vinefield had occupied a year earlier. Given the obvious similarity in their names, it is possible that in 1910 Fields operated a second brothel under the pseudonym of Mollie Vinefield, a name produced solely for the benefit of census takers.

Unlike Vinefield's house of prostitution, which was on the northern edge of the district, Hattie Jackson's house sat virtually in the heart of Levee traffic. Jackson managed a resort at 2106 Dearborn Court, a narrow street between Dearborn and State. A twenty-seven-year-old woman originally from Arkansas, Jackson employed two younger black women: nineteen-year-old Lenora Warren from Kentucky and twenty-year-old Eva Newton from Missouri. A small place, Jackson's establishment was of little importance. Yet it was not isolated from other leisure institutions. Her resort shared a building with a poolroom and was next door to a saloon.[61] Tellingly, Jackson's small brothel did not occupy a main street within the Levee. Very likely, proprietors of small sex enterprises found accommodations on the major streets that housed large brothels and disorderly saloons unaffordable. Establishing small, out-of-the-way brothels was the one opening that most black women sex entrepreneurs found within the Levee economy. Yet even modest, out-of-the-way resorts operated by black women were few and far between.

The businesses conducted by Vina Fields, Mollie Vinefield, Maggie Douglas, and Hattie Jackson represent black sex entrepreneurs' varying adaptations to white male entrepreneurship within and syndicate control of the Levee. If such control limited black women's options for making money on Levee streets, it did not altogether drive them from this terrain. Furthermore, as map 4.2 shows, syndicate coverage of the district was not complete. Indeed, Vina Fields's house at 1834 Dearborn Street and Mollie Vinefield's brothel across the street at 1900 Dearborn were north of syndicate territory. This positioning may have resulted from the business choices made by both women (if indeed they are separate individuals). As longtime sex entrepreneurs, they eschewed the protection provided by syndicates, perhaps bristling at the duties and obligations expected of them in such an arrangement. On the other hand, perhaps neither of them was welcomed in the Levee. Indeed, the 1907 Health Department targeting of Fields's resort on Armour Avenue may have been the outcome of syndicate irritation with her independence. These are all speculations. Whether or not these women operated on the fringes of the Levee by choice, their location beyond the reach of syndicate-brokered protection exposed them to greater police harassment. It also removed them from the steady traffic of white men that flowed through the heart of the district just a few blocks to the south.

The Closing of the Levee

By 1910 the anti-Levee and anti-vice activism of white middle-class church groups, neighborhood associations, and women's organizations had gained momentum. Dramatic public demonstrations staged against Levee institutions and the persistent outcry of leaders in white middle-class neighborhoods adjoining segregated districts riveted public attention to the city's tolerance of sexual commerce. Perhaps most important for the foes of segregated sexual commerce, new research that both examined the causes and detailed the social costs of "the social evil" helped to validate their position.[62] The concerted efforts of moral, neighborhood, and academic leaders eventually forced public officials to take a stance against Chicago's segregated prostitution district. Giving in to escalating public pressure, in October 1911 Mayor Carter Harrison ordered the closing of the city's most famous brothel, the Everleigh Club.[63]

The municipal assault on the Twenty-Second Street Levee escalated in the second half of 1912 and came to a head in October, when State's Attorney John Wayman issued 135 warrants for the arrests of keepers of Levee resorts.[64] Wayman's attack and the subsequent closing of Levee brothels and disorderly saloons were more spectacular than complete. In 1913 investigators for the Committee of Fifteen—an anti-vice organization formed in 1911—found prostitutes freely circulating in red-light district saloons.[65] However, the era of *officially* tolerated red-light districts in Chicago had come to an end. By 1915 the remnants of the Twenty-Second Street Levee had all but disappeared.

The 1912 closing of Chicago's Twenty-Second Street Levee represents one dramatic episode in the development of urban sexual commerce.[66] For black men and women involved in the South Side sex economy, however, it was not a defining moment. Geographical changes and institutional transformations that defined their work environment had commenced years earlier. This transformation—in effect the expulsion of black sex workers, entrepreneurs, and clients from the Levee—began at the turn of the century and ended well before authorities shut down the Twenty-Second Street Levee for good. Several factors contributed to the spatial separation of black and white sexual commerce, the most concrete of which being the inability of black women and men to meet the financial demands of either paying for protection or operating without it in the Levee, a marketplace in the control of white syndicates. Yet the sex trade's changing economic climate did not on its own bring about the exodus of African Americans from the district. Syndicate operatives, and the corrupt police officials in their pay, had their own reasons for wanting to rid the Levee of black women and men. By keeping black sex workers and black male customers out of the Levee, syndicates likely hoped to fend off some of the scrutiny of increasingly well-organized and vocal anti-prostitution reformers alarmed by what they believed was the unbridled sexual exploitation of innocent white girls at the hands of unsavory foreign men and men of color.[67] The exclusion of black sexual commerce might help to sever the association of the Levee sex trade with illicit interracial sex and what many imagined to be white women's ultimate degradation. Syndicate efforts to keep most black men and women out of the Levee also reflected the racial hostilities of syndicate leaders and police officers, most of whom were immigrants.[68]

Over the course of its existence, Chicago's largest municipally segregated prostitution district served several purposes. Like urban red-light districts throughout the country, the Levee was a geographical embodiment of a middle-class desire to keep moral and sexual danger at a safe remove from respectable commerce and residence. Chicago's Levee, however, was the most infamous of the more than thirty tolerated red-light districts existing in the United States between 1900 and 1912.[69] These red-light districts functioned to demarcate lines—spatially and cognitively—that defined and bolstered white middle-class respectability. Yet just as the drawing of clear boundaries *around* the most visible manifestations of the urban sex trade eased the worries of white middle-class men and women, so did the erection of boundaries *within* the segregated sex district. Although preceding the Great Migration of the World War I era, the steady movement of African Americans to urban areas between 1890 and 1910 generated increasing alarm among white urbanites. This alarm was registered in fears about racial intermixture in urban nightlife and particularly in sexual commerce, both of which were becoming visible and seemingly uncontrolled features of modern city living.

In response to all of these changes in Chicago's social and recreational landscapes, by 1910 the South Side sex district had become an almost entirely racially homogeneous leisure district. The racial segregation of sexual commerce within the Levee served to contain the spread of a moral contagion considered by many white urbanites to be more dangerous than prostitution itself—the promiscuous racial intermingling that characterized the old Levee. Ironically, ridding the Levee trade of black men and women might also protect the district's illicit businesses from the actions of a mounting reform movement. In either instance, the exclusion of African American men and women from the Levee helped to preserve among white urbanites a sense of their own racial superiority in an increasingly racially and ethnically diverse city.

FIVE

Leisure Culture and the Commercialization of Black Women's Sex Work, 1900–1920

Before the end of the nineteenth century, African Americans moved away from the cramped and unsavory neighborhood near the central business district, seeking better housing and more comfortable surroundings for their families, institutions, and businesses. As early as 1885 a significant number of the black community's professional, business, labor, and institutional elite settled as far south as Thirty-Fifth Street.[1] Working-class men and women who wanted to convert the fruits of their labor into affordable and comfortable housing soon followed the middle-class African Americans who pioneered this migration. By 1900 African Americans of varying means lived within a narrow belt stretching south from Twelfth Street to Thirty-Ninth Street and bordered on the west by Wentworth and on the east by Wabash.[2] Prodded by the southward advance of light manufacturing, commerce, and railway freight yards, by 1910 most blacks had abandoned the area north of Twenty-Second Street. The heaviest concentration of black Chicagoans now centered on Thirty-Fifth Street, with some African Americans moving into quiet neighborhoods south of Thirty-Ninth Street. By 1912 Chicago's black citizens lived in an area bordered by Twenty-Second Street

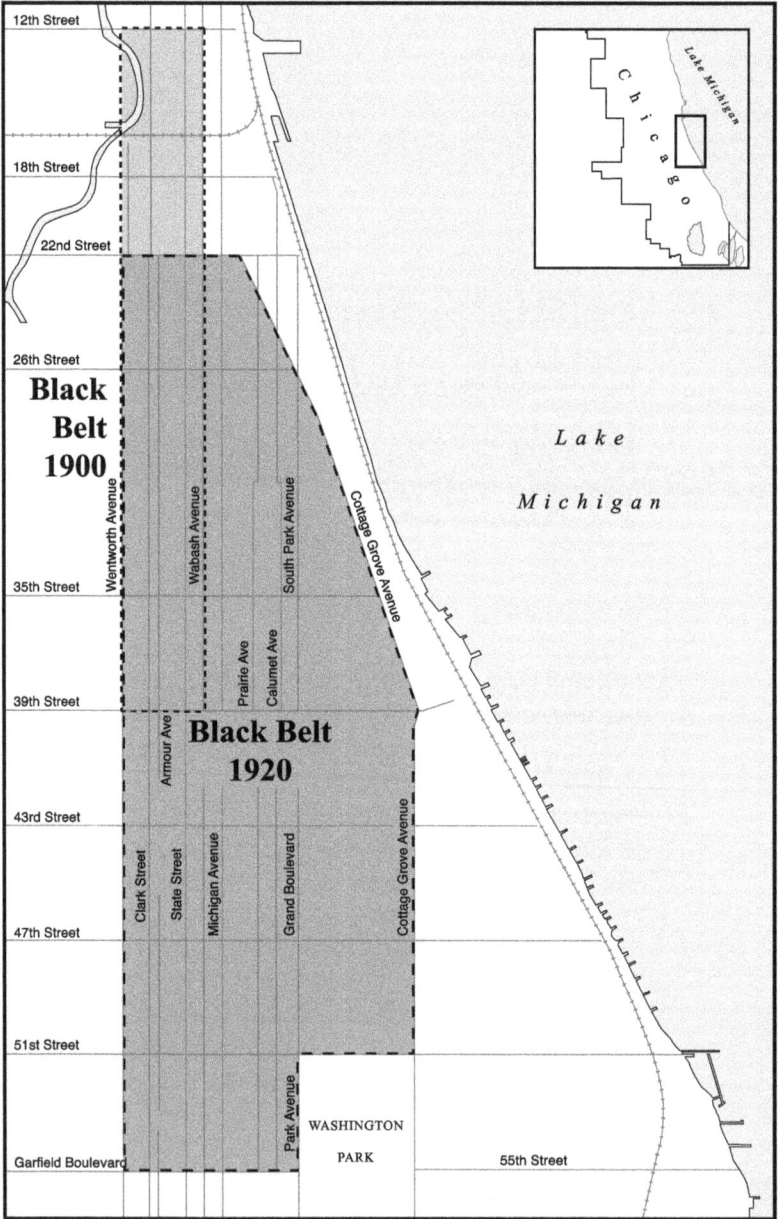

Map 5.1   The Black Belt, 1900 and 1920. *Source*: Rand McNally and Co., *Street Guide Map of Chicago* (Chicago: Rand McNally and Co., between 1897 and 1899), http://www.lib.uchicago.edu/e/su/maps/chi1890/G4104-C6-1897-R3.html.

on the north, Fifty-Fifth Street on the south, the railroad tracks on the west, and Wabash on the east (map 5.1).[3]

A vibrant assortment of recreational institutions grew within Chicago's South Side Black Belt. Playhouses, moving-picture theaters, restaurants, cafés, and eventually cabarets and nightclubs crowded into the major thoroughfares of the expanding black neighborhood. Well before World War I–era migrations swelled the ranks of South Siders seeking respite from the difficulties of making ends meet in the urban economy, African American men and women put their leisure time to good use.[4]

African American prostitution flourished within the context of this developing commercialized leisure culture. The transplanting of black women's sex work from the red-light district to black community leisure networks was both geographical and institutional. This transformation of the context of African American women's sex work was significant for several reasons. First, black women's use of alternative ways of organizing and selling their sexual labor coincided with the declining importance of brothel-based sex work. As white brothels continued to prosper in the Levee, the number of black women working in brothels diminished. Black women working outside brothels found themselves removed from the protections that houses of prostitution offered. Yet they also enjoyed freedom from the constraints of brothel work. Women working through saloons, cabarets, or even residential hotels rarely engaged in the domestic performances that customers frequently expected in residentially based sex work. Significantly, as black women's work in brothels waned, the role that black male leisure entrepreneurs played in the sex economy expanded considerably.

Second, the inroads African American women made into Black Belt leisure institutions placed them within a world of leisure that was increasingly heterosocial. Where red-light district resorts most often catered to men of leisure, most Black Belt entertainments courted the patronage of both men and women. The movements of black sex workers into diverse amusements highlight the gendered organization of black leisure in the early twentieth century.

Finally, in moving from a terrain that had been identified explicitly with sexual commerce and other illicit pursuits to one that was increasingly associated with the everyday movements of black men and women, black sex workers redefined the relationship of prostitution to black urban leisure and to black community areas. In the late nineteenth century, African American prostitutes labored within a landscape only intermittently associated with areas of black residence. They also worked within an economy in which they shared immoral city terrain with white prostitutes. Though the presence of black sex workers could trouble working-class black South Siders who lived near them or frustrate black religious and business leaders who had loftier hopes for the race, these women still occupied terrain that was separate from respectable black neighborhoods. The existence of a segregated sex district allowed Chicago's African Americans to establish and constantly hold up to view the boundaries that separated black Levee inhabitants from blacks struggling to live respectably beyond the district's borders.

The racial configuration of the Twenty-Second Street Levee economy gradually exposed the difficulty of maintaining such an opposition between respectable black community spaces and the locales of the community's "immoral" members. As black sex workers sought and found opportunities for trade within the leisure networks of the black community, they intermingled with the respectable—and not-so-respectable—men and women who themselves took advantage of expanded leisure opportunities within the Black Belt.

Commercialized amusements did not supplant older leisure practices of South Side residents, however. Churches, men's fraternal organizations, women's lodges, and a host of social clubs continued to provide entertainment and opportunities for respectable association beyond the home.[5] However, after the turn of the century, men, women, and children channeled their energies and financial resources into new arenas of recreation.

The Commercialization of Black Belt Leisure

The network of entertainments that emerged within the South Side's black neighborhoods before 1915 was characteristic of the commercialization of leisure taking place throughout the city, attracting Chicagoans of every class and ethnic group to the new forms of urban amusement. Among the most important aspects of the expanding entertainment landscape at the turn of the century were the active efforts of businessmen to incorporate women consumers into the culture and economy of urban leisure. From vaudeville theaters to amusement parks to nightclubs, women were invited to take part in commercial amusements, and they did so in unprecedented numbers. Theater owners and saloon keepers who catered to a white middle-class trade tried by various means to make their establishments acceptable to the "gentler sensibilities" of middle-class women, as well as to respectable men. A similar trend expanded the amusements open to working-class women.

By toning down the bawdier aspects of saloons and theaters that had previously thrived on male camaraderie and by creating diversions like dime museums and amusement parks that invited the whole family, entrepreneurs strove to create commercialized amusements that would appeal to women. Whereas in the second half of the nineteenth century, middle- and working-class men predominated in institutions providing nighttime recreation, by 1900 women increasingly spent money on entertainment and rubbed elbows in new settings with anonymous hordes of men and other women.[6]

Although the Illinois Civil Rights Act of 1885 made it illegal to exclude African Americans from public accommodations, discriminatory practices persisted, and blacks were frequently shunned in leisure resorts situated downtown or in white ethnic communities. Despite this exclusion black residents actively and creatively pursued amusement in the expanding leisure economy. Just as working-class immigrant communities throughout the city looked to neighborhood institutions to supply their entertainment needs, African Americans' leisure activities took place within community spaces. However, unlike residents of other communities, who might venture beyond the neighborhood for entertainment, black Chicagoans rarely traversed city space to partake of amusements offered elsewhere without meeting some form of resistance. In the first decades of the twentieth century, the expanding Black Belt became the focal point of African American leisure.[7]

To meet the needs of a growing black population, African American men and women ventured into the arena of providing commercial entertainment. State Street stood at the center of the Black Belt's emerging recreation district. "The Stroll"—a segment of State Street that stretched southward from Twenty-Sixth to Thirty-Ninth Street—was the home of black commerce and consumption, leisure, and public sociality (map 5.2).[8] An enthusiastic *Chicago Defender* reporter described the lively and infectious atmosphere that gripped the Stroll, or the Great Light Way, on a warm spring night:

With the coming of real summer weather "the Great Light Way" . . . has blossomed forth in all its glory. From 26th street south it has become the popular promenade for the masses and classes. As soon as the lights are turned on they turn out and even Coney Island and Atlantic City are forgotten in the enjoyment of its varied attractions. . . . Every amusement to be found elsewhere is to be found here.[9]

After 1900, theaters, movie houses, restaurants, and nightclubs flourished along this major avenue, drawing African American men and

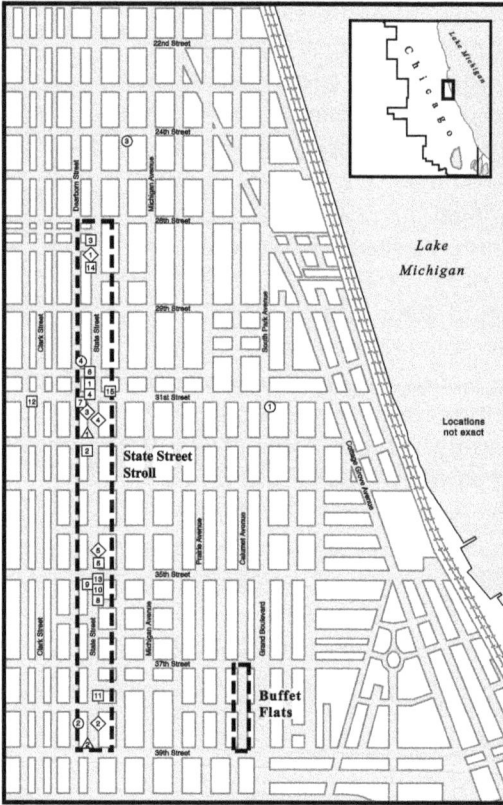

Churches

① Olivet Baptist Church
② Institutional Church and Social Settlement
③ Quinn Chapel A.M.E.
④ Bethel A.M.E. (1910–1922)

Theaters

◇ Robert Motts's Pekin Theatre (1910s–1920s)
◇ Star Theater
◇ Grand Theater (1908–1930)
◇ Vendome Theater (1910s–1940s)
◇ Monogram Theater (1910s)

Billiard Halls

△ Queen Solace
△ Scott and Stanton's Pool Room and Billiard Hall

Nightclubs, Saloons, and Cabarets

1 John Fry's Keystone Hotel and Saloon
2 Hugh Hoskins's Iowa Club
3 Johnnie Seymore's Saloon
4 The New Elite Café and Buffet (1915–1928)
5 Elite #2 (1910–1928)
6 William Bowman's Marquette Club (1912–?)
7 Jack Johnson's Café du Champion (1912–1913)
8 Mineral Springs Club Buffet and Café (1912–?)
9 Dreamland Ballroom (1910–early 1920s)
10 The De Luxe Café (ca. 1912–?)
11 The Roumania Buffet (ca. 1912–?)
12 Royal Gardens (1910s)
13 Panama Club (1910s–1920)
14 Pekin Café/Pekin Cabaret (1910s–1920s)
15 Schiller Café (1916–?)

Map 5.2   The State Street Stroll, 1910s–1920s. *Source*: Rand McNally and Co., *Street Guide Map of Chicago* (Chicago: Rand McNally and Co., between 1897 and 1899), http://www.lib.uchicago.edu/e/su/maps/chi1890/G4104-C6-1897-R3.html.

women out of their homes and into a lively public arena. In 1904 saloon keeper and restaurateur Robert Motts transformed his popular beer garden, the Pekin Inn, into the Pekin Temple of Music. A venue for black musical performers and vaudeville acts, the Pekin quickly attracted widespread attention.[10] In 1906 the Pekin was again transformed, this time into the Pekin Theatre. The theater soon became an important establishment that offered a varied fare of musical entertainment, theatrical performance, and film exhibition to the growing black community.[11] Motts annexed a saloon and restaurant to the theater, further diversifying the offerings of this entertainment hub (fig. 5.1). Others tried to join Motts as purveyors of entertainment to Black Belt residents. The Dunbar Theater and Byron's Temple of Music followed in the Pekin's footprints,

5.1   The Pekin Theatre (1900s or 1910s). Courtesy of the John Steiner Collection, Chicago Jazz
       Archive, Special Collections Research Center, University of Chicago Libraries.

offering both "vaudeville de luxe" and "the best motion pictures."[12] These black-owned theaters were joined by a growing number of white-owned establishments, which, like the Pekin, featured a blend of motion pictures, vaudeville shows, and musical entertainment.[13]

Along with entertainment venues, restaurants invited "the masses and the classes" to the Stroll. Several elegant establishments offered special culinary attractions; but most black restaurateurs operated small affairs offering modest lunches and inexpensively priced dinners. Smith and Sons' State Street Restaurant provided "Extra Fine Home Cooking," and Mrs. Mable Martin's Restaurant at Twenty-Eighth and State offered, simply, "Home Cooking" served at all hours.[14] A 1901 survey found fifteen restaurants along the strip of State Street between Twenty-Sixth and Thirty-Third streets. In 1908 a black business directory listed twenty-four South Side restaurants owned by African Americans. Ten of these were along State between Twenty-Sixth and Thirty-Second streets; of the remainder, a few could be found as far south as Fifty-Third Street, but most were north, sprinkled along State, Dearborn, and Armour. A survey taken five years later found ten restaurants along the section of the Stroll south of Thirtieth Street.[15]

Entrepreneurs developed inventive ways to satisfy the recreational needs of a community frequently unable to gain admittance to the city's music and dance halls and outdoor amusement parks. In 1907 two African American men, lawyer and businessman Beauregard Moseley and former-postal-worker-turned-publisher Robert Jackson, opened the Chateau de Plaisance on the 5300 block of State Street. Moseley and Jackson designed the resort to meet virtually every amusement need of the South Side community. Announcing itself as "the only Amusement Park Pavilion and Stadium owned and controlled by negroes in the world," the summer resort offered "Band Concerts, Vocal Solos, Roller Skating and the Best Meals procurable after a few of the Open Air Attractions." By 1909 the owners had expanded its attractions to include a "Big Musical Program," "Swings and Easy Chairs," and "Pictures that Move." The Chateau Gardens (its name had changed by 1909) offered these grand amusements for an admission price of only ten cents. It appears not to have survived beyond 1910.[16] Despite its apparent failure, the Chateau was an ambitious enterprise responding to the needs of an underserved community. By establishing ventures like the Chateau and the Pekin, Moseley, Motts, and other leisure entrepreneurs hoped to prove to Black Belt residents that "every amusement to be found elsewhere is to be found here."

Drinking and Gender: The Stroll and Beyond

Perhaps the most abundant of nighttime leisure resorts along the Stroll and other Black Belt streets were the saloons. In the first decades of the twentieth century, the saloon and the sample room continued to be important business institutions within the black community. As commercial ventures they offered African American men unparalleled opportunities for financial success. Numerous men—and a few women—took their chances with an industry that required little investment capital but promised substantial returns.[17]

The actual number of saloons owned by black Chicagoans is difficult to pinpoint. The 1900 federal census counts forty-eight black-owned saloons in Chicago, while a 1905 source tallied forty-one. Three years later a black business directory listed the names of only nineteen saloons, though the 1910 census counted thirty-three black saloon owners in the city.[18] Like restaurants, which were often attached to saloons, the majority of Black Belt saloons were modest enterprises that existed for only a few years. Many saloon keepers found themselves entangled in unprofitable contracts with brewers, who supplied them with fixtures and furniture, often at exorbitant rates.[19] Yet, as one saloon keeper went out of business, other hopeful entrepreneurs waited in the wings for their chance in liquor retailing. The high rate of turnover reveals the unstable existence of small liquor enterprises. At the same time it discloses the consistent demand among black South Siders for places that supported social drinking.

Saloons filled Black Belt streets. The Stroll alone boasted fifty-two saloons in 1910, though not all of these were black owned. The majority of Black Belt saloons were small-scale enterprises nestled between the stores, business offices, restaurants, theaters, and rooming houses that defined the busiest sections of black community terrain. On residential streets like Wabash and Dearborn, saloons occupied modest corner storefronts.[20]

In the early twentieth century, smaller drinking establishments along side streets and on residential thoroughfares included a network of African American working-men's and working-women's saloons, whose patronage came mainly from nearby rooming houses and apartment buildings. The names of these neighborhood spots are irretrievable today. Unlike the openings of the larger and fancier saloons and cabarets that came to dominate nightlife in the Black Belt after 1910, the openings of these virtual holes-in-the-wall did not receive laudatory attention within the *Broad Ax* or the *Defender*. Nor did their owners advertise in these newspapers. These little joints built patronage almost exclusively through local word of mouth and by attracting passersby. If they did enter the public record, it was most often after some disturbance, perhaps a dispute between patrons, that required police intervention. For example, a "difficulty" occurred in an otherwise-anonymous saloon at 2832 State Street when its proprietor, Robert Marshall, shot and killed a patron, Jeff Carpenter, in self-defense.[21]

The often rough-and-tumble world of small community establishments did not exclude women, although saloon keepers complied with the letter of the law by prohibiting women from the front bar area. To accommodate female patrons, and the men desiring their company, neighborhood saloon owners, like saloon owners throughout the city, provided back-room accommodations. Interested patrons accessed back rooms from a back or side entrance, often called the "ladies" entrance. Together, the back room and the ladies' entrance facilitated women's entry into saloons by offering them a "protected" realm of public drinking separate from the more boisterous festivities in the barroom—at least this was the theory. Although the side entrance was designed to circumscribe women's access to public drinking establishments, black women used the side door as their special entrance into the world of the saloon.[22] Entertainer and internationally known saloon keeper Ada "Bricktop" Smith recalled that, in the first decade of the twentieth century in Chicago, "saloons were a part of our everyday life. No one thought anything bad about his neighbor going into them to relax and unwind, and of course us kids knew that the women patronized the saloons by way of the back door." Besides the mixed company of men and women, other attractions that were prohibited in the front bar found outlet here. Musicians, singers, and dancers offered entertainment to the patrons gathered in back rooms. Bricktop was captivated by the glimpses of merriment she witnessed as a young girl sneaking peaks under the back-entrance doors of State Street saloons. These were "mysterious and exciting places," she said, from which music and laughter streamed. No doubt older women in her neighborhood were drawn to these morally charged places for the same reason.[23]

Although proscribed by prevailing gender conventions, women's participation in saloon life took a variety of forms. In 1905 one observer noted with particular disdain that "women of the Town of Lake" (a community south of Thirty-Ninth Street annexed by Chicago in 1889) openly entered saloons on the corners of Forty-Seventh and State, Forty-Seventh and Dearborn, Forty-Ninth and State, and Forty-Seventh and Armour. These "shameless" women walked out of area saloons toting beer and whiskey in portable containers. Some women even sent their young children to saloons to fetch alcohol for a parent's or a neighbor's home use. Bricktop reminisced that as a child she included regular saloon trips among the errands she ran for women in her neighborhood. "In a neighborhood with a lot of saloons, like ours, the women were always sending youngsters out to 'rush the can.'" Despite the newspaper reporter's clear concern about the impropriety of this behavior, some manner of gender, and generational, protocol is revealed in the practice of beer or whiskey runs. Both women and children could enter these saloons, but they did so in distinct and observable ways. This suggests that in their day-to-day operation, many neighborhood establishments were governed by intricate rules of gender propriety. In some bars such propriety could take the form of strict rules excluding women. For example, a prominent black-owned drinking institution such as John Fry's Keystone Hotel and Saloon, at 3022 State Street, was proud of its policy of restricting its patronage to men. However, saloons like the unnamed ones in the Town of Lake that allowed women and children to enter and leave toting alcohol for private consumption appear to have been governed by a competing community ethos. These community saloons trod a fine line. Whether on the corners of residential streets or along a business thoroughfare, they visibly occupied family terrain. Saloon owners, and perhaps neighbors or family members, set firm limits on the nature of family participation, however. Women's involvement was circumscribed, but it was not altogether excluded from this locus of male sociality.[24]

Not all neighborhood spots restricted women's participation in public drinking. Women were frequently found in what contemporaries contemptuously referred to as "dives." However, it is possible that these "dives" were merely unassuming places where working men and working women congregated to share a relaxing concoction of humor, petty gambling, dancing, flirtation, and public drinking. This realm of black working-class leisure is obscure to us today, though men and women walking to and from work or coming home from a shopping trip or an errand on State Street must have been attuned to the intricate network of saloons that dotted Black Belt streets.[25]

Sporting Taverns and Gambling Saloons

Several of these smaller resorts shaded into sporting saloons, places that catered to petty gamblers, high rollers, and men and women whose lifestyle and manner flouted standards of respectability. The stories of most of these resorts are lost, though a few names surface here and there: Johnnie Seymore's Saloon, Big Jim's Saloon, Hugh Hoskins's Iowa Club. These were not only saloons but early nightclubs that provided musical entertainment to an exclusively black clientele. Although after 1910 rising jazz singers and musicians played at larger and more popular Black Belt clubs and cabarets, most newcomers to the city hoping to break into the local music scene got their start in the smaller clubs.[26] These venues were also hangouts for men and women involved in the South Side's illegal economies.

When young blues singer Alberta Hunter arrived in Chicago in about 1910, one of her earliest singing gigs was at Hugh Hoskins's Iowa Club, a nightclub located at Thirty-Second and State. Hunter recalls Hoskins's place, a small club, as "a sporting house for high-class Black con men." Hoskins employed a singer and a piano player for the pleasure of an audience that included sporting men and female con artists. These women were mostly pickpockets who—like women who worked sex district streets in the late nineteenth century—seductively approached traveling businessmen and other obvious out-of-towners downtown or at train stations and lifted any item of value from their unguarded pockets.[27] In the late hours these women and men would converge at Hoskins's club, tally the evening's spoils, and spend a healthy portion of their "earnings" on drinks and entertainment.[28]

When pianist and composer Perry Bradford arrived in Chicago in 1908, he soon found himself thrust into a circuit of saloons and after-hours clubs where musicians, actors, and sporting men and women worked and played. After disembarking from a train at the Forty-Seventh Street depot, Bradford was immediately greeted by a streetwalking "chick" who told him about a piano-playing contest at Johnnie Seymore's Saloon at Twenty-Seventh and State. "When we arrived," he reminisced, "what a sight! All the landladies and their stables were in full bloom: 'High Yellows' and seal skin Browns with their 'Birds of Paradise' feathers draped on down with diamonds that looked like electric lights." Bradford won the piano contest "hands down," after which another prostitute escorted him to a club at Twenty-Ninth and Dearborn. Like Seymore's, Big Jim's Saloon was a hangout for members of the black underworld. Just as Hoskins's place advanced the career of Alberta Hunter, this sporting tavern gave Bradford steady employment and exposure within Chicago's musical circles. He played there until he left for New York City in 1910.[29]

These glimpses into the world of small prewar nightclubs reveal the ways that African American sex workers were becoming part of an economy that had roots in institutions other than the brothel. Furthermore, black women—whether "landladies," their "stables," professional prostitute-pickpockets, or street workers—had begun to move into a marketplace that was geographically separate from Levee traffic and removed from the sex district's organization of white male leisure. Between 1900 and 1915 African American sex workers found a niche within multiplying Black Belt drinking establishments, a great number of which offered some form of live musical entertainment. They entered the more unassuming of these black-owned saloons as patrons; these clubs offered protection from police officers and relaxation after a hard day's work in the underground economy. Black Belt bars also afforded sex workers access to new customers. And as prostitutes moved into these settings that supported both work and leisure, they rubbed elbows with black South Siders who, like them, were drawn to emerging forms of musical entertainment. Thus, at the same time that these clubs nursed the careers of piano players and singers who might eventually move on to larger and better-paying venues, they also provided a place where the black sporting set could mingle leisurely with working-class men and women.

Few of the saloons appear on maps of early jazz or blues performance in Chicago.[30] Nor were they identified in early-twentieth-century investigations of sexual commerce in the city. Their existence nevertheless attests to a hidden economy that supported both black nighttime leisure and sexual commerce. Along the continuum of working-men's and working-women's saloons, these clubs carved out a special niche at the intersection of black Chicago's sporting, leisure, and informal economies.

However plentiful these resorts may have been, they shared Black Belt streets with another type of bar that was more flagrant in its cultivation of a sporting clientele: the gambling saloon. These saloons, holdovers from the late nineteenth century, were more visible exemplars of turn-of-the-century sporting institutions. According to jazz historian William Kenney, they united African American men, "slumming young upper-class whites, . . . downtown politicians, artisans, actors, and immigrants to the city from many lands" in "an informal brotherhood of pleasure-seeking bachelors."[31] These were interracial, male leisure reserves that catered to a wider swath of men than small-time nightclubs did. At the same time that an interracial sporting fraternity lost ground within the Levee, it found fertile soil within the Black Belt leisure economy. African American proprietors of gambling saloons were highly visible, gaining notoriety for their personal and entrepreneurial extravagance and, frequently, for their political aspirations.

John "Mushmouth" Johnson, whose saloon was located at 464 South State Street, was among the first African American saloon keepers to gain fame within Chicago's sporting crowd. Once a porter in a white gambling house, in 1890 Johnson took his earnings and his experience and built an elaborate gambling emporium of his own.[32] Its plush interiors rivaled the most ornate houses of prostitution. Until Johnson's death in 1907, his resort remained a prominent institution for Chicago's black, white, and Chinese professional gambling elite and for small-time gamblers as well. Chicago businessman and community historian Dempsey Travis wrote that "Johnson's attracted gamblers of all colors from every economic and social spectrum: for those with lean purses there was a poor man's game." Travis's father's reminiscences underscore the special significance that Johnson's place had for many African American working men: "'Mushmouth' Johnson had the cheapest action in downtown Chicago. Boy! Where else could a country boy go just ten days out of Georgia and feel like a big time gambler for only a nickel?"[33]

In its extravagant decor Johnson's saloon mirrored the opulence of 1890s parlor houses and, like them, cultivated the atmosphere of elite male pleasure. However, by offering games of chance that drew in, as

Harold Gosnell described, the "nickels, dimes, and quarters that were sometimes referred to as 'chicken feed'" by white gamekeepers, Johnson effectively extended the atmosphere of racially exclusive parlor houses and gambling resorts to black and white men of limited means.[34] Johnson's gambling saloon also expanded men's access to black sex workers. Sexual commerce was both tolerated and encouraged—indeed, Johnson employed "voluptuous waitresses [who] served the tables" and made arrangements for private liaisons.[35]

Robert Motts furthered this more equitable approach to sporting culture. After Johnson's death, Motts became, in the words of Allan Spear, "the gambling lord of the South Side." Significantly, his respectable Pekin Theatre was bankrolled by money that Motts had amassed in his long career among the shadier elements of Chicago's saloon trade. Motts began his career in the 1890s as an employee in Johnson's notorious saloon and gambling den. Having received ample training there in mixing gambling and alcohol sales, he established a partnership with successful saloon keepers William Beasley and Samuel Snowdon and opened a saloon at 480 South State Street. With the profits from this venture, Motts opened his own beer garden at 2700 State Street, which by 1900 had become, like Johnson's place, a well-known hangout for an interracial sporting fraternity.[36] Gambling and prostitution flourished in Motts's saloon. In 1902 Julius Taylor, publisher of the *Chicago Broad Ax*, called the saloon a "hell-hole of iniquity" where a "number of our seemingly promising young girls . . . have lost their virtue."[37]

With the opening of the Pekin Theatre, Motts had turned his profits from the sale of alcohol and the shady transactions involved in gambling into respectable leisure that invited both men and women. The relationship that Motts established between saloon and theater enterprises was not unique. After 1900, Chicago saloon keepers were among the top three occupational groups to move into film exhibition.[38] Motts's venture, however, was singular among African American leisure entrepreneurs at this time and was directed at a black community eager to support its own entertainment resorts. In bridging the gap between disreputable and legitimate entertainment, Motts stood first in a line of businessmen who, a decade later, would help extend a previously circumscribed sporting culture into the commercialized leisure culture of the Black Belt.[39]

Other prominent saloon keepers showed an interest in expanding their saloons into more diversified and presumably more lucrative, though not necessarily more reputable, leisure enterprises. Along with Motts, Pony Moore was among the first resort keepers to expand the audience for the sporting life. However, while the Pekin Theatre can be seen as a successful effort by Motts to transform his image from that of a keeper of a notorious dive to that of a civic-minded purveyor of family entertainment, Moore's new business direction was born of a less lofty desire. Moore's entrepreneurial endeavors were among the earliest to transform South Side saloon culture itself and to insert a new breed of leisure resorts into the South Side landscape. Moore's career presages the institutional evolution and geographical shift of black sporting culture in the first decade of the twentieth century.

Since at least 1897 Pony Moore had operated a saloon and hotel at 171 Twenty-Second Street in the Twenty-Second Street Levee. According to Detective Clifton Wooldridge, Moore's Turf Exchange was not simply a saloon but "a wide-open, carefully guarded gambling resort." The saloon was elegantly fitted out, with lavishly decorated wine rooms and private rooms. Moore's resort supported an assortment of games, including craps and betting on horse races, and drew a large part of its late-night gambling clientele from red-light district saloons and restaurants that had closed for the evening. His customers included not only patrons who had left closing resorts in the area but also the waiters, piano players, and prostitutes who worked in other Levee resorts. At the turn of the century, the Turf Exchange was incorporated into the economies of late-night entertainment, gambling, and sexual commerce that defined the district.[40]

In 1899 Moore's Twenty-Second Street resort was the object of increasing, if uneven, police attention. While flagrant gambling played a large part in provoking police attacks on the resort, Moore's Turf Exchange was notorious for another reason. Here, according to Detective Wooldridge, "depraved women, both white and black," congregated. They catered to black and white men. And if this indiscriminate mixing were not offensive enough, Moore's saloon "was also frequented by Chinamen and Japanese."[41] The conspicuous presence of sexual interchange, especially interracial commerce, troubled city officials and civic leaders alike. The *Chicago Tribune* reported that "not in years . . . was there a time when no women of questionable character were in the place." After an arrest that netted over forty wrongdoers, Police Chief Collins testified that not only was Moore's resort "one of the worst gambling resorts in town" but that "brazen-faced white and Colored women hung out in his saloon and Hotel De moore."[42]

In November 1905 things came to a head when, after a series of raids, the city revoked the license for Moore's resort. Praise for the move appeared in the *Tribune* and the *Record-Herald*. Even the *Portland (OR)*

Advocate expressed relief at the closing of Moore's saloon. Said the *Advocate*, "Many a young girl in Chicago who is now leading a life of shame and disgrace owe their downfall to this stink-hole."[43] The *Chicago Broad Ax*—whose editor claimed no little responsibility for shining a light on Moore's resort—gleefully reported Police Chief Collins's assessment of the resort. According to the police chief, Moore's place "had become so notoriously bad that it was a stench in the nostrils of all decent and law abiding people, [and] that many of the best class of Colored people— those who believe in morality and decency— . . . had written him letters highly commending him for revoking [Moore's] license, and closing up his joint."[44] The specific source of the "stench" goes unstated, but it was very likely due to Moore's promotion of a dangerous mixture of both casual and commercial interracial sexual contacts.

The closing of Moore's Twenty-Second Street saloon proved to be only a temporary business setback. In early 1906 reports circulated that he planned to open another resort, and in May 1906 Moore's Palace Theater opened its doors on Thirty-First Street near Dearborn. Like Robert Motts, Moore hoped to draw patrons who were looking for expanded entertainment fare within the Black Belt. Guests of his grand opening were treated to "a fairly good vaudeville show" and could purchase soft drinks. However, Moore had not dissociated himself from his earlier clientele. According to the ever-watchful *Broad Ax*, "Many of the leading sports in the 'Red Light District' were there." Also present were "many ladies, both white and colored, whom it is claimed are not above flirting with gentleman [sic] who have plenty of money to burn and assist them to scatter a little red paint around the town."[45]

Moore's new entertainment emporium catered simultaneously to a growing and underserved audience for vaudeville and a group of black and white sporting men and women seeking light diversion. Indeed, the Palace Theater appeared to be a sure thing—theater, saloon, gambling house, and site for illicit sexual transactions. Moore's venture was not as successful as Motts's Pekin, however. In 1907 he declared bankruptcy, owing his many creditors in excess of $30,000.[46]

Despite the failure of the Palace Theater, Moore's efforts expose important features of the South Side's prewar sex economy. First, the institutional contexts of black women's sex work were transformed. Whereas in the late nineteenth century black prostitutes worked in a sex industry that was for the most part well defined and separate from other kinds of leisure, after the turn of the century the sex economy increasingly overlapped with a growing entertainment economy. Often the proprietors of saloons for the black or interracial sporting fraternity ventured into more reputable amusements. The line that separated these spheres of nighttime leisure was not always clearly drawn. Second, the business ventures of Pony Moore, Robert Motts, and John "Mushmouth" Johnson reveal the intertwining geographies of reputable black entertainment and an intraracial sex trade. As economic and institutional links between respectable amusements and disreputable leisure were strengthened, so the presence of black sex workers increased in the resorts and along the streets where black men and women took their leisure.

Additionally, black male entrepreneurs became important investors in the South Side sex economy. Those operating leisure resorts—sporting taverns, small nightclubs, and theaters—provided black sex workers with new opportunities to meet potential customers. Some proprietors profited directly from sexual transactions initiated in their establishments. Others simply took advantage of the flow of customers that prostitutes brought to their resorts.

At the same time that owners of leisure establishments profited from sexual exchanges, other black men played more direct roles in the organization of the trade itself—as procurers of prostitutes, marketers of their services, and recipients of a significant portion of black women's earnings. Pimps had for decades been an element of Chicago's sporting scene.[47] After the turn of the century, they became a standard fixture in the nightclubs and sporting saloons that were multiplying within the Black Belt.

The image of the pimp calls to mind an exploitative relationship defined by men's physical domination and economic exploitation of women and women's psychological dependency on abusive men. In many instances relations between prostitutes and the men in their lives took this form. Timothy Gilfoyle finds that, in the second half of the nineteenth century, "a visible, well-established system of pimps existed in New York" that was characterized by the intimidation and control of prostitutes. Ruth Rosen has found that in several cities the pimp as abuser of impoverished, defenseless women was an important feature of the turn-of-the-century sex trade, especially for women unattached to brothels or for street workers who sought protection from police harassment or customer violence. Pimps and prostitutes in Chicago did not conform neatly to these outlines, however. While the existence of pimps was often noted in the late-nineteenth-century reform and police literature, anti-prostitution crusaders used the word "pimp" quite loosely, referring as often to lovers or husbands as to men who clearly took advantage of women's economic and physical vulnerability and lived off their earnings.[48] Most often the term reflected reformers' inability to comprehend women's willing involvement in the sex trade and their assumptions about (white) women's innate innocence.

Between 1900 and 1920 the world of pimps in Chicago began to resemble more closely the image of the male exploiter. Yet even during this period the pimp played a variety of roles in the lives of sex workers, ranging from the lover and business partner who provided companionship, protection, and bail money to the abusive controller of one or more prostitutes' labor and earnings.[49] The latter role emerged most clearly after the closing of the Levee, when women, black and white, worked independently of brothels. Still, for most black sex workers (and for some white ones), the African American pimp remained a petty sex merchant rather than an established fixture in an intricately orchestrated sex economy. The network of hardened pimps who not only dominated groups of women but shaped the sex trade itself would not develop in Chicago until the 1920s (see the epilogue).[50] Until then, most black sex workers managed to maintain a considerable degree of independence within the trade.

Even though black women were not on the whole dependent on pimps in the first two decades of the twentieth century, black men were ever more central to the operation of the Black Belt sex economy. The interests of black prostitutes and male entrepreneurs became intricately intertwined. Bricktop's recollections about South Side saloons after the closing of the Levee are illuminating: "It was a fantastic time for the saloon business in Chicago. The city was on a big crusade against vice and had shut down all the whorehouses, but that just made business better in the saloons, and didn't stop prostitution. The girls simply moved into the saloons, . . . and the pimps and madames moved into the saloons to keep an eye on what was going on."[51] Whether or not black sex workers and madams were financially obligated to saloon or nightclub proprietors, their earnings from sexual labor became increasingly dependent on the ability to make arrangements with, and in some cases work for, male leisure entrepreneurs.

Cabarets and After-Hours Clubs

Perhaps the most successful of ventures that linked sporting men and women, on the one hand, and amusement-seeking South Siders, on the other, were the cabarets, which grew in number after 1910. Like the lesser-known sporting hot spots, they featured a lively mixture of

musical entertainment and social drinking. At the same time they borrowed equal doses of ornament and entrepreneurial prestige from the
gambling saloon. In melding these entertainment values, entrepreneurs
courted the patronage of women and men who assiduously avoided the
disreputable sporting scene.

Turn-of-the-century cabarets were innovative entertainment venues that transformed the culture and physical makeup of the saloon by
providing a space for musicians and dancers to perform and to mingle
with enthusiastic audiences.[52] Like saloons these new leisure spots supported public drinking, serving food and alcoholic beverages to men
and women in rooms separated from the main bar area. However, cabarets offered something more. In these rooms—often very large spaces
occupying an entire floor above a saloon—singers and dancers provided
entertainment ranging from vaudevillian musical productions to early
jazz and blues. Indeed, cabarets, or cafés as they were also called, were
important outlets for early jazz musicians and dancers. Between 1910
and 1915 the South Side witnessed a wave of cabaret openings. In addition, many longtime saloon owners renovated their establishments
to meet the swelling demand among black and white Chicagoans for
drinking establishments that offered lively musical entertainment,
spectacular dance performances, and opportunities for social dancing.
Just as the elaborately furnished saloons and gambling houses eclipsed
the run-of-the-mill barrooms that dotted the Stroll and side streets of
the Black Belt in the first decade of the century, cabarets would soon
overshadow these saloons and gambling houses.[53]

The earliest and brightest light among Black Belt cabarets was Henry
Jones's establishment. Since the late nineteenth century Henry "Teenan"
Jones had been proprietor of the Senate, a gambling saloon located at
5532 Lake Avenue in Hyde Park. But in 1910 Jones closed down his
long-running establishment and joined forces with white businessman
Art Codozoe to take over proprietorship of the New Elite Café and Buffet, a saloon at 3030 State Street. After the Elite Café opened, it quickly
became one of the South Side's hot spots for respectable dining and musical entertainment.[54] Riding the success of the Elite, in 1915 Jones ventured out on his own to open the Elite #2, located four blocks south at
3445 State Street. The *Indianapolis Freeman* predicted that the opening of
the second Elite would be "one of the biggest events of the year 1915."
Echoing the *Freeman*'s enthusiasm about the opening of this high-
profile black business, the *Chicago Defender* dubbed Jones's establishment "a Mecca for High-Class Amusement."[55] Among prewar black cabaret owners, Jones was perhaps the most prominent.[56] However, many

other men tried to make money in the café business. One was William H. Bowman, who, "after looking around for a business opening on the South Side or on the stroll," opened an "elegantly decorated saloon" at 3010 State Street. According to the *Chicago Broad Ax*, in 1911 Bowman was "putting the finishing touches on the interior of the second floor which will be used for a first class café." In 1912 the *Chicago Defender* wrote, "Among the establishments for the supply of wines and other choice beverages along 'the Stroll' none stand out more prominently than the Marquette Club." With its impeccable service, "splendid and artistic decorations," and fine musical entertainment, Bowman's club attracted black political figures and celebrities alike. Even heavyweight boxing champion Jack Johnson, the paper reported, counted it among his favorite "stopping places" in the city.[57]

Perhaps spurred by the achievement of the Marquette, Johnson himself decided to join the ranks of cabaret owners in 1912. This undertaking was no new idea to the champion. In 1904 Johnson and prominent vaudeville comedian and producer Sherman H. Dudley attempted to open a café and bar at 2442 State Street. The fate of their joint venture is unclear. If it ever opened, it quickly and quietly faded from the South Side entertainment landscape.[58] After winning the heavyweight boxing championship in 1910, Johnson had amassed both sufficient financial resources and notoriety[59] and was finally able to return to his earlier plan of opening a cabaret. On July 4, 1912, Johnson opened his Café de Champion. It was located at 41 West Thirty-First Street—significantly, it occupied the premises of Pony Moore's failed Palace Theater. (Not to be outdone, Moore proposed to open a resort next door to the Café de Champion. The rival cabaret seems never to have opened. Moore died in October 1913.)[60]

The Café de Champion was large and extravagantly outfitted. Johnson recalled that, "in the furnishing and decoration of the cabaret, I had spared no expense or effort." Although he insisted that "the appearance of the interior was neither gaudy nor vulgar," some contemporary observers thought otherwise. Local white newspapers ridiculed the café's decorative excesses—its artwork, its silver cuspidors, its ornate woodworking. However, in its size, its furnishings, and its display of black wealth and urbanity, Johnson's cabaret sat firmly within the tradition of turn-of-the-century gambling saloons. As such it drew crowds who were attracted to the sporting culture nurtured by its antecedents.[61]

Johnson hoped that the Café de Champion would appeal to a clientele of respectable men and women as well as a sporting crowd. Fifteen years after the club's demise, he wrote: "Throughout the entire existence of the cabaret it was successful financially and otherwise, and I sought at all times to conduct it, not only in accordance with the law, but with as good taste and as strictly as a business of that kind can be conducted." Johnson defensively acknowledged that respectability was frequently undermined within his establishment. "Naturally," he conceded, "it attracted classes of people desiring lively times. All sorts of patrons came within its doors and there were those, of course, who would have caused difficulties wherever they went."[62]

Indeed, federal investigators, eager to undermine the stature of the controversial figure, searched for and found reason to question the Café de Champion's claim of social propriety. Justice Department officials took note of the champion's easy and frequent association with black and white prostitutes, several of whom worked for him in various capacities, including waitresses, entertainers, and his personal assistants.[63] Johnson insisted that he never personally or as a club owner "profited financially through his transactions with . . . prostitutes,"[64] but for a brief while his cabaret occupied an important place on the changing map of the South Side sex economy.

The Café de Champion was short-lived. In 1913 Johnson was convicted of violating the 1910 Mann Act (the White-Slave Traffic Act).[65] After his conviction he fled the country, leaving the club to an uncertain future. Despite its short life, Johnson's café was an important institution. As Bricktop proudly remembered, "Jack Johnson had given Chicago something different—an elegantly furnished, racially integrated saloon." Although it had predecessors in the field of black-owned cabarets, the Café de Champion proved that cabarets and the saloon culture that spawned them could draw a large interracial patronage that included respectable men and women. Surprisingly, they could do this even when they also attracted a sporting trade. Dempsey Travis recalled that his father described Johnson's cabaret as "the classiest black and tan public club in the country."[66] Many cabarets, cafés, and buffets were indeed classy nightspots, vigilantly limiting their customers to respectable men and women. Others, like Moore's and Johnson's establishments, walked a precarious line that simultaneously separated and joined a reputable entertainment venture and illicit, if hidden, sexual commerce. Many men and women, black and white, happily walked this fine line themselves as they enjoyed a vast new world of heterosocial, often racially mixed, urban entertainment.[67]

Between 1910 and 1915 black and white leisure entrepreneurs clamored to stake a claim in the South Side's cabaret market (map 5.2). In this short period black-owned establishments multiplied. These included the Mineral Springs Club Buffet and Café (3517 South State), the Roumania Buffet (3759 South State), the Belle Meade Club (5059 Armour Avenue), the Bachelor Buffet (4704 South State), the Dreamland Ballroom (3520 South State), and the De Luxe Café (3503 South State). They competed with a growing number of white-run places such as the Pompeii on Thirty-First Street and the Panama at Thirty-Fifth and State. To varying degrees, these nightclubs became major venues for early jazz performance. As such they were all important sites of Black Belt leisure.[68] Whether black-owned nightspots proudly waving the banner of race enterprise or white-owned businesses respectfully courting the patronage of Black Belt residents, numerous resorts began to assemble under one roof respectable African American men and women, an interracial sporting set, and, ever so quietly, black prostitutes.

Teenan Jones's two Elites occupied one end of the spectrum of resorts fostering such intermingling. Despite the lavish praise contemporaries heaped on his respectable amusement ventures, Jones maintained close associations with the underworld. A 1916 *Chicago Daily News* report on blacks in the city described "Teenan" as the "colored ruler of [the South Side] underworld district," controlling gambling and prostitution in his cabarets and throughout the Black Belt.[69]

Most resorts were less deeply involved in the underground gambling and sex economies; however, the intermingling of patrons and of licit and underground activities was nonetheless important to the culture of the South Side's saloons and emerging nightclubs. Bricktop described the mix that characterized Chicago's prewar club scene: "A quick glance separated the entertainers from the prostitutes. The entertainers wore long skirts and blouses. The prostitutes dressed to the teeth, and wore their skirts several inches above the ankle." As for customers, Bricktop stated that they "cut right through American life—on any given night you could find the steady family man, the politician, the gambler, the pimp." And among women in attendance, "some were ladies with husbands; some were with other ladies' husbands, offering companionship for the night."[70] As the bright lights of the Stroll burned brighter, the sex trade found new avenues for expansion.

Along with sophisticated cabarets and a vital network of lesser-known clubs and saloons that harbored small-time musicians and petty dealers in the underground economy, another nighttime institution helped transform the structure of black women's sex work. Some women worked well into the morning hours through an alternative network of nightclubs known as after-hours clubs. In Chicago, after-hours clubs emerged in the first decade of the twentieth century and functioned to extend the hours and supplement the offerings of more "official" nighttime amusements. The festivities in after-hours clubs began after other bars officially closed their doors at 1 a.m. in compliance with the city's closing ordinance. Although the name suggests that late-night revelry found release in autonomous and hidden institutional spaces, after-hours clubs were not always separate from other leisure resorts. They were frequently attached to saloons and cabarets or located in back rooms, basements, or rooms above the main barroom. In fact, some bars transformed themselves into late-night spots in clear violation of the closing ordinance—at one o'clock they simply closed off the main entrance and directed traffic to a side or alley entrance. Piano player and jazz innovator Jelly Roll Morton recalled that, in Chicago and in the other cities where he played piano in the first decades of the century, "the saloons closed at 1:00 but that didn't make no difference, they just pulled down the shades."[71] Other after-hours hangouts were more circumspect in their defiance of the ordinance, finding ways to manipulate openings in the law. Some after-hours clubs designated themselves as membership clubs. As private organizations, membership clubs were not required to close at one o'clock in the morning, nor were they obliged to restrict the attendance of women when they served alcoholic beverages.[72] Whatever strategy late-night resorts used to circumvent city ordinances, women, who during normal business hours were required to enter through a side entrance and remain in back rooms, could freely mingle with men and other women after hours.[73]

After-hours clubs emerged in part to supply a leisure space for the growing numbers of local and traveling entertainers who hoped to make a name for themselves in Chicago's early-twentieth-century theater and cabaret scene. Entertainers, like black locals, were for the most part excluded from other late-night resorts. Many after-hours joints thrived on the patronage of musicians and theater folk who desired an atmosphere of easy conviviality and relaxation after a night's work. Stage performer Ada Smith (Bricktop) remembered her prewar days of performing in Roy Jones's saloon and cabaret in the Levee. After she and her coworkers "sang and danced from seven p.m. to one a.m.," she would either "go straight home [or] I'd go to some after-hours place with friends."[74] Alberta Hunter also frequented after-hours clubs when she finished work at Teenan Jones's Elite, Isadore Levine's Panama Club, or the Dreamland Ballroom. However, Hunter went not so much for diversion as to earn some extra money entertaining late-night crowds. According to her biographer, "She worked on days off or after hours as a drop-in girl, a singer who circulated from one club to another, at places like the Pekin (which became a cabaret around 1915), Packy Mc-Farland's, Lorraine Garden #2 . . . , Elite Number Two and the Entertainer Café." Hunter often worked the after-hours club scene until eight or nine in the morning.[75]

As after-hours clubs grew in number, they were also patronized by men and women who wanted to continue an evening's fun in settings that were more intimate and less restrained than most saloons and cabarets. In after-hours joints, male entertainers, sporting men, and neighborhood residents mingled freely with female singers, dancers, and women selling their sexual services. All imbibed alcohol, enjoyed impromptu musical performances, danced, and flirted. Many took part in the gambling that was a staple attraction of after-hours affairs. Others found opportunities to arrange sexual liaisons, taking their partners, or their customers, to a nearby rooming house or hotel. These standing late-night parties extended the spaces in which black sex workers were able to find trade within the Black Belt. As institutions that operated both within and beyond the boundaries of municipal law, after-hours clubs provided important links between legitimate leisure institutions, Chicago's burgeoning entertainment community, and the South Side's underground economies of gambling and prostitution. Significantly, when they were located within saloons and cabarets, after-hours clubs bolstered the role played by male proprietors in the South Side sex economy.

Black Belt Streets

Rarely the primary focus of commercial activity in South Side leisure spots, prostitution nevertheless flourished within State Street institutions—whether cabarets, gambling saloons, or sporting taverns. It also thrived in the public spaces that surrounded these resorts—along the Stroll and along busy side streets. As in the nineteenth-century Levee, the street continued to be an important site of the sex trade. Black women's presence on State Street was not simply the result of their being removed from Levee brothels. Many black women who shunned or were excluded from red-light district establishments found accommodations within one or another of the growing number of Black Belt institutions. Rather, several factors led some black women to work neighborhood streets. Like their nineteenth-century counterparts, many preferred the relative independence that street work offered. Others may have sought to work in cabarets and nightclubs but may not have been welcomed by management hoping to avoid the attention of police officers. Other women strategically chose street work as a way to profit from the lively traffic of amusement-seeking men. In this respect, street workers were like other leisure entrepreneurs who set up shop in the Black Belt. Black sex workers were drawn to places where men pursued entertainment and relaxation. Interestingly, although women were invited to join men in the many resorts that invigorated State Street nightlife, the main street of the Black Belt remained in many ways identified with male traffic and male leisure.

The *Chicago Defender* said as much when it gushed, "Every man of color in Chicago, young or old, if he has any leisure time generally wends his way" to the corner of Thirty-First and State streets. On a street that in the daytime drew African American women into groceries, five-cent theaters, and clothing stores, the most public of spaces was reserved for the fellowship of men. "Here," the writer continued his celebration of this busy corner, the man of color

can meet all of his friends and here he can talk "shop" to his "heart's content" and learn in an hour everything of interest that has occurred during the last day, week or year. Here congenial souls in all walks of life meet in a happy half hour's chat. Sometimes old cronies renew friendships over a game of billiards, but as a rule the evening out is spent along the curbstone in enjoyment of the "after-dinner" cigar.[76]

By 1910 Thirty-First Street was indeed a busy thoroughfare for fun-seeking black men. Men gathered in the saloons and clubs that crowded into the two blocks that stretched in both directions from Thirty-First Street (map 5.2). Even as many saloons transformed themselves into cabarets and cafés, several resorts maintained an exclusively male clientele. The Keystone Hotel and Saloon at 3022 State Street—Keystone Hotel and Buffet by 1913—was one of these institutions. The Keystone, observed the *Broad Ax*, "was for many years the headquarters for all the out of town men who visited Chicago, no women being allowed in it or around or about it."[77] In addition to saloons like the Keystone, other kinds of leisure spots continued to cultivate a male clientele at a time when black women, in pursuit of commercial entertainment, were traversing the same paths as men. Pool and billiard parlors were prominent among these resorts and proliferated along the main and side streets of the Black Belt. Some were attached to enterprises that catered to both men and women. At the Hotel Brunswick at 3004 State, the buffet may have served women, but its poolrooms were reserved for men's amusement. Other billiard halls operated solely for the enjoyment of men.

The Queen Solace operated at Thirty-Second and State; Scott and Stanton's Pool Room and Billiard Hall conducted business at Thirty-Ninth and State. Both offered their patrons cigars and tobacco, and the Queen Solace even provided laundry service to its bachelor clientele. Pool halls were sprinkled along the Stroll and on side streets between Twenty-Sixth and Thirty-Ninth. Some proprietors located their resorts beyond this area. In doing so they extended the geography of male leisure into newly forming districts of black residence. For example, Wilbur Holmes operated his "High Class Billiard and Pool Parlor" on Fifty-First Street. Like other billiard hall proprietors, Holmes anticipated the needs of his patrons by offering diverse services: the Holmes Pool Parlor also had a "First Class Barber in Connection."[78] Thus, at the same time that a growing assortment of heterosocial amusements defined the Black Belt leisure terrain, an intricate network of male leisure resorts continued to flourish.

On the streets of the Black Belt, black sex workers sought unobstructed access to momentarily unattached men roaming about in search of entertainment. Their bold activity did not go unnoticed by citizens concerned about upholding standards of public morality. In 1907 the Anti-Crime League, a white reform organization, sent a report to the chief of police on the conditions of vice throughout the city. The report stated that women "accost pedestrians nightly along Thirty-First Street between State and Cottage Grove." A few years later the *Broad Ax*, ever watchful for signs of moral impropriety within the black community, sounded a similar alarm. The reporter noted with particular concern that many women and young girls "congregate around 31st and State streets, some of them tender in years, but very bold in manner and conduct. They hold out all kinds of inducements for men to approach them, and if they are disinclined to do so they will boldly make advances towards the men in order to induce them to part with enough money to pay their way into cheap theaters and other places of amusement."[79]

As the *Broad Ax*'s warning indicates, not all the women and girls seeking the attentions of men on Thirty-First Street were soliciting for prostitution. Many were women, though "tender in years," who were expressing emerging ideas about sexual exploration. Like the young immigrant women who, according to historian Kathy Peiss, found in the streets the freedom to pursue flirtations away from cramped living quarters and beyond the reach of parental authority, black women and girls took to the streets to explore both commercial amusements and the possibility of sexual experience. Like the men with whom they flirted, black women and girls were attracted to State and Thirty-First streets—thoroughfares "painted and spangled [and] made seductive by brilliant lights, laughter and music."[80] Most were working-class women who on their own could not afford the area's nightclubs or restaurants. By brazenly flirting with men, they hoped to entice new male companions to escort them into area resorts. Young women who sought access to amusements in this way were keenly aware that in exchange for such financial assistance they might be expected to bestow sexual favors.[81] These leisure-seeking women may only occasionally have parlayed their sexual capital into access to the Black Belt's vibrant nightlife. Yet in the minds of many onlookers, they were dangerously close to women who systematically worked the streets in search of opportunities for commercial sexual exchange.

The traffic in pleasure-seeking men and trade-seeking women along State Street did not deter the flow of respectable citizens along this exciting thoroughfare. Indeed, it occasioned the nightly intermingling of members of the sporting set, young men and women exercising new sexual ideals, and proper African American residents, both in the public spaces of the street and within the semiprivate confines of commercial entertainment resorts. Such intermingling proved troubling for black leaders hoping to maintain clear distinctions between the reputable and disreputable members of the race. Yet for increasing numbers of men and women in pursuit of fun, there were few attractive alternatives to the bright lights of State Street. As the *Defender*'s drama critic Sylvester Russell observed in 1910, "The best class of people of the colored race are compelled to be mixed with the undesirable or remain at home in seclusion." Weighing these options, many black South Siders chose to brave the crowded and morally fraught terrain of the Great White Way.[82]

Black Women's Sex Entrepreneurship and Residential Prostitution

Not all nighttime resorts were in the bright-light entertainment district. Nor were they all operated by male leisure entrepreneurs. Another late-night entertainment option surfaced in the form of the "buffet flat." Buffet flats were late-night institutions that grew virtually in tandem with the after-hours clubs. However, most proprietors of buffet, or "good-time," flats were women. Called "landladies" by urbanites-in-the-know, the operators of these flats did not directly compete with saloon-based after-hours clubs. Instead, they were part of the late-night party circuit and established their special niche by providing an assortment of racy amusements to men and women pursuing titillating diversion.

Generally, buffet flats were located in private dwellings, usually in apartments. Landladies entertained their guests with a wide range of amusements: in addition to the sale of alcohol and occasionally food, good-time flats offered piano players and singers. Many buffet flats were famous for featuring sexual entertainment—either the services of prostitutes for men or live sex shows for a mixed and adventurous audience. The buffet flat was a hybrid institution. On the one hand, it borrowed from the brothel, whose main purpose was to excite, satisfy, and make money from male sexual curiosity. On the other hand, the buffet flat drew liberally from the permissive cabaret atmosphere that gave non-monetary heterosocial interchange a spirited musical backdrop.

The buffet flat most likely evolved around the turn of the century in rooming houses where beds and entertainment were furnished and sexual liaisons arranged for traveling Pullman porters who could not find other accommodations in the towns along their routes.[83] After World War I–era migration to cities in the South and North, these apartment-based resorts became prominent sites of entertainment within developing black neighborhoods. Urban buffet flats achieved the height of their visibility and vitality after the passage of the Volstead Act in 1919, when they furnished an illegal combination of raunchy entertainment and bootleg alcohol. During the 1920s these resorts attracted a growing number of white "slummers." Thomas Dorsey recalled that more buffet flats opened after "the town went dry. . . . It was nothing strange for one of the landladies to call me at 2 or 3 a.m., saying 'I have a swell bunch from the north side and they want music.' The word[s] 'swell bunch' meant they had money. I would get dressed, hop a cab, rush over and sometimes the bunch would stay until daybreak. I would leave with $15 or $20."[84]

Notwithstanding their growth in the late teens and throughout the twenties, a network of buffet flats filled out Chicago's Black Belt leisure landscape before 1910. In this early incarnation they were, in the words of dance sociologist Katrina Hazzard-Gordon, "after-hours joints that served the general black community."[85] If their original function was to nurture the leisure and sexual proclivities of Pullman porters, they quickly became popular among a broad spectrum of black pleasure-seekers. The popularity of buffet flats sprang both from their presentation of innovative musical performance and from their continued association with relaxed sexual mores and commercialized sexual experimentation.

Like after-hours clubs, buffet flats were very much a part of the leisure and work circuit of Chicago entertainers. Bricktop described prewar buffet flats in Chicago as "the type of place where gin was poured out of milk pitchers. The customers paid ridiculous prices for watered-down liquor, and there was a joke that they even watered the ginger ale. It didn't matter. Nobody drank very much."[86] Bricktop and her friends used buffet flats as places where they could "sit around and harmonize." Others frequented these parties for purely sexual purposes. A significant proportion of the customers were men and women seeking freedom to socialize and to engage in sexually charged flirtations. One writer testily observed that "seemingly bright and promising young girls and married women to[o] for that matter frequent [good-time houses] with their gentlemen friends and fill up on bottled beer and other good things."[87] However, in their pursuit of sexual play, these reckless women and girls rubbed elbows with other late-night revelers seeking more commercial sexual engagements. Early-twentieth-century performers, especially piano players, took in stride the conspicuous presence of black sex merchants at underground apartment gatherings. For example, Perry Bradford joined a group of "pimps with their gals" as they moved their party from Big Jim's Saloon to Ann Brown's buffet flat.[88]

Joining other after-hours establishments, buffet flats provided sex workers ample opportunity to drum up business among late-night partygoers. Many were run by women who had been madams in the red-light district. In a series of articles in 1909, the *Broad Ax* complained about the influx of these undesirable elements into respectable, middle-class sections of the Black Belt. "Two Colored women who not so long ago conducted fancy rooming h[o]uses further down the line, near 21st and D[e]arborn street [in the Levee] and still farther downtown are now located on Wabash ave., between 31st and 34th streets." Indeed, Wabash Avenue "in the past few years . . . has become the grand parade or boulevard of the Colored people, and the result is that the sporting element both men and women are flocking to it at a rapid rate." Good-time houses were apparently wide open along Calumet Avenue between Thirty-Fifth and Thirty-Seventh streets as well, causing a reporter to complain that "one section of the Red Light District has been transferred to Calumet avenue"[89] (map 5.2). Summarizing the troubling goings-on in increasingly visible buffet apartments, the *Broad Ax* reporter declared that sporting-house keepers "sell bottled beer, they rent out their rooms to men and women for a long or short time, they pull off cat hops or dances at any time and they sing loud and bang away on the piano at all hours of the day and night."[90]

By providing entertainers and late-night pleasure-seekers the space to mingle and enjoy each other's company, buffet flats extended the leisure geography of the South Side well beyond the Great White Way of State Street. They also extended the physical terrain in which black women's entrepreneurial capabilities operated within the urban sex trade. In the buffet flat, black women's sex entrepreneurship moved beyond both the red-light district (dominated by white male and female proprietors) and the bright-light areas of South State Street (the preserve of black businessmen). To the embarrassment of respectable middle- and working-class people, these resorts popped up east of State Street along the once-dignified thoroughfares of Wabash, Vernon, and Calumet. Before 1910 the *Broad Ax* had attacked real estate agents for selling houses "on practically all streets and avenues east of State Street" to "Colored ladies" from the red-light district. By 1914 the newspapers identified a new gate-crasher: a *Defender* editorial lamented the complete takeover of the State Street area by "a certain class of intruders." In resigned tones, it concluded that "east of State Street does not mean so much today as it did a few years ago."[91]

Buffet flat proprietors not only claimed new (and contested) territory for the urban leisure and sex trades but also operated within a competitive context of proliferating commercialized amusements. The form of the buffet flat reflected entrepreneurial efforts to carve out a unique niche in the leisure economy. However much buffet flats were patterned on the atmosphere of State Street cafés, landladies saw little use in draping their amusements in the garb of respectability. Unlike cabaret proprietors, who were often at pains to mask, and at times suspend, their legally questionable activities, landladies openly participated in the neighborhood's informal economies. Even before Prohibition some conducted a vigorous trade in alcohol. Notwithstanding Bricktop's assertion that little alcohol was consumed at the flat parties she attended, one woman who ran a house on Vernon boasted that she made between $20 and $30 a night from the sale of beer alone.[92] Other proprietors set aside rooms or tables for gambling parties.[93] Landladies oiled the wheels of underground commerce, and increased an evening's profits, by inviting or employing women to circulate among male partyers and encourage them to linger and dance, drink, gamble, watch a sex show, or enter into a private commercial transaction. Hidden amid neighborhood apartments and homes, quiet buffet flats could escape police detection.

However, the often-raucous goings-on frequently exposed many flats to police surveillance. One observer remarked that buffet flats "make a better harvest for the police than the saloons."[94]

Buffet flats were not exclusive to the Black Belt. As early as 1907 antivice reformers and white neighborhood associations expressed outrage at the growth of good-time flats in apartment buildings in white neighborhoods on the North and Far South Sides. This form of residentially based prostitution was an adaptation to the constricted opportunities prostitutes and madams faced within the South Side Levee. It was also an innovative response to demands for new forms of heterosocial leisure among white urbanites. Property owners in Kenwood (a white middle-class neighborhood southeast of the Black Belt) complained to the police that "women of questionable repute are moving into flat buildings along Oakendale, Lake, Berkeley and other avenues offending their neighbors by their conduct." The Douglass Neighborhood Association repeatedly directed police attention to the operation of disorderly flats within the white residential district just east of the Black Belt.[95] Disorderly flats were plentiful on the North Side as well. Apartment buildings on Erie Street were "visited by loads of men and women in automobiles every night." A distressed neighbor of a white buffet flat on Ontario complained about the "simply awful" piano-playing and incessant partying. "The women in the house are shouting and singing at all hours of the night. . . . These women give regular vaudeville shows in their rooms, and men and women flock to the place."[96]

Even within the Black Belt, buffet flats were not the exclusive preserve of African American women. Witnessing the attraction that black entertainment and black women's sexual favors held for many white pleasure-seekers, several white madams situated their businesses within or near the growing entertainment district of the South Side. Marie Walsh operated one such resort near Thirty-Fifth Street and South Park Avenue. Apparently trying to drum up business in a saloon at Thirty-Fifth and State, Walsh boasted to undercover investigators that she ran what she called a "cheap place" at Twenty-Second and Wabash and had just spent $8,000 to fix up her new Thirty-Fifth Street resort.[97] Other women tailored their businesses to satisfy a specialized market: black men in search of white women's sexual services. In especially disparaging tones, the *Broad Ax* reported on a madam who ran this type of good-time house on Calumet Avenue: "Each evening after business is over down in the Red Light District and the fancy houses closed up for the night, [the landlady] has the low white women, who are not engaged with sporting white men, to come to her house on Calumet ave., where they meet Colored men, and they spend the remainder of the night in drinking beer and cheap whisky and in having a high old time."⁹⁸ Entrepreneurs like this landlady capitalized on the exclusion of black men from most of the resorts within the Levee.

Notwithstanding these competitors, black women dominated the city's buffet flat circuit, thanks largely to their integration in black entertainment circles. Performers of all stripes looked to the buffet flat as a place to unwind; to develop their skills before a receptive audience; to secure future jobs; and to gather in the generous tips from late-night revelers.⁹⁹ Patrons who were not show people benefited from a landlady's connections and were able to participate—in a less formal way than at the theater, the cabaret, or even the saloon—in a vibrant world of heterosocial amusement.

Buffet flats varied in size from nondescript apartments with a few rooms for dancing, drinking, and flirtation to large enterprises with several venues, each featuring a different diversion. In the larger good-time flats, prostitutes employed by the landlady could take customers to back rooms or to rooms elsewhere in the building. However, it appears that most buffet parties provided merely the occasion for sexual solicitation. Sex workers frequenting buffet flats could take their customers to nearby rooming houses, hotels, and private apartments. Buffet flats, then, were woven into a network of residential institutions that further extended black women's sex work into black neighborhoods.

Residential places for assignation—whether private or commercial— were nothing new. In the nineteenth century they thrived in the vicinity of brothels and disorderly saloons. After the turn of the century, however, they took on new life as they moved beyond areas of concentrated sexual commerce and spread into neighborhoods not primarily identified with sexual commerce. On the city's South Side they made this move along with saloons, after-hours clubs, cabarets, and buffet flats. And like these entertainment venues, they profited from both commercial assignation and from casual, nonmonetary sexual liaisons. In 1910 places for sexual assignation maintained important economic links to other leisure establishments, but geographically they were entrenched in an urban terrain defined by middle- and working-class home life and legitimate neighborhood commerce.

As prostitutes and sex entrepreneurs searched for quieter and less public areas in which to conduct their trade, apartment buildings away from the bright lights of the Levee and South State Street offered inviting opportunities. Prostitution conducted in apartments or furnished rooming houses is perhaps the most difficult for the historian to investigate. These were subterranean operations that readily masked their true character—if not always from neighbors, very often from police officers. Unlike buffet flats, which regularly announced their goings-on to neighbors and partyers in the know, apartment prostitution generally survived only as long as proprietors and participants maintained some degree of decorum. These scattered places for prostitution rarely appeared in vice investigations. Only after 1920, when white urbanites began to take part in the leisure offerings of South Side nightclubs in significant numbers, did the apartment-based sex trade within the Black Belt receive regular attention from white reform agencies. Even then, only the most flagrant resorts—specifically those fostering interracial sex contacts—received sustained attention.

Perhaps the most commercial assignation houses were the "disorderly hotels" that popped up here and there within the Black Belt. Some, like Pony Moore's Hotel de Moore and the hotel attached to the Pompeii, were situated above the saloons where sex workers solicited customers; others were just a stone's throw away from saloons and other area nightspots. Unlike the grand hotels downtown, most neighborhood hostelries were small enterprises and may have been no more than lodging houses for working-class men and women. A few, like one at 3120 State, were tucked away above storefronts on the Stroll. The operations of these nameless resorts remain obscure to us today. One exception was the Columbia Hotel located "at the top of 'The Stroll,'" at the corner of Thirty-First and State streets. From at least 1910 through the 1920s, the Columbia operated in the heart of the café and theater district. According to pianist Willie "The Lion" Smith, "anyone in show business could get a room for a buck and a half a night (one dollar, if you were pressed for funds)."[100] Given the easy association between entertainers and members of the "underworld," men and women not in show business very probably could secure short-time accommodations here as well.[101]

Despite these examples, hotels and commercial lodging houses in the Black Belt were scarce before the 1920s. Such enterprises required considerable capital for the purchase and upkeep of property and for day-to-day operations. It was an investment that few South Siders could afford, and white entrepreneurs resisted investing in an area where providing inexpensive accommodations did not guarantee large profits. Thus, before the war, hotels were not as important to the neighborhood sex trade as they were downtown and in other sections of the city.[102] Rather, less formal accommodations provided in rooming houses and boardinghouses and in unobtrusive apartments away from the bright-light district provided necessary shelter for sex workers and their customers.

Rooming houses were central to the evolution of both South Side housing and the South Side sex trade. Rooming houses and boarding-houses were informal adaptive housing forms that emerged in response both to a restricted urban housing market and to the persistent economic insecurity of black South Siders.[103] In a city where single-family dwellings and apartments were priced beyond the budgets of most working-class men and women, the practice of renting meager space in family homes served the needs of a diverse population: it provided temporary accommodations for black travelers, transitional housing for families, homelike dwellings for unattached men, and shelter for single working women. The benefits of lodging accrued not only to migrating tenants but to host households as well: it was an economic exchange that offered families and individual women who took in paying guests a means of offsetting financial instability.[104]

Boardinghouses and rooming houses pervaded virtually every neighborhood of the black community. Keepers advertised annually in local business directories and weekly in the *Defender*.[105] The locations of rooming houses advertised in the *Defender*, however, reveal only part of the evolving residential geography of the Black Belt. Between 1910 and 1915 the majority of keepers who placed ads in the weekly paper operated houses east of State Street, where, according to one study, "many of the colored people who desire a better neighborhood" dwelled.[106] However, many rooming houses were located west of State, an area rarely discussed in newspaper coverage of community happenings.

The oldest and poorest housing within the Black Belt was situated in the western section of the community. Between State Street and the railroad tracks just west of Federal Street, African Americans—mostly single men and women—created homes in dwellings deemed "old, dingy, [and] frequently broken-down" by social reformers. The rooming houses here did not advertise in the city's black newspapers, yet they were tremendously important to the housing of poorer black South Siders. They were also important to the spread of sex work beyond the State Street entertainment corridor. While both the *Defender* and the *Broad Ax* expressed outrage at the spread of good-time flats and "fancy rooming houses" into the impressive housing structures along Wabash, Forest, Calumet, and Vernon, prostitution conducted in the furnished rooms in the unprepossessing district to the west continued virtually ignored.[107]

One reformer observed in 1912 that, although the western section of the black community was some distance from "the district of segregated vice, . . . it was hardly possible that the residents of these blocks can escape its influences."[108] Indeed, the sex trade did infiltrate this district. Fragmentary court records collected between 1911 and 1915 by the Committee of Fifteen, an anti-vice reform organization, afford us a partial view of this area of sexual commerce. In several cases brought before criminal court, black women figured prominently as prostitutes, panderers, or keepers of houses of ill fame. Black men appear in these documents as well, though usually as panderers and pimps, most often of white women.

Many of the addresses cited were between Twenty-Fifth and Thirty-Fifth streets along Dearborn and Federal streets. For example, in 1911 black sex entrepreneur Alma Kendall was found guilty of forcing two young black girls—fourteen-year-old Mary Gray and seventeen-year-old Georgia Baker—to work as prostitutes in a colored boardinghouse at 2735 Dearborn Street. In 1913 Mrs. Allie Crass brought charges against Allen Samuels for forcing her to entertain men in a small apartment at 2714 Dearborn. In 1915 Alfred Dobbins was found guilty of procuring Pearl Foggy for houses of prostitution—one at 3525 Wabash, the other at 2450 Federal Street. White women found employment in this area of the Black Belt sex trade as well. In 1911 Roberta Drew, a black woman, employed at least one white woman in her dwelling at 3021 Dearborn, which catered to "colored men." Roberta Drew was not alone in exploiting black men's willingness to pay for white women's sexual services. In 1915 James Miller was charged with forcing his white wife, Grace, to entertain men in their room at 2546 Federal Street. The same racialized sex economy that had excluded black men from full participation in both the old Levee and the Twenty-Second Street Levee created opportunities for small-time sex entrepreneurship, and in many instances exploitation, in hidden neighborhood spaces.[109]

These addresses indicate the scattering of prostitution beyond the western border of State Street. They offer a glimpse into the emerging structure of prostitution in poorer sections of the community. Like the "fancy" rooming houses and buffet flats to the east, disorderly flats and rooming houses in this district demonstrated the ability of black sex entrepreneurs to adjust to shifting contexts of commerce, geography, and policing. The inexpensive rooms and apartments were ideal places for short and apparently inexpensive commercial liaisons. Unlike buffet flats, which offered at the very least live musical entertainment and alcohol, rooming houses and apartments off the beaten path supported prostitution that was quick and unencumbered with nonsexual superfluities. These exchanges suited the pockets of neighborhood working men. Furthermore, accommodations for sexual leisure west of State Street—whether rooming houses or rented flats—lacked the buffet flats' connection with the entertainment scene. Some women—whether on their own or with the assistance of increasingly important male "agents"—found customers in neighborhood saloons; however, others secured a portion of their trade on nearby streets.[110]

The same racially organized sex economy that had excluded black men from participation as customers in the Twenty-Second Street red-light district created opportunities for black men's and women's entrepreneurship within neighborhood spaces—whether State Street or the respectable residential districts to the east of State. Plotting the addresses of rooms and rooming houses that supported black women's sex work locates these opportunities not only along the main entertainment thoroughfares but in areas where women and men of limited means struggled to achieve economic security in the urban economy. These random addresses afford a glimpse into the emerging structure of prostitution in poorer sections of the community.

Residential prostitution offered many women a means of eluding black (and white) male control of the Black Belt sex economy. In buffet flats black women incorporated the leisure activities that were making nightclubs so attractive to a broadening array of city dwellers—bottled beer and, above all, music. Assignation rooms further multiplied the locations of sexual exchange. Because they could pop up anywhere and required no extra capitalization, places for assignation increased opportunities for small-time entrepreneurs to tap into the sex economy. Veiled by the privacy of apartment buildings and rooming houses and nestled among reputable households, buffet flats and assignation houses could also evade police surveillance. However, residentially based sex resorts assumed their own risks. Located along the thoroughfares of Wabash, Forest, and Calumet to the east and Dearborn and Armour to the west, they were very often neighbors of men and women who would gladly seek police assistance in removing them from their buildings and their streets. Despite the increased chance of neighbor surveillance, apartment-based prostitution allowed female entrepreneurs to maintain an important foothold within the sex marketplace.

Conclusion

By the time of its official closing in 1912, the area designated as Chicago's red-light district held declining importance in the business of black women's sexual services. However, well before 1910 black male and female entrepreneurs organized black women's sexual labor within a different geography and within a different leisure economy. A burgeoning district of entertainment and black residences on the South Side provided new outlets for the circulation and intermingling of black sex workers and their customers. It also allowed for the intermingling of black prostitutes with other South Siders in search of an evening's entertainment.

The nature of black women's sex entrepreneurship changed as well. Many madams transferred their base of operation to saloons, cabarets, and after-hours clubs. As saloon owners gained respectable status within the black community, their businesses provided outlets for black women who had moved beyond the rigid confines of the brothel trade, which continued to dominate the red-light district. The growing importance of Black Belt nightlife had contradictory consequences for sex entrepreneurs and workers. At a time when black women's stock was declining within the Levee, their success as madams operating within the Black Belt depended on maintaining cordial and profitable relations with male proprietors. For the individual sex worker unattached to a madam or to a nightclub owner, cabarets and after-hours clubs could offer greater control over the patterns of her labor. Despite the benefits that might have accrued to casual prostitutes, the expanding male control of Black Belt entertainment enterprises undermined the prominence of women sex entrepreneurs within the most visible institutions of nighttime leisure.

Although new institutional forms supported black women's sex work in the first decade of the twentieth century, a relationship continued between the old-style brothel madams working in the Levee and the proprietors of saloons, after-hours clubs, buffet flats, and rooming houses that proliferated in the Black Belt. Indeed, old-school madams often associated with younger saloon owners and landladies. When Perry Bradford arrived at Johnnie Seymore's Saloon in 1908 for his first piano contest, he found in attendance two of "the celebes of the Sporting Madams . . . Viney Fields and a sister of ebony hue known as Black Mag."[111] These Sporting Madams not only moved through a sporting saloon circuit but also frequented recreational events that catered to respectable black men on the South Side. In 1905 the *Broad Ax* reported that "Miss Ellen French and Miss Black Mag, the two most popular landladies in the sporting or 'Red Light District,' were in evidence at the Knight Templars' ball at the Coliseum annex Monday Evening. Miss French wore a beautiful baby blue dress, with opera coat and hat to match. Miss Black

Mag looked very charming in her black skirt, white silk waist and her Easter hat."[112] As these accounts reveal, black madams had established a presence within expanded spheres of black male recreation—not just as dispensers of sexual pleasure but also as welcome associates in leisure. And, significantly, not just for sporting men.

The *Broad Ax*'s sarcastic description of the attire of these "popular landladies" barely veils an underlying concern with the porous barriers separating respectable men and women from the disreputable elements of Chicago's black society. The permeability of these barriers became ever more obvious as the decades progressed. Black prostitutes and madams moved increasingly freely through the leisure resorts and neighborhood spaces of the Black Belt. Due to the institutional and geographical shift of black women's sex work away from the Levee, black prostitution became almost exclusively identified with the landscape of black community residence. The editor of the *Broad Ax*, a vigilant enemy of sexual license, was not the only one to issue warnings about the dire repercussions that sexual immorality in general and the traffic in black women in particular had for respectable men and women of the race.

By 1910 African Americans in Chicago were engaged in a simultaneously forceful and muted discussion of prostitution. This discussion, however, was shaped only in part by a concern for the experiences and well-being of black sex workers. Rather, the meanings that community leaders gave to black women's sexual labor were deeply enmeshed in larger ongoing struggles over black citizenship. In these early-twentieth-century battles, aggressively waged on contested urban turf, black people's sexuality was ever at issue.

SIX

Rage and Rescue: African American Anti-Vice Reform Strategies

In the early 1900s middle-class discourses of respectability greatly influenced public reaction among African Americans to prostitution within the Black Belt. Such discourses had multiple audiences. Middle-class black men and women directed their exhortations to public propriety, thrift, cleanliness, and sexual morality initially at themselves, providing themselves with a guide to personal success and racial betterment. They also encouraged working-class and poor blacks to accept the ideals of public and private morality. Through upright living, members of Chicago's black middle class laid the tracks by which less fortunate blacks could find their way to respectability, economic stability, and social purity. To the extent that middle-class uplift ideologies converged with their own conceptions of respectability, working-class men and women did embrace middle-class ideals of public and private conduct. This was the case, for example, in matters of personal and domestic cleanliness. The resonance between working-class and middle-class notions of respectability was especially strong in efforts to protect young girls and working women from association with sexual immorality and to shield them from sexual exploitation by white male employers.[1]

Middle-class discourses of respectability were a "bridge discourse," as Evelyn Brooks Higginbotham argues, by which black men and women hoped to communicate with and garner the support of sympathetic whites.[2] Indeed, criticisms of the backwardness and immorality among poor, urbanizing blacks served simultaneously to establish connections to middle-class whites and to position the black middle class as both exemplars and arbiters of the race's social progress. To be sure, most blacks (middle class as well as working class) did not view the discourse of respectability as primarily a political strategy. For those who embraced it, respectability was a deeply felt value system, a necessary guide for righteous living. Yet for several prominent community leaders concerned with upholding and demonstrating the sexual purity of the race, it was also a political discourse, one that extended beyond attempts to find a common ground with whites. Many used respectability to challenge whites who themselves either failed to support black efforts for racial betterment or who were directly responsible for those instances when black Chicagoans veered from the path of respectability.

It is in this latter mode that many of Chicago's black middle-class men and women registered their concern about the sex economy that after the turn of the century was rapidly emerging in their midst. Between 1900 and 1920 middle-class African Americans in the Black Belt leveled increasingly loud charges against white municipal authorities, who they believed allowed prostitution to move into areas of black residence and to flourish unchecked within black community spaces. They criticized white reformers who professed that they wanted to save women from sexual exploitation but who showed little interest in rescuing black prostitutes. Black leaders also condemned white men for coming into the Black Belt in search of sexual entertainment. The discourse of respectability helped them frame each of these critiques. Yet it did not allow black leaders to either address the economic circumstances that led so many black women to turn to prostitution or publicly acknowledge the hardships these women faced as sex workers.

The events surrounding the case of one black girl elucidate the ways that black middle-class Chicagoans negotiated the realities of black prostitution. They did this, significantly, not by addressing black women's prostitution directly. Indeed, the girl, Mator McFerrin, was in no way involved in the South Side sex trade. Yet the attention her circumstances generated exposed the centrality of prostitution to ideas of black women's sexual vulnerability in the turn-of-the-century city. Through a campaign in defense of one unfortunate girl, middle-class blacks leveled their gaze at the hypocrisy of white municipal authorities and reformers whose neglect of black girls and women imperiled the virtue of black womanhood. At the height of Chicago's white slavery scare, and at a

moment when city officials were waging an attack on the Levee, this
charge was strategic.

"The Worst Scandal in Years"

On October 26, 1912, the *Chicago Defender* covered a story titled "Colored Girl Outraged in Cook County Hospital." The article began:

One of the most pathetic as well as unfortunate cases in years has come before the
citizens of Chicago. A young girl, seventeen years of age, about to become a mother
in a month. . . . Without a penny, without clothes, she f[a]ces the world, poor crea-
ture. Such is the case of Mator McFerrin, who never knew a father's love or care,
never had the love of a mother, [and] who has lived in hospitals or in charity institutions the greater part of her life.[3]

The site of Mator's outrage, or rape, was Chicago's Cook County Hospital, where she received treatment for tuberculosis. There the seventeen-
year-old girl met Frank Chaplin, a white man also being treated for TB.
While recovering, the two worked together in the hospital's kitchen.
Chaplin was the "culprit" responsible for what the *Defender* called "the
worst scandal in years."

Mator McFerrin's case could easily have gone unnoticed. Indeed, her
predicament escaped the concern of Chicago's white daily papers. Her
case easily fit prevailing white explanations of black women's sexual behavior. White reporters likely saw the story of a black girl's illegitimate
pregnancy as one more example of black women's sexual immorality
and thus did not consider it newsworthy. In taking up her cause, the
Defender challenged what it viewed as the conspiracy of silence surrounding poor McFerrin's circumstances.

Yet the *Defender*'s editor did not immediately grasp the implications
of McFerrin's story. At the time that the first article appeared about Mc-
Ferrin, she was already eight months pregnant. Furthermore, the article
appeared on the second page of the paper, flanked by "Sarah Bernhardt's
Wealth" and an "Explanation of the Workings of Somnambulism."
While the editor saw McFerrin's case as sad and beseeched readers to
"open your hearts, [and] give what you can" to help "poor Mator," the
child's story did not warrant front-page attention.

Two overlapping national dramas—each of which played out with
particular intensity in Chicago—propelled McFerrin's case to the *Defender*'s headlines. The first of these dramas, the scare over white slavery

that peaked between 1900 and 1915, registered and heightened a national panic over women's increasing mobility and the growth of prostitution in the nation's cities. The alarm over white slavery eventually led to the official closing of Chicago's Levee. The controversy surrounding heavyweight boxing champion Jack Johnson furnished the second national drama framing the *Defender's* coverage of McFerrin's case. In 1912 federal authorities arrested the fighter for violating the Mann Act (the White-Slave Traffic Act) and the following year secured his conviction. The outrage that consumed white civic leaders and moral reformers in reaction to white slavery did not extend to black women, who, if arrest rates accurately reflect their participation in prostitution, were "trapped" in the web of the urban sex trade to a greater degree than white women. The public outcry generated by the white slavery scare and the passage of the Mann Act simultaneously enraged black Chicagoans and provided men and women of Chicago's black middle class with a language and a strategy with which to challenge black women's exclusion from national and local deliberations about the dangers facing young, unprotected women in the city. For three months in 1912, the convergence of events surrounding Jack Johnson's arrest mobilized the anger and resources of Chicago's African American women's clubs, men's clubs, business owners, and church leaders in defense of Mator McFerrin.

African American leaders had been waging a battle against sexual commerce in the emerging Black Belt since 1900. In the first decade of the century, most anti-vice activity took place in church pulpits and through the uplift work of church groups, men's and women's clubs, and a few social settlements. Yet white anti-vice activities incited by the white slavery scare spurred African Americans to make increasingly vocal protestations about the sex trade. After 1910, black leaders in Chicago began to press city officials to take note of the dangers that unchecked prostitution posed to the Black Belt community. Black church and civic leaders complained that police anti-vice policies contributed to the spread of sexual commerce in the Black Belt. Between 1907 and 1912 Chicago city government, through police raids, concentrated its efforts on shutting down brothels and disorderly saloons in the Levee. Many Black Belt residents argued that such closings only dispersed prostitution into the neighboring community.

Increasingly, black leaders came to see that city government caused a large part of the community's "vice" problem.[4] Inconsistent anti-vice policies, neglect of the growth of the sex trade within the Black Belt, and practices of policing black prostitution encouraged sexual commerce to grow in the Black Belt and posed dangers for unprotected black girls. Middle-class leaders took their concerns about the city's complicity in the community's escalating vice problem to the pages of the black press, to city council representatives, and to white reform agencies. Yet addressing their concerns to white city leaders, black leaders confronted a major obstacle in white slavery discourse. Largely excluded from public conversations on the city's prostitution conditions, African Americans had to find a pathway into this discussion whose power relied on a construction of female innocence that stood in opposition to popular white representations of black women. To enter the debate about public sexuality, African American community leaders had both to maneuver around the racial specificity of white slave discourse and to preempt imputations of black women's sexual depravity. This dilemma necessitated an interpretation of the Black Belt's vice problem as one not emerging from within the Black Belt. Rather, black women were the victims of a vice economy run rampant. In trying to include black women under the protective arm of municipal and reform agencies, African American leaders acceded to ideas of female vulnerability at the heart of white slave discourse.

The *Chicago Defender*'s construction of Mator McFerrin's image strategically intervened in the anti-vice debate raging in the city. Her life, as pieced together by the *Defender*'s reporters, consisted of a series of dislocations punctuated by physical traumas. According to the paper, McFerrin was a "penniless" and motherless child of seventeen who, "without a single friend in the world," had to face a pregnancy resulting from a rape. The sexual assault took place in a hospital where she had been recovering from tuberculosis. This "unfortunate" girl, who had only a fourth-grade education, the October 26 article went on to say, suffered pneumonia at age eleven, for which she received treatment and was discharged from a Cook County children's hospital, only to suffer a relapse, and while recovering at another hospital, she suffered a blow to the head with a bottle. She sustained minor injuries and recuperated in yet another Chicago hospital. After McFerrin's recovery the Cook County Juvenile Court—her legal guardian—placed her in a home for girls on the city's far South Side. It was there that she contracted tuberculosis. McFerrin, the reporter despairingly concluded, had "not been properly cared for by those who had her in [their] charge."[5] Young Mator, the *Defender* insisted, was a child abused by a system of institutional neglect. Such neglect not only endangered her health but made possible her sexual violation directly under the noses of her supposed custodians.

McFerrin was a pitiable figure indeed. Yet the crusade in her defense would gain momentum only as controversies surrounding Jack Johnson began to escalate. A week before McFerrin first appeared in the *Defender*, Chicago police arrested heavyweight boxing champion Jack Johnson on charges of abducting Lucille Cameron, a nineteen-year-old white woman who had recently moved to Chicago from Minneapolis. In Chicago Cameron worked in Johnson's South Side club, the Café de Champion, and it was there that a romance between the two began.

As world heavyweight champion, Jack Johnson commanded a great deal of attention. His flamboyant demeanor, his history of romantic relations with white women, and his 1910 defeat of white boxing hopeful Jim Jeffries contributed to Johnson's notoriety among whites and his grudging celebrity among blacks. But it was his well-known sexual liaisons with white women that made him the target of local and federal investigations.[6]

Lucille Cameron's mother initiated the case against Johnson, pressing the charge of abduction after learning of Lucille's association with the black fighter. In the case that local and federal authorities tried to build against him, Johnson, along with his accomplices in an alleged interracial prostitution ring, reportedly lured Cameron from her Minneapolis home. The elements of Cameron's case fit well into the structure of white slave narratives: a young white woman comes to Chicago from a midwestern town, works in a saloon adjacent to the Levee, and fraternizes with a disreputable set; a distraught mother seeks to rescue her daughter from the clutches of an evil seducer against whom the innocent young woman is helpless.

Nationally and locally African Americans reacted negatively to this portrayal of Johnson. Some saw the federal government's attack on the fighter as an effort to strip a successful black man of his fairly earned wealth and status. For others it represented a tacit endorsement of southern violence against black men accused of raping or otherwise sexually menacing white women.[7] Many, though, could not avoid the conclusion that a black woman in a similar situation would never engender the public outrage provoked by the figure of Lucille Cameron. The hush surrounding the sexual assaults of black women galled black observers of the Johnson episode. An editorial appearing in the *Muskogee Cimeter* and reprinted in the *Defender* plainly makes the point: "We cannot forget that *white men* have been, and are even now, using innocent and ignorant colored girls and women in the same way. . . . White men . . . should quit their devilment, because they are the *white Jack Johnsons*, and are just as detestable in every way to decency."[8]

The figure of Lucille Cameron herself seemed to insult black observers the most. Her mother's attorney built his case against Johnson with the suggestion of Cameron's naïveté and prior sexual purity. Mrs. Cameron-Falconet's testimony played a pivotal role in the construction of her daughter's victimization. Replying to the outpouring of support from white men and women across the country, she proclaimed: "I am in the fight for my daughter and justice. I will see this case through to the finish."[9] The image of the victimized innocent did not sit well with black observers, and many commented on Cameron's unworthiness of the outpouring of protective outrage reflected in the white press. The *Chicago Broad Ax*, a black weekly newspaper, did not bother to hide its contempt for Cameron and her supporters. In a bitingly worded attack, the paper's editor denounced her and those who hypocritically had come to her defense against Johnson: "The people in Chicago and throughout the country . . . permitted themselves to go crazy not in behalf of a pure and innocent young lady; far from it but they worked themselves up to fever pitch over a lady much older than sweet 19 who understands the art of making love to both White and Colored gentlemen, providing that they have plenty of money in their pockets."[10] The *Defender*, in less acerbic tones, criticized Chicago's white newspapers for "entwining a halo of purity" around Cameron.[11]

African American observers felt no surprise when federal investigators disclosed that, months before she met Johnson, Cameron had been a prostitute in Chicago.[12] Furthermore, Lucille herself refused to testify against Johnson. The disclosure of Cameron's sexual past vindicated the fighter in the minds of most African Americans. More than this, it underscored the hypocrisy at the root of white slave discourse. But federal authorities compounded the insult when they looked to Belle Schreiber to salvage their case against Johnson. Schreiber, an unrepentant Chicago prostitute and a longtime friend of Johnson's, provided the evidence that investigators needed to secure their case against the fighter. With her testimony federal agents arrested Johnson on November 7 and prosecuted him for transporting Schreiber across state lines for immoral purposes. Though authorities eventually acquitted him on the charge of abducting Cameron, in May 1913 Johnson was convicted for violating the Mann Act.

For African American leaders intently watching the drama of Jack Johnson's persecution, the disreputable characters of Cameron and Schreiber made even more galling the exclusion of black women and girls from the enforcement efforts of local and federal authorities hoping to protect endangered womanhood. The fallen figures of Cameron and Schreiber fueled middle-class African Americans' attempts to grab the banner of sexual purity for black womanhood. Nationally and in Chicago black men and women did so in a way that directly challenged the silences surrounding the historical and, tragically, continuing sexual assault of black women and girls by white men. The renewed campaign to prove black women's sexual innocence framed the *Defender*'s championing of Mator McFerrin's cause.

"FOR GOD'S SAKE HELP ME. . . . Women of my race, I have been taken advantage of by a White Gentleman who, I thought, I had to obey." A week after her story first appeared in the *Defender*, McFerrin's desperate words screamed out on the front page of the paper. In her plea, no doubt reworded by the *Defender*'s editor, McFerrin made explicit the crime that brought her to such a tragic state. To be sure, her tragedy centered on her rape and pregnancy. Yet the sexual assault of a defenseless black girl did not alone put McFerrin's story in the *Defender* headlines.[13] The deplorable offense that brought the newspaper to McFerrin's defense was the fact that a "white gentleman" had raped the young, helpless girl. Her violation, the *Defender* lamented, was "more disgraceful than anything that has ever happened in the city of Chicago." In fact, the story of McFerrin's rape stood out as "the most pathetic case ever heard in the city courts."[14]

If the implied parallel between McFerrin's case and the Jack Johnson affair did not immediately strike the *Defender*'s readers, one angry man's letter to the editor clarified the issues at the heart of young Mator's story:

Let us as a race come together, to shelter and protect this child as a race should.

Had this case been a white child one whole side of the white papers would be full of it. Now I am surprised at our preachers, our lawyers, our doctors, our leading men and women making such great demonstration over Jack Johnson's case when here is one a great deal worse.[15]

For this outraged reader, the contrasting figures of the disreputable Lucille Cameron and the innocent Mator McFerrin undergirded his criticism of local white newspapers that championed the former while overlooking the circumstances of the latter. At the same time he admonished the "leading men and women" of the race who in defending a morally questionable Jack Johnson shared guilt with white Chicagoans who had neglected the sorry case of one of the race's most vulnerable.

In the pages of the *Defender*, McFerrin occupied a moral universe completely removed from the world of disreputable cafés, free-flowing

This is the first photograph of Mator McFerrin who became a mother at the Cook County Hospital. This photograph was taken in the city hall on Monday last during the morning and afternoon session of the Court of Domestic Relations when the culprit, Frank Chaplin, was tried and found guilty of his outrageous crime.

6.1 "Little Mator McFerrin and Her Son Clarence." Front page of the *Chicago Defender,* November 30, 1912. Courtesy of the *Chicago Defender.*

liquor, and prostitution in which Cameron circulated. In implicitly, and at times explicitly, constructing McFerrin as Cameron's opposite, the paper admonished its readers to live up to their racial duty to protect McFerrin, who, unlike Cameron, had neither family nor friend to advocate for her rescue.

The *Defender* constructed McFerrin as a truly pitiable figure (fig. 6.1). Readers learned that young Mator had been "a victim of neglect" for most of her life. Her mother was "responsible for the present condition of her daughter," accused the paper. Jessie McFerrin, who had died two years earlier, was a woman of "questionable character," and officers of the juvenile court had to remove young Mator from her care on several occasions.[16] Her father's whereabouts were unknown, and Mator lost contact with her grandmother through her successive moves. The juvenile court was McFerrin's only true protector, according to the *Defender,* and as her legal guardian had on several occasions tried to secure for the child a decent home. One woman with whom McFerrin lived for a short while provided the *Defender* with additional clues to the child's past. Most importantly, she attested to McFerrin's good character. "She was a loveable child," Nancy Smith recalled, "and tried to help herself in every way. She had no vices and I was surprised to hear of her present plight, also of her mother's death. *But she is not to blame*" (emphasis in original).[17]

McFerrin's young age added further proof of her victimhood, though it took *Defender* reporters a while to determine her exact age. When McFerrin first appeared in the paper, readers learned that she was seventeen. A week later the headline read: "15 Year Old Child Soon to Be Mother." The following week the headline announced: "Mother at Fifteen . . . is the Fate of Little Mator McFerrin." From then on her age remained pegged at fifteen. In December, apparently relieved, the *Defender* assured it readers that "conclusive proofs of her age . . . have been established."[18]

The *Defender*'s insistence that McFerrin was fifteen and not seventeen served two purposes. First, the newspaper sought to ensure the continued protective services of the juvenile court. As a ward of the state, McFerrin could expect their assistance only until her eighteenth birthday.[19] If she were seventeen the juvenile court's help in her case would soon end. Second, the newspaper's editor clearly understood that the closer a young black girl's age was to the age of consent (eighteen in Illinois), the less believable her charge of rape against a white man before a white judge or jury. At the same time that the *Defender* sought to heighten the outrage of the race's leading men and women, it also endeavored to erase any cause for doubt that McFerrin could be anything other than an unwilling victim of Frank Chaplin's sexual advances.

Fears that McFerrin's virtue might be called into question by readers and white onlookers shaped the *Defender*'s characterization of McFerrin's assailant. The newspaper alternately referred to Chaplin as a "cowardly, dastardly white brute," the "white monster," and the "culprit." In naming Chaplin a "brute," the *Defender* encouraged its readers to see in McFerrin's case, not just one white man's attack on a poor black girl, but the long history of white men's sexual abuse of black women. In fact, as a "southern white gentleman" Chaplin carried this history in his blood. Chaplin, the *Defender* asserted, was a "scoundrel suffering from the ravages of the 'white plague,' brought on from his inheriting the blood of his vile and degenerate parents who thrust themselves upon their enslaved female servants and sold in cold blood their own offspring for paltry sums of gold." To the *Defender* and its readers, Chaplin embodied white southern men's historical attacks on black female virtue. As the object of the *Defender's* contempt, Chaplin provided readers with an opportunity to avenge this history of sexual abuse. In reality Chaplin bore little resemblance to a southern "gentleman." Like McFerrin he received medical treatment at Cook County, a public hospital. Nevertheless, the *Defender* used Chaplin's southern origins and the history of black women's sexual abuse to frame McFerrin's case and to expose the inadequacy of white slavery discourses that overlooked the continuing sexual violation of black women. The *Defender* leveled criticism at city officials, whose neglect of black womanhood placed McFerrin at moral risk, and at the city's white newspapers, which "failed to mention anything about the cowardly . . . white brute."[20]

The front-page layout of the November 16 *Defender* boldly drew connections between McFerrin's story, Chaplin's savagery, Jack Johnson's persecution, and the anti-vice climate in the city (fig. 6.2). Three stories vied for the attention of readers. The main headline read: "Negroes Uphold Mann Act." "But," this article went on to argue, "the United States government should prosecute white men who are importing colored women into the North from the South and buying homes for them, and living with them . . . ; is this not a violation of the Mann Act? . . . The culprits can be brought to justice and a step to save our young women will be made for the first time in the history of America." Below this appeared an update of events in the Johnson case titled "All White People Up, All Black People Down, Policy of U.S. Government." And across from this article a reader could not miss the following announcement: "Little Mator M'Ferrin Becomes Mother in the Cook County Hospital Wednesday . . . Youthful Mother Passes Ordeal Successfully."[21]

Through the selection and arrangement of stories on the front page, the *Defender's* editor sought to knit an intricate web connecting the Mann Act, Jack Johnson's prosecution for trafficking in white women, and Mator McFerrin's case. The newspaper pushed readers to see McFerrin's case as one episode in a larger battle. By bringing McFerrin's case to light and by inserting her rape at the hands of a white man into national debates about endangered womanhood, the *Defender* laid bare the racialism at the center of white slavery discourse. In appealing to the race loyalty of black men and women, the newspaper challenged its readers to take up McFerrin's cause as a racial duty. In coming to her aid, black Chicagoans would combat black women's exclusion from the moral indignation and legal protection of the state.

Negroes Uphold Mann Act

who are importing colored women into the North from the South and buying homes for them, and living with them, is it said, in the summer, is this not a violation of the Mann Act? Information can be given of such persons to the government by phone or letter, and the culprits can be brought to justice and a step to save our young women will be made for the first time in the history of America. Hot Springs, Arkansas, should be watched in this particular as it is said is a hotbed of such filth. Revenge is sweet and the Mann Act affords the only hope for the saving of our girls from the whites who would use them for immoral purposes. See to it then that your surroundings are not contaminated by women of this stripe here in the North.

ALL WHITE PEOPLE UP
ALL BLACK PEOPLE DOWN
POLICY OF U. S. GOVERNMENT

6.2 Front page of the *Chicago Defender*, November 16, 1912. Courtesy of the *Chicago Defender*.

As the *Defender* hoped, McFerrin's story inspired considerable outrage among Chicago's black leadership, especially after the birth of her son, Clarence. To financially assist the young mother, the editor established the Mator McFerrin Relief Fund. Individuals, churches, hotel employees, railroad men, and the prestigious North Shore Men's Club offered their financial assistance to "little Mator."[22] Contributions came from as far as Mackinaw City, Michigan, and Nelson, British Columbia. Joining the fund-raising efforts of the *Defender*, the W. T. Jackson Music School held a benefit concert for McFerrin and her son. Even those unable to give money found ways to lend support. The young girl's plight so touched Mrs. John Freehart that she provided baby Clarence with a complete wardrobe of twenty-two handmade garments.[23]

McFerrin's supporters knew that the new mother desperately needed material assistance. But ensuring the just outcome of the impending court battle against Chaplin was equally, if not more, pressing in the eyes of those who rallied to McFerrin's defense. "Justice," the *Defender* asserted, "is the wish of the people." The newspaper assured it readers that, with its vigilance, the "white brute" would be given "the severest punishment of the law."[24]

The initial legal attack on Frank Chaplin commenced swiftly; but the juvenile court, not her newfound champions, prosecuted the case against McFerrin's assailant. On November 25, less than two weeks after McFerrin gave birth to Clarence, Chaplin was found guilty of bastardy in the Court of Domestic Relations. Given the *Defender*'s insistence that Chaplin had sexually assaulted the young girl, it is surprising that the juvenile court did not seek his prosecution on the charge of rape. Most likely, juvenile court officers in charge of McFerrin's case believed that, even if she had been raped, the young mother most urgently needed ongoing financial support for Clarence. Furthermore, officers of the juvenile court may not have been fully convinced that Chaplin raped McFerrin. If the charge of bastardy did not vindicate McFerrin's rape claim, Chaplin's conviction nevertheless established that he had sexual relations with the underage girl and proved his responsibility for the newborn baby. This represented no small victory for a young black girl whose claim of sexual violation could easily have been dismissed by an unsympathetic white judge. The advocacy of the juvenile court no doubt bolstered McFerrin's credibility in the eyes of the judge.

Nevertheless, in the opinion of her new friends the support of the juvenile court proved insufficient. Answering McFerrin's desperate call to "women of my race," many of Chicago's African American clubwomen came out in full force to show their support during her appearance before the Court of Domestic Relations. The "pathetic" court scene, the *Defender* reported, featured "a mere child clad in clothes of cheap material and make, almost . . . pleading for justice" from the judge. McFerrin did not face the judge alone, however. "Members of the unfortunate girl's race were out in large number," the *Defender* reported. "The majority of them were women, representing the various women's clubs that

have interested themselves in the case."[25] Behind McFerrin as she testified and holding baby Clarence sat Joanna Snowden, a volunteer probation officer of the juvenile court and a prominent woman in the City
Federation of Colored Women's Clubs.[26] Although the *Defender* had in-
augurated the crusade for McFerrin's honor, on the day of her trial the
Chicago colored women's clubs were the most visible champions of the
young girl's innocence. The presence of these women in the courtroom
served two main purposes. First, they hoped to give McFerrin moral
support as she laid bare "a part of her young life that was repulsive to
her and her hearers." Perhaps more importantly, although these "rep-
resentative women" offered no testimony on McFerrin's behalf, their
presence served to frame Chaplin's assault as both a violation of an innocent child and an affront to respectable black womanhood. After the
trial Snowden and Mrs. Lou Ella Young, president of the T. E. Butler Art
Club and officer in the City Federation of Colored Women's Clubs, escorted McFerrin out of the courtroom.

The clubwomen's attentiveness to McFerrin did not end with the
trial. Upon securing her release from Cook County Hospital, Snowden
and Young found a comfortable home for McFerrin and Clarence on
the South Side. If Chicago's clubwomen felt vindicated at the trial's outcome, Chaplin's bastardy conviction did not satisfy their call for justice.
Nor did the *Defender* rest in its advocacy of McFerrin's case. Weeks before McFerrin's case appeared before the Court of Domestic Relations,
representatives from the paper and from the Men's Protective Association endeavored to secure "the ablest lawyers of the race, who will
see that the full extent of the law is given the scoundrel."[27] However,
clubwomen, not the men's organization, took the case further. In its
November 31 meeting the City Federation of Colored Women's Clubs
engaged the services of Edward Alexander, a prominent black attorney,
this time to prosecute Chaplin on the charge of rape. In its December 7
issue the *Defender* proclaimed, "Justice for the girl is assured, declare the
attorneys and clubs interested."[28]

Unfortunately, evidence of further legal action against Frank Chaplin has not survived in either extant newspaper or court records.[29] Indeed, except for a December 21 article gleefully announcing that "Mator McFerrin and Baby Clarence Will Hang Up Stockings in Anticipation
of a Visit from Dear Old Santa," the *Defender*'s coverage of Mator Mc-
Ferrin's story ends rather abruptly. Her departure from the pages of
the newspaper was as sudden as her appearance six weeks earlier, and
equally revealing. In its first article on McFerrin, the *Defender* recruited
its readers to the cause of a black girl, abused, pregnant, and aban-

doned; but in the ensuing weeks it became clear that the *Defender* had recruited McFerrin herself to help subvert existing white discourses that vilified the sexual morality of black women and girls. That the newspaper ended its fight for McFerrin after Chaplin's bastardy conviction seems curious, since its coverage focused not only on her pregnancy but also on her rape by a white man and on the institutional neglect that made her defilement possible. Yet just as the editor's decision to champion McFerrin's cause points to the immediate circumstances that made its intervention necessary—the eruption of the Jack Johnson episode and the strengthening hold of the image of the "white slave" over anti-vice reform activity in Chicago—the decision to relinquish its position as McFerrin's leading advocate highlights the limits of the *Defender's* designs on McFerrin's story. While genuine concern for the girl's welfare spurred the *Defender's* support, this concern eventually took a backseat to the larger and intertwined goals of proving black women's sexual vulnerability, inserting black women and girls into white slavery debate, and exposing white men's sexual depravity.

"Reformation for These Beautiful Creatures of God"

Though designed to challenge the legal attack on Jack Johnson, the exposure of Mator McFerrin's plight did not shame federal or local officials into backing away from their support of the morally questionable Lucille Cameron and Belle Schreiber. In May 1913 Johnson was convicted of violating the Mann Act. Nor did the crusade for McFerrin spur city officials to examine their disregard for the violation of black girls. To the frustration of black leaders, the sexual victimization of young black girls remained beyond the purview of most of the city's anti-vice crusaders. Yet McFerrin's story nevertheless galvanized Chicago's black leaders as they strove to formulate a response to the growing problem of prostitution within the expanding Black Belt.

Members of the T. E. Butler Art Club were so moved by the "agonizing tones" of the *Defender's* coverage of McFerrin's story that they redirected their "attention from the work we had organized to do to that of helping little Mator McFerrin." One visit to the child in Cook County Hospital gave club members, in the words of club president Lou Ella Young, "new inspiration to seek out and lift up the fallen."[30] Given the outlines of McFerrin's case as so strenuously presented by the *Defender*, McFerrin's "fall" did not result from her own misguided actions. Yet the specter of the fallen black women working in Chicago's sex industry spurred McFerrin's newfound protectors to wage a battle on the girl's behalf. Indeed, concern about African American women's involvement in the local sex trade drove the *Defender* and McFerrin's other advocates to drape McFerrin in a cloak of innocence and to surround her with maternal and paternal protection. As they endeavored to take on the racial exclusivity of white slavery discourse, most middle-class proponents of respectability sought also to undermine the dominant beliefs about black women's sexuality. For most this precluded dealing with the fallen women working in Black Belt resorts and living in neighborhood apartments.

Chicago's black leaders could not ignore the growing problem of black prostitution, however. Clubwomen had long been aware of the dangers that led young women into the sex trade. In 1904 active local clubwoman Fannie Barrier Williams warned of the "dangers of city life and well dressed idleness" that lured young city women away from the path of propriety. To be sure, engaging in prostitution was just one way that a young woman could succumb to the traps of city living. Precocious sexual activity could lead a girl "on the downward path" ending not in prostitution but in "the forced marriage."[31] However, the growing specter of neighborhood vice engendered the most pained debates about the moral safety of young black women living in the city. Such fears underlay schemes designed to neutralize the dangers facing vulnerable black girls migrating to the city.

Concerned Black Belt residents developed a variety of programs and institutions to protect and uplift young neighborhood girls. In 1903 Mrs. Fannie Ralston formed the Colored Women's Twentieth Century Penny Club. The aim of the club was to "aggregate finances" to build a home for black women unable to afford Chicago rents. Ralston warned readers of the *Broad Ax* that the pool of unprotected colored women served as prey for unscrupulous men and women. While the penny contributions would come primarily from club members, she urged men reading the *Broad Ax* to contribute to the fund as well. She admonished male readers to "visit the slums and see if you, as wealthy men, are not spiritually advised to build a home of reformation for these beautiful creatures of God which, by discouragement and hardship has driven them" to lives of shame.[32] In the attempt to address the needs of women who for whatever reason had already turned to the sex trade, Ralston's Penny Club project was uncommon. Most clubwomen worked for the prevention of prostitution and the alleviation of conditions that surrounded still "innocent" young black women.

The Phyllis Wheatley Home exemplified this model of preventative uplift. Established by the Phyllis Wheatley Women's Club, the home opened in 1907 with the goal of helping black women who migrated to the city to find lodging, respectable work, and a wholesome social environment. Clubwomen involved in the creation of the home recognized that "many of these girls were going astray by being led unaware into disreputable homes, entertainment and employment." Yet caretakers of the home admitted only the "the colored girl or woman of good character who come to Chicago for the purposes of advancement."[33] To address the lure of "disreputable entertainment," the Phyllis Wheatley Women's Club led a campaign to shut down saloons close to neighborhood schools. They succeeded in "closing one that was particularly disreputable." The Phyllis Wheatley Women's Club also organized a "Sunshine Club" to keep vulnerable girls aged nine to eighteen occupied and out of harm's way.[34]

The Phyllis Wheatley Home was one of several homes that clubwomen established to protect young women at moral risk in the city. For example, in 1912 Joanna Snowden and Ida Lewis, two women who had been prominent in the care of young Mator McFerrin, participated in an effort to establish a home for dependent girls and young black working women living on the city's West Side. Like many such efforts at institution building within the black community, the home quickly faced financial difficulties. Ongoing uplift work required a steady stream of money. Even the most vigorous fund-raising efforts of Chicago's clubwomen could not sustain the numerous institutions that middle-class black women realized were necessary for the protection of young, vulnerable girls. By 1913 the West Side home no longer existed as an independent institution but had been taken over by the Amanda Smith Home for "colored and dependent children."[35]

The coordinated efforts of the city's clubwomen made the Phyllis Wheatley Home the most successful home for young black women in Chicago. Numerous colored women's clubs, in addition to the Phyllis Wheatley Women's Club, regularly made monetary or in-kind contributions to the home. They also participated in events designed to raise money for the institution.[36] This preexisting network of women's clubs, ready and able to mobilize for the care of dependent girls and unprotected young women, stepped forward in McFerrin's campaign and took over when the *Defender* lost interest in the girl's case.

Chicago's colored women's clubs played a central role in creating and maintaining institutions and running programs for the protection of young black women. Yet individual women also participated in the care and guidance of endangered black girls. Several, like Joanna Snowden, volunteered their time and personal resources to advocate for the interests of young girls and boys appearing before juvenile court.[37] African American clubwomen were well aware of the limited resources available for the care of black children caught in Chicago's jim crow social service system and strove to intervene in the adjudication of cases of dependent or "delinquent" black children. Through their work as probation officers in juvenile court, middle-class black women had their most direct dealings with girls who were in danger of taking or had already taken seriously wrong turns on their way to adulthood.

Though records of their work with young women in houses of prostitution have not survived, most black probation officers probably resembled Elizabeth McDonald, the first black woman probation officer in the country. Using her own financial resources, McDonald proudly claimed that she rescued young girls from "shameful lives" and led many away from immoral Black Belt resorts. On at least one occasion she rescued a girl from a house of prostitution and secured a place for her in one of the few industrial schools that accepted African American girls.[38] In their capacity as probation officers, black clubwomen directly encountered delinquent girls who worked in Chicago's houses of prostitution. Of 2,241 young girls of all races and nationalities brought before juvenile court in the first decade of the twentieth century, between 65 and 80 percent were charged with "offenses involving sexual irregularity," a designation that included promiscuity and prostitution.[39] Juvenile court records do not disclose what proportion of these girls were African American. However, through the apparatus of this court, black women could identify and intervene in the lives of both innocently erring black girls and willfully wayward ones.

Significantly, only as advocates of child welfare did clubwomen directly engage the issue of prostitution. Working through the juvenile court, black women intervened in the lives of young fallen girls at a stage when they were believed to be most receptive to—and most in need of—moral instruction and industrial training. Clubwomen avoided, however, dealing with adult fallen women. The matrons of homes specifically designed to provide safe and wholesome living spaces for adult women trying to avoid immoral surroundings generally refused admittance to known prostitutes. By excluding black prostitutes, matrons of women's homes could view their inmates as innocents requiring their protection.

In their work as probation officers and as supporters of homes for women and girls, black clubwomen revealed their ideas about prostitution. The sources of commercial sex included an immoral urban environment; neglectful parents; a juvenile court system that failed to provide adequate services for black boys and girls; a municipal government that refused to provide proper recreational facilities for Black Belt youth; and unscrupulous white and black men who preyed on the morally unformed colored girl. As they worked to tackle these causes of prostitution, middle-class women also revealed an inability, or perhaps a refusal, to address a fundamental fact: the overwhelming majority of women working in Black Belt houses, cabarets, buffet flats, and after-hours clubs were not naive girls but grown women in their twenties and thirties who worked in prostitution because they lacked other opportunities.

Working on the moral front, middle-class women rarely focused their attention on the reasons that adult black women turned to prostitution. Homes for working women did provide inexpensive and safe housing, yet too few existed to answer the housing needs of the growing numbers of independently living working women in Chicago's Black Belt. Nor could the model of respectability offered in homes for working women or in recreational activities for girls and women sponsored by colored women's clubs offer an adequate response to all women struggling to find employment in the city.

One prominent clubwoman came close to acknowledging why some women and girls chose prostitution as a means of making money in Chicago. Writing in 1920 when World War I–era migrations had swelled the city's black population, Irene McCoy Gaines penned "A Plea for Our Girls." "The white girl," Gaines attested, "is given the opportunity to choose her employment from all the trades, crafts, arts and professions." Yet "the Colored girl is almost without employment, except of the most menial sort, and receives less protection from public opinion than from the law." This appeal, printed in the *Defender*, echoed the charge central to the defense of Mator McFerrin—that black girls were victims of the hostility of local whites and the failure of municipal and state authorities to protect their interests. Though Gaines pinpointed the economic, legal, and social impediments to the progress of "the potential mother of the race," she ended her plea with a rather general admonition to black men and women to attend to the needs of the colored girl. In a later, slightly altered draft of this plea addressed to members of the YWCA, she turned to a topic that occupied many black reformers in the 1910s and 1920s: the need for "constructive, wholesome recreation for young women."[40]

The *Defender* most forthrightly acknowledged the connection that existed between the conditions of black women's employment and the participation of so many in the sex trade. Writing in response to a state-sponsored investigation of vice conditions in Illinois that blamed, among other things, the immoral environment of the factory for white women's entrance into prostitution, the paper argued:

Though the shops and factories are closed to [the colored working women of this state], there are thousands in domestic service whose moral condition is as important and as much menaced by low wages as those in the so-called industries of the state. In fact in many instances they are far worse off, being in the camp of the enemy. And yet what are they to do? A living must be made at any cost, they are barred from the stores, factories, mills, etc., on account of their color, and it seems the bars are being built higher and higher each day. Is it to be wondered at that they constitute an ever increasing class from whose ranks the vice centers of the state are constantly recruiting their victims?[41]

Obliquely referring to white men's sexual abuse of black women whom they employed to work in their homes, the *Defender* crafted an argument about the moral consequences of black women's economic subjection. In highlighting black women's status as domestic workers, the *Defender* put forth an argument about prostitution that never again appeared in its pages, nor in its competitor the *Broad Ax*.

Nor would middle-class clubwomen publicly entertain the notion that some women turned to prostitution out of economic necessity. Addressing the financial pressures that led some black women to see sex work as an alternative to service work fell beyond the scope of the discourse of respectability. Rather, through industrial training programs and classes in the domestic arts, black clubwomen concentrated much of their anti-vice efforts on making domestic service a reputable employment for working black women.[42] Furthermore, middle-class black women viewed prostitution as the sad outcome of the lack of moral guardianship. Unable to understand sex work outside a moral framework, clubwomen did not speak to the concrete issue facing individual working-class and poor black women: the need for survival in a hostile urban economy.

Beyond the purview of clubwomen's uplift efforts, black women who ran buffet flats, worked in disreputable cafés, or looked for trade along Thirty-Ninth and Forty-Seventh streets served as unsightly warnings that spurred middle-class black women into action to protect those not yet fallen. Mator McFerrin was a perfect recipient of the focused attention of Chicago clubwomen who publicly lamented the gauntlet of dangers facing young women in the Black Belt. Though herself blameless, McFerrin's desperate circumstances could easily have led her to seek help in the wrong places. McFerrin, then, represented all the poor colored girls who faced similar circumstances of neglect and violation. Without the protective advocacy of clubwomen or the aggressive intervention of white anti-vice crusaders, these girls formed a sad gallery of wasted potential as they plied their trade along Thirty-Ninth and Forty-Seventh streets.

"The Lust of White Men"

Though the *Defender* abruptly ended its crusade on Mator McFerrin's behalf, it continued to point out the hypocrisy at the heart of white slavery discourse. In September 1913 the paper reprinted a one-sentence report that originally appeared in the *Chicago Record-Herald*. In a bold type that took up nearly as much space as the story it announced, the headline read: "Jack Johnson Juror Violates Mann Act."[43] Few details were given in the snippet that followed, though it appears that the woman transported from Chicago to California for "immoral purposes" was white. But then again, details were not necessary. The headline said it all. White men—in fact, the very ones who appointed themselves protectors of white women's virtue—presented as much a danger to white womanhood as they had accused Jack Johnson of being. Not only did lecherous white men pose a danger to black women, but they imperiled women of their own race. The exposure of this duplicity no doubt gave the *Defender*'s editor and the paper's readers a certain degree of satisfaction; it did not, however, get at what readers believed to be the real problem, one that remained unuttered in the white papers: white men's continuing sexual assaults of black women and girls.

The *Defender* was not alone in alerting black Chicagoans to the racial limits of the swirling white slavery debate. In the midst of Jack Johnson's legal ordeal, the *Broad Ax*, in somewhat-subdued tones, posed the question: "If the [white slave traffic] law is for justice to all then why not term it the 'female slave traffic'?"[44] A few weeks after the boxer's 1913 conviction, the *Broad Ax* printed a story that more forcefully addressed the stakes for black men and women in the white slavery debates: "Convicted under Mann Act. White Man and Negro Woman." The story, which had initially appeared in a St. Paul, Minnesota, newspaper, gave an account of the conviction of a white man and a black brothel keeper for transporting Frankie Allen, a black woman, from Chicago to St. Paul to work in the woman's house of prostitution. The report concluded with a comment that must have echoed the sentiments of *Broad Ax* readers: "[A f]ew more convictions and this traffic will be stopped among Negro women, who feel that they were on account of color immune from this law."[45] In this exceptional case—few white judges and juries convicted white men for "trafficking" in black women[46]—a white man was found guilty of preying on black womanhood. That a black woman from Chicago had been transported across state lines to work in a house of prostitution only amplified the relevance of the case for Chicago readers. Interestingly, the article made no remark about the black woman, who was also convicted for illegally transporting Frankie Allen across state lines.

As it had in the *Defender*, the Jack Johnson controversy suffused the ways that the *Broad Ax* interpreted prostitution for its readers. However, an incident occurring in September 1913 revealed that even after the uproar over Johnson had subsided and the boxer had fled to Paris to escape imprisonment, black leaders continued to fight against Black Belt vice by seeking justice against white men who sexually assaulted black women and girls. A raid of a notorious neighborhood buffet flat provided the *Defender* with disturbing evidence that lecherous white men went to great lengths to satisfy their lust for innocent black girls. Chicago police officers raided a flat located at Thirty-Second and Wabash where they found sixteen young black women and sixteen white men who, the *Defender* emphasized, were between the ages of twenty-five and forty-five. "Each of these innocent girls was between the ages of fourteen and sixteen," the reporter stated. The writer went on to make clear that the arrested girls were "under the age of consent." The house, according to the report, had long been "a mecca for white men to assault colored girls at the tender age, and the crimes committed there became so numerous and dastardly that the police made the raid." Yet as sensational as the raid was and as shocking its findings, "not a reporter for the white dailies appeared on the scene nor a line the next day in the papers." In the aftermath of the wave of anti-vice activity that in the previous year had shut down the Levee and had dominated the front pages of Chicago's white newspapers, the reporter found the deliberate inattention to what he described as the worst vice conditions in the Black Belt especially enraging. Reiterating the charge that shaped many black Chicagoans' reactions to the city's anti-prostitution campaign, the *Defender* inveighed: "Had it been white girls and colored men there would have been glaring headlines in every daily paper and sympathy would have gone out toward the 'white angels.' But when it comes to colored girls, they put the lid on the press and close their eyes to the lust of white men."[47]

In all of these cases Chicago's black press characterized the Black Belt sex trade as a problem with very clear and narrow outlines: white men regularly and without obstruction made their way into the Black Belt to exploit black girls. As in the McFerrin case, framing the issue of prostitution as a problem caused by lustful white men provided community spokespersons with a wedge into anti-vice debates from which white anti-vice crusaders had excluded them. In the case of the raided Wabash Avenue buffet flat, white men's depredations and black girls' innocence could not be ignored, even by usually derelict city authorities. In exposing such blatant cases of abuse, the *Defender* and the *Broad Ax* hoped to shame reformers and the police into protecting "race girls." Yet expanding the scope of Chicago's vice prevention drive was only one goal of black leaders determined to highlight the vulnerability of black girls and expose the activities of white men. A multilayered politics developed to designate white men as the source of the community's prostitution problem and black girls as their victims.

First, through this focus journalists and editors hoped to direct the gaze of readers and city officials away from black women involved in the neighborhood sex trade, real-life embodiments of white stereotypes of the race's sexual immorality. In the place of the sinful, inveterate prostitute, newspaper writers presented the image of the helpless black girl entangled in a system of sexual slavery from which she could find no escape on her own. In keeping this pitiable figure at the forefront of anti-prostitution discussions, black leaders engaged in an ingenious balancing act. On the one hand, at the height of the city's anti-vice drive, black leaders felt compelled to acknowledge the existence of prostitution within the Black Belt. On the other hand, the actions of the black prostitutes who walked neighborhood streets, beckoned from flat windows, or circulated in saloons and cabarets presented serious obstacles to inclusion in an anti-vice rhetoric based on the protection of the innocent and vulnerable. By focusing on black girls and young women under the age of eighteen—"girls" whom the law deemed unable to voice consent—newspaper writers conveniently recharacterized neighborhood prostitution. In doing so, they sidestepped the politically tricky issues of black *women* in prostitution and black women's *consent* to their own sexual servitude. Like the contemporaneous uplift work of black clubwomen, the newspapers' preoccupation with young, vulnerable women avoided bringing to view the majority of African American prostitutes, who for financial reasons sought refuge in the Black Belt's growing sex economy.

Second, in addition to eliding black women prostitutes in their emerging anti-vice campaign, black spokespersons simultaneously deployed the distressing image of an invading army of lustful white men. Descriptions of the predatory behavior of white men further obscured the agency of black women. Yet the focus on the white patrons of neighborhood prostitutes served another function as well. In the process of constructing the portrait of commercial sex in the Black Belt as an economy fueled by the illicit desires of white men, black leaders like the *Defender*'s Robert Abbott and the *Broad Ax*'s Julius Taylor defined prostitution as a system of coercion and entrapment that, significantly, emanated from outside the community.[48] Not only were black girls blameless in their moral decline, but the community at large held little direct responsibility for the flourishing of the Black Belt sex trade. Indeed, it too fell victim to the steady influx of white male pleasure-seekers.

Together, the intertwined images of the innocent race girl and the besieged Black Belt provided ammunition in black leaders' battle to prove the race's respectability and to define the community's worthiness for inclusion in the city's cleanup campaigns. More broadly, black leaders hoped these images would overcome prevailing white notions of the race's sexual immorality, a notion that the neighborhood sex trade seemed to substantiate.

Faced with this conundrum, middle-class men and women engaged in the struggle for sexual respectability in complementary ways. For black women working through Chicago's women's clubs, a young woman's respectability required sexual purity or, in its absence, evidence of blamelessness for her sexual or moral misstep. Clubwomen's efforts to guide promising young women along the path of sexual rectitude and to uplift the nearly fallen attest to a general discomfort with black women's sexual, as well as economic, agency. For black men, establishing sexual respectability required that they also take a stance regarding the protection of black girls. Yet their construction of their own respectability also included a more direct offensive, at least on paper, against white male debauchees. The assault on white men's sexual license was only partially a reaction to existing prostitution conditions in the Black Belt. This attack arose as well from middle-class black men's need to retaliate against the historical sexual privileges of white manhood. "White slavery," the *Defender* editorialized, "is nothing compared with the black slavery which white men have insidiously practiced upon the Negro race, leaving a trail of bastardy from the waters of Dan to the gulf of Beersheba. . . . And the emancipation of the race did not stop it either."[49]

Significantly, in fastening the public's attention to the image of the white scoundrel, middle-class black men, in particular the editors of the city's leading black papers, enforced a silence that was central to the construction of black male respectability. Public outcries against commercialized sex in the Black Belt rarely targeted African American men. Neither as customers nor as lustful manipulators did they appear in discussions of prostitution conditions plaguing the community. This silence proved as significant as the suppression of the image of the consenting black prostitute. The invisibility of black men—who provided an increasingly important source of employment for neighborhood sex workers after 1900 and who continued to provide black prostitutes with clientele—further underscored the argument that white men visited the moral plague of prostitution upon the Black Belt.

Certainly exceptions to this trend existed. The *Broad Ax*'s Julius Taylor had early on tried to draw attention to the role that certain black saloon keepers and café owners played in the growth of the Black Belt sex trade. On several occasions he had criticized "Bob Motts' notorious joint, where many young girls are led to the brink of ruin in each year." On other occasions he set his sights on Pony Moore's ventures. He blamed Moore for operating a "place of sin" where "white men slip in and out . . . in the dark hours of the night" and "look upon all colored women as wenches." He reserved his sharpest censure for "the colored men who hang around [Moore's place] and spend their money there, which they need to support their families, on cheap or common white women that no decent man would wipe his feet on." Taylor also criticized church leaders who, he lamented, refused to come out strongly against leaders of commercialized vice in the Black Belt.[50] By 1912, though, the vituperative Taylor had toned down his critique of black leisure entrepreneurs and other internal sources of Black Belt prostitution. His paper joined the *Defender* in emphasizing the external origins of the threats to community morality.

The erasure of the black male figure from the Black Belt sex trade gave middle-class black men the moral footing from which they could level an attack on white male "viciousness." This deletion also gave black men the basis for asserting their patriarchal right to community leadership. In the years following the anti-vice crusades and the official closing of the Levee, black men would repeatedly invoke this right.

"Guard against the Unlawful Invasions"

Together, the interlocking themes of black women's sexual vulnerability, white men's responsibility, and black men's invisibility constituted a formulation of the Black Belt's prostitution problem that many leaders hoped would undermine white Chicagoans' understanding of the issue. Moreover, this formulation could both force the inclusion of black women in contemporary debates about endangered womanhood and prop up black middle-class male respectability. These underlying goals continued to shape black anti-vice rhetoric well into the 1920s. Yet the specific elements of this rhetoric would change in the years after the closing of the Twenty-Second Street Levee.

Just as the convergence of the events surrounding Jack Johnson's trial and Mator McFerrin's case drew blacks into the local white slavery debate, the closing of the red-light district drew a range of usually reticent community leaders into a public discussion of the neighborhood's vice conditions. Faced with the closing of the segregated sex district, African American leaders articulated an even more forceful condemnation of white anti-vice activities. They argued that the city's war against the "social evil" not only left black women and girls unprotected but in fact posed a serious threat to the moral outlines of the black community as a whole.

The *Defender* articulated the urgency of the state of affairs brought on by State's Attorney Wayman's drive against Levee resorts:

The present vice crusade in this city is of considerable moment to its Negro citizens. After a week or more of spectacular acting on the part of the state's attorney's office, the many arrests by the police and special detectives, the acting of the various reform associations and the daily newspaper publicity of the matter has only resulted in scattering the denizens of the red light district and menacing the residence districts of the race.[51]

In the view of the *Defender*, the official closing of the red-light district had brought a new threat to Chicago's black community. Middle-class blacks feared that, with the end of segregated prostitution, the South Side sex trade would find a new home in the Black Belt. Again, the threat was external, resulting from the actions of the state's attorney, city police, white reform agencies, and the city's white press. And, indeed, as these agencies clamored to clean up the city, their actions had dire consequences for the moral geography of the black community.

In vocalizing fears about potential repercussions of the city's new anti-prostitution crusade, the *Defender* revealed that community members had, albeit with some reservations, accepted the city's former prostitution policies. Since moving to areas south of Twenty-Second Street, many black residents had relied on the municipal policing of the boundaries that separated the segregated red-light district from the growing black community. Though concerned about the ability of the police to contain the spread of prostitution and other illicit enterprises, one minister announced that, like many community leaders, he was "a firm believer in the segregation of vice." The *Defender* also supported the containment of vice, asserting that, in regard to "the inmates of the various Red Light Palaces," the goal of "both police officers and reformers" should be to "keep them from roaming."[52] The desire to protect the moral outlines of the community led many who were otherwise morally opposed to the sex trade to nonetheless embrace a municipal policy that promised to patrol the boundary separating the Black Belt from the Twenty-Second Street Levee. Years after the closing of the Levee, black Chicagoans continued to express support for a segregated prostitution district. Speaking to an interviewer for the Chicago Commission on Race Relations, an embalmer worried that, because vicious elements could roam free throughout the Black Belt, "his wife, who is frequently obliged to return home late at night, is subjected to insults from men in the neighborhood."[53]

Yet even supporters of a segregated sex district did not always have faith in the city's ability to confine the sex trade to red-light district limits. In 1907 the Reverend W. S. Braddon of Berean Baptist Church, located at Forty-Eighth and Dearborn, sounded early warnings about the fragility of the borders securing the segregated red-light district. In that year Chicago's chief of police announced the city's new commitment to limit sexual commerce to the area enclosed by Wabash Avenue, Clark Street, Eighteenth Street, and Twenty-Second Street. Reverend Braddon, however, expressed his doubts. "To my mind or to the mind of any one who has taken the time to study the under element of the South Side this boundary is wholly inadequate and, it will be only a comparatively short time, say two or three years before the boundary will be broadened" until it reached as far south as Thirtieth Street. In the meantime, Braddon warned, the community would be forced to endure the indignities of a tolerated vice district distressingly close to their homes. Living in morally intolerable conditions had already forced black Chicagoans to "leave old Fourth avenue" near the nineteenth-century Levee, with its abundance of "vice and crime." Ultimately, Braddon warned, the insufficiency of the red-light boundaries and the inability of city authorities to prevent incursions into respectable areas would disrupt nearby black communities, as well as destabilize established churches in the northern section of the Black Belt. All church leaders and concerned churchgoers, Braddon ominously predicted, "must sooner or later awake to the fact that the present and ultimate boundary lines of the Red Light district has [*sic*] and will completely change . . . the religious geography of the South Side." Certain that the vice landscape would soon spill across the boundary lines drawn by city officials, Braddon encouraged community members to build for the future and invest in churches as far away from the red-light district as possible.[54]

Braddon's church, at the southern edge of black settlement, had much to gain from this call to look southward. Not all leaders were so calculating about the inevitable dismantling of the barrier protecting Black Belt residents. Although most similarly feared the southward creep of the red-light district borders, many African American leaders believed that, short of the mass relocation of community members to other sections of the city, segregation provided the best safeguard against the wholesale infiltration of vice in black neighborhoods.

The dramatic reversal of municipal vice policies in 1912 forced black leaders to reformulate their analysis of the neighborhood's prostitution problem and to rethink their own anti-vice strategies. If in the first decade of the twentieth century silence about black men's and women's active participation in the Black Belt sex trade had been a tactical maneuver designed to deny white Chicagoans evidence of the race's moral failings, the closing of the red-light district presented a new set of circumstances requiring a new response from black leaders.

"Now," the *Defender* urged its readers, "there must be a determined and combined effort on the part of the race in this present moment against the 'Red-lighters' or you will awaken some morning to find that your next-door neighbor is the famous 'Miss X,' who formerly had a pretentious establishment around or about 21st and Armour or Dearborn Street."[55] Black churches seemed prepared to answer this call. On Sunday, October 13, in the midst of Wayman's raids, churches throughout the Black Belt deliberated about the implications of the closings of Levee brothels for their congregations and their neighborhoods. The pastor of Bethel A.M.E (located at Thirtieth and Dearborn in 1912) exhorted his congregants to "stand as a mighty front and guard against the unlawful invasions." Community members tried in various ways to prevent the tide of "red light denizens" from sweeping over the Black Belt.[56] Residents frequently called police officers to quiet or expel particularly disorderly neighbors. Through their complaints, the *Defender* reported, "residents of the better residence districts" were sometimes able to "rout" many "undesirables." Their efforts were not always effectual, however. One *Daily News* reporter noted that the "protests of colored families against the painted women in their neighborhood, the midnight honking of automobiles, the loud profanity and vulgarity are usually ignored by the police."[57]

The reluctance of police officers to clean up the Black Belt made it clear to community observers that their desires for a wholesome neighborhood flew in the face of the plans of city officials to disband the Levee. Leaders quickly pointed out that the troubles that descended on the Black Belt after the district's closing had been initiated by the joint efforts of white reform organizations, the state's attorney's office, the city government, and a police force that demonstrated little concern about the consequences of the end of vice segregation for the "residence districts of the race." In the martial terms that male leaders frequently adopted to describe the Black Belt as a community under attack, the *Defender* encouraged women's clubs and real estate dealers to "go to the front for the race" and to confront "these officials and reformers who are making such a racket at this time."[58] Faced with the neglect of municipal authorities and the influx of "red lighters," the black press and church leaders, as well as clubwomen, framed the growing sex trade in the Black Belt as an external threat to the community's moral well-being and geographical integrity.

In shining the spotlight on the city's complicity in the unleashing of sexual depravity on a beleaguered black neighborhood, race leaders employed a strategy that both acknowledged the neighborhood's growing sex economy and affirmed the black community's sexual respectability. Yet focusing attention on the unwelcome movement of the sex economy into community territory was not merely a rhetorical strategy. Despite residents' various efforts to prevent the influx of disreputable elements, black South Siders witnessed a gradual transformation in the shape of sexual commerce in the Black Belt in the years following the Levee's closing.

Within months of the raids on the Levee, white saloon and brothel keepers who had prospered in the Levee sought out new opportunities in other parts of the city. Some Levee proprietors moved to sections of the North Side, such as the bright-light area that had existed on North Clark Street since the turn of the century. Others found cover in the rooming house districts north and west of downtown.[59] But, as African American community leaders had feared, many Levee entrepreneurs moved into the Black Belt.

The black South Side appeared inviting to white leisure and sex entrepreneurs for several reasons. With a major transportation artery at its center—the State Street Stroll—the Black Belt was easily accessible to visitors from other parts of the city. With its saloons, cafés, and buffet

flats, the neighborhood already had a dense network of nightlife institutions with which white establishments could easily intermingle.
Perhaps the most attractive feature of the Black Belt was that the most
active anti-vice reform agencies—the Committee of Fifteen and the Juvenile Protective Association—had yet to concern themselves with the
sex trade there. Preoccupied with keeping Levee resorts closed and with
patrolling establishments in other parts of the city that they believed
led white girls down "the road to destruction," these and other reform
organizations largely ignored prostitution in the Black Belt.[60]

White sex enterprises began to move into the Black Belt after 1912,
spurring a correspondent for the *Indianapolis Freeman*, a black weekly
paper with a regional focus, to warn readers that "a white sporting element planned to form a red light district within a boundary starting
from 31st street and the elevated railroad station east to Cottage Grove
avenue, invading the territory south of 31st street. . . . The red light
district dive keepers are fostering their way south."[61] Fears of an impending white vice invasion escalated with each opening of a nightclub
and each discovery of an assignation house catering to white men and
women. Although white sex entrepreneurs indeed relocated businesses
to the Black Belt after 1912, the flow of white nightclubs and houses of
prostitution to the area increased considerably in the years after 1915,
when World War I–era black migration to the city swelled the neighborhood. Ten years after the closing of the Levee, the *Chicago Whip*, another black weekly, proclaimed that "the southside will soon be the real
redlight district of the city if houses of prostitution continue to increase
within its limits."[62]

White houses of prostitution, buffet flats, and disorderly saloons
popped up on the major thoroughfares and along the side streets of
the Black Belt. As they had in the Levee, many of these resorts catered
exclusively to white patrons. The *Chicago Whip* complained that the
women working in Black Belt houses of prostitution "are almost all
white and they cater almost exclusively to white men." However, to the
shame of many Black Belt leaders, a growing number of white-owned
resorts entertained a mixed clientele. "Here and there," one *Whip* reporter remarked, "we find one [house of prostitution] which invites any
and all who have two or three dollars."[63] Along with concern about the
increasing number of interracial houses of prostitution, community
leaders voiced distress about interracial nightclubs known as black-and-
tans.[64] Many believed that such places exposed unsuspecting black girls
to the unrestrained lusts of white men and pushed them down the road
to destruction. They shared this concern with white reformers, who re-

served some of their strongest criticism for interracial leisure resorts in the Black Belt.

The Black Belt became one of several urban playgrounds in which largely middle-class white men and women sought out sexual excitement. The Black Belt also became an important workplace for white sex workers. In early-twentieth-century America, slumming was a ritual of urban exploration in which white men and women sought out excitement, entertainment, and release from the strictures of a Victorian sexual morality.[65] Slumming expeditions to areas of black residence were not new, but as black South Siders knew too well, they increased in frequency in the late 1910s. In exploring the limits of modern sexuality in sections of the city believed to be exotic and governed by a "foreign" or "primitive" moral code, white Chicagoans of means engaged in a leisure practice based on the construction and commercialization of opposing moral regions within the urban landscape. The practice of slumming, then, sexualized not only the leisure institutions within the Black Belt but all of black community space.

For respectable Black Belt residents, what appeared to be the wholesale transplanting of white people's sexual immorality to the landscape of African American homes, churches, schools, and reputable businesses represented both a moral affront and a spatial violation. To the frustration of community leaders, this influx demonstrated the race's inability to protect the community's moral boundaries. Resorts of the type that "would not be tolerated in any other part of the city since the old 22nd street levee was broken up" made an unwelcome appearance in the neighborhood. One reporter complained, "White proprietors have brought them into the district and many of them are patronized largely by crowds from other parts of the city. The resorts are forced on the colored people."[66]

Black Belt residents discussed the sexualization of community terrain in dire terms. Departing from the martial imagery often used by the *Defender*, the *Indianapolis Freeman* characterized the influx of white sex resorts, prostitutes, and patrons as "the white plague system." As commonly used, this expression referred to tuberculosis; employed by the *Freeman*, however, it graphically illustrated the external sources of the neighborhood's growing prostitution problem. Resuscitating a familiar argument, the *Freeman* intoned that at the heart of the white plague system was the "mobilization of white men in search of negro women." Yet, the reporter made clear, white women also played a part in the community's new vice outbreak. "White girls, some taking care of colored men and others soliciting them, are frequenting the district after 1 o'clock as an accessory to the plague."[67] As another paper summarized it, "Don't you know that an influx of white hoodlums and vile women now infest your best districts?"[68] By evoking the specter of contagion, black newspapers dramatized the dangers that the infestation of white sexual immorality posed to the moral health of the race.[69] Sadly, journalists noted, the contaminating alliance between vicious white men and women found support in a city government that neither recognized nor protected the rights of Black Belt residents to live in a morally clean community.

In criticizing whites—whether invading businessmen, customers of black prostitutes, or city officials—black leaders continued to refine the anti-vice strategy that had guided the crusade for Mator McFerrin. Just as church leaders, newspaper editors, and black clubwomen refused to admit that women of the race might willingly engage in the neighborhood sex trade, they resisted acknowledging the prostitution that had thrived in the neighborhood before white businessmen and businesswomen shifted their vice operations to the Black Belt. As was the case during the white slavery hysteria, in years after 1915 African Americans formulated an attack on the neighborhood's prostitution problem that highlighted the nefarious agency of white men. Yet they broadened the scope of the attack to include the white prostitutes who set up houses of prostitution near schools and churches, often, race leaders believed, with the purpose of preying on black men. In characterizing prostitution as a system engineered by white men and in defining prostitutes as primarily white women, Black Belt leaders hoped to divert the attention of white onlookers from the black women working in the trade. Other than as targets of the wiles of "vile white women," black men remained invisible in the developing discourse about community prostitution.

Conclusion

For middle-class Black Belt leaders during the era of migration, the struggle against the invasion of white sex entrepreneurs, prostitutes, and nightclubs was inextricably linked to the struggle for racial equality. Their outcries about the imperiled moral health of the black community revealed underlying concerns about the position African Americans would hold in the social and economic life of the city. One reporter drew clear links between the municipal toleration of sexual commerce on the South Side and the lack of power that African Americans wielded in city politics:

From the plague spots of the districts of Chicago in which colored people dwell, where disorderly saloons, "buffet" flats, gambling houses and other symptoms of commercialized vice are tolerated by the police, the chain of politics stretches upward. . . . The colored citizen does not get his share of opportunities and advantages which the city and state offer and has more than his share of the vice and demoralization thrust upon him by white politicians.[70]

Another writer put it succinctly: "White people are cultivating the social evil instead of civil rights."[71]

As waves of black migrants moved to the South Side neighborhood, concern about civil rights, political power, and social acceptance weighed heavily on the minds of race leaders. In attempting to galvanize black public sentiment against the licentious use of community terrain, church leaders, clubwomen, and other prominent community members waged a battle over the meanings that the Black Belt would hold in the civic imagination.[72] While this most often led to a criticism of the hypocrisy of white Chicagoans, it frequently involved looking inward.

"Much to the humiliation of all respectable classes of Colored citizens," one *Defender* reporter stated, many migrants had "given our enemies ground for complaint."[73] To counteract the negative image of blacks in the white mind, neighborhood leaders called upon black men and women to police their own behavior as well as the behavior of others—by limiting their association with disreputable people and by shunning all but the most respectable amusements. The outcome of such self-policing would be the eventual elimination of buffet flats and assignation houses and the curtailment of the spread of vice through the Black Belt. Ultimately, it was hoped, such vigilance would sever the connection that existed between evidence of neighborhood immorality and black Chicagoans' restricted economic and political opportunities in the city.

Black leaders directed their call for self-policing not only at ill-behaved working-class men and women. On at least one occasion, black middle-class men and women held themselves up to harsh scrutiny, exposing their own responsibility for the spread of prostitution in the Black Belt. In 1917 the *Defender* wrote a surprisingly sympathetic article about the black women who had been forced into lives of prostitution by harsh economic circumstances or tricked into the trade by the treachery of men. After describing in detail the cases of a few black women who found themselves before the city's Morals Court, the angry reporter asked readers "Who cares" for the "girls who have fallen by the wayside?" (The Morals Court was established in 1913 by Chief Justice Harry Olson of the Municipal Court of Chicago. This specialized court handled all the cases related to prostitution.)[74] In tones both despairing and accusatory, the writer answered, "Few of our race." In fact, to the apparent irritation of the reporter, white court officials regularly commented on the lack of support black women appearing before the Morals Court on prostitution-related charges received from "clubwomen, ministers, priests," and "sisters of the church." It was a shame, one bailiff stated, that "the Colored people did not do something" to aid the "poor girl of the Race." The reporter concluded: "The clubwomen are asleep; the ministry is asleep."[75]

In calling respectable black men and women into action for the protection of black womanhood, the *Defender* article took a surprising departure from the usual course of its anti-vice arguments. Instead of concentrating on girls below the age of sexual consent caught in the net of prostitution, the reporter focused on women over eighteen who, unlike young women and girls appearing in juvenile court, had no standing from which to appeal to the state for protection. In the eyes of the court, these women were consenting adults. The *Defender's* campaign for the intervention of respectable men and women of the race on behalf of adult prostitutes appearing in court on criminal charges was short-lived. Very soon, the *Defender's* anti-prostitution crusade reverted to its old outlines. Yet this article embodied much more than a momentary shift in the *Defender's* editorial policy toward neighborhood prostitutes. In pointing out the silence of black leaders on the matter of adult prostitutes, the *Defender* piece identified the limits of anti-vice activism among middle-class men and women.

The activities of grown sex workers presented specific problems for proponents of an anti-prostitution discourse based on the image of endangered female innocents. Adult women working in neighborhood assignation houses, buffet flats, and cabarets apparently could not be imagined as victims of white male trickery or lust. Similarly, unlike minors, who by law could always point to an older sexual partner as an assailant, adult prostitutes had no such recourse. In law and in the minds of many Black Belt residents, these women had consented to their downfall. The reach of the maternalist discourse of clubwomen and the paternalist stance of male race leaders did not extend to fully grown women who actively participated in immoral sexual behavior. Beyond moral reform, these women were of little symbolic use in the struggle for racial justice in the city's court system or as a means of uncovering the corrupting influence of white male lust on the Black Belt's moral geography.

The politically strategic discourse of respectability and the equally strategic goals of racial uplift required that the condition of African American prostitute women and their increasing involvement in Chicago's criminal justice system remain beyond the focus of anti-vice activism. The sexual politics of black leaders involved establishing a moral distance between respectable blacks and black prostitutes and between vulnerable black girls and mature black prostitutes. Black leaders' responses to the growth of the Black Belt sex trade remained largely the same into the 1920s. In newspaper articles and in the activities of churches and black women's clubs, middle-class men and women continued to be preoccupied with innocent young girls and with white outsiders who despoiled young womanhood and contaminated the neighborhood.

The argument here is not that black middle-class men and women could have changed the circumstances that kept race women in prostitution if they had directed their attention to the plight of black sex workers. The reasons women entered prostitution, how they made use of the trade, and their choice to remain sex workers were well beyond the scope of the discourse of respectability. Any intervention by Black Belt leaders would likely have been concerned primarily with behavioral modification and moral reformation. Neither goal addressed the economic hardships that black women working as prostitutes struggled to ameliorate. Yet if black middle-class involvement in the struggles of black prostitutes might not have helped these sex workers *out* of the trade, the intervention of the middle class in Chicago's court system might have mitigated black women's difficulties *within* the trade by minimizing their exposure to the harsh penalties municipal judges increasingly meted out to black prostitutes after 1915. However, these were not the goals of Black Belt leadership. With their eyes on the prize of racial advancement and equal involvement in the city's civic life, black leaders ignored the economic and social realities of Chicago's growing sex trade.

As they struggled to cope with the challenges of Chicago's labor market, black women who worked in the sex industry were most likely indifferent to their representation in the political discourse of middle-class blacks. They had more pressing concerns. As the sex trade expanded in the years following massive black migration to Chicago's South Side, black sex workers encountered an array of new obstacles: a sex marketplace that was increasingly in the control of black businessmen, a local policing agenda that increasingly targeted black women as threats to community health, and a court system that vigorously punished black women's violations of sexual propriety and dominant ideas of racial order.

"This Way of Livin'
Sure Is Hard"

"Want to spend $1.00, honey?" BLACK SEX WORKER INVITING A VICE INVESTI-
GATOR TO HER FURNISHED ROOM ON SOUTH DEARBORN STREET, 1923[1]

Annual arrest statistics from the Chicago Police Department present a puzzling portrait of African American
women working in the city's sex economy in the 1920s.
In 1922 African American women accounted for one-third
of all women arrested as inmates of houses of prostitution in Chicago. By 1924 black women consistently composed more than half of all women arrested for working
in a house of prostitution. At the outset of the Great Depression, black women's proportion of all such arrests had
increased to an astounding 78 percent. The same pattern
held for women arrested as keepers of houses of prostitution. In 1922, 28 percent were African American, but in
1930, 70 percent of all women arrested for running a house
of prostitution were black (see tables E.1 and E.2).[2]

Black women not only continued to be overrepresented
among the city's sex workers but their overrepresentation
snowballed in the 1920s. And, contrary to historians' frequent assumption that black women working in the sex
industry were mostly street workers, in Chicago black prostitutes did not labor primarily on the streets. In fact, in
the 1920s considerably more black women were arrested
as inmates of houses of prostitution than for soliciting on
the street. For example, in 1928, 2,183 black women were

Table E.1. Women charged in municipal court as inmates and keepers of houses of ill fame, 1906–1930

	1906	1912	1916	1920	1922	1924	1928	1930
Female inmates of houses of ill fame	849	979	23	70	154	889	4,359	2,559
Native-born white women	604 (71%)[a]	674 (69%)	17 (74%)	56 (80%)	100 (65%)	339 (38%)	2,114 (48%)	542 (21%)
Black women	53 (6%)	211 (22%)	Nil Nil	10 (14%)	49 (32%)	536 (60%)	2,183 (50%)	2,000 (78%)
Female keepers of houses of ill fame	564	296	4	33	83	294	1,417	195
Native-born white women	309 (55%)	139 (47%)	2 (50%)	10 (30%)	55 (66%)	121 (41%)	734 (52%)	55 (28%)
Black women	61 (11%)	98 (33%)	1 (25%)	5 (15%)	23 (28%)	159 (54%)	639 (45%)	136 (70%)

Source: City of Chicago, Police Department of the City of Chicago, Annual Report, 1906, 1912, 1916, 1920, 1922, 1924, 1928, 1930.
[a]Number (and percentage) of native-born white women or black women in the general category. For example, of the 849 total female inmates of houses of ill fame charged in 1906, 604 (71%) were native-born white women.

Table E.2. Women charged in municipal court with streetwalking and soliciting for prostitution, 1906–1930

	1906	1912	1916	1920	1922	1924	1928	1930
Female streetwalkers	2,437	1,439	1,994[a]					
Native-born white women	1,694 (70%)[b]	983 (68%)	1,312 (66%)					
Black women	252 (10%)	266 (19%)	463 (23%)					
Females soliciting for prostitution				151[c]	440	450	670	198
Native-born white women				90 (60%)	259 (59%)	208 (46%)	205 (31%)	113 (57%)
Black women				54 (36%)	162 (37%)	236 (52%)	453 (68%)	83 (42%)

Source: City of Chicago, *Police Department of the City of Chicago, Annual Report*, 1906, 1912, 1916, 1920, 1922, 1924, 1928, 1930.

[a] The last year that streetwalking was listed as a misdemeanor offense in the Chicago municipal code was 1914. The 1,994 figure is for 1914.

[b] Number (and percentage) of native-born white women or black women in the general category. For example, of the 2,437 total female streetwalkers charged in 1906, 1,694 (70%) were native-born white women.

[c] Soliciting for prostitution replaced streetwalking as a misdemeanor offense in the municipal code in 1915.

charged for being inmates, but only 453 black women appeared before the court as streetwalkers. While black women consistently accounted for more than 40 percent of arrested streetwalkers in the 1920s, most African American sex workers appearing in court worked in a "house of ill fame," a term capacious enough to embrace boardinghouses, furnished rooms, apartments, and call flats. (Call flats were apartments or rooms used for sexual exchanges arranged via telephone.)[3] By the 1920s, whether they worked in houses or solicited on the streets, black women were not merely prominent in the sex trade but had become the most visible and vulnerable prostitutes working in Chicago's sex industry.

These prostitution-related arrest figures force us to reconsider the conclusions that several historians have reached about urban prostitution after the era of the red-light district. Several scholars of early-twentieth-century prostitution have argued that sexual commerce assumed new forms after the closing of sex districts across the nation in the 1910s. No longer working in brothels concentrated in well-defined urban sex districts, most prostitutes worked in scattered call flats or solicited trade on the streets of poor urban districts. Banished to the fringes of urban life, hidden away in apartments, and accessible only to men in the know, the trade diminished in the frequency of its occurrence as well.

Scholars point to numerous factors that contributed to the decline in urban prostitution in the early twentieth century. Expanded job opportunities for white women meant that fewer found it necessary to sell their sexual services. Additionally, the decline in immigration gradually dried up the pool of young, unattached, working-class men who in previous decades paid frequent visits to prostitutes.[4] Historians of urban sex work have also attributed the assumed decline in the trade to the changing sexual culture of white middle- and working-class Americans. The modernization of sexuality—the liberalization of men's and women's sexual attitudes and practices both within and outside marriage—ultimately diminished men's demand for women's paid sexual services. With fewer women needing to earn money in the sex economy and fewer men seeking women's paid sexual services, it would seem that in the 1920s prostitution became all but obsolete.[5]

Yet in Chicago, rather than a decline in prostitution, the 1920s witnessed an expansion of the urban sex trade, and not just for black women. Police data record this important shift (table E.3). Except for streetwalking, the number of prostitution-related arrests throughout the decade for all women exceeded that of the 1910s. Changes in the geography of Chicago's sex trade in the 1920s contributed to the aggressive policing that resulted in increased arrests over the decade. No

Table E.3. Prostitution-related charges in Chicago municipal courts, 1906–1930

	1906	1912	1916	1920	1924	1928	1930
Inmates of houses of ill fame	1,210	1,663	61	392	3,249	7,925	2,919
Keepers of houses of ill fame	649	396	16	64	582	2,214	291
Streetwalkers[a]	2,437	1,516	2,006[a]				
Soliciting for prostitution[b]			742	167	498	745	254

Source: City of Chicago, Police Department of the City of Chicago, Annual Report, 1906, 1912, 1916, 1920, 1924, 1928, 1930.
[a]The last year that streetwalking was listed as a misdemeanor offense in the Chicago municipal code was 1914. The 2,006 figure is for 1914.
[b]Soliciting for prostitution replaced streetwalking as a misdemeanor offense in the municipal code in 1915.

longer concentrated in the red-light district, prostitution for all women moved into neighborhoods throughout the city where it did not earlier exist. The trade required more vigorous policing to slow and, city authorities hoped, reverse prostitution's expansion into respectable neighborhoods. In addition, arrest figures reveal that throughout the 1920s many black and white women continued to turn to the trade as a means of earning money, challenging the conclusion that fewer women relied on the sex economy for work. Furthermore, what appears to be the postwar *growth* of prostitution in Chicago suggests, not a waning of interest in commercialized sex, but a transformation of the role that paid sexual relations played in modernizing sex lives. Rather than eschewing prostitution for the pleasures attainable in more open heterosexual dating practices or the new playground of the marital bed, many men incorporated sexual commerce into their understanding and experience of modern sexuality.

In the context of the geographical dispersal of prostitution throughout Chicago and the overall increase in the city's sex trade as reflected in 1920s arrest rates, black women's overwhelming prominence in the sex economy is striking. Black women's escalating overrepresentation among arrested prostitutes had numerous sources, including the changing and perhaps more racially adventurous sexual habits of white middle- and working-class urbanites. But it also reflected the city's emerging racial geography during and after World War I and exposed city leaders' heightened concern about black sexual "deviance."[6]

The rapid rise in the proportion of black women in Chicago who were prostitutes coincided with the Great Migration of southern blacks to Chicago and to other cities in the Midwest, Northeast, and South. Between 1916 and 1930 migratory waves of African Americans from the rural districts and towns of the South swelled Chicago's black population from 2 percent of city residents to 7 percent. In 1920 the number of black residents was nearly 110,000, and by 1930 the number had more than doubled to reach 234,000.[7] Migrating women had hoped, like their male counterparts, to find in Chicago's industrial economy "a path leading to new vistas," yet they generally faced disappointment.[8] Unlike black men, many of whom secured industrial jobs, black women could only rarely expect to find factory work in the city. While black men could find positions as unskilled laborers in Chicago's stockyards, packinghouses, and steel industries, the job market remained severely limited for African American women. Restricted to service work and making only incremental gains as unskilled laborers in Chicago's factories, on the eve of the Great Depression black women toiled on the lowest rung of the city's economic ladder.[9] In many ways, black women in Chicago experienced continuity in their employment opportunities in the first decades of the twentieth century. This continuity extended not only to their relegation to the least remunerative and most demeaning employments but also to their struggle to escape domestic work whenever possible.[10] For some women, prostitution continued to provide an avenue leading away from service work.

The growing numbers of black women of working age who could find no suitable employment in Chicago's wage economy explains why more black women worked in the sex industry in the 1920s than in earlier decades. But the rapid growth of the Black Belt population alone cannot explain why black women were overrepresented in *police* records. Even contemporary observers questioned whether black women's predominance among prostitution-related arrests accurately represented their participation in the sex economy. One Morals Court judge tried to explain the disproportionate presence of black defendants in his court. Dismissing the conclusion that "there is any greater percentage of immorality" among black women, Judge Wells Cook opined that "colored people, living largely in one section of the city . . . are apt to congregate in places and in resorts where the police could more easily raid them, and are much more easily apprehended."[11] Judge Cook's comments highlight three intertwined factors that contributed to the preponderance of black women appearing in court on "morals" charges: racial segregation, the concentration of prostitution in the Black Belt, and increased police attention to the Black Belt sex trade. An examination of each of these three factors bears out their interrelatedness.

First, the waves of African Americans moving to Chicago's South Side after World War I placed pressure on living space within the existing Black Belt. Blacks seeking to move beyond the borders of the neighborhood faced often-violent resistance from whites living in communities to the south, east, and west of the Black Belt.[12] White resistance took many forms, but the most effective methods for limiting black inroads were violence and the organized campaigns of white property owners.[13] Despite white resistance, the Black Belt was able to expand incrementally. By 1930 blacks lived in a "rigidly segregated ghetto" that extended from Twenty-Second Street to Sixty-Third Street between Wentworth and Cottage Grove. This was a densely crowded area, with blacks living in cramped, subdivided houses and apartments. Not only were blacks confined to a narrow strip of Chicago land, but racial segregation within areas of black residence—a process that began before the turn of the century—accelerated dramatically. Between 1920 and 1930 the proportion of African Americans living in areas 90 percent black grew from zero to two-thirds. In the words of historian Arnold Hirsch, by 1930 "the borders of [Black Chicago] were sharp and clear."[14]

Second, within this clearly defined Black Belt, institutions of sexual leisure grew in number and visibility over the decade. The Chicago Commission on Race Relations, an organization formed to investigate the causes of the 1919 race riot, noted with concern that prostitution seemed to spread southward as the Black Belt expanded. Plotting the geography of defendants found guilty in Morals Court against the map of the South Side, the commission's study noted "the gradual drift of prostitution southward coincidentally with the expansions of the main area of Negro residence."[15] Prostitution thrived both clandestinely and quite openly from Twenty-Second Street to as far south as Fifty-Fifth Street (figs. E.1 and E.2). Another study concluded that "the greatest concentration of vice resorts both in 1920 as well as in 1930 has occurred in the tracts possessing the highest percentages of Negro population."[16] The increased concentration of prostitution within the Black Belt only heightened black leaders' alarm about the hazards that the mushrooming vice industry posed to the morals of unprotected women and youth of the community (fig. E.3). Yet the growth of Black Belt prostitution also led directly to the third factor contributing to black women's high arrest rates: intensified policing of the Black Belt sex trade.

Although Judge Cook's comments illuminate why Black Belt prostitution in general, white and black, would be the object of heightened police attention, these three factors do not explain why Chicago police officers focused so much attention on *black* prostitutes. The sources of the criminalization of black women reside in the racial organization of the Black Belt sex industry itself.

African American women tended to work in areas of the trade most

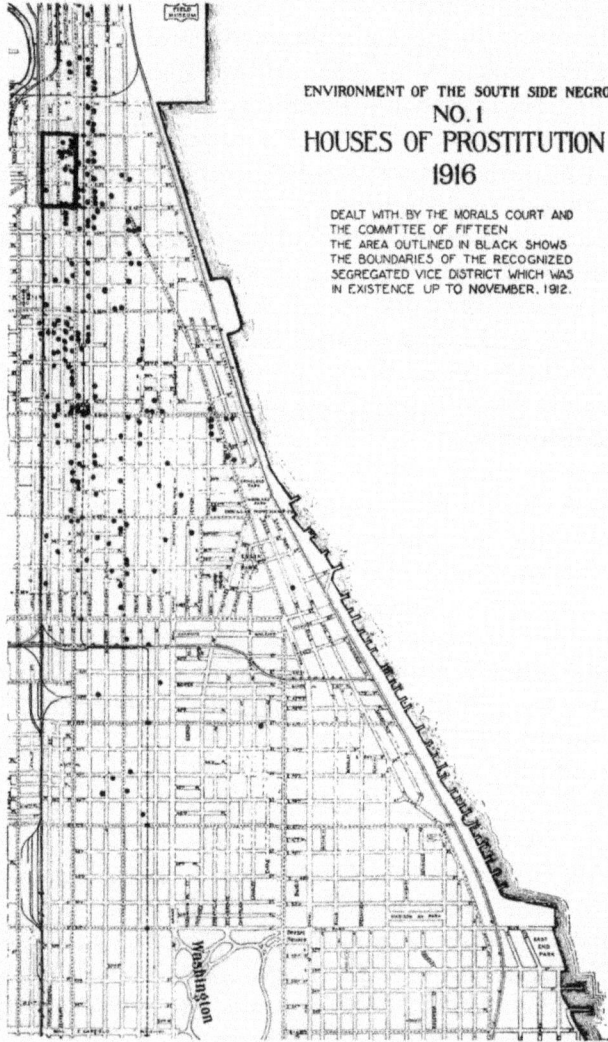

Map E.1   "Houses of Prostitution, 1916." From Chicago Commission on Race Relations, *The Negro in Chicago* (Arno Press and the New York Times, 1922). Courtesy of Special Collections, University of Illinois at Chicago Library.

ENVIRONMENT OF THE SOUTH SIDE NEGRO

NO. 3

RESORTS

SUMMER OF 1919

HOUSES OF PROSTITUTION----- ●
SALOONS---------------------- ▲
BILLIARD HALLS--------------- ■
GAMBLING PLACES-------------- ✚
CABARETS--------------------- ℭ

Map E.2   "Resorts, Summer of 1919." From Chicago Commission on Race Relations, *The Negro in Chicago* (Arno Press and the New York Times, 1922). Courtesy of Special Collections, University of Illinois at Chicago Library.

The Menacing Hand!

E.1 "The Menacing Hand!" From *Chicago Defender,* June 3, 1922. Courtesy of the *Chicago Defender.*

vulnerable to police harassment. Yet, police statistics notwithstanding, prostitution in the Black Belt was not exclusively African American. Cabarets, saloons, and parlor houses run by white men and women, employing white women, and catering to an exclusively white clientele dotted the Black Belt. However, many of these resorts were under the control of increasingly powerful vice syndicates, crime organizations able to broker protection from politicians and police for their enterprises. While it is difficult to determine how many resorts were controlled by syndicates, it appears that most white women who worked in the Black Belt worked in connection with a syndicate. A large proportion of Black Belt resorts operated without syndicate protection, however.[17] Black women tended to work in nightclubs and apartment-based houses that existed beyond vice networks. Lacking the cover and protection of the syndicates, black prostitutes encountered police harassment much more often than did white prostitutes working on the South Side.

Additionally, continuing a trend that had begun in the previous decade, during the 1920s an increasing number of black women worked outside cabarets, nightclubs, and saloons. Sociologist Walter Reckless referred to such women as "an unregimented class of professional, semi-professional, and amateur prostitutes." Rather than laboring in the establishments that provided institutional "organization" for the sex industry, these sex workers, according to Reckless, "have taken to street walking, rooming houses, hotels, assignation places, and call flats where prostitution is conducted on a more independent, clandestine basis."[18] Notwithstanding Reckless's assessment, these "independent" prostitutes were neither "unregimented" nor isolated individuals. Rather, many worked in teams or small groups that rented and shared furnished rooms and small apartments and coordinated their daily work schedules. They worked "independently," then, not because they labored alone, but because they shunned male control of their earnings in cabarets and the financial obligations of working in a syndicate house. These women braved the Black Belt sex marketplace on their own and consequently suffered police detection and frequent arrest. Although some white women also worked independently in the Black Belt, African American women were the most visible of these "independent" prostitutes. The criminalization of black women in the 1920s, then, arose in large part from their concentration in areas of the sex trade beyond male protection, whether that protection came in the form of an employer or a syndicate agent.

Yet the criminalization of black women not only reflected their concentration in the least protected areas of the sex industry but also represented city officials' response to the crumbling of racial boundaries within the Black Belt sex trade. Black women's involvement in interracial sexual exchanges made them targets for city officials bent on policing—albeit unevenly—both sexual commerce and increasingly rigid racial lines in the city. Throughout the 1920s anti-vice reformers regularly and vociferously expressed discomfort with the interracial trade that characterized all branches of the South Side sex industry. Investigators from the Juvenile Protective Association—an organization that worked to protect Chicago's youth from the scourge of commercialized vice—repeatedly noted in their field reports the extent of interracial interaction. One investigator reported that, in the crowded Schiller Cabaret on Thirty-Fifth Street, "75 couples [were] present, about 20 unescorted colored women and 4 unescorted white women. Of the 75 couples present the majority of the men were white while their companions were colored. There were also 4 white women in the company of colored men."[19] At the Dreamland Café at Thirty-Fifth and State, another investigator witnessed "approximately 25 unaccompanied prostitutes present," of whom 15 were black and 10 white. "Both the colored and white prostitutes were seen boldly to accost unaccompanied men."[20] At the Lorraine Cabaret an investigator counted "approximately 35 couples present," 25 of whom "were white persons who were apparently visiting the place on a slumming tour; the remainder," he concluded, "appeared to be prostitutes and pimps." The investigator himself was "solicited by two colored prostitutes" who "offered to commit an act of prostitution with me for $3.00."[21]

The Juvenile Protective Association investigators witnessed the flourishing of the "Negro Vogue," the white middle-class fascination with black culture that simultaneously commodified and sexualized racial difference in cities like Chicago and New York.[22] Since 1910, Black Belt residents had noticed with horror the increasing traffic of white slummers seeking sexual titillation and "new" sexual experiences in South Side resorts. But slumming became a full-fledged feature of the Black Belt sex trade in the 1920s. While black and white women working in popular cabarets could easily attract the attention of pleasure-seeking white men, those working outside these resorts took advantage of the flow of white men through neighborhood streets. As one investigator walked in front of a furnished rooming house on South State Street at 1:15 a.m., he was "accosted by three colored prostitutes." As he walked away he noted that "all three prostitutes were seen to accost white men and to take these men whom they accosted, to their rooms upstairs."[23] A black prostitute sitting in a window of a furnished room motioned to this same investigator, inviting him to enter her room. Such women fully expected that men, white and black, would sooner or later make their way past their doors and their windows. These "unregimented" prostitutes extended the interracial sex trade beyond the institutions of commercialized nightlife, turning large tracts of the Black Belt into fields of racialized sexual play for white men.

The policing of black prostitutes served as a mechanism for policing the most visible form of sexual commerce in the Black Belt—the trade between black women and white men. Although white prostitutes worked in neighborhood cabarets that were open to an interracial clientele, black women far outnumbered them in these resorts. Similarly, while some white women worked in the area's furnished rooms, inviting both black and white men to their rooms, most worked in more clandestine houses of prostitution. Though not always successful, these houses increased their chance of avoiding detection by reformers by excluding black patrons.

Traditionally, white Americans believed that black men posed the biggest threat to racial boundaries and to the ideal of white racial purity in American society. For some white northern urbanites in the 1920s, black women increasingly embodied this threat. This refiguring of racial threat developed in the modern northern city at a time when "sharp and clear" spatial boundaries that defined emerging Black Belts successfully served to limit white women's interactions with black men. Indeed, even as white women were increasingly mobile and able to navigate city spaces on their own,[24] few crossed the sexualized spatial divide that protected respectable white women from moral downfall. Those brave few who did foray into Chicago's Black Belt on a slumming tour did so on the protective arms of white men. White women's mobility, then, rarely translated into sexual exploration across the color line. White men, however, could investigate the Black Belt on their own, negotiating sexual exchanges on streets that white women would never dream of walking alone.

Black sex workers, then, labored on the front lines of both the sexualization and policing of racial boundaries in the city. Working on the front lines was fraught with contradiction, however. While the commercialization of racial boundaries expanded black sex workers' opportunities for earning money, the rigid policing of black women's bodies by white urban reformers and keepers of social order depressed their wages. In the context of their intense criminalization, black sex workers continued to struggle for some measure of economic security and at the same time carve out an arena for self-dominion. Earning between $1 and $3 for their services, their efforts rarely met with success.

The arrival of the Great Depression made their struggle even harder. It swiftly diminished men's earnings and shriveled the commercial leisure economy that enlivened the 1920s Black Belt sex trade. For most black women working in Chicago's sex industry, the outcome of the decades-long battle for financial independence was increasingly grim.

"I've Got to Make My Livin'"

African American women working in the early-twentieth-century sex economy labored to earn money at the intersection of several processes

central to urban development—the shifting geography of the sex industry, the growth of the commercialized leisure industry, African American
urbanization, the racialization of urban space, the sexualization of racial
boundaries, the development of black urban reform ideologies, and the
modernization of sexuality. These processes had roots in the nineteenth
century but flowered after the turn of the century. Together, these processes affected prostitutes' ability to earn money in an early-twentieth-
century urban economy that continued to situate black women at the
bottom of the urban labor hierarchy.

The voices of black women working in Chicago's early-twentieth-
century sex economy seem almost inaudible to us today, much as the
substance of the experiences of late-nineteenth-century sex workers
nearly eludes the grasp of contemporary researchers. Yet here and there
the economies and choices of black prostitutes have emerged into public light. In 1930 blues singer Lucille Bogan wrote and recorded "They
Ain't Walking No More." Although in this study I have endeavored to
show how black sex workers labored within a variegated sex economy, I
use this blues recording about streetwalking to illustrate the ways black
prostitutes understood the turf—geographical and economic—in which
they worked and lived.

Sometimes I'm up, sometimes I'm down,
I can't make my livin', around this town,
'Cause tricks ain't walkin', tricks ain't walkin' no more,
I said tricks ain't walkin', tricks ain't walkin' no more,
And I've got to make my livin', don't care where I go.
· · · · · · · · · · · · · · · · · ·
I got a store on the corner, sellin' stuff cheap,
I got a market 'cross the street, where I sell my meat,
But tricks ain't walkin', tricks ain't walkin' no more,
I said tricks ain't walkin', tricks ain't walkin' no more,
And I can't get a break, don't care where I go.

This way of livin' sure is hard,
Duckin' and dodgin' the Cadillac Squad,
But tricks ain't walkin', tricks ain't walkin' no more,
I said tricks ain't walkin', tricks ain't walkin' no more,
And if you think I'm lyin', follow me to my door.[25]

At first glance, Lucille Bogan's street worker personifies the tenuous
grip that many black sex workers had on financial security within the

urban economy and reveals the lengths to which some women were forced to go in order to stay afloat in the city. Away from the glamour of the nightclub or the sophistication of the cabaret, these poor working women appear to embody the lowly position that black women occupied—as workers and as sexual commodities—in the city. This struggle was not unique to women who used the streets, however. Although their working conditions seem to suggest their peculiar vulnerability in the urban sex marketplace, their plight simply reveals the relations of economic and sexual domination confronted by all women laboring as prostitutes in the early-twentieth-century urban economy. These conditions only got worse during the Great Depression.

In tracing the movement of black sex workers from random pockets within the central business district of mid-nineteenth-century Chicago to the community spaces of the Great Migration–era black community, I have tried to outline black women's often-ingenious adaptations to the racial, geographical, and institutional permutations of Chicago's changing sex economy. In part a story of the spatial transformation of urban prostitution and the sexual policing of urban race relations, this has also been a story of black women's hard work, entrepreneurial acumen, and savvy (if inadequately remunerative) manipulation of oppressive racial and gender relations in the city. In every sexual transaction— whether it took place in brothels, nightclubs, furnished rooms, buffet flats, hotel rooms, or the streets—black women bore the weight of the racial organization of urban sexual culture and the gender organization of the urban economy. That so many black women engaged in transactions that were sometimes economically unprofitable and always ideologically fraught underscores the failure of the urban economy to fully incorporate black women into modern, industrial prosperity.

Notes

INTRODUCTION

1.   Washington Intercollegiate Club of Chicago, *Book of Negro Achievement Featuring the Negro in Chicago, 1779–1929* (Chicago, 1929), 5, 257.
2.   Bertha "Chippie" Hill, "Street Walker Blues," June 15, 1926, Chicago, Okeh 8437. Bertha Hill, a singer who had worked in New York City cabarets and saloons, moved to Chicago in the mid-1920s and worked the South Side cabaret circuit through the 1930s. It is possible that Hill had herself been a prostitute before arriving in Chicago. In the early twentieth century "Chippie" was a common slang term for prostitute. Hill tells a different story about her nickname. According to Hill, a Harlem club owner named her "Chippie" because of her youth when she performed in his clubs in the early 1920s. The lyrics to "Street Walker Blues" may represent Hill's own experiences as a prostitute or may express her deep empathy for the women she witnessed working the streets of New York's Tenderloin and Chicago's Black Belt (*Record Changer*, April 11, 1948, 11).
3.   Daphne Duval Harrison, *Black Pearls: Blues Queens of the 1920s* (New Brunswick, NJ: Rutgers University Press, 1988), 232–34; Dempsey J. Travis, *An Autobiography of Black Jazz* (Chicago: Urban Research Institute, 1983), 134.
4.   Luise White has argued strenuously that prostitution is above all a means of capital accumulation for women. In her study of colonial Nairobi, White reconstructs the labor relations of prostitution and uncovers the well-articulated structure of women's sexual labor in an African city under British colonial rule. This influential book has informed my own analysis of black women's prostitution in the United

States. See Luise White, *The Comforts of Home: Prostitution in Colonial Nairobi* (Chicago: University of Chicago Press, 1990).

5. For further discussion of African American women's work in cities, see Jacqueline Jones, *Labor of Love, Labor of Sorrow: Black Women, Work and the Family from Slavery to the Present* (New York: Vintage Books, 1985); Tera W. Hunter, *"To 'Joy My Freedom": Southern Black Women's Lives and Labors after the Civil War* (Cambridge, MA: Harvard University Press, 1997); Elizabeth Clark-Lewis, *Living In, Living Out: African American Domestics in Washington, D.C., 1910–1940* (New York: Kodansha International, 1996); Gretchen Lemke-Santangelo, *Abiding Courage: African American Migrant Women and the East Bay Community* (Chapel Hill: University of North Carolina Press, 1996); Sharon Harley, "'Working for Nothing but for a Living': Black Women in the Underground Economy," in *Sister Circle: Black Women and Work*, ed. Sharon Harley and Black Women and Work Collective (New Brunswick, NJ: Rutgers University Press, 2002), 48–66.

6. Alecia P. Long, *The Great Southern Babylon: Sex, Race, and Respectability in New Orleans, 1865–1920* (Baton Rouge: Louisiana State University Press, 2004); Tera Hunter, *"To 'Joy My Freedom,"* 112–14; E. Susan Barber, "Depraved and Abandoned Women: Prostitution in Richmond, Virginia, across the Civil War," in *Neither Lady nor Slave: Working Women of the Old South*, ed. Susanna Delfino and Michele Gillespie (Chapel Hill: University of North Carolina Press, 2002), 155–73; Timothy J. Gilfoyle, *City of Eros: New York City, Prostitution, and the Commercialization of Sex, 1790–1920* (New York: W. W. Norton and Co., 1992), 41–43, 47–48, 209–10; Gilbert Osofsky, *Harlem: The Making of a Ghetto* (New York: Harper and Row, 1966), 14–15; David M. Katzman, *Before the Ghetto: Black Detroit in the Nineteenth Century* (Urbana: University of Illinois Press, 1975), 171–72; W. E. B. DuBois, *The Philadelphia Negro: A Social Study* (Philadelphia: University of Pennsylvania Press, 1899; repr., Philadelphia: University of Pennsylvania Press, 1996), 313–14; Kenneth L. Kusmer, *A Ghetto Takes Shape: Black Cleveland, 1870–1930* (Urbana: University of Illinois Press, 1976), 48–50.

7. George Kibbe Turner, "The City of Chicago, a Study of the Great Immoralities," *McClure's Magazine* 28, no. 6 (April 1907): 576–79; Ernest A. Bell, *Fighting the Traffic in Young Girls* (Chicago: n.p., 1910); Robert O. Harland, *The Vice Bondage of a Great City; or, The Wickedest City in the World* (Chicago: Young People's Civic League, 1912); Eric Anderson, "Prostitution and Social Justice: Chicago, 1910–15," *Social Service Review* 48, no. 2 (1974): 203–28; Mark Thomas Connelly, *The Response to Prostitution in the Progressive Era* (Chapel Hill: University of North Carolina Press, 1980); Mara L. Keire, "The Vice Trust: A Reinterpretation of the White Slavery Scare in the United States, 1907–1917," *Journal of Social History* 35, no. 1 (2001): 5–41.

8. Vice Commission of Chicago, *The Social Evil in Chicago: A Study of Existing Conditions with Recommendations* (Chicago: Gunthorp-Warren, 1911).

9. See Ruth Rosen, *The Lost Sisterhood: Prostitution in America, 1900–1918* (Baltimore, MD: Johns Hopkins University Press, 1982); Connelly, *Response to Prostitution.*

10. Deborah Gray White, *Too Heavy a Load: Black Women in Defense of Themselves, 1894–1994* (New York: W. W. Norton and Co., 1999), 23, 24, 53–54.

11. DuBois, *Philadelphia Negro,* 313.

12. On the politics of respectability, see Evelyn Brooks Higginbotham, *Righteous Discontent: The Women's Movement in the Black Baptist Church, 1880–1920* (Cambridge, MA: Harvard University Press, 1993), 185–229. See also James R. Grossman, *Land of Hope: Chicago, Black Southerners, and the Great Migration* (Chicago: University of Chicago Press, 1989), 145–55; Victoria W. Wolcott, *Remaking Respectability: African American Women in Interwar Detroit* (Chapel Hill: University of North Carolina Press, 2001); Deborah White, *Too Heavy a Load,* esp. 87–109. See also Darlene Clark Hine, "Rape and the Inner Lives of Black Women in the Middle West: Preliminary Thoughts on the Culture of Dissemblance," *Signs: Journal of Women and Culture in Society* 14 (Summer 1989): 912–20. For a treatment of the role of respectability in contemporary black politics, see Cathy J. Cohen, *Boundaries of Blackness: AIDS and the Breakdown of Black Politics* (Chicago: University of Chicago Press, 1999).

13. Michele Mitchell, "Silences Broken, Silences Kept: Gender and Sexuality in African-American History," *Gender and History* 11, no. 3 (1999): 433–44; Evelynn M. Hammonds, "Toward a Genealogy of Black Female Sexuality: The Problematic of Silence," in *Feminist Genealogies, Colonial Legacies, Democratic Futures,* ed. Chandra Talpade Mohanty and M. Jacqui Alexander (New York: Routledge, 1997), 170–82.

14. Ruth Rosen, *Lost Sisterhood;* Christine Stansell, *City of Women: Sex and Class in New York, 1789–1860* (Urbana: University of Illinois Press, 1987), 171–92; Gilfoyle, *City of Eros.*

15. Ruth Rosen, *Lost Sisterhood,* 14–68; Kathy Peiss, *Cheap Amusements: Working Women and Leisure in Turn-of-the-Century New York* (Philadelphia: Temple University Press, 1986), 163–84.

16. Kevin J. Mumford, *Interzones: Black/White Sex Districts in Chicago and New York in the Early Twentieth Century* (New York: Columbia University Press, 1997); Wolcott, *Remaking Respectability;* Long, *Great Southern Babylon.* See also Tera Hunter, *"To 'Joy My Freedom";* Gilfoyle, *City of Eros;* Angela Davis, *Blues Legacies and Black Feminism: Gertrude "Ma" Rainey, Bessie Smith, and Billie Holiday* (New York: Vintage Books, 1998).

17. Hazel Carby, "Policing the Black Woman's Body in an Urban Context," *Critical Inquiry* 18 (Summer 1992): 738–55.

18. Judith R. Walkowitz, *City of Dreadful Delight: Narratives of Sexual Danger in Late-Victorian London* (Chicago: University of Chicago Press, 1992); Gail Hershatter, *Dangerous Pleasures: Prostitution and Modernity in Twentieth-*

Century Shanghai (Berkeley and Los Angeles: University of California Press, 1997).

19. This is a reference to the subtitle of Deborah Gray White's *Too Heavy a Load: Black Women in Defense of Themselves, 1894–1994*.

20. The historical literature on enslaved women's sexual oppression at the hands of slaveholding men and on free black women's sexual abuse at the hands of white employers is extensive. See Deborah Gray White, *Ar'n't I a Woman? Female Slaves in the Plantation South* (New York: W. W. Norton and Co., 1985); Brenda Stevenson, *Life in Black and White: Family and Community in the Slave South* (New York: Oxford University Press, 1996); Hine, "Rape and the Inner Lives of Black Women"; Jacqueline Dowd Hall, "'The Mind That Burns in Each Body': Women, Rape, and Racial Violence," in *Powers of Desire: The Politics of Sexuality*, ed. Ann Snitow, Christine Stansell, and Sharon Thompson (New York: Monthly Review Press, 1983), 328–49.

21. On historical memory, see Catherine Clinton, "'With a Whip in His Hand': Rape, Memory, and African American Women," in *History and Memory in African-American Culture*, ed. Genevieve Fabre and Robert O'Meally (New York: Oxford University Press, 1994), 205–18; David Blight, "'For Something beyond the Battlefield': Frederick Douglass and the Struggle for the Memory of the Civil War," *Journal of American History* 75 (March 1989): 1156–78.

22. See, e.g., Jones, *Labor of Love, Labor of Sorrow*, 181.

23. Jody Raphael, *Listening to Olivia: Violence, Poverty, and Prostitution* (Boston: Northeastern University Press, 2004), 123–26; Alexa Albert, *Brothel: Mustang Ranch and Its Women* (New York: Random House, 2001), 77–79; Chicago Coalition for the Homeless, "Unlocking Options for Women: A Survey of Women in Cook County Jail" (Chicago, 2002).

24. Gilfoyle, *City of Eros*, 91, 105; Marilynn Wood Hill, *Their Sisters' Keepers: Prostitution in New York City, 1830–1870* (Berkeley and Los Angeles: University of California Press, 1993), 267–78; Ruth Rosen, *Lost Sisterhood*, 76.

25. Tera Hunter, *"To 'Joy My Freedom,"* 154; Wolcott, *Remaking Respectability*, 106–13.

26. For a discussion of the challenges of conducting historical research on prostitutes, see Timothy J. Gilfoyle, "Prostitutes in the Archives: Problems and Possibilities in Documenting the History of Sexuality," *American Archivist* 57, no. 3 (Summer 1994): 514–27.

27. The Great Migration is the name given to the movement of over a million African Americans out of the South from 1915 to 1930. Deborah Gray White, *Ar'n't I a Woman?*; Martha Hodes, *White Women, Black Men: Illicit Sex in the Nineteenth-Century South* (New Haven, CT: Yale University Press, 1997); Hannah Rosen, "'Not That Sort of Women': Race, Gender, and Sexual Violence during the Memphis Riot of 1866," in *Sex, Love, Race:*

NOTES TO PAGES 19–21

Crossing Boundaries in North American History, ed. Martha Hodes (New York: New York University Press, 1999), 267–93.

CHAPTER ONE

1. *Chicago Times*, November 27, 1870.
2. *The Sporting and Club House Directory* (Chicago: Ross and St. Clair Publishing, 1889); Allan H. Spear, *Black Chicago: The Making of a Negro Ghetto, 1890–1920* (Chicago: University of Chicago Press, 1967), 12.
3. Dorothy Salem, *To Better Our World: Black Women in Organized Reform, 1890–1920* (Brooklyn: Carlson, 1990); Deborah Gray White, *Too Heavy a Load*.
4. Spear, *Black Chicago*, 7–8; Estelle Hill Scott, *Occupational Changes among Negroes in Chicago* (Chicago: Works Progress Administration, 1939), 27–38, 63–72.
5. Scott, *Occupational Changes*, 38. Of foreign-born women in service in 1890, 25 percent were from Germany, 28 percent were from Ireland, and 30 percent were from Sweden and Norway. U.S. Bureau of the Census, *Eleventh Census of the United States, 1890, Compendium*, pt. 1, *Population*, 650–51. In 1900 Richard R. Wright Jr. found that "where the work of the house is specialized and there are three or four servants, fashion dictates that they be Swedes or of some other foreign nationality. Here the Negro is generally shut out except, perhaps, a cook." See his "The Industrial Condition of Negroes in Chicago" (BD thesis, University of Chicago Divinity School, 1901), 26.
6. U.S. Bureau of the Census, *Negro Population, 1790–1915* (Washington, DC: GPO, 1918), 156–57; U.S. Bureau of the Census, *Eleventh Census, 1890, Compendium*, pt. 1, 674–75; U.S. Bureau of the Census, *Twelfth Census of the United States, 1900*, vol. 2, *Population*, pt. 1, 314; Joanne J. Meyerowitz, *Women Adrift: Independent Wage Earners in Chicago, 1880–1930* (Chicago: University of Chicago Press, 1988), 9, 11. In 1890 and 1900 males accounted for 56 percent and 53 percent of Chicago's black population, respectively. In most eastern and southern cities, women outnumbered men as migrants. Between 1890 and 1900, for example, only 46 percent of Philadelphia's and 45 percent of New York City's black population was male. Noting the "excess" of black women in these cities, W. E. B. DuBois suggested that, unlike black men, for whom job opportunities were few, black women could easily get work in the homes of middle-class and elite urban families (*Philadelphia Negro*, 54–55). For a discussion of women's labor migration to the urban South, see Tera Hunter, *"To 'Joy My Freedom,"* 21–25. Chicago was not out of step with other midwestern cities, however. In Cleveland, for example, in both 1890 and 1900 women were only 47 percent of the black population. In 1900 black males outnumbered black females in thirteen of the nation's thirty-four largest northern cities

(U.S. Bureau of the Census, *Negro Population*, 156–57). See also Kelly Miller, "Surplus Negro Women," in *Race Adjustment: Essays on the Negro in America* (New York: Neale Publishing Co., 1908), 172, 180–81; Jones, *Labor of Love, Labor of Sorrow*, 156; Kusmer, *A Ghetto Takes Shape*, 39; David A. Gerber, *Black Ohio and the Color Line, 1860–1915* (Urbana: University of Illinois Press, 1976), 276n10.

7. Scott, *Occupational Changes*, 43, 47, 68, 72, 83–85.

8. As was the case for black women, black men found work in service more than in any other area of employment. Still, in the late nineteenth century black men who settled in Chicago faced a more varied job horizon than black women. In 1890, when 47 percent of black men worked as servants, a significant proportion, 15 percent, were employed as unskilled laborers in the city's commercial establishments, factories, and railroad yards. Ibid., 32.

9. Tera Hunter, *"To 'Joy My Freedom"*; Clark-Lewis, *Living In, Living Out*; David M. Katzman, *Seven Days a Week: Women and Domestic Service in Industrializing America* (New York: Oxford University Press, 1978), 84–93.

10. The literature on the informal economy is voluminous. On the concept's origins, see Victor E. Tokman, "The Informal Sector in Latin America: From Underground to Legality," in *Beyond Regulation: The Informal Economy in Latin America*, ed. Victor E. Tokman (Boulder, CO: Lynne Rienner Publishers, 1992), 3–4; Philip Harding and Richard Jenkins, *The Myth of the Hidden Economy: Towards a New Understanding of Informal Economic Activity* (Philadelphia: Open University Press, 1989), 16. See also the articles in *SAIS Review* 21, no. 1 (Winter–Spring 2001).

11. The assortment of economic pursuits that exist beyond officially regulated networks of exchange is vast, ranging from the friendly exchange of goods and services between neighbors to the sale of drugs. Students of the underground economy have debated whether criminal activities, especially those, such as theft and drug trafficking, that have victims, are properly embraced by the concept of the informal economy. Historian Mark H. Haller limits his analysis of underground economic activity, or "illegal enterprise," to "the sale of illegal goods or services to *customers who know that the goods and services are illegal*" (emphasis mine). Prostitution, loan-sharking, gambling, and the sale of pornography, drugs, and bootleg liquor all exist within this category of economic behavior. Yet even though criminal exchanges are at the center of Haller's definition of illegal enterprise, Haller separates them from criminal transactions that prey on victims, such as theft and forced prostitution. See his "Illegal Enterprise: A Theoretical and Historical Interpretation," *Criminology* 28, no. 2 (1990): 207. In a somewhat different formulation, sociologist José Blanes Jiménez analytically separates criminal economic transactions from other informal-sector activities. Yet, unlike Haller, he explores a connection between these two "spheres"

of informality in his analysis of the relations between the traffic in cocaine and the informal economy in La Paz, Bolivia. See his "Cocaine, Informality, and the Urban Economy in La Paz, Bolivia," in *The Informal Economy: Studies in Advanced and Less Developed Countries*, ed. Alejandro Portes, Manuel Castells, and Lauren A. Benton (Baltimore, MD: Johns Hopkins University Press, 1989), 135–49. Sociologist J. J. Thomas offers a definition of the informal economy that more fully reflects its economic and social complexity. Addressing the broad range of unregulated economic practices, Thomas has formulated a theory that divides "informal economic activity" into four distinct sectors: the household, the irregular, the criminal, and the urban informal. He distinguishes these sectors by the extent of their involvement with market transactions and the legality of the production and distribution of either legal or illegal goods and services. By distinguishing between the criminal sector and the urban informal sector, yet maintaining them within the category of "informal economic activity," Thomas offers a useful way of incorporating criminal transactions—including those with victims—within discussions of informality. See his *Surviving in the City: The Urban Informal Sector in Latin America* (London: Pluto Press, 1995), 11–15. More recently, Sudhir Alladi Venkatesh has employed a similarly capacious definition of the informal economy in his illuminating examination of "the underground economy of the urban poor" living on Chicago's South Side at the turn of the twenty-first century. He studies the vast network of exchanges that constitute a clandestine economy, ranging from off-the-books car repair to local drug dealing. In the process he explores in great detail the ways that these exchanges have given rise to an intricate social structure, one linking local preachers and store owners to prostitutes and dealers in stolen goods, a structure upon which poor blacks rely both for much-needed cash and for some semblance of social order. See Venkatesh, *Off the Books: The Underground Economy of the Urban Poor* (Cambridge, MA: Harvard University Press, 2006).

12. Policy was a lottery game in which players made bets, usually small, on daily drawings. Drawings were run by dealers who oversaw a highly organized operation that provided work for men and women who took bets door-to-door and business owners whose establishments were used as policy stations. Mathilde Bunton, "Policy," pp. 2–3, box 35, Illinois Writers' Project, "The Negro in Illinois," Vivian Harsh Collection, Carter G. Woodson Regional Library, Chicago Public Library; St. Clair Drake and Horace R. Cayton, *Black Metropolis: A Study of Negro Life in a Northern City* (New York: Harcourt, Brace and Co., 1945; repr., Chicago: University of Chicago Press, 1993), 470–72; Mark H. Haller, "Policy Gambling, Entertainment, and the Emergence of Black Politics: Chicago from 1900 to 1940," *Journal of Social History* 24, no. 4 (Summer 1991): 719–40. Analyses of the policy business in urban black communities has largely focused on the post–World War I period, and few have focused on the activity of

women—as players, numbers runners, or dealers—within policy organizations. An important exception is Victoria W. Wolcott, "The Culture of the
Informal Economy: Numbers Runners in Inter-war Black Detroit," *Radical
History Review*, no. 69 (Fall 1997): 46–75; see also her *Remaking Respectability*, 121–26.

13. On John "Mushmouth" Johnson and Robert Motts, see Spear, *Black
Chicago*, 76–77; Herbert Asbury, *Gem of the Prairie: An Informal History of
the Chicago Underworld* (New York: Alfred A. Knopf, 1940; repr., DeKalb:
Northern Illinois University Press, 1986), 167–68. For an example of an-
other black-owned saloon, see George Cross's advertisement in I. C. Harris,
Colored Men's Professional and Business Directory of Chicago (Chicago: I. C.
Harris, 1885), 61. On gambling in the nineteenth century, see Ann Fabian,
*Card Sharps, Dream Books, and Bucket Shops: Gambling in 19th-Century
America* (Ithaca, NY: Cornell University Press, 1990).

14. In 1904 Chicago clubwoman Fannie Barrier Williams warned readers of
the problem facing educated black women: "Hundreds of young women
who have been trained for something better than menial service, failing
to find such employment, fall easy victims to the flattering inducements
of a well-dressed-idleness, the handmaid of shame." See her "The Need of
Social Settlement Work for the City Negro," *Southern Workman* 33, no. 9
(September 1904): 502. On the economic vulnerability of professionally
trained black women in the city, see Stephanie Shaw, *What a Woman Ought
to Be and to Do: Black Professional Women Workers during the Jim Crow Era*
(Chicago: University of Chicago Press, 1996), 118–19. For an example of
the difficulties a trained nurse faced in securing a job in Cleveland around
1910, see Jane Edna Hunter, *A Nickel and a Prayer* (Cleveland, OH: Elli Kani
Publishing Co., 1940), 70–72.

15. In 1890, 232 African American women were classed as dressmakers, milliners, or seamstresses not working in factories; in 1900, 400 black women
were dressmakers and milliners (Scott, *Occupational Changes*, 47, 84). Eileen
Boris notes a more pronounced trend in New York City, where between
1890 and 1900 the number of black women dressmakers and seamstresses
increased fourfold. See her "Black Women and Paid Labor in the Home:
Industrial Homework in Chicago in the 1920s," in *Homework: Historical and
Contemporary Perspectives on Paid Labor at Home*, ed. Eileen Boris and Cynthia R. Daniels (Urbana: University of Illinois Press, 1989), 36. As suggestive
as these figures are about the importance of sewing skills for black women's
work opportunities, they do not reveal how many black women otherwise
employed may have augmented their income by taking in sewing work. Nor
does the casual aspect of sewing register in these statistics. Whether working primarily as a dressmaker who eventually sought to establish her own
shop, occasionally securing sewing or mending jobs to fill in gaps within
a personal or family budget, or running a stable bedroom sewing business,

black women sought access to much-needed income through home-based
needlework. Independent dressmaking was an important business in a
city where black women were restricted from garment industry employment and where those seeking the latest in fashion might be unwelcome
in fashionable dry goods establishments or simply unable to pay the price.
The seemingly inexorable march forward of ready-to-wear did not wipe out
skilled women workers. In fact, the racial exclusion in both manufacturing
and retailing helped black seamstresses remain important to community
residents. See William Leach, *Land of Desire: Merchants, Power, and the Rise of
a New American Culture* (New York: Pantheon Books, 1993), 92–95.

16. There were a few early efforts to establish hair salons for black women during this period. In 1885, when I. C. Harris's black business directory listed
thirty-one barbershops, there was one hair establishment for the care of
women's hair—Miss Gillespie's Hair Bazaar. In 1896 Mrs. Grace Garnett-
Abney opened a beauty parlor at 2808 South State Street. Other women
probably opened shops around the turn of the century as well. In the 1900
census for Chicago, seventy-six women were classified as hairdressers or
barbers. Where they worked—at home, in a barbershop, or in a beauty
parlor—is unclear; but many probably worked in the growing number of
salons that catered to black women's hair care. Beauty salons, however,
would not become a prominent institution within Chicago's South Side
until after 1915. At the end of the nineteenth century, the ventures of
aspiring businesswomen like Gillespie and Garnett-Abney did not replace
private networks of beauty culture. See Harris, *Colored Men's Professional and
Business Directory*, 23; Scott, *Occupational Changes*, 83; Mathilde Bunton,
"From an Interview with Mrs. Grace Garnett-Abney," Illinois Writers' Project, "The Negro in Illinois," box 25, Vivian Harsh Collection, Carter G.
Woodson Regional Library, Chicago Public Library, Chicago. See also Kathy
Peiss, *Hope in a Jar: The Making of America's Beauty Culture* (New York: Met-
ropolitan Books, 1998).

17. Tera Hunter, *"To 'Joy My Freedom,"* 58.

18. Joanne Meyerowitz underscores the attraction of the sex industry for many
urban women: "Of the unskilled women adrift [self-supporting women],
only the sexual service workers were not paid as dependent daughters"
(*Women Adrift*, 40).

19. Ruth Rosen, *Lost Sisterhood*, 81. To be sure, other sites of sexual exchange
competed with the brothel in Chicago, as elsewhere. As the nineteenth
century drew to a close, furnished rooms, saloons, and hotels were as
prominent as brothels in some cities. Timothy Gilfoyle has shown that
as early as 1880 these workplaces actually outnumbered brothels in New
York City (*City of Eros*, 394n2). While there was variation among cities, the
brothel remained the dominant institution of the urban sex trade in the
United States through the end of the nineteenth century.

20. Jane Addams and Frances Kellor were notable exceptions among white reformers at the turn of the century. See Jane Addams, *A New Conscience and an Ancient Evil* (New York: Macmillan Co., 1912), 169; Frances Kellor, "Assisted Emigration from the South: The Women," *Charities* 15, no. 1 (October 7, 1905): 12–13.

21. The federal manuscript census is a rich repository of information about late-nineteenth-century prostitution, especially prostitution existing within geographically circumscribed sex districts. Although the literature on prostitution in turn-of-the-century U.S. cities is voluminous, surprisingly few historians have used the census to explore urban sex work or to identify urban sex workers. Three notable exceptions—each recovering the worlds of prostitution in nineteenth-century western mining communities—are Marion S. Goldman, *Gold Diggers and Silver Miners: Prostitution and Social Life on the Comstock Lode* (Ann Arbor: University of Michigan Press, 1981); Alexy Simmons, *Red Light Ladies: Settlement Patterns and Material Culture on the Mining Frontier*, Anthropology Northwest, no. 4 (Corvallis: Department of Anthropology, Oregon State University, 1989); Paula Petrik, "Capitalists with Rooms: Prostitution in Helena, Montana, 1865–1900," *Montana: The Magazine of Western History* 21, no. 2 (Spring 1991): 28–40.

22. The census is simultaneously a valuable and a frustrating starting point for the study of urban prostitution. First, federal data present only one branch of Chicago's sex industry: brothel prostitution. Although this covers a variety of settings and financial arrangements between workers and madams, it does not encompass the experiences of all women working in the sex trade. Those women who worked on their own—in assignation houses, in saloons, or on the streets—were invisible to enumerators. In addition, the wariness of prostitutes themselves could render the census officials' attempts at accurate enumeration incomplete. Reluctant to disclose the illegal source of their income to representatives of the government, many prostitutes concealed their labors from census takers by claiming to be engaged in some type of reputable employment, such as seamstress, laundress, or milliner; other women claimed no occupation at all. Furthermore, census takers may have designated women as prostitutes who were in fact not in the trade but who shared living quarters with women who were. One can easily imagine how this might have been the case for black women. Census takers, the vast majority of whom were white men, were no doubt as influenced by prevailing myths about black women's sexual nature as were the compiler of the 1889 Chicago brothel directory and many of the period's moral and social reformers. Some may have listed incorrectly as "prostitute" black women living on their own in the boardinghouses and rooming houses in the Levee neighborhood. Further evidence of census takers' reticence (or their refusal to include prostitutes in their tallies) was that many houses of prostitution were passed over by enumerators in their canvassing of streets within the vice district. In both

1880 and 1900 addresses shown in other sources to house prostitutes are conspicuously absent from the manuscript data. For a variety of reasons, then, establishing a completely accurate count of Chicago's prostitutes is impossible. However, I have been able to identify women sex workers in addition to those who explicitly and freely identified themselves as prostitutes to census takers. Listed below are my criteria for identifying houses of prostitution, prostitution boardinghouses, and individual prostitutes within the 1880, 1900, and 1910 manuscript censuses. (Census takers in 1910 no longer listed women as "prostitutes." Although "prostitute" was not used as an occupation in the enumeration districts that made up the South Side sex districts, "houses of ill-fame" were clearly designated as such, and their residents were listed as "keepers" and "inmates.")

1. The clearest case is presented by addresses that are listed as boardinghouses and that boarded self-avowed prostitutes. These were more numerous in the 1880 census, when women appeared less reluctant to claim prostitution as a vocation.

2. Some houses were listed as boardinghouses, but the residents, rather than being identified as "prostitute," either had no occupation or were listed simply as "boarder." I have identified such houses as brothels or brothel boardinghouses when they were clustered within a strip of known brothels and when the makeup of the house resembled that of neighboring houses of prostitution—that is, when there were between three and ten young women boarders, and when the keeper of the house was a woman. This is admittedly a risky method; yet its value is borne out by several cases in which houses of prostitution headed by well-known brothel madams—all of whom were listed as keepers of boardinghouses—were inhabited by young female boarders claiming no occupations. For example, in 1880 prominent white madams Lizzie Allen and Carrie Watson were identified as keepers of boardinghouses with boarders who claimed no occupations.

3. A different problem emerges when sex workers did report occupations other than prostitute to census enumerators. I count these women as prostitutes only when they are found at well-known brothel addresses—that is, when other sources show the address to have been a house of prostitution. For example, in 1900 the black women living at 138–140 Custom House Place claimed to work in a range of jobs, including seamstress, dressmaker, and cook. Yet for several years before and after 1900, a brothel known to be run by black madam Vina Fields operated at this address.

23. Unless otherwise noted, statistics on prostitutes in Chicago have been derived from federal manuscript census schedules: U.S. Bureau of the Census, Tenth Census (1880), Chicago Manuscript Schedules (microfilm), Enumera-

tion Districts 5, 8, and 9; U.S. Bureau of the Census, Twelfth Census (1900), Chicago Manuscript Schedules (microfilm), Enumeration Districts 12, 21, 24, 30, 38, 42, 43, and 161. Figures do not include madams.

24. Bessie Louise Pierce, *A History of Chicago*, vol. 3, *The Rise of the Modern City, 1871–1893* (New York: Alfred A. Knopf, 1957), 515–16, 519.

25. Immigrant parents' attempts to maintain firm control over the behavior of daughters may have successfully kept young immigrant women from entering the ranks of prostitutes in the early twentieth century as well. Ruth Rosen, *Lost Sisterhood*, 141–42; Mary E. Odem, *Delinquent Daughters: Protecting and Policing Adolescent Female Sexuality in the United States, 1885–1920* (Chapel Hill: University of North Carolina Press, 1996), 43–46; Meyerowitz, *Women Adrift*, 9–11.

26. Meyerowitz, *Women Adrift*, xvii–xxiii.

27. Pierce, *History of Chicago*, vol. 3, 516; Meyerowitz, *Women Adrift*, 7–8.

28. Peiss, *Cheap Amusements*, 62–76.

29. State-of-birth figures for African Americans in 1900 are taken from Spear, *Black Chicago*, 13. Comparable statistics are not available for 1880.

30. On chain migration, see Grossman, *Land of Hope*, 89–94.

31. Perry R. Duis, *Challenging Chicago: Coping with Everyday Life, 1837–1920* (Urbana: University of Illinois Press, 1998), 248–49.

32. I found the May Churchill quotation in Donald Miller, *City of the Century: The Epic of Chicago and the Making of America* (New York: Simon and Schuster, 1996), 506.

33. William T. Stead, *If Christ Came to Chicago* (Chicago: Laird and Lee, 1894; repr., Evanston, IL: Chicago Historical Society Bookworks, 1990), 247.

34. *Chicago Daily News*, May 16, 1881; *Chicago Tribune*, May 16, 1881.

35. In 1880 African Americans comprised 2.4 percent of Detroit's population. David Katzman estimates that at the turn of the century "a significant number of Negroes, possibly 10 percent of the adult working black population, earned a living as entrepreneurs or employees in the city's illegal saloon, gambling, and prostitution industries" (*Before the Ghetto*, 62, 67, 171). Blacks accounted for 1.3 percent of Cleveland's population in 1880. By the early twentieth century a red-light district existed near what had become the city's black neighborhood. See Kusmer, *A Ghetto Takes Shape*, 10, 12–13.

36. *Chicago Daily News*, May 16, 1881.

37. For an example of reform literature targeting the vices of drink, gambling, and prostitution in Chicago, see George Wharton James, *Chicago's Dark Places* (Chicago: Craig Press and Women's Temperance Publishing Association, 1891).

38. For a discussion of women's ability to leave prostitution without suffering social stigma and either find wage work or eventually get married, see Ruth Rosen, *Lost Sisterhood*, 144–45. See also Judith R. Walkowitz's analysis of

the occupational mobility of working-class prostitutes before the passage of Britain's Contagious Disease Acts in 1864, 1866, and 1869: *Prostitution and Victorian Society: Women, Class and the State* (New York: Cambridge University Press, 1980), 192.

39. U.S. Bureau of the Census, Tenth Census (1880), Chicago Manuscript Schedules, Enumeration District 9.

40. Ibid.

41. Young girls between the ages of fifteen and eighteen made up a small segment of black and white sex workers (4 percent and 2 percent, respectively).

42. Gilfoyle also notes the "aging of New York's prostitutes" in the first decade of the twentieth century (*City of Eros*, 293). In her study of prostitution in Victorian England, Judith Walkowitz observes that, between 1866 and 1883 in areas where the Contagious Disease Acts were enforced, the average age of registered prostitutes increased. Furthermore, after the repeal of the acts in 1886, this "aging" trend among prostitutes continued nationally (*Prostitution and Victorian Society*, 196, 209–10).

43. U.S. Bureau of the Census, Tenth Census (1880), Chicago Manuscript Schedules, Enumeration District 9; U.S. Bureau of the Census, Twelfth Census (1900), Chicago Manuscript Schedules, Enumeration Districts 21, 42, and 43.

44. Duis, *Challenging Chicago*, 208, 248–51; Spear, *Black Chicago*, 2–3; Meyerowitz, *Women Adrift*, 12.

45. Stead, *If Christ Came to Chicago*, 248.

46. In 1900 Richard R. Wright Jr. found that "most of the Negro service is in families where there is one and rarely two servants" ("Industrial Condition," 26). This suggests that black women worked, not for the wealthy, but in middle-class households.

47. As Tera Hunter (*"To 'Joy My Freedom"*) and Elizabeth Clark-Lewis (*Living In, Living Out*) have shown, black women at the end of the nineteenth century were slowly trying to remove themselves from the ranks of domestic servants.

48. Arriving at a similar conclusion, Walkowitz argues that the changing age profile of English prostitutes between 1866 and the early twentieth century reveals that "as prostitutes became public figures through the registration process, it became increasingly difficult for them to gain respectable employment, and to move in and out of their other social identities" (*Prostitution and Victorian Society*, 210).

49. U.S. Bureau of the Census, Tenth Census (1880), Chicago Manuscript Schedules, Enumeration District 9; U.S. Bureau of the Census, Twelfth Census (1900), Chicago Manuscript Schedules, Enumeration District 30.

50. U.S. Bureau of the Census, Tenth Census (1880), Chicago Manuscript Schedules, Enumeration District 9; U.S. Bureau of the Census, Thirteenth Census (1910), Chicago Manuscript Schedules, Enumeration District 161.

51. U.S. Bureau of the Census, Tenth Census (1880), Chicago Manuscript Schedules, Enumeration District 9; U.S. Bureau of the Census, Twelfth Census (1900), Chicago Manuscript Schedules, Enumeration District 42.
52. Stead, *If Christ Came to Chicago*, 247; *Lakeside Annual Directory of the City of Chicago* for the years 1879, 1883, and 1888 (for Vina Fields); U.S. Bureau of the Census, Tenth Census (1880), Chicago Manuscript Schedules, Enumeration District 9; U.S. Bureau of the Census, Thirteenth Census (1910), Chicago Manuscript Schedules, Enumeration District 161.
53. For Lillian Richardson, see *Lakeside Annual Directory*, 1888; *Sporting and Club House Directory*, 39.
54. U.S. Bureau of the Census, Twelfth Census (1900), Chicago Manuscript Schedules, Enumeration Districts 42 and 43.
55. U.S. Bureau of the Census, Tenth Census (1880), Chicago Manuscript Schedules, Enumeration Districts 5, 9, and 16; U.S. Bureau of the Census, Twelfth Census (1900), Chicago Manuscript Schedules, Enumeration District 30.
56. U.S. Bureau of the Census, Tenth Census (1880), Chicago Manuscript Schedules, Enumeration District 9.
57. Ibid., Enumeration Districts 5, 16; U.S. Bureau of the Census, Twelfth Census (1900), Chicago Manuscript Schedules, Enumeration Districts 21, 43.
58. U.S. Bureau of the Census, Tenth Census (1880), Chicago Manuscript Schedules, Enumeration Districts 5, 9.
59. *Sporting and Club House Directory*, 7–39.
60. Ibid., 38–39.
61. *Chicago Times*, November 27, 1870.
62. As Victoria Wolcott has argued, being able to make it financially in the city reaped more immediate benefits than adhering to the discourse of virtuous womanhood ever could (*Remaking Respectability*, chap. 3, esp. p. 95).

CHAPTER TWO

1. The *Chicago Record-Herald* (October 28, 1907) reserved the name "the jungle" for this area of concentrated sexual commerce. See also Walter Reckless, "The Natural History of Vice Areas in Chicago" (PhD diss., University of Chicago, 1925), 34.
2. Thomas Lee Philpott, *The Slum and the Ghetto: Immigrants, Blacks, and Reformers in Chicago, 1880–1930* (New York: Oxford University Press, 1978), 135.
3. Fewer than 33 percent of Chicago's Germans were unskilled laborers, whereas more than half of the city's Irish were employed as unskilled workers. A Swedish community was established along the north branch of the Chicago River. However, for the most part, areas of settlement for Swedes, Norwegians, and Danes were scattered. Bessie Louise Pierce, *A History of Chicago*, vol. 2, *From Town to City, 1848–1871* (New York: Alfred A. Knopf,

1940), 13, 16–21, 150–52, 482; Homer Hoyt, *One Hundred Years of Land Values in Chicago: The Relationship of the Growth of Chicago to the Rise in Its Land Values, 1830–1933* (Chicago: University of Chicago Press, 1933), 96–97, 85–86; U.S. Bureau of the Census, *Ninth Census of the United States, 1870*, vol. 1, *Population*, 380–85.

4. An 1880 school census suggests that 45 percent of the over 5,000 African Americans enumerated lived in the Second Ward, between Harrison Street on the north, Sixteenth Street on the south, the Chicago River on the west, and Lake Michigan on the east. They made up at least 11 percent of that ward's population. Monroe Nathan Work, "Negro Real Estate Holders of Chicago" (MA thesis, University of Chicago, 1903), 13. I use this census cautiously because it records only 5,159 African Americans within Chicago, while the federal census documents a total of 6,945.

5. *Chicago Times*, July 15 and 16, 1874; *Chicago Tribune*, July 15, 1874.

6. U.S. Bureau of the Census, *Eighth Census of the United States, 1860, Population*, 90. Citywide in 1890, 55.6 percent of the African American population were men. Comparing ward and citywide figures for 1890 is problematic. Ward data counted black men and women among the city's "colored population," defined as "persons of negro descent, Chinese, Japanese and civilized Indians." Figures for the entire city, however, were given for "persons of negro descent." The total "colored" male population was 8,502, while the total number of males "of negro descent" was 7,938—a difference of 564. The total number of "colored" females was 6,350, while there were 6,333 females "of negro descent"—a difference of only 17. Therefore, the ward breakdown of males of "negro descent" must be postulated with caution. U.S. Bureau of the Census, *Eleventh Census, 1890, Compendium*, pt. 1, 675; U.S. Bureau of the Census, *Eleventh Census of the United States, 1890*, vol. 15, *Population*, pt. 1, 884.

7. U.S. Bureau of the Census, *Eleventh Census, 1890, Compendium*, pt. 1, 674–75; U.S. Bureau of the Census, *Twelfth Census, 1900*, vol. 2, *Population*, pt. 1, 613. In 1890 and 1900 the sex ratios of African Americans in the First Ward were comparable to the sex ratios of white native- and foreign-born First Ward residents. In 1890, 64 percent of native-born whites and 63 percent of foreign-born whites were male. In 1900, 72 percent of both native- and foreign-born whites were male.

8. Rather, studies have invariably focused on white men's patronage of black prostitutes, interpreting the paid sexual encounter as evidence of white men's ongoing sexual exploitation of black women. For example, see John D'Emilio and Estelle B. Freedman, *Intimate Matters: A History of Sexuality in America* (New York: Harper and Row, 1988), 297. To the extent that the sex trade victimized women, incorporating black men into this examination of Chicago's sex economy challenges the unstated assumption that white men perpetrated the most egregious sexual abuse of black women.

9. In a Chicago guidebook prepared for world's fair visitors, John J. Flinn described the housing along State Street south of Congress Street, where a large proportion of the area's African Americans lived: "The upper floors of the stores which are not given over to rooms, furnished and unfurnished, are occupied as hotels." Here, he observed, "Black and White mingle almost indiscriminately." See *The Standard Guide to Chicago* (Chicago: Standard Guide Co., 1893), 71.

10. *Sporting and Club House Directory*; Clifton R. Wooldridge, *Hands Up! In the World of Crime* (Chicago: Police Publishing Co., 1901), 60. Between 1901 and 1906 several editions of *Hands Up!* were published, with some differences distinguishing each. In this study I have used three editions, each published in 1901. In subsequent notes, I will distinguish them by referring to the publisher.

11. Most black houses of prostitution were modest establishments, such as the eleven black houses of prostitution on Fourth Avenue south of Polk Street that the *Sporting and Club House Directory* designated as "coon dives." In many cases brothel keepers, black and white, ran their establishments in apartments at the same address. For example, in 1889 white madams Mollie Fitch and French Amie both had brothels at 114 Fourth Avenue. See *Sporting and Club House Directory*, 17, 41, 43–45.

12. U.S. Bureau of the Census, Tenth Census (1880), Chicago Manuscript Schedules, Enumeration District 9.

13. Many prostitutes were listed as "mulatto" in the census. I have designated these women as black for the purposes of counting. Mulattoes were not defined as a separate social category or a distinct class of people. However, for many white customers, purchasing the sexual services of a mulatto woman was preferable to buying sex from a Negro woman. While this distinction is visible in the late nineteenth century, it becomes clearer in the twentieth-century Levee.

14. U.S. Bureau of the Census, Tenth Census (1880), Chicago Manuscript Schedules, Enumeration District 9.

15. Estimates of prostitutes' earnings are based on prices listed for "Colored Houses" in the *Sporting and Club House Directory*, 38–39; Isabel Eaton, "Special Report on Negro Domestic Service in the Seventh Ward," in *The Philadelphia Negro: A Social Study*, by W. E. B. DuBois (Philadelphia: University of Pennsylvania Press, 1899; repr., Philadelphia: University of Pennsylvania Press, 1996), 449; Ruth Rosen, *Lost Sisterhood*, 76. See also Meyerowitz, *Women Adrift*, 40–41.

16. Timothy Gilfoyle suggests that by "mixing sex with nonerotic entertainments, the concert saloon [in New York City] effectively pushed the boundaries of prostitution into new areas of leisure" (*City of Eros*, 225). I would argue that the brothel itself underwent a transformation as it encountered the challenges posed by other places of male leisure, such as the concert saloon. Significantly, unlike in the concert saloon, where, as Gilfoyle

points out, sex was "only one item available for purchase from the menu of pleasures" (225), in the parlor house and in lesser brothels sex was still the main course.

17. *Sporting and Club House Directory*, 42–46.
18. For an analysis of the politics of Victorian domestic architecture and furnishings in Chicago, see Gwendolyn Wright, *Moralism and the Model Home: Domestic Architecture and Cultural Conflict in Chicago, 1873–1913* (Chicago: University of Chicago Press, 1980), 9–102 passim.
19. *Sporting and Club House Directory*, 11, 16, 27. Timothy Gilfoyle has noted that parlor, or private, houses in antebellum New York City "reflected an emphasis on replicating the atmosphere, privacy, and physical environment of the middle-class home" (*City of Eros*, 164). By the end of the century in Chicago, parlor house decor had extended beyond the quieter tastes of middle-class domesticity and moved into a realm that combined home touches with expensive flamboyance. Extravagant parlor houses could be found in vice districts throughout the country at the turn of the century. See Ruth Rosen, *Lost Sisterhood*, 87–89.
20. *Sporting and Club House Directory*, 33–34.
21. See, e.g., ibid., 21, 23. Virtually every entry advertised the sale of either wine or beer.
22. Ibid., 15.
23. On the skills required for running a "high-class" brothel, see Ruth Rosen, *Lost Sisterhood*, 87–88; Goldman, *Gold Diggers and Silver Miners*, 74–76.
24. *Sporting and Club House Directory*, 39.
25. This name for Vina Fields's resort appears in Bill of Indictment, Case File no. 2682, Criminal Case Files, U.S. District Court for the Northern District of Illinois, Northern Division (Chicago), District Courts of the United States, General Records, Record Group 21, National Archives and Records Administration—Great Lakes Region (Chicago).
26. William T. Stead found that Vina Fields employed over sixty black women during the world's fair. A year later she had only thirty or forty (Stead, *If Christ Came to Chicago*, 247). These numbers were probably inflated. In the 1900 census, enumerators counted twenty women in Fields's House of Pleasure. In 1892 many feared that the World's Columbian Exposition would draw criminal elements to Chicago. "It is a known fact," wrote one reporter, "that already the worst criminals in the country are flocking to Chicago in anticipation of a rich harvest during the World's Fair" (*Chicago Daily News*, February, 6, 1892). Women as well as men sought to take advantage of the opportunities offered by the festive occasion of the fair, and prostitutes from other cities migrated to Chicago, many staying only for the duration of the fair.
27. Stead, *If Christ Came to Chicago*, 249.
28. Ibid.
29. Ibid., 459.

30. *Sporting and Club House Directory*, 17.
31. Ibid., 39.
32. Several historians have explored the exclusion of black women from nineteenth-century Victorian ideals of womanhood. See Patricia Morton, *Disfigured Images: The Historical Assault on Afro-American Women* (Westport, CT: Praeger, 1991), 17–54; Hine, "Rape and the Inner Lives of Black Women." For discussions of black women's struggle to claim Victorian ideals of home, womanhood, and sexual morality, see Shaw, *What a Woman Ought to Be*; Higginbotham, *Righteous Discontent*, 185–229; Victoria Wolcott, "Bible, Bath, and Broom: Nannie Helen Burroughs's National Training School and African-American Racial Uplift," *Journal of Women's History* 9, no. 1 (Spring): 88–110.
33. Stead, *If Christ Came to Chicago*, 247.
34. Reckless, "Natural History of Vice Areas," 23.
35. *Sporting and Club House Directory*, 38–39, 7–37 passim.
36. On the ever-present threat of sexual violation that black domestic workers faced, see Hine, "Rape and the Inner Lives of Black Women"; Shaw, *What a Woman Ought to Be*, 23–25; Angela Davis, *Women, Race, and Class* (New York: Random House, 1981), 90–98.
37. With the exception of Vina Fields's house, none of the black houses of prostitution identified as such in the 1880 census employed servants.
38. Reckless, "Natural History of Vice Areas," 23.
39. Wooldridge, *Hands Up!* (Police Publishing Co.), 237.
40. On the madam's duties and the demands she placed on brothel workers, see Ruth Rosen, *Lost Sisterhood*, 87–90; Marion Goldman provides an example of one madam who controlled her brothel with an iron fist (*Gold Diggers and Silver Miners*, 77–78).
41. Reckless, "Natural History of Vice Areas," 55; James, *Chicago's Dark Places*, 40–42. Several furnished rooming houses were promised to be "exclusive" and "perfectly safe in every sense of the word" (*Sporting and Club House Directory*, 8, 37).
42. Wooldridge, *Hands Up!* (Police Publishing Co.), 243.
43. One "lowly" institution in which nineteenth- and early-twentieth-century street prostitutes found work was the "crib house." In western frontier communities a crib house amounted to a shack or other small dwelling that was subdivided into rows of cubicles that provided only enough space for a cot and perhaps a night table and washstand. For a flat rate a prostitute rented a crib space by the night or by the month and brought customers to her room for quick and cheap service. Cribs were used by the women least desirable to predominantly white miners and laborers: black, Mexican, and poor white women. When cribs emerged outside the West in cities like Hartford, Connecticut, and New Orleans, black women and the most vulnerable white women worked there. See Anne M. Butler, *Daughters of Joy, Sisters of Misery: Prostitutes in the American West, 1865–90* (Urbana:

University of Illinois Press, 1985), xviii; Ruth Rosen, *Lost Sisterhood*, 80, 94. Cribs were not common in late-nineteenth-century Chicago. The few cases of crib prostitution that existed, however, were connected to black sex workers. In the 1870s the Black Hole, a collection of saloons, gambling dens, and brothels west of downtown at Washington and Halsted streets, contained some partitioned rooms in which mostly black streetwalkers serviced their clients. By the 1880s the Black Hole had vanished, but several black crib houses, known as Noah's Ark, appeared along South State Street between Harrison and Taylor. Aside from these examples, crib houses were never very important to streetwalkers working in Chicago. See Al Rose, *Storyville, New Orleans: Being an Authentic, Illustrated Account of the Notorious Red-Light District* (Tuscaloosa: University of Alabama Press, 1974), 92–96, 159; Goldman, *Gold Diggers and Silver Miners*, 93; Asbury, *Gem of the Prairie*, 102–3, 122; *Chicago Times*, August 5, 1877.

44. For several historians, whether of prostitution or of black life, African American sex workers have embodied the "extreme" oppression that black women faced in their efforts to find work in the city. These women experienced a unique form of degradation as workers in the prostitution economy. According to Barbara Hobson, streetwalkers were "the most powerless individuals" at work in the urban sex trade and were "drawn disproportionately from the ranks of racial minorities, the poor, [and] the very young." See Barbara Meil Hobson, *Uneasy Virtue: The Politics of Prostitution and the American Reform Tradition* (New York: Basic Books, 1987), 35–36. In her study of black women's work, Jacqueline Jones concluded that during the First Great Migration, "as a group, black prostitutes represented an extreme form of the victimization endured by all black women workers in terms of their health, safety, and financial compensation" (*Labor of Love, Labor of Sorrow*, 182). In 1944 Gunnar Myrdal noted that the "ordinary Negro streetwalker" scrambled for money in "an unprotected, economically disadvantaged and overcrowded occupation." See his *An American Dilemma: The Negro Problem and Modern Democracy* (New York: Harper and Bros., 1944), 332. In their history of sexuality in the United States, John D'Emilio and Estelle B. Freedman have likened the experiences of black prostitutes at the hands of white male clients to the sexual exploitation suffered by enslaved women and girls: "customers might come from the ranks of white laborers or office workers who drove through the black district or roamed central city neighborhoods filled with seedy hotels, in search of quick sexual release. What white southerners had once taken from the black women they owned as slaves, northerners now bought in a sexual marketplace" (*Intimate Matters*, 297).

45. *Chicago Tribune*, March 29, 1883. On ladies "thronging" Chicago's downtown thoroughfares, see Louis Schick, *Chicago and Its Environs* (Chicago: Louis Schick, 1893), 100–103. For example, Schick comments: "There is a steady stream of ladies, almost always in parties of two or three, passing

along Adams Street in either direction, and, as they meet the throng on
State Street, there is a good humoured crush in which the male pedestrian
feels that he is sadly out of place" (103). For a general discussion of women
in public spaces in the nineteenth century, see Mary P. Ryan, *Women in
Public: Between Banners and Ballots, 1825–1880* (Baltimore, MD: Johns Hopkins University Press, 1990), chap. 2.

46. Stead, *If Christ Came to Chicago*, 38.
47. Clifton R. Wooldridge, *Hands Up! In the World of Crime* (Chicago: Thomp-
    son and Thomas, 1901), 482–83.
48. Ibid., 290.
49. Joseph Kirkland, "Among the Poor of Chicago," in *The Poor in Great Cities*,
    ed. Robert Woods et al. (New York: Charles Scribner's Sons, 1895; repr., New
    York: Arno Press, 1971), 228. Kirkland distinguished the Bad Lands from
    other areas in the Levee by describing it as "the abode of vice and crime
    rather than of poverty" (203).
50. *Chicago Daily News*, January 19, 1892.
51. *Chicago Tribune*, June 5, 1880.
52. *Chicago Times*, July 17 and December 19, 1880; *Chicago Tribune*, May 10,
    1893.
53. Panel houses were not unique to Chicago but could be found in the red-
    light districts of most large cities (Gilfoyle, *City of Eros*, 172–74).
54. *Chicago Morning News*, April 1, 1881.
55. Wooldridge, *Hands Up!* (Thompson and Thomas), 79, 150.
56. Ibid., 40–47.
57. Ibid., 203, 303.
58. *Chicago Tribune*, May 16, 1881. On December 23, 1880, the *Tribune* reported
    that "Eliza Dennis, a notorious negress who has gotten away with more
    money from more men than any other cyprian within the city limits, was
    locked up last night at the West Madison Street Station upon the charge of
    larceny. This time she stole $20 only, but it was all her victim had all the
    same. John Dwyer is his name, and to all appearances he is as green as he
    claims to be." See also *Chicago Daily News*, May 16, 1881.
59. *Chicago Tribune*, November 5, 1899, 8; Wooldridge, *Hands Up!* (Thompson
    and Thomas), 47.
60. Clifton R. Wooldridge, *Hands Up! In the World of Crime* (Chicago: Stanton
    and Van Vliet Co., 1901), 203–6.
61. Wooldridge, *Hands Up!* (Police Publishing Co.), 238.
62. *Chicago Tribune*, February 23, 1893, 7. See also February 28, 1893, 1;
    March 2, 1893, 3; March 10, 1893, 6.
63. Case nos. 32299, 36021A, and 34787, Records of the Chicago Criminal
    Court (microfilm), Circuit Court of Cook County Archives, Richard J.
    Daley Center, Chicago; *Chicago Tribune*, May 28, 1893, 5; *Chicago Tribune*,
    August 17, 1893, 6. For Wooldridge's descriptions of his arrests of Shouse,
    see his *Hands Up!* (Police Publishing Co.), 233–35, where he details appre-

hending Shouse in the Barland case. His dates do not exactly correspond with newspaper and court records, but the general facts of the case and the last name of the plaintiff are the same.

64. *Chicago Morning News*, April 1 and 9, 1881; Wooldridge, *Hands Up!* (Thompson and Thomas), 46–47.
65. Wooldridge, *Hands Up!* (Police Publishing Co.), 60–61, 200.
66. Ibid., 60–61; Wooldridge, *Hands Up!* (Thompson and Thomas), 79, 187–88.
67. *Chicago Daily News*, February 1 and March 10, 1876.
68. Residents of Hull House, *Hull House Maps and Papers: A Presentation of Nationalities and Wages in a Congested District of Chicago* (New York: Thomas Y. Crowell and Co., 1895), Wage and Nationalities Maps; Stead, *If Christ Came to Chicago*, 448–49; *Sporting and Club House Directory*, 43–45.
69. Case no. 192577, Paul Brown, Receiver, vs. Vina Fields, 1899, Records of the Chicago Criminal Court (microfilm), Circuit Court of Cook County Archives, Richard J. Daley Center, Chicago.
70. Hoyt, *One Hundred Years of Land Values*, 201–2; Wooldridge, *Hands Up!* (Thompson and Thomas), 290, 483–84.
71. *Sporting and Club House Directory*, 41.
72. U.S. Bureau of the Census, Tenth Census (1880), Chicago Manuscript Schedules, Enumeration District 9; *Sporting and Club House Directory*, 42. House number 465 Clark Street (Georgia Styles's former resort) is not listed in Stead's Black List of Clark Street properties (*If Christ Came to Chicago*, 446). Residents of Hull House, *Hull House Maps and Papers*, Wage and Nationalities Maps.
73. Wooldridge, *Hands Up!* (Thompson and Thomas), 484.
74. Miss Mattie Lee appears in the 1896 *Lakeside Annual Directory* at 150 Custom House Place and in 1898 at 143 Custom House Place. See also Wooldridge, *Hands Up!* (Thompson and Thomas), 203–6.
75. U.S. Bureau of the Census, Tenth Census (1880), Chicago Manuscript Schedules, Enumeration District 9. Moving about could bring financial stability and even success to some black madams. One such madam may have been Elizabeth Morris, who, after appearing in the 1880 census and the 1880 city directory at 116 Custom House Place, disappeared from available sources. A Mrs. Morris appears in Stead's 1894 Black List as keeper of a colored house of prostitution at 182 Custom House Place. Perhaps this was Elizabeth Morris. If so, it suggests that, even when their activities went unnoticed by directory compilers, police officers, or reformers, some black women were able to stay in business within the district for extended periods of time. Stead, *If Christ Came to Chicago*, 451.
76. *Lakeside Annual Directory*, 1893; Stead, *If Christ Came to Chicago*, 451. By 1893 Butterfield had been renamed Armour Avenue. Ella White appears in the city directory as Ellen White; in Stead, she appears as Allon White.
77. On the long and colorful careers of Lizzie Allen and Caroline (aka Carrie) Watson, see Asbury, *Gem of the Prairie*, 135–40. In 1880 Lizzie Allen ran a

resort at 47 Congress, where she employed eight white women and three servants. U.S. Bureau of the Census, Tenth Census (1880), Chicago Manuscript Schedules, Enumeration District 5.

78. *Lakeside Annual Directory*, 1879–1904. Fields is listed in the 1879 directory as "Miss Venie Fields"; in the 1880 directory as Mrs. Fanny Fields; in the 1882 directory as Mrs. Vinie Fields; and in the 1888 directory as Miss Vinia Fields. After this, she or the directory compilers settled on Vina as her first name, though her marital status continued to fluctuate.

79. On Lizzie Allen see Asbury, *Gem of the Prairie*, 138; Stead, *If Christ Came to Chicago*, 451. Marilynn Wood Hill found that, in New York City in the 1850s, as many as 40 percent of female property owners in the city's vice districts were known sex entrepreneurs. Hill discusses prostitution as a "means of accumulating property" in *Their Sisters' Keepers*, 96–103.

80. Stead, *If Christ Came to Chicago*, 448, 450. Entries from the *Chicago Street Gazette* in the late 1870s show that Ritchie did not simply rent out her property to other madams but would at times set a friend up with her own establishment. Asbury, *Gem of the Prairie*, 131, 135. This may have been the case in 1900 when Ritchie identified herself to census enumerators as a servant working at 2034 Dearborn Street. Her properties at 2020 and 2024 Dearborn were enumerated as sex resorts but were under the management of other white madams. Marilynn Wood Hill found similar networking among New York City prostitutes in the middle of the nineteenth century (*Their Sisters' Keepers*, 102).

81. Wooldridge, *Hands Up!* (Police Publishing Co.), 60.

82. Stead, *If Christ Came to Chicago*, 247, 449.

83. Ibid., 449; Residents of Hull House, *Hull House Maps and Papers*, Wage and Nationalities Maps.

84. Stead's Black List of "Occupiers, Owners and Tax-Payers of Property Used for Immoral Purposes" provides the addresses of many Levee property owners (*If Christ Came to Chicago*, 446–51). In a note accompanying this Black List, Stead warns his readers against too quickly drawing conclusions as to the responsibility of all listed owners for the immoral use of their property. He states: "It is only just to remember that persons who pay taxes as agents for property have often no means of controlling the disposition of that property. It is also well to state that in many cases the owners of the houses are only owners of the ground on which the houses stand, with next to no power of control over the tenants of the houses built on their land. In other cases they have inherited the property and do not know what to do with it" (451). Stead's disclaimer points to the difficulty that I confronted when I attempted to recover the history of ownership of Levee properties. While some cases of ownership are substantiated in other sources (such as Fields's ownership of the property at 138–140 Custom House Place), others are much more difficult to corroborate with extant sources. Nevertheless,

Stead's Black List provides useful clues to the web of property relations that shaped the Levee sex economy.

85. C. E. Robinson's estate took advantage of the high returns earned from renting property for immoral purposes: in 1893 Stead found that Robinson's estate paid taxes on ten properties in the Near South Side Levee and five in the vice district developing south of Twentieth Street (*If Christ Came to Chicago*, 446–51).

86. Ibid., 450.

CHAPTER THREE

1. *Chicago Times*, July 15, 1874.
2. See n. 4 in chap. 2.
3. Spear, *Black Chicago*, 14. Spear points out that in 1900 African Americans could still be found throughout the city: fourteen of the city's thirty-five wards were at least 1 percent black.
4. *Chicago Times*, July 15, 1874.
5. While the destruction of the Little Fire was significant—approximately $3.5 million in property damage—the extent of the damage was not nearly as great as that occasioned by the 1871 fire, which destroyed over $200 million worth of property. See Pierce, *History of Chicago*, vol. 3, 308; Joseph Kirkland, *The Story of Chicago*, 2d ed. (Chicago: Dibble Publishing, 1892), 355.
6. *Chicago Times*, July 16, 1874; *Chicago Evening Journal*, July 15, 1874; *Chicago Tribune*, July 15, 1874.
7. *Chicago Times*, July 15, 1874.
8. Ibid.
9. Ibid.
10. *Chicago Tribune*, July 16, 1874.
11. Ibid.
12. *Chicago Times*, July 16, 1874.
13. Kathleen M. Brown has discussed the racialization of the term "wench" in colonial Virginia. She has observed that, while in the seventeenth and early eighteenth centuries "wench" was used to designate "English women of low birth," by the middle of the eighteenth century the term had come almost exclusively to describe women of African descent. See her *Good Wives, Nasty Wenches, and Anxious Patriarchs: Gender, Race, and Power in Colonial Virginia* (Chapel Hill: University of North Carolina Press, 1996), 370.
14. *Chicago Times*, November 27, 1870.
15. *Chicago Times* in 1876, quoted in Asbury, *Gem of the Prairie*, 112. On Dan Webster's notoriety as a gambler, saloon keeper, brothel owner, and "professional bailer of the colored people," see *Chicago Tribune*, August 25, 1874, 5; October 3, 1875, 16; October 24, 1876, 8; November 3, 1876, 3; July 6, 1879, 2; July 9, 1879, 5; March 10, 1881, 7.

16. *Chicago Tribune*, January 10, 1880. In I. C. Harris's 1885 colored men's business directory, Mortimer appears in a joint venture with Daniel Smith and J. Hunter at 103 E. Harrison (*Colored Men's Professional and Business Directory*, 34).

17. Residents of Hull House, *Hull House Maps and Papers*, 23.

18. *Chicago Tribune*, January 10, 1880.

19. Harold Wentworth and Stuart Berg Flexner, eds., *Dictionary of American Slang* (New York: Crowell, 1960; 2d supp. ed., 1975). Irving Lewis Allen notes that the term "dive" was "an Americanism of the 1860s" that "originally denoted a disreputable drinking place, often in a basement, that one figuratively 'dived' into, as though to escape public view." See his *The City in Slang: New York Life and Popular Speech* (New York: Oxford University Press, 1993), 146–48, esp. 147.

20. Harold Vynne, *Chicago by Day and Night: The Pleasure Seeker's Guide to the Paris of America* (Chicago: Thomson and Zimmerman, 1892), 201–3; L. O. Curon, *Chicago, Satan's Sanctum* (Chicago: C. D. Phillips and Co., 1899), 118–19.

21. In his study of prostitution in nineteenth-century New York City, Timothy Gilfoyle found that most African American prostitutes worked in Tenderloin "dives" and in "rundown brothels" in Greenwich Village (*City of Eros*, 209–10, 213–25).

22. *Chicago Tribune*, September 18, 1905, 2.

23. Vynne, *Chicago by Day and Night*, 202–4.

24. *Chicago Daily News*, March 10, 1878.

25. *Chicago Tribune*, January 26, 1936, D7; Asbury, *Gem of the Prairie*, 65; see also Lloyd Lewis and Henry Justin Smith, *Chicago: The History of Its Reputation* (New York: Harcourt, Brace, and Co., 1929), 98.

26. Asbury, *Gem of the Prairie*, 106.

27. T. A. Larson, *History of Wyoming*, 2d ed. (Lincoln: University of Nebraska Press, 1978), 202–4; Writers' Program of the Works Projects Administration, Wyoming, *Wyoming: A Guide to Its History, Highways, and People* (Wyoming: Works Projects Administration, 1941; repr., Lincoln: University of Nebraska Press, 1981), 186.

28. Allen, *The City in Slang*, 178.

29. Wooldridge, *Hands Up!* (Police Publishing Company), 60.

30. Asbury, *Gem of the Prairie*, 106–7; Wooldridge, *Hands Up!* (Thompson and Thomas), 289–92.

31. Wooldridge, *Hands Up!* (Thompson and Thomas), 242–44, 48–49. In 1892 Emma Ford was convicted of larceny and sentenced to five years in Joliet Correctional Center. During sentencing Judge Baker said to Ford: "You have been a perfect terror until finally justice, in a measure, has been meted out to you." According to a *Tribune* reporter, "the prisoner laughed and told the court she had got 'just enough to make me feel good'" (*Chicago Tribune*, April 17, 1892, 5). Her defiance sealed her status among the dangerous

black women of the Levee. Prison did not end her career as a thieving prostitute, however. In 1901 Ford appeared again in criminal court, this time for stealing $14 from a Colorado doctor, for which she received one year in the house of correction. The police credited Ford "with being the cleverest pickpocket in Chicago" (*Chicago Tribune*, January 3, 1901, 1).

32. Dorothy Hammond and Alta Jablow, *The Africa That Never Was: Four Centuries of British Writing about Africa* (New York: Twayne Publishers, 1970), 149–56; see also Patrick Brantlinger, "Victorians and Africans: The Genealogy of the Myth of the Dark Continent," in *"Race," Writing, and Difference*, ed. Henry Louis Gates Jr. (Chicago: University of Chicago Press, 1986), 194–95.

33. Hammond and Jablow, *The Africa That Never Was*, 94–95; Fawn M. Brodie, *The Devil Drives: A Life of Sir Richard Burton* (New York: W. W. Norton and Co., 1967), 212.

34. Jean Burton, *Sir Richard Burton's Wife* (New York: Alfred A. Knopf, 1941), 128; Edward Rice, *Captain Sir Richard Burton: The Secret Agent Who Made the Pilgrimage to Mecca, Discovered the Kama Sutra, and Brought the Arabian Nights to the West* (New York: Scribner's, 1990), 474–75.

35. The *Chicago Tribune* periodically printed communiqués from the Welsh explorer Henry M. Stanley's African expeditions. For example, see the report titled "Stanley in Africa," September 5, 1883. On May 10, 1893, the *Chicago Daily News* provided a brief lesson about Dahomey to its readers: "Dahomey has been brought by the recent French invasion into the light of the world's attention." Among "the more interesting features of this African State [are] the now famous body guards of 6000 Amazons who are well disciplined and formidable warriors." The sketch stressed the "extreme barbarism" of the Dahomeans, who "have been accustomed to practice cruel outrages upon travelers and missionaries in the past."

36. The caricature of the black urban Amazon was not unique to Chicago. Historian Kali N. Gross has examined the popularization of this image of black women's criminality in Philadelphia at the turn of the twentieth century. Gross has found that the Amazon figure that emerged in Philadelphia newspapers reflected white concerns about black women's criminality and "embod[ied] that which many whites found wholly objectionable about city life." In Chicago the figure of the Levee's brutish black women reflected similar anxieties among whites about black urbanization but more specifically reflected fears of paid interracial sex in the city's prostitution economy. See Kali N. Gross, *Colored Amazons: Crime, Violence, and Black Women in the City of Brotherly Love, 1880–1910* (Durham, NC: Duke University Press, 2006), 101–26.

37. Edward D. McDowell, "The World's Fair Cosmopolis," *Frank Leslie's Popular Monthly* 36, no. 4 (October 1893): 415.

38. This phrase was used under the photograph of the Dahomean Village in *Midway Types: A Book of Illustrated Lessons about the People of the Midway Plaisance* (Chicago: Engraving Co., 1893), vol. 12, not paginated.

39. John C. Eastman, "Village Life at the World's Fair," *The Chautauquan* 17, no. 5 (August 1893): 603. Robert W. Rydell discusses the educative mission of the Midway in "The World's Columbian Exposition of 1893: Racist Underpinnings of a Utopian Artifact," *Journal of American Culture* 1, no. 2 (Summer 1978): 253–75.
40. Eastman, "Village Life," 603–4. Literary critic Denton J. Snider remarked that "one of the marvelous facts of Dahomey is that of the Amazons." See his *World's Fair Studies* (Chicago: Sigma Publishing Co., 1895), 331.
41. "Four Amazons," in *Midway Types*.
42. McDowell, "World's Fair Cosmopolis."
43. Snider, *World's Fair Studies*, 329; McDowell, "World's Fair Cosmopolis."
44. Frederick Douglass's speech at Colored American Day, August 25, 1893, is quoted in Christopher Robert Reed, *"All the World Is Here!": The Black Presence at White City* (Bloomington: Indiana University Press, 2000), appendix 1. Douglass had earlier surmised that, "as if to shame the Negro, the Dahomians are also here to exhibit the Negro as a repulsive savage"; see Ida B. Wells et al. *The Reasons Why the Colored American Is Not in the World's Columbian Exposition*, ed. Robert W. Rydell (Urbana: University of Illinois Press, 1999), 13.
45. Vynne, *Chicago by Day and Night*, 202–3.
46. John J. Flinn, *The Best Things to Be Seen at the World's Fair* (Chicago: Columbia Guide Co., 1893), 577.
47. Wooldridge, *Hands Up!* (Police Publishing Co.), 200.
48. Wooldridge, *Hands Up!* (Thompson and Thomas), 289–92. Herbert Asbury offers an embellished retelling of Wooldridge's account of the arrest of Susan Winslow: "Wooldridge removed the back door [of Winslow's resort] from its hinges and sawed out the frame and about two feet of wall." After tying the rope around Winslow's waist, Detective Wooldridge shouted: "Giddap! The horse lunged forward, and Black Susan was dragged out of her chair and skittered up the plank for about three feet before she began shrieking. . . . When the rope was removed, she waddled painfully up the planks." During the ride to the police station, another woman, arrested with Winslow, pulled splinters from Winslow's prostrate body (*Gem of the Prairie*, 107–8).
49. Like the travel narratives of Stanley and Burton, Detective Clifton Wooldridge's sensational and self-aggrandizing account of his one-man fight against crime in Chicago was popular reading for Chicagoans. Between 1899 and 1901 *Hands Up!* went through at least three editions, and another appeared in 1906.
50. Kali Gross has found that in turn-of-the-century Philadelphia, news accounts applied the Amazon figure even to domestic servants and in so doing "ridiculed and demonized African-American women's desire for better employment and better wages" (*Colored Amazons*, 114).

51. From the *Chicago Conservator*, quoted in St. Clair Drake, *Churches and Voluntary Associations in the Chicago Negro Community* (Chicago: Illinois Works Projects Administration, 1940), 83.
52. See, e.g., Mumford, *Interzones*, 26. On the Levee as a "segregated vice district," see also Perry R. Duis, *The Saloon: Public Drinking in Chicago and Boston, 1880–1920* (Urbana: University of Illinois Press, 1983), 204, 253.
53. *Chicago Times*, July 15, 1874.
54. Bethel African Methodist Episcopal was founded around 1860 and was located on Third Avenue north of Harrison until at least 1885 (Drake, *Churches and Voluntary Associations*, 73).
55. St. Clair Drake cited *The Morris Dictionary of Chicago Churches*, which listed the following among Chicago's black churches: Herman Baptist; the Free Will Church; Hyde Park People's Church A.M.E.; St. Mark's A.M.E.; St. John's A.M.E.; St. Mary's Mission A.M.E.; Wayman Mission A.M.E.; and Walter's Metropolitan Zion. The addresses of these were not noted. See *Churches and Voluntary Associations*, 106.
56. I. C. Harris, *Colored Men's Professional and Business Directory*, 15–20; *Chicago Conservator*, November 18, 1882.
57. John J. Flinn, *Chicago: The Marvelous City of the West* (Chicago: National Book and Picture Co., 1893), 124; Schick, *Chicago and Its Environs*, 378; Drake, *Churches and Voluntary Associations*, 65; Pierce, *History of Chicago*, vol. 3, 50n85, 431–32n24, 470–71; *Chicago Conservator*, December 16, 1882; David Nasaw, *Going Out: The Rise and Fall of Public Amusements* (Cambridge, MA: Harvard University Press, 1993), 12.
58. Nasaw, *Going Out*, 13. See also theater listings in guidebooks.
59. Pierce, *History of Chicago*, vol. 3, 431–32, 432n24, 470–471; Nasaw, *Going Out*, 13–14.
60. Violators were subject to fines ranging from $25 to $500 and faced up to one year in prison.
61. Claudia D. Johnson, "That Guilty Third Tier: Prostitution in Nineteenth-Century Theaters," *American Quarterly* 27, no. 5 (December 1975): 575–84.
62. Nasaw, *Going Out*, 10–11; *Chicago Daily News*, March 16, 1888.
63. The *Minneapolis Western Appeal*, March 24, 1888, expressing a hopeful sentiment that was no doubt shared by its readers, concluded that "the proprietors will soon learn that Colored people know their rights and dare maintain them." On Wilkins, see Drake, *Churches and Voluntary Associations*, 69.
64. Flinn, *Chicago*, 127; Pierce, *History of Chicago*, vol. 3, 470–73; *Chicago Daily News*, March 28, 1885.
65. Stead, *If Christ Came to Chicago*, 258–59; Vynne, *Chicago by Day and Night*, 34–36.
66. *Chicago Daily News*, March 16, 1888.
67. *Chicago Tribune*, March 16, 1888.

68. Duis, *Saloon*, 192–96. See also Royal Melendy, "The Saloon in Chicago," *American Journal of Sociology* 6, no. 3 (November 1900): 289–306, on the saloon as a social institution for working-class men. Although this study did not look at saloons in African American neighborhoods, its conclusions are helpful in examining the evolution of saloons as a public institution serving the needs of black urban communities.

69. Duis, *Saloon*, 47. The financial arrangement between breweries and keepers frequently led to keepers' financial dependency and ultimately to business failure.

70. I. C. Harris, *Colored Men's Professional and Business Directory*, 35; Mathilde Bunton, "The Negro in Business: Taverns," Illinois Writers' Project, "The Negro in Illinois," box 25, Vivian Harsh Collection, Carter G. Woodson Regional Library, Chicago Public Library. After the turn of the century, it appears that some black-owned bars continued to prohibit the entrance of women. For example, see the *Chicago Broad Ax*, October 12, 1907, and October 2, 1909. Regarding Harris's *Colored Men's Professional and Business Directory*, it is important to stress that there were many businesses not listed within its pages. St. Clair Drake wonders why three prominent churches were not listed in the directory (*Churches and Voluntary Associations*, 72).

71. Schick, *Chicago and Its Environs*, 105.

72. *Indianapolis Freeman*, August 30, 1890; I. C. Harris, *Colored Men's Professional and Business Directory*, 35; *Chicago Conservator*, December 18, 1886.

73. Duis, *Saloon*, 64.

74. *Indianapolis Freeman*, August 8, 1890; I. C. Harris, *Colored Men's Professional and Business Directory*, 23, 26, 28, 46, 52, 61, 63.

75. *Chicago Conservator*, December 18, 1886, and November 18, 1882.

76. See George Cross's advertisement in I. C. Harris, *Colored Men's Professional and Business Directory*, 61. On Johnson and Motts, see Spear, *Black Chicago*, 76–77; Asbury, *Gem of the Prairie*, 167–68.

77. *Chicago Daily News*, May 4, 1893, and January 19 and 20, 1892.

78. On white gamblers and craps, see *Chicago Daily News*, February 12 and 13, 1892; *Chicago Tribune*, May 10, 1893.

79. *Indianapolis Freeman*, August 30, 1890; *Chicago Daily News*, January 1, 1894.

80. *Chicago Tribune*, May 17, 1887.

81. *Chicago Tribune*, January 6 and August 31, 1893. In the 1880s Daniel Scott owned Scott and Hunter's Sample Room and Billiard Parlor with J. H. Hunter. See I. C. Harris, *Colored Men's Professional and Business Directory*, 63. Daniel Scott died in 1895. The *Tribune* reported that he was "one of the wealthiest colored men in Chicago, and a resident of the city for thirty years" (*Chicago Tribune*, August 25, 1895).

82. Stead, *If Christ Came to Chicago*, 448; *Chicago Tribune*, January 9, 1890; *Indianapolis Freeman*, August 30, 1890. In April 1890 Scott was twice indicted for keeping a gambling house (*Chicago Tribune*, April 10, 1890, 3).

83. Such concerns were regularly expressed in the *Chicago Conservator*. See the reminiscences of the *Conservator*'s editor, Ferdinand L. Barnett, recorded in Drake and Cayton, *Black Metropolis*, 48; Ralph Nelson Davis, "The Negro Newspaper in Chicago" (MA thesis, University of Chicago, 1939), 16–17; I. C. Harris, *Colored Men's Professional and Business Directory*, 21, 28, 52, 56. Regarding the men who worked for the *Conservator*, Ralph Davis wrote: "Associated with Mr. Barnett in the work of the *Conservator* were Dr. J. E. Henderson, Mr. Alexander Clark, and Mr. A. T. Hall. Dr. J. E. Henderson, a practicing physician, was a graduate of Fisk University and the medical school of Northwestern University. Mr. Alexander Clark was a leader in a Masonic Lodge, and the nature of duties as a national officer included traveling over the midwest sections of the country. He was reputed to be the best known and most influential man in the midwest. Through his work he had contact and exercised influence with the masses and the classes. The office of the *Conservator* was in charge of Mr. A. T. Hall who had some newspaper experience. He was also the city editor" ("Negro Newspaper," 26). Arriving at a different conclusion regarding the drink habit among blacks in Philadelphia in the 1890s, W. E. B. DuBois found that, while "the increase of beer-drinking among all classes, black and white, is noticeable," "the saloon is evidently not so much a moral as an economic problem among Negroes" (*Philadelphia Negro*, 277, 282).
84. *Chicago Tribune*, June 21, 1877, 7.
85. Drake and Cayton, *Black Metropolis*, 48.
86. From the *Chicago Conservator*, quoted in Drake, *Churches and Voluntary Associations*, 82.
87. Ibid., 83–84.
88. Ibid., 83.
89. Tera Hunter, *"To 'Joy My Freedom,"* 82–85.

CHAPTER FOUR

1. Stead, *If Christ Came to Chicago*, 248; "Real Estate Transfers," *Chicago Daily Tribune*, January 20, 1909, 13; U.S. Bureau of the Census, Twelfth Census (1900), Chicago Manuscript Schedules, Enumeration District 21; affidavit of Lucinda Webb, December 4, 1896, Case File no. 2682, Criminal Case Files, U.S. District Court for the Northern District of Illinois, Northern Division (Chicago), District Courts of the United States, General Records, Record Group 21, National Archives and Records Administration—Great Lakes Region (Chicago).
2. U.S. Bureau of the Census, Thirteenth Census (1910), Chicago Manuscript Schedules (microfilm), Enumeration District 160.
3. On the fame of Chicago's Twenty-Second Street Levee, see Emmett Dedmon, *Fabulous Chicago* (New York: Random House, 1953), 251–69; Lloyd Wendt and Herman Kogan, *Lords of the Levee: The Story of Bathhouse John*

     and Hinky Dink (Indianapolis: Bobbs-Merrill Company, 1943); Asbury, *Gem of the Prairie*, 242–319.

4.   Mayor Carter Harrison reminisced that it was at the stroke of his pen that the Near South Side vice district met its end. Carter H. Harrison, *Stormy Years: The Autobiography of Carter H. Harrison, Five Times Mayor of Chicago* (New York: Bobbs-Merrill Co., 1935), 311.

5.   Earl Shepard Johnson, "The Natural History of the Central Business District with Particular Reference to Chicago" (PhD diss., University of Chicago, 1944), 584–85.

6.   Hoyt, *One Hundred Years of Land Values*, 142; Richard C. Lindberg, *To Serve and Collect: Chicago Politics and Police Corruption from the Lager Beer Riot to the Summerdale Scandal* (New York: Praeger, 1991), 130. On the spatial relation of vice and railroads, Walter Reckless wrote in 1925: "This growing vice area on the South Side, along its entire stretch, from downtown out, bordered on the railroad tracks and terminals. The vice areas in many of the large cities have been near railroad yards. The property about railroad tracks in the central parts of the city has always been undesirable for residential purposes, and the poor and criminal elements have congregated there" ("Natural History of Vice Areas," 32). While Reckless pointed out the relationship between railroad tracks and concentrated districts of vice, he overlooked the fact that contests between real estate developers and railroad companies over tracts of inexpensive land influenced the shape of urban vice districts and the placement of railway lines. Moreover, his analysis cannot account for the ever-changing geography of sexual commerce in the city.

7.   Stead, *If Christ Came to Chicago*, 450. On the displacement of Italian families, see Edith Abbott, *The Tenements of Chicago, 1908–1935* (Chicago: University of Chicago Press, 1936), 111–12.

8.   Carter Harrison, *Stormy Years*, 312. See also U.S. Bureau of the Census, Twelfth Census (1900), Chicago Manuscript Schedules, Enumeration District 30; Asbury, *Gem of the Prairie*, 244; Alson J. Smith, *Chicago's Left Bank* (Chicago: Henry Regnery Co., 1953), 138–39.

9.   Carter Harrison, *Stormy Years*, 311.

10.   City of Chicago, *Report of the General Superintendent of Police of the City of Chicago to the City Council, 1904* (Chicago, 1904), 26; City of Chicago, *Report of the General Superintendent of Police of the City of Chicago to the City Council, 1906* (Chicago, 1906), 6.

11.   Pierce, *History of Chicago*, vol. 3, 22–32; Duis, *Challenging Chicago*, 74–75, 81–83.

12.   Abbott, *Tenements of Chicago*, 94–95, 113; Hoyt, *One Hundred Years of Land Values*, 312–13. Many of the Levee residents who lived in working-men's lodging houses along State and Clark found accommodations in the rooming house districts that formed on the edges of working-class communities

on the Near North and West Sides (Hoyt, *One Hundred Years of Land Values*, 202).

13. Philpott, *The Slum and the Ghetto*, 153. Internal transportation improvements hastened the movement of older immigrants away from the central city, as new cable and electric car lines opened up western and southern sections of the city to working-class and middle-class families able to take advantage of new housing opportunities. See Abbott, *Tenements of Chicago*, 111–13; Harold M. Mayer and Richard C. Wade, *Chicago: Growth of a Metropolis* (Chicago: University of Chicago Press, 1969), 154, 262.

14. *The Sporting and Club House Directory*, 7–41 passim.

15. Stead, *If Christ Came to Chicago*, 450–51; Wendt and Kogan, *Lords of the Levee*, 80. For a map of Chicago's internal transit system in 1893, see Mayer and Wade, *Chicago*, 137.

16. As early as 1856 keeping either a disorderly house or a house of ill fame was prohibited in the municipal code. See City of Chicago, *The Charter and Ordinances of the City of Chicago* (Chicago, 1856), 296. Keeping an assignation house was first made a misdemeanor offense in the 1881 code. See City of Chicago, *The Municipal Code of Chicago, 1881* (Chicago, 1881), 375–76; see also City of Chicago, *The Revised Municipal Code of Chicago of 1905* (Chicago, 1905), 405.

17. *Chicago Record-Herald*, May 31, 1905.

18. Ibid., June 1, 1905.

19. As we have seen, in the late nineteenth century some form of vice "toleration" had long been standard police practice. Yet in the early twentieth century the context and terms of "segregation" underwent a transformation. The emergence of a regular system of payments to police officers and ward politicians bolstered the resolve of public officials to keep prostitution and gambling in segregated urban areas.

20. Charles Washburn, *Come into My Parlor: A Biography of the Aristocratic Everleigh Sisters of Chicago* (New York: National Library Press, 1936); Asbury, *Gem of the Prairie*, 247–55; Wendt and Kogan, *Lords of the Levee*, 284–85. On the closing of the Everleigh Club, see *Chicago Record-Herald*, October 26, 1911; Carter Harrison, *Stormy Years*, 306–12.

21. Asbury, *Gem of the Prairie*, 263; Wendt and Kogan, *Lords of the Levee*, 282–83.

22. Vice Commission of Chicago, *Social Evil*, 357; U.S. Bureau of the Census, Thirteenth Census (1910), Chicago Manuscript Schedules, Enumeration Districts 160–62.

23. U.S. Bureau of the Census, Twelfth Census (1900), Chicago Manuscript Schedules, Enumeration Districts 21 and 42; U.S. Bureau of the Census, Thirteenth Census (1910), Chicago Manuscript Schedules, Enumeration District 162.

24. *Chicago Daily News*, May 24, 1907; *Lakeside Annual Directory*, 1908, 1911; U.S. Bureau of the Census, Thirteenth Census (1910), Chicago Manuscript Schedules, Enumeration District 160. Fields does not appear in city directories after 1911.

25. Minnie Shima operated a Japanese house of prostitution at 2026 Armour Avenue as early as 1894. She was still there at the time of the 1910 census. See Stead, *If Christ Came to Chicago*, 451; U.S. Bureau of the Census, Thirteenth Census (1910), Chicago Manuscript Schedules, Enumeration District 160.

26. As partial payment for the $29,000, Fields received another property—a ten-flat building on Wentworth Avenue. In 1908 the purchaser of the building at 132 Custom House Place, Mrs. Harriet Blair Borland, was acquiring several holdings along Custom House Place. According to the *Chicago Tribune*, "The purchases were made for investment purposes [and were] to be occupied by the printing and kindred industries" (October, 3, 1908, 15).

27. The intricate web of property relations that linked madam landlords and renting brothel managers is discussed in chapter 2.

28. In attempting to trace the chain of ownership in Cook County records of Levee district properties, I have confronted nearly insurmountable obstacles. While records for property transactions go back as far as 1871 at the Tract Department of the Cook County Recorder of Deeds, following the chain for properties that no longer exist or on streets that have been renamed and renumbered has been incredibly difficult. Because that research tack proved fruitless, I have used other sources. Especially useful were the "Real Estate Transfers" published weekly in the *Chicago Tribune* at the turn of the century. These postings recorded the location and a brief description of properties being sold, the names of sellers and buyers, as well as the sale price. I have used this detailed information to corroborate accounts from less-official reports of property ownership in the nineteenth- and twentieth-century Levees.

29. Case no. 192577, Paul Brown, Receiver, vs. Vina Fields, 1899, Records of the Chicago Criminal Court (microfilm), Circuit Court of Cook County Archives, Richard J. Daley Center, Chicago. Although Fields agreed to pay this exorbitant rent, she stopped payment and left the property after being informed that "the city authorities would not permit [her] to further use the premises for the purposes intended." The owner of the property, Paul Brown, sued Fields for the months she did not pay rent and for attorney's fees. Brown won his case in Chicago Circuit Court. However, the bold and business-savvy Fields appealed the case to the Court of Appeals of Illinois, which affirmed the judgment of the circuit court. Undaunted, Fields pressed her case to the Illinois Supreme Court, which overturned the appellate court ruling and remanded the case to the circuit court. In its ruling, the state supreme court stated: "One who leases a house with full knowledge it is leased by the tenant for the purpose of keeping a house of

ill-fame or place for the practice of prostitution, and afterwards receives rent therefor and permits the house to be so used, is guilty of a violation of the statute, and on principles of public policy ought not to be permitted to invoke or obtain the aid of the courts to enforce stipulations in the contract letting which will enable him to secure a judgement by confession for rent due for such use of the house." *Fields v. Brown*, [no numbers in original], Court of Appeals of Illinois, First District, 90 Ill. App. 195; 1899 Ill. App. LEXIS 774, October 1899, Decided, July 10, 1900, Opinion Filed. *Fields v. Brown*, [no numbers in original], Court of Appeals of Illinois, First District, 89 Ill. App. 287; 1900 Ill. App. LEXIS 5, March 1900, Decided, May 10, 1900, Opinion Filed. *Fields v. Brown*, Supreme Court of Illinois, 188 Ill. 111; 58 N.E. 977; 1900 Ill. LEXIS 2437, December 20, 1900.

30. *Chicago Daily News*, May 24, 1907. This quarantine occurred at a time of heightened anti-vice activity. It came on the heels of the influential George Kibbe Turner exposé "The City of Chicago: A Study of the Great Immoralities." For Turner's discussion of the social evil, see 580–82. The attack on Fields's house occurred only days after Precinct Captain Edward McCann vowed to attack vice in the Twenty-Second Street Levee, "the wickedest district in Chicago" (*Chicago Record-Herald*, May 23, 1907).

31. On the Everleigh sisters' inheritance and their investment in their Chicago resort, see Asbury, *Gem of the Prairie*, 248–49.

32. *Chicago Record-Herald*, October 15, 1909; Asbury, *Gem of the Prairie*, 263. As a result of the raids, which swept through the Levee from October through December 1912, Roy Jones closed his Dearborn Street saloon. He eventually reopened at 2037 Wabash. Jones was a key figure in early-twentieth-century vice syndicates in Chicago. See Asbury, *Gem of the Prairie*, 304–5; Wendt and Kogan, *Lords of the Levee*, 135, 303. One student of organized crime in Chicago called Jones's Wabash Avenue café "one of the most notorious resorts in the levee district." See John Landesco, *Organized Crime in Chicago*, pt. 3, *Illinois Crime Survey* (Chicago: Illinois Association for Criminal Justice, 1929), 848–49n1. The Illinois Senate investigations of vice conditions throughout the state show that in 1913 Jones's resort continued to be a target of vice reformers, this time for the indecent dancing of black performers. Illinois General Assembly, Senate Vice Committee, *Report of the Senate Vice Committee* (Chicago: n.p., 1916), 469–76, 503–9.

33. Asbury, *Gem of the Prairie*, 262–63; Landesco, *Organized Crime in Chicago*, pt. 3, 845–48.

34. U.S. Bureau of the Census, Thirteenth Census (1910), Chicago Manuscript Schedules, Enumeration District 162. After 1914 Jordan operated "cheap all-night cafes on South State Street" (Wendt and Kogan, *Lords of the Levee*, 329). See also Asbury, *Gem of the Prairie*, 276.

35. Report of Investigation, March 14, 1913, p. 2, Clifford Barnes Papers, Chicago Historical Society.

36. *Chicago Record-Herald*, June 16, 1908.

37. *Chicago Daily Tribune*, February 18, 1893. Scott is discussed in chapter 3.

38. On property relations in New York City vice districts, see Gilfoyle, *City of Eros*, 34–54, 197–223.

39. Ruth Rosen, *Lost Sisterhood*, 71–76. See also Walter Reckless, *Vice in Chicago* (Chicago: University of Chicago Press, 1933), 32–54.

40. Ruth Rosen, *Lost Sisterhood*, 77.

41. Wendt and Kogan, *Lords of the Levee*, 282–83; Asbury, *Gem of the Prairie*, 262–66, 273–75; William Howland Kenney, *Chicago Jazz: A Cultural History, 1904–1930* (New York: Oxford University Press, 1993), 63.

42. For discussions of the consequences of the capitalization of the urban sex trade, see Ruth Rosen, *Lost Sisterhood*, 70–72; Gilfoyle, *City of Eros*, 197–223.

43. Asbury, *Gem of the Prairie*, 320–74; Reckless, *Vice in Chicago*, 69–98; Landesco, *Organized Crime in Chicago*, pt. 3, 815–919; Lindberg, *To Serve and Collect*, 119–45; Gilfoyle, *City of Eros*, 251–69.

44. See, e.g., Lindberg, *To Serve and Collect*, 147–218.

45. *Chicago Record-Herald*, October 11, 1909.

46. Asbury, *Gem of the Prairie*, 307; Lindberg, *To Serve and Collect*, 119–36. For a detailed history of the long and shady careers of Michael "Hinky Dink" Kenna and "Bathhouse" John Coughlin—two powerful First Ward aldermen—see Wendt and Kogan, *Lords of the Levee*.

47. Lindberg, *To Serve and Collect*, 126; Asbury, *Gem of the Prairie*, 267, 304–5. See Gilfoyle, *City of Eros*, 251–69, for discussion of the growing importance of syndicates in early-twentieth-century New York City.

48. For a discussion of the sporting fraternity, see Gilfoyle, *City of Eros*, 92–116, 236–39; Christopher Robert Reed, *Black Chicago's First Century: 1833–1900* (Columbia: University of Missouri Press, 2005); Robert M. Lombardo, "The Black Mafia: African-American Organized Crime in Chicago, 1890–1960," *Crime, Law, and Social Change* 38, no. 1 (July 2002): 33–65.

49. *Chicago Broad Ax*, December 2, 1905.

50. For an example of a white house of prostitution on the North Side being pressured to pay $200 for protection, see Illinois General Assembly, Senate Vice Committee, *Report of the Senate Vice Committee*, 529–31.

51. *Chicago Tribune*, September 18, 1905.

52. *Chicago Record-Herald*, August 31, 1908; Bricktop, *Bricktop*, with James Haskins (New York: Atheneum, 1983), 38–41; Frank C. Taylor, *Alberta Hunter: A Celebration in Blues* (New York: McGraw-Hill, 1987), 25–28.

53. Meyerowitz, *Women Adrift*, 103–11; Peiss, *Cheap Amusements*, 88–114; Lewis A. Erenberg, *Steppin' Out: New York Nightlife and the Transformation of American Culture, 1890–1930* (Chicago: University of Chicago Press, 1981), 60–145.

54. For a discussion of the charged meanings that black male/white female sexual relations held for white men and women in early-twentieth-century America, see Mumford, *Interzones*, esp. 1–18. Also, in their 1913 interviews

with proprietors, Illinois Senate investigators demonstrated a preoccupation with the racial makeup of cabaret and dance hall employees and patrons. See, e.g., Illinois General Assembly, Senate Vice Committee, *Report of the Senate Vice Committee*, 451, 470–71, 503–6.

55. U.S. Bureau of the Census, Twelfth Census (1900), Chicago Manuscript Schedules, Enumeration District 42; U.S. Bureau of the Census, Thirteenth Census (1910), Chicago Manuscript Schedules, Enumeration District 162; *Chicago Record-Herald*, October 5, 1912; Asbury, *Gem of the Prairie*, 264; Wendt and Kogan, *Lords of the Levee*, 283.
56. According to Herbert Asbury, she offered "the most bestial circuses ever seen in the United States" (*Gem of the Prairie*, 264). "Circuses" were staged performances in which two or more women engaged in sex with one another for an audience of brothel guests. Some houses conducted circuses at the occasional request of patrons; others were known for these shows and offered them as standard fare. See Reckless, "Natural History of Vice Areas," 53–54n3.
57. Eric Lott, *Love and Theft: Blackface Minstrelsy and the American Working Class* (New York: Oxford University Press, 1993), 38–39.
58. *Chicago Record-Herald*, October 5, 1912. See *Chicago Tribune*, October 7, 1912, on Wayman's fight for the suppressed key to the Vice Commission of Chicago report, *Social Evil*. See also Asbury, *Gem of the Prairie*, 264; Reckless, "Natural History of Vice Areas," 53–54n3; Junius B. Wood, *The Negro in Chicago* (Chicago: Chicago Daily News, 1916), 27.
59. Asbury suggests that there were two Chinese brothels and two brothels with Japanese women. I found information about only one of these resorts: the house run by the Japanese keeper Minnie Shima. See n. 25 above.
60. U.S. Bureau of the Census, Thirteenth Census (1910), Chicago Manuscript Schedules, Enumeration District 162.
61. Ibid.; Sanborn Fire Insurance Maps of Chicago (1910), vol. 3, map 42, Richard M. Daley Library, University of Illinois at Chicago.
62. Vice Commission of Chicago, *Social Evil*; Addams, *New Conscience*. On the formation of the Vice Commission of Chicago, see Graham Taylor, "The Story of the Chicago Vice Commission," *Survey* 6 (May 1911): 239–47. See also Clifford W. Barnes, "The Story of the Committee of Fifteen of Chicago," *Social Hygiene* 4, no. 2 (April 1918): 145–56. An early and influential exposé of corruption and immorality in Chicago was Turner's "City of Chicago."
63. Asbury, *Gem of the Prairie*, 281–88, 296; Reckless, *Vice in Chicago*, 1–6.
64. *Chicago Record-Herald*, October 6, 10, and 11, 1912.
65. Report of Investigation, March 14, 1913, Clifford Barnes Papers, Chicago Historical Society.
66. Beginning in 1912 municipalities across the country gradually closed districts of tolerated sexual commerce. On the closing of red-light districts, see Thomas C. Mackey, *Red Lights Out: A Legal History of Prostitution, Disorderly*

      Houses and Vice Districts, 1870–1917 (New York: Garland, 1987); see also
      Ruth Rosen, *Lost Sisterhood*, 28–32.

67. On the white slavery scare of the early twentieth century, see Ruth Rosen,
      Lost Sisterhood, 112–35; Keire, "Vice Trust."

68. Lindberg, *To Serve and Collect*; Landesco, *Organized Crime in Chicago*, pt. 3,
      815–917.

69. Neil Larry Shumsky, "Tacit Acceptance: Respectable Americans and Segre-
      gated Prostitution, 1870–1910," *Journal of Social History* 19, no. 4 (1986):
      666, 671–72; Reckless, *Vice in Chicago*, 2.

CHAPTER FIVE

1.   Prominent among these men and women of means was a small group
      of black professionals. For example, of the four "Leading Physicians and
      Surgeons" advertised in an 1886 business directory, three had office ad-
      dresses beyond the Near South Side district. Dr. J. Milton Williams's office
      was located on the 2900 block of South Dearborn; Dr. Mary Green had two
      offices, one on Twenty-Second Street, the other on the 2600 block of State
      Street; and Dr. Daniel Hale Williams, perhaps the city's most prominent Af-
      rican American physician, had his office at Thirty-First Street and Michigan
      Avenue. Attorney John G. Jones resided at 3717 Butterfield Avenue (later
      Armour Avenue, later Federal Street). Businessmen and businesswomen
      were also drawn to this emerging southern neighborhood, many seizing
      the opportunity to build an interracial clientele outside the main black
      residential areas to the north. Several black men owned barbershops with
      addresses between Twenty-First and Twenty-Ninth streets on State Street
      and Butterfield Avenue. Mrs. George Taylor was the proprietor of a laundry
      at the corner of Twenty-Eighth and State. Skilled workmen such as black-
      smith H. Branham and contractor D. W. Sanders also established businesses
      south of Twenty-Second Street. Perhaps the clearest sign of the southward
      move of Chicago's black elite and middle class was the construction of
      churches at considerable distances from the older black neighborhood. In
      1885 Emanuel Congregational Church occupied an edifice at 2945 Dear-
      born, and Bethesda Baptist held services at Thirty-Fourth and Butterfield.
      By 1894 two of Chicago's most prominent black churches eventually joined
      other churches in the move southward. Quinn Chapel A.M.E. had settled at
      Twenty-Fourth and Wabash, and Bethel A.M.E. was located at Thirtieth and
      Dearborn. Within a short time Olivet Baptist would leave its home on Har-
      mon Court to occupy a new building at Twenty-Seventh and Dearborn. In
      1917 Olivet moved to the corner of Thirty-First Street and South Park Way.
      See I. C. Harris, *Colored Men's Professional and Business Directory*, 10–12, 15,
      23, 37, 52; Drake, *Churches and Voluntary Associations*, 104–5; Wallace Best,
      Passionately Human, No Less Divine: Religion and Culture in Black Chicago,
      1915–1952 (Princeton, NJ: Princeton University Press, 2007), 46–47.

2. Chicago Commission on Race Relations, *The Negro in Chicago: A Study of Race Relations and a Race Riot* (Chicago: University of Chicago Press, 1922; repr., New York: Arno Press and the New York Times, 1968), 107; Spear, *Black Chicago*, 12–15.

3. Alzada P. Comstock, "Chicago Housing Conditions, VI: The Problem of the Negro," *American Journal of Sociology* 18, no. 2 (September 1912): 241–42; Spear, *Black Chicago*, 20–21.

4. The body of scholarship on the commercialization of urban amusements is large and steadily growing. Students of urban leisure have traced the uneven process by which market relations came to organize the leisure time activities of white middle- and working-class men and women. They have also explored the social and cultural transformations brought about by the changing economies of leisure in the city. Some have looked closely at struggles waged by middle-class men and women over working-class women's sexuality, while others have explored the ways that urban leisure practices aided in the reconfiguring of urban gender ideals among a range of urban men and women. Some have focused on the intergenerational conflicts sparked by clashing leisure sensibilities; others have questioned whether the mass dissemination of commercialized amusements occasioned the erosion of ethnic borders within the industrial city. Examinations of leisure, class, and gender in the early twentieth century include Roy Rosenzweig, *Eight Hours for What We Will: Workers and Leisure in an Industrial City, 1870–1920* (Cambridge: Cambridge University Press, 1983); Peiss, *Cheap Amusements*; Gilfoyle, *City of Eros*; Meyerowitz, *Women Adrift*; Erenberg, *Steppin' Out*; Lizabeth Cohen, *Making a New Deal: Industrial Workers in Chicago, 1919–1939* (Cambridge: Cambridge University Press, 1990), 99–158. These studies have provided innumerable insights into white leisure at the turn of the century. However, how African Americans participated in urban leisure has only recently begun to receive attention. African Americans were avid consumers of urban entertainments. And black communities faced new leisure opportunities with as much ardor and ambivalence as did white middle-class men and women and working-class immigrant communities. Examinations of the ways that African Americans pursued urban amusements in the early twentieth century include Tera Hunter, *"To 'Joy My Freedom,"* 145–86; Mary Carbine, "'The Finest outside the Loop': Motion Picture Exhibition in Chicago's Black Metropolis, 1905–1928," *Camera Obscura* 23 (May 1990): 9–41; Katrina Hazzard-Gordon, *Jookin': The Rise of Social Dance in African-American Culture* (Philadelphia: Temple University Press, 1990), 63–171; Gregory Waller, *Main Street Amusements: Movies and Commercial Entertainment in a Southern City, 1896–1930* (Washington, DC: Smithsonian Institution Press, 1995), 161–79; Davarian L. Baldwin, *Chicago's New Negroes: Modernity, the Great Migration, and Black Urban Life* (Chapel Hill: University of North Carolina Press, 2007), 91–154.

5. Drake, *Churches and Voluntary Associations*, 122–31; Grossman, *Land of Hope*, 92.

6. Peiss, *Cheap Amusements*; Erenberg, *Steppin' Out*, esp. 60–87; Gilfoyle, *City of Eros*, 224–250.

7. For a discussion of the ways that ethnic and African American working-class men and women integrated popular culture into community life in 1920s Chicago, see Lizabeth Cohen, *Making a New Deal*, 100–158.

8. Grossman, *Land of Hope*, 86; Kenney, *Chicago Jazz*, 14; Baldwin, *Chicago's New Negroes*, 44–52.

9. *Chicago Defender*, June 18, 1910.

10. Kenney, *Chicago Jazz*, 5–6; Henry T. Sampson, *Blacks in Blackface: A Source Book on Early Black Musical Shows* (Metuchen, NJ: Scarecrow Press, 1980), 115–16; *Indianapolis Freeman*, June 18, 1904; *Minneapolis Western Appeal*, May 28, 1904.

11. Indeed, the breadth of Motts's venture has allowed historians studying different areas of early-twentieth-century black leisure history to claim the Pekin as the starting point for their particular branch of black entertainment. Jazz historian William Kenney refers to the Pekin as "the most important South Side club and musical theater before 1910 and the first to employ musicians who were closely associated with ragtime and pre-jazz popular culture" (*Chicago Jazz*, 5). Henry Sampson, in his history of black musical theater, calls the Pekin "the first legitimate black theatre in the United States" deserving "a special place in the history of American theatricals." "At the time of [Motts's] death," Sampson states, "nearly every large city in the United States had a black theatre patterned after the idea he originated" (*Blacks in Blackface*, 119). Film historian Mary Carbine refers to the 1905 opening of the Pekin Theatre as the inauguration of an important pattern of black film spectatorship that linked the new medium of mass-produced film and live black entertainment. According to Carbine the Pekin and later "picture houses provided a space for consciousness and assertion of social difference as well as the consumption of mass amusements" ("'The Finest Outside the Loop,'" 9).

12. *Chicago Broad Ax*, July 4 and 18, 1908; *Chicago Defender*, July 19, 1909.

13. Carbine, "'The Finest Outside the Loop,'" 16. For a list of theaters on the South Side between 1909 and 1928, see Carbine, "'The Finest Outside the Loop,'" 40; Henry T. Sampson, *The Ghost Walks: A Chronological History of Blacks in Show Business, 1865–1910* (Metuchen, NJ: Scarecrow Press, 1988), 281; Sampson, *Blacks in Blackface*, 75, 119.

14. *Chicago Defender*, June 22, 1912, September 3, 1910, and July 12, 1909.

15. Spear, *Black Chicago*, 112; H. W. Rhea, *Rhea's New Citizens' Directory of Chicago, Ill.* (Chicago: W. S. McCleland, 1908), 131–32; Louise De Koven Bowen, *The Colored People of Chicago: An Investigation Made for the Juvenile Protective Association* (Chicago: Juvenile Protective Association, 1913), not paginated.

16. Spear, *Black Chicago*, 117. Advertisements for the resort were placed in Rhea's *New Citizens' Directory* and ran regularly in the *Chicago Broad Ax*. See, e.g., June 13, 1909. The proprietors of the Chateau de La Plaisance (as its name appears in a 1910 advertisement) were aware of the competition it faced from cheaper movie theaters. To attract potential customers away from movie houses, one advertisement warned, "Go where you will, pay what you may, but the CHATEAU leads in real wholesome, health-giving entertainment. Come away from the stuffy, tubercular 5c death-giving, cheap theater and enjoy the invigorating, health-giving atmosphere of the CHATEAU" (*Chicago Defender*, February 12, 1910).

17. In 1913 Louise De Koven Bowen of the Juvenile Protective Association wrote: "The commercial amusements found in the neighborhoods of colored people are of the lowest type of pool rooms and saloons, which are artificially numerous because so many young colored men find their first employment in these two occupations and with their experience and very little capital are able to open places for themselves" (*Colored People of Chicago*). She found one woman who owned a State Street saloon.

18. Duis, *Saloon*, 158; Mathilde Bunton, "The Negro in Business: Taverns," 1–2, Illinois Writers' Project, "The Negro in Illinois," box 25, Vivian Harsh Collection, Carter G. Woodson Regional Library, Chicago Public Library; Rhea, *New Citizens' Directory*, 132–33.

19. Louise De Koven Bowen commented on "the ephemeral life of the pool rooms and saloon, only one of which has survived [more than five years], while eleven others have changed proprietors recently." She attributed this "ephemeral" existence to the eagerness of "breweries and the pool room manufacturers [to] readily accommodate their salesmen with their goods and other fittings." Unfortunately, the Black Belt proprietor had to "respond to the pressure of the large concern who is his creditor" (*Colored People of Chicago*). Perry Duis has found that in 1916 brewing companies owned the fixtures in two-thirds of Chicago's saloons (*Saloon*, 25–26). Roy Rosenzweig discusses brewer control over saloons in Worcester, Massachusetts, in *Eight Hours for What We Will*, 184–85.

20. Sanborn Fire Insurance Maps of Chicago (1910), vol. 3, maps 82–83 and 113–16; vol. 4, maps 21–22, 52–53, 76–77, 115–16, and 129–30; Richard M. Daley Library, University of Illinois at Chicago.

21. *Minneapolis Western Appeal*, March 19, 1904.

22. One 1913 study found that 72 percent of South Side saloons surveyed had back rooms. Although in their canvass, the investigators bypassed areas where black men and women may have frequented saloons in significant numbers, their figures reveal the prevalent use of back rooms by women in Chicago. According to the investigators' alarmed estimation, in any twenty-four-hour period more than 14,000 women and girls entered these "agencies for demoralizing the sex." See Chicago South Side Club, *Survey*

of the Conditions Demoralizing to Women and Girls in the Saloons of Chicago (Chicago, 1913), 3, 7–8.

23. Bricktop, *Bricktop*, 18.
24. *Chicago Broad Ax*, December 16, 1905; Bricktop, *Bricktop*, 14. On the Keystone Hotel and Saloon, see *Minneapolis Western Appeal*, May 6, 1905; *Chicago Defender*, February 12, 1910. "Can rushing" was by no means a practice exclusive to black neighborhoods. Perry Duis discusses can rushing in white working-class saloons: "The afternoon hours saw a busy trade at the back or side door, when women would come to the barroom entrance or send their children after a can of beer or a little whisky or wine for 'cooking' purposes" (*Saloon*, 106). For a discussion of African American women and social drinking in another city, see Tera Hunter, *"To 'Joy My Freedom,"* 162–66.
25. For an early discussion of African American women's patronage of urban saloons, see DuBois, *Philadelphia Negro*, 277–82.
26. Mike Rowe, *Chicago Blues: The City and the Music* (New York: Da Capo Press, 1975), 41.
27. Alberta Hunter is quoted in Daphne Harrison, *Black Pearls*, 203. See also Frank Taylor, *Alberta Hunter*, 28–31. Saloons in other cities sheltered the activities of sporting men and women. See Katzman, *Before the Ghetto*, 171–73; Kusmer, *A Ghetto Takes Shape*, 48–49.
28. *Chicago Daily News* reporter Junius Wood lists Hugh Hoskins's place as one of "the principal gambling places in the [Black Belt] district" (*The Negro in Chicago*, 28). In 1911 an advertisement for the Iowa Club ran in the *Chicago Defender* touting the club's "High Class Entertainers" and notifying readers of the "Neatly Furnished Rooms in Connection." See, e.g., *Chicago Defender*, May 13, 20, and 27, 1911.
29. Perry Bradford, *Born with the Blues: Perry Bradford's Own Story* (New York: Oak Publications, 1965), 33–34, 135, 166.
30. See P. E. Miller and R. Venables, eds., *Esquire's 1946 Jazz Book* (New York: A. S. Barnes, 1946), which provides valuable essays on Chicago jazz history and a useful pair of maps of "Chicago Jazz Spots" from 1914 to 1928. See also *The New Grove Dictionary of Jazz* (New York: Macmillan, 1988), 195–205, for a comprehensive historical listing of jazz venues in Chicago.
31. Kenney, *Chicago Jazz*, 6.
32. Harold F. Gosnell, *Negro Politicians: The Rise of Negro Politics in Chicago* (Chicago: University of Chicago Press, 1935), 125–27; Spear, *Black Chicago*, 76; Asbury, *Gem of the Prairie*, 167–68.
33. Travis, *Autobiography of Black Jazz*, 26.
34. Gosnell, *Negro Politicians*, 126.
35. Travis, *Autobiography of Black Jazz*, 26.
36. Spear, *Black Chicago*, 76; Kenney, *Chicago Jazz*, 5–6.
37. *Chicago Broad Ax*, February 22, 1902.
38. Duis, *Saloon*, 293.

39. Kenney, *Chicago Jazz*, 27; Carbine, "'The Finest Outside the Loop."
40. Wooldridge, *Hands Up!* (Police Publishing Co.), 322–28; *Chicago Broad Ax*, November 18, 1905.
41. Wooldridge, *Hands Up!* (Police Publishing Co.), 324.
42. *Chicago Tribune*, November 11, 1905; *Chicago Broad Ax*, September 30 and November 18, 1905, and March 17, 1906.
43. See *Chicago Tribune*, November 11, 1905; *Chicago Record-Herald*, November 11, 1905; *Portland (OR) Advocate*, n.d. Each paper is quoted at length in the *Chicago Broad Ax*, December 2, 1905.
44. *Chicago Broad Ax*, March 17, 1906.
45. Ibid., May 19, 1906.
46. Ibid., August 10, 1907.
47. Since the middle of the nineteenth century, newspapers classed the city's pimps among "the gamblers, . . . the burglars, the pocket-book dropper, the confidence men, and several other species not necessary now to be mentioned" ("Loafing in Chicago: The Knaves and What Should Be Done with Them," *Chicago Tribune*, June 21, 1864, 4). Through their criminal behavior such men plagued the city and its hardworking citizens. Significantly, in such representations of this character, the pimp was not linked directly, or even tangentially, to prostitutes or the sex economy. Rather, this figure was associated with a collection of parasitic, apparently unemployed men who hung about the city streets and frequented watering holes and gambling dens. See, e.g., "The Loafing Nuisance," *Chicago Tribune*, April 26, 1868, 2.
48. Gilfoyle, *City of Eros*, 89–91; Ruth Rosen, *Lost Sisterhood*, 108–10.
49. Vice Commission of Chicago, *Social Evil*, 184–85.
50. Drake and Cayton, *Black Metropolis*, 611.
51. Bricktop, *Bricktop*, 28–29.
52. Erenberg, *Steppin' Out*, 113–45.
53. William Kenney discusses the evolution of the early cabaret and jazz scene on Chicago's South Side in *Chicago Jazz*, 8–34.
54. See the advertisement announcing new ownership of the Elite in the *Chicago Defender*, August 27, 1910. See also Kenney, *Chicago Jazz*, 9–14; Gosnell, *Negro Politicians*, 128–30.
55. *Indianapolis Freeman*, January 2, 1915; *Chicago Defender*, January 23, 1915.
56. In the late teens Henry "Teenan" Jones was the proprietor of the Star Theater, located at 3937 State Street (Carbine, "'The Finest Outside the Loop,'" 36n43).
57. *Chicago Broad Ax*, December 30, 1911; *Chicago Defender*, June 15, 1912. As popular as the Marquette may have been in 1912, by 1915 it had become the Ranier Buffet and Cabaret under the proprietorship of Walter Speedy. Speedy was a member of the South Side gambling fraternity and openly challenged the power of such gambling lords as Henry "Teenan" Jones, leading to frequent police raids on Speedy's club. Speedy apparently dabbled in the South Side sex trade as well. In 1916 he was found guilty

of pandering. See *Indianapolis Freeman*, October 9, 1915; Wood, *The Negro in Chicago*, 28.

58. Sampson, *Ghost Walks*, 319, 462, 525; Jack Johnson, *The Autobiography of Jack Johnson: In the Ring and Out* (Chicago: National Sports Press, 1927), 62–65.

59. In 1909 *Variety* remarked on Johnson's popularity on the black vaudeville circuit: "Johnson is a drawing card, and seems to attract even those hostile to him through his color. His bearing . . . proved the black champion is no novice on the stage" (*Variety*, April 3, 1909, quoted in Sampson, *Ghost Walks*, 462).

60. *Chicago Defender*, June 8, 1912; *Chicago Broad Ax*, October 18, 1913.

61. Randy Roberts, *Papa Jack: Jack Johnson and the Era of White Hopes* (New York: Free Press, 1983), 138–39; Bricktop, *Bricktop*, 45; Jack Johnson, *Autobiography*, 66–68.

62. Jack Johnson, *Autobiography*, 66–68.

63. Randy Roberts, *Papa Jack*, 138–67.

64. Ibid., 167.

65. Much has been written about Jack Johnson's 1913 conviction for violation of the Mann Act. Two studies have offered important analyses of what the Johnson case illuminates about race, gender, and sexuality in the early twentieth century: Mumford, *Interzones*, 3–18; Gail Bederman, *Manliness and Civilization: A Cultural History of Gender and Race in the United States, 1880–1917* (Chicago: University of Chicago Press, 1995), 1–10.

66. Bricktop, *Bricktop*, 44; Travis, *Autobiography of Black Jazz*, 69.

67. Kenney, *Chicago Jazz*, 11–23.

68. Ibid., 9–10, 17–18; *Chicago Defender*, July 22, 1912; *Chicago Broad Ax*, December 23, 1911. See *Chicago Broad Ax*, August 17, 1912, on the opening of the Mineral Springs. Reports of Chicago's cabaret scene regularly appeared in the *Indianapolis Freeman*. See, e.g., February 20, March 20 and 27, and October 9, 1915.

69. Wood, *The Negro in Chicago*, 25, 27. Teenan Jones's gambling lordship ended in 1917 when State's Attorney Maclay Hoyne arrested him, along with Second Ward alderman Oscar DePriest and Captain Stephen Healy of the Chicago Police Department, in connection with graft and vice. See Gosnell, *Negro Politicians*, 130; Grossman, *Land of Hope*, 169–70.

70. Bricktop, *Bricktop*, 28–29.

71. *The Saga of Mr. Jelly Lord*, vol. 5, Library of Congress audio recording, quoted in Hazzard-Gordon, *Jookin'*, 85.

72. Randy Roberts, *Papa Jack*, 138–39; Bricktop, *Bricktop*, 45. On the rise in membership clubs in black urban neighborhoods, see Hazzard-Gordon, *Jookin'*, 135–41. The intersection between membership clubs and urban entertainment can be seen in the evolution of William Bowman's Marquette Club from a private gentleman's club for black men to full-blown cabaret in 1911 (*Chicago Broad Ax*, December 30, 1911).

73. On "dangerous back-rooms," see Chicago South Side Club, *Survey of the Conditions*, 7–8.
74. Bricktop, *Bricktop*, 42.
75. Frank Taylor, *Alberta Hunter*, 33, 40.
76. *Chicago Defender*, February 12, 1910.
77. *Chicago Broad Ax*, February 1, 1913; see also *Minneapolis Western Appeal*, May 6, 1905.
78. *Chicago Defender*, July 13, 1909, and September 3, 1910; *Chicago Broad Ax*, December 23 and 30, 1911.
79. *Chicago Tribune*, October 3, 1907; *Chicago Record-Herald*, October 4, 1907; *Chicago Broad Ax*, June 22, 1911.
80. Peiss, *Cheap Amusements*, 53–55, 108–12; *Chicago Record-Herald*, October 28, 1907.
81. Peiss, *Cheap Amusements*, 108–14; Meyerowitz, *Women Adrift*, 102–3. For a full exploration of working-class "treating" and the relation between modernizing sexual mores and changing patterns of urban prostitution, see Elizabeth Clement, *Love for Sale: Courting, Treating, and Prostitution in New York City, 1900–1945* (Chapel Hill: University of North Carolina Press, 2006).
82. *Chicago Defender*, April 9, 1910. Debates about the moral character of State Street, especially at its intersection with Thirty-First Street, were ongoing in the pages of the *Defender*. See, e.g., May 11 and June 15, 1912, and May 21, 1914.
83. Michael Harris, *The Rise of the Gospel Blues: The Music of Thomas Andrew Dorsey in the Urban Church* (New York: Oxford University Press, 1992), 51; Chris Albertson, *Bessie* (New York: Stein and Day, 1972), 122–23.
84. Thomas Dorsey quoted in Michael Harris, *Rise of the Gospel Blues*, 52.
85. Hazzard-Gordon, *Jookin'*, 90. Although white male pleasure-seekers were drawn to stops on the buffet circuit before 1915, it appears that they did not infiltrate these community institutions in significant numbers until the early 1920s. Even during Prohibition many buffet flats operated below the radar of North Side slumming parties. Diverging audiences for jazz and blues performance may explain this. Historians of early-twentieth-century jazz and urban blues have suggested that there was a relatively sharp class and racial divide in the followers of these musical styles. In Chicago, as in other cities in the 1920s, jazz was performed in cabarets. This musical form was distinct from the piano-based blues that was performed in "hole-in-the-wall" saloons and along buffet flat and rent party circuits. White musical slummers, and many middle-class African Americans, shied away from the slower blues and the venues in which it was played. Most South Side buffet flats were underground community spaces that catered predominantly to black men and women. See Michael Harris, *Rise of the Gospel Blues*, 51–63; Margaret McKee and Fred Chisenhall, *Beale Black and Blue: Life and Music on Black America's Main Street* (Baton Rouge: Louisiana State University Press, 1981), 218–19.

86. Bricktop, *Bricktop*, 57.
87. *Chicago Broad Ax*, September 4, 1909.
88. Bradford, *Born with the Blues*, 34.
89. *Chicago Broad Ax*, September 4 and 18, 1909.
90. Ibid., September 4, 1909.
91. *Chicago Defender*, May 30, 1914; *Chicago Broad Ax*, October 2, 1909. In 1916 *Chicago Daily New* reporter Junius Wood remarked that "the borderland of a colored residential district is the haven" for buffet flats (*The Negro in Chicago*, 26). But by 1915 they had already established niches *within* black residential terrain.
92. *Chicago Broad Ax*, September 25, 1909.
93. Albertson, *Bessie*, 122.
94. Wood, *The Negro in Chicago*, 26; Hazzard-Gordon, *Jookin'*, 89–91; Michael Harris, *Rise of the Gospel Blues*, 51–53.
95. *Chicago Daily News*, October 7, 1907; *Chicago Record-Herald*, July 15 and 22, 1908, and September 6, 1909.
96. *Chicago Record-Herald*, July 30, 1908.
97. *Chicago American*, September 16, 1909, quoted in *Chicago Broad Ax*, September 18, 1909.
98. *Chicago Broad Ax*, September 18, 1909.
99. See Michael Harris, *Rise of the Gospel Blues*, 52; Albertson, *Bessie*, 122–23.
100. Willie "the Lion" Smith, *Music on My Mind: The Memoirs of an American Pianist*, with George Hoefer (Garden City, NY: Doubleday and Co., 1964), 123. Further information about the Columbia and the hotel at 3120 State is from Sanborn Fire Insurance Maps of Chicago (1910), vol. 3, map 114, and vol. 4, map 21, Richard M. Daley Library, University of Illinois at Chicago.
101. Given the moral danger that could greet respectable residents in neighborhood lodging houses, a few black-owned establishments prided themselves on accommodating men only. The best known were the Keystone at 3022 State (mentioned above), and the Douglass Hotel at 2906 State. That these hotels insistently advertised their policy of excluding women suggests that their owners felt it necessary to distinguish their establishments from others that were not selective about the moral status of the women and men to whom they rented rooms. See advertisement for Douglass Hotel in *Chicago Broad Ax*, August 17, 1912.
102. See Reckless, "Natural History of Vice Areas," 154–58.
103. African Americans looking for housing in Chicago had early taken advantage of the financial flexibility afforded by boarding and lodging in the homes of families. On August 30, 1890, the *Indianapolis Freeman* pointed out the importance of this informal housing practice when it observed that "many families [in Chicago] make a practice of keeping roomers, and excellent accommodations are secured that way." A 1902 investigation of black real estate ownership in Chicago noted the high rate of lodging among black renters. See Work, "Negro Real Estate Holders of Chicago," 30.

In 1913 a study of the economic and social conditions facing Chicago's African Americans found that almost one-third of the residents of the South Side were lodgers and boarders in private homes or in rooming houses (Bowen, *Colored People of Chicago*).

104. Paul Groth, *Living Downtown: The History of Residential Hotels in the United States* (Berkeley and Los Angeles: University of California Press, 1994), 121–22. Whether keepers were wives seeking to extend the earnings of husbands, widows trying to maintain a household, or single mothers struggling to support a family in the face of unmanageably high rents, black women who kept lodgers found an important means of earning much-needed money within the confines of their homes.

105. For some women who relied primarily on their roomers' rent for income, advertising further formalized their status as housing entrepreneurs. For example, six keepers advertised their accommodations in Rhea's 1908 directory (*New Citizens' Directory*). Many more advertised regularly in the *Chicago Defender*'s classifieds. In both cases it is clear that black women dominated this neighborhood economy. Of the six rooming houses listed in Rhea's directory, five were run by women.

106. Comstock, "Chicago Housing Conditions," 242.

107. Sophonisba P. Breckinridge and Edith Abbott, "Chicago's Housing Problem: Families in Furnished Rooms," *American Journal of Sociology* 16, no. 3 (November 1910): 291; *Chicago Broad Ax*, October 2, 1909.

108. Comstock, "Chicago Housing Conditions," 243.

109. Committee of Fifteen, MS 1028, vol. 25, 158, 171, 327, 379, 386, 393, Chicago Committee of Fifteen Papers, Special Collections, Joseph Regenstein Library, University of Chicago. Alfred Dobbins's case is Case no. 119204, June 11, 1915, Records of the Chicago Criminal Court (microfilm), Circuit Court of Cook County Archives, Richard J. Daley Center, Chicago.

110. In the cases followed by the Committee of Fifteen, women frequently complained that they had been forced to "go out on the street[,] solicit men[,] and take them" either to their rooms or "to where prostitution was practiced." See, e.g., Committee of Fifteen, MS 1028, vol. 25, 376, 386, 393, Chicago Committee of Fifteen Papers, Special Collections, Joseph Regenstein Library, University of Chicago.

111. Bradford, *Born with the Blues*, 34.

112. *Chicago Broad Ax*, April 29, 1905.

CHAPTER SIX

1. Wolcott, *Remaking Respectability*, 22–27.

2. Higginbotham, *Righteous Discontent*, 197; Anne Meis Knupfer, *Toward a Tenderer Humanity and a Nobler Womanhood: African American Women's Clubs in Turn-of-the-Century Chicago* (New York: New York University Press, 1996), 11–29.

3. *Chicago Defender*, October 26, 1912.

4. In turn-of-the-century reform literature and in everyday parlance, the word "vice" connoted several concepts simultaneously. At its most general, the word referred to depraved or immoral habits and the acts that contributed to moral corruption. After the turn of the century, the meaning of the term began to narrow. Moral reformers, police officers, and urbanites concerned about sexual immorality increasingly applied the word to prostitution alone, though distress about the dangers of gambling persisted. In the midst of the anti-prostitution crusades of the 1910s and 1920s, the word was applied not only to prostitution but specifically to organized prostitution. The term, then, reflected public concern both with sexual immorality and increasingly with the *criminality* of sexual commerce within the urban economy. When used in this book, the term "vice" is meant to evoke the simultaneity of these meanings for black and white Chicagoans.

5. Ibid.

6. Al-Tony Gilmore, "Jack Johnson and White Women: The National Impact, 1912–1913," *Journal of Negro History* 58, no. 1 (January 1973): 18–22; Randy Roberts, *Papa Jack*, 138–68.

7. At the same time, there was an undercurrent of disapproval of Johnson's choice of white women. Booker T. Washington sounded the loudest blast at Johnson, saying, "It is unfortunate that a man with money should use it in a way to injure his own people in the eyes of those who are seeking to uplift his race and improve its conditions. . . . In misrepresenting the colored people of the country this man is harming himself the least" (*Chicago Tribune*, October 20, 1912).

8. Quoted in *Crisis* 5, no. 2 (December 1912): 73.

9. *Chicago Daily News*, October 19, 1912.

10. *Chicago Broad Ax*, November 9, 1912.

11. *Chicago Defender*, October 26, 1912. Among Chicago's white papers, the *Chicago Tribune* (October 20, 1912) engaged in just such characterizations of Lucille Cameron: "the negro made his first advances to the girl after he had invited a slumming party of which she was a member to his rooms upstairs over his café. According to the report Johnson gave all his guests many drinks and made his first approaches to the girl after she had become intoxicated."

12. Gilmore, "Jack Johnson and White Women"; Randy Roberts, *Papa Jack*, 138–68.

13. *Chicago Defender*, November 2, 1912.

14. Ibid., November 16 and 30, 1912.

15. Ibid., November 9, 1912.

16. Ibid., November 2, 1912.

17. Ibid.

18. Ibid., October 26, November 2 and 9, and December 7, 1912.

19. Hurd's Revised Statutes of Illinois (1909), chap. 23, secs. 175 and 176, quoted in Vice Commission of Chicago, *Social Evil*, 350–53. Through the advocacy of the Cook County Juvenile Court, McFerrin's guardianship was given to any institution or individual in whose care she was placed. At the time of her rape, Cook County Hospital was her legal guardian.
20. *Chicago Defender*, November 16, 1912.
21. Ibid.
22. Ibid., November 9 and 30 and December 7, 1912.
23. Ibid., November 9 and December 7, 1912.
24. Ibid., November 9 and 16, 1912.
25. Ibid., November 30, 1912.
26. Elizabeth Lindsay Davis, *Lifting as They Climb* (n.p.: National Association of Colored Women, n.d.), 133; Knupfer, *Toward a Tenderer Humanity*, 154.
27. *Chicago Defender*, November 16, 1912.
28. Ibid., December 7, 1912.
29. In a March 13, 1913, article covering the quarterly meeting of the City Federation of Colored Women's Clubs, the *Chicago Defender* announced: "Report [was] made on the Mator McFerrin Case"; however, a summary of the report did not make it into the article. Other than in the pages of the *Defender*, traces of Mator McFerrin and her plight are all but impossible to recover. McFerrin's case involved both Cook County Juvenile Court and the Court of Domestic Relations. In the Circuit Court of Cook County Archives—which houses records for both courts—no juvenile court records before 1950 are available. Nor does McFerrin's name appear in the small collection of extant juvenile delinquency cases held in the Circuit Court of Cook County Archives. Records from the Court of Domestic Relations for 1912 and 1913 have been destroyed. Finally, in the Indictment Index of Criminal Felonies, 1912–14, there is no record of an indictment against Frank Chaplin.
30. *Chicago Defender*, November 16, 1912.
31. Ibid., September 13, 1913.
32. *Chicago Broad Ax*, December 31, 1904.
33. Elizabeth Lindsay Davis, *The Story of the Illinois Federation of Colored Women's Clubs, 1900–1922* (n.p., 1922), 16, 95–96. See also Wanda Ann Hendricks, "The Politics of Race: Black Women in Chicago, 1890–1920" (PhD diss., Purdue University, 1990), 119–20; W. E. B. DuBois, *Some Efforts of American Negroes for Their Own Social Betterment* (Atlanta, GA: Atlanta University Press, 1898), 100.
34. Elizabeth Davis, *Illinois Federation of Colored Women's Clubs*, 16; *Chicago Broad Ax*, February 9 and 16, 1901.
35. Knupfer, *Toward a Tenderer Humanity*, 76–77, 151.
36. Ibid., 83–84.
37. The Cook County Juvenile Court adjudicated cases of dependent and delinquent boys under the age of seventeen and girls under the age of eighteen.

According to Illinois statutes, the dependent child over whom the court
had guardianship was one who, "for any reason, is destitute, homeless or
abandoned; or dependent on the public for support; or has not proper parental care or guardianship; . . . or is found living in any house of ill-fame
or with any vicious or disreputable person." Extreme poverty, parental
neglect, and residence in a house of prostitution could bring a "dependent"
child's case to the attention of the court. The municipal code defined the
delinquent child, in contrast, as one who violated a state law, "knowingly
associates with thieves, vicious or immoral persons," or knowingly engaged
in gambling, drinking, or prostitution. See Hurd's Revised Statutes of Illinois (1909), chap. 23, secs. 175 and 176, quoted in Vice Commission of
Chicago, *Social Evil*, 350.
38. *Chicago Broad Ax*, November 14, 1903; Cook County Juvenile Court Report,
1906, p. 4.
39. Vice Commission of Chicago, *Social Evil*, 174.
40. Irene McCoy Gaines, "A Plea for Our Girls," *Chicago Defender*, February
28, 1920, Irene McCoy Gaines Collection, box 1, Notebooks, 1911–18+,
Chicago Historical Society; see also January 27, 1922, letter to "Presidents,
Officers, and Members" of the YWCA, Gaines Collection, box 1, folder
1912–26.
41. *Chicago Defender*, April 5, 1913. This article was written in response to
early reports of the findings of the Senate Vice Committee. The report was
eventually published in 1916. See Illinois General Assembly, Senate Vice
Committee, *Report of the Senate Vice Committee.*
42. See Elizabeth Davis, *Illinois Federation of Colored Women's Clubs*; Knupfer,
Toward a Tenderer Humanity, 104–6.
43. *Chicago Broad Ax*, November 9, 1912.
44. *Chicago Defender*, September 13, 1913.
45. Ibid., June 21, 1913.
46. See David J. Langum, *Crossing of the Line: Legislating Morality and the Mann
Act* (Chicago: University of Chicago Press, 1994).
47. *Chicago Defender*, September 16, 1913.
48. This characterization of the Black Belt's "vice" problem mirrors the belief
shaping much white slavery discourse: that immigrant men were responsible for corrupting the virtue of innocent white (American) girls and
leading, at times forcing, them into prostitution. See Ruth Rosen, *Lost
Sisterhood.*
49. *Chicago Defender*, December 14, 1912.
50. *Chicago Broad Ax*, February 22, 1902, October 5, 1907, and September 30,
1905.
51. *Chicago Defender*, October 12, 1912.
52. Ibid.
53. Chicago Commission on Race Relations, *The Negro in Chicago*, 181.
54. *Chicago Broad Ax*, June 1, 1907.

55. *Chicago Defender*, October 12 and 19, 1912.
56. While mainline AME and Baptist churches were most prominent in their fight against the spread of prostitution through Black Belt streets, storefront churches were equally invested in the struggle for the neighborhood's moral geography. Wallace Best argues: "More than any other religious institutional development, storefronts indicated that urban space—the streets themselves—would be contested space. Each time a storefront church was established, usually along the State and Federal streets corridor, the congregation demarked a bit of sacred space alongside commercial ventures, entertainment venues, and vice." See his *Passionately Human, No Less Divine*, 51.
57. *Chicago Defender*, October 12, 1912; Wood, *The Negro in Chicago*, 26.
58. *Chicago Defender*, October 12 and 19, 1912.
59. Harvey Warren Zorbaugh, *The Gold Coast and the Slum: A Sociological Study of Chicago's Near North Side* (Chicago: University of Chicago Press, 1929), 115–21. On prostitution in the rooming house district on LaSalle and Clark streets between the Chicago River and Chicago Avenue, see Kimball Young, "A Sociological Study of a Disintegrated Neighborhood" (PhD diss., University of Chicago, 1918). See also Joanne J. Meyerowitz, "Sexual Geography and Gender Economy: The Furnished Room Districts of Chicago, 1890–1930," in *Gender and American History since 1890*, ed. Barbara Melosh (New York: Routledge, 1993), 43–71.
60. On the dangers of dance halls, see Louise De Koven Bowen, *The Public Dance Halls of Chicago* (Chicago: Juvenile Protective Association, 1917); and Louise De Koven Bowen, *The Road to Destruction Made Easy in Chicago* (Chicago: Juvenile Protective Association, 1916).
61. *Indianapolis Freeman*, March 11, 1916.
62. *Chicago Whip*, December 16, 1922.
63. Ibid.
64. On black-and-tans in Chicago, see Kenney, *Chicago Jazz*, 16–17, 23–24; Mumford, *Interzones*, 30–33.
65. Kenney, *Chicago Jazz*, 15; Mumford, *Interzones*, 133–56.
66. Woods, *The Negro in Chicago*, 25; *Chicago Whip*, December 16, 1922.
67. *Indianapolis Freeman*, April 1, 1916.
68. *Chicago Whip*, December 23, 1922.
69. African American community leaders had long described the threat posed by the proximity of sexual commerce to the Black Belt in terms of dirt and disease. On September 13, 1913, the *Defender* complained, "What we consider a disgrace to the race in this city is the way that the unemployed, the dope fiends, the drunkards, the thieves, the gamblers, the pickpockets, the prostitute women and their lovers line 18th street. Unmolested by the police they lounge along the side walk to the disgust of all the decent people of this town. They need to be cleaned out and it is certainly up to the police department to do so. It is a living hell hole, a breeding spot of evil, a breeding spot for contagious diseases and filth."

70. Wood, *The Negro in Chicago*, 29.
71. *Indianapolis Freeman*, April 1, 1916.
72. On the community-based crusade against neighborhood resorts run by vice syndicates, see *Chicago Whip*, December 2 and 16, 1922.
73. *Chicago Defender*, May 17, 1919.
74. Michael Willrich, *City of Courts: Socializing Justice in Progressive Era Chicago* (Cambridge: Cambridge University Press, 2003), 121, 172–207.
75. *Chicago Defender*, May 12, 1917.

EPILOGUE

1. "Furnished Room, 2621 S. Dearborn Street, ground floor, north," April 28, 1923, folder 92, Juvenile Protective Association Papers, Special Collections, Richard M. Daley Library, University of Illinois at Chicago.
2. Between 1906 and 1930 police statistics for "offenses preferred before criminal and municipal courts" were organized according to gender, racial group, and country of birth. Tables E.1 and E.2 focus exclusively on women appearing in court for prostitution-related offenses. Although men were at times prominent among defendants charged with these offenses, I am primarily concerned with the criminalization of women. Tables E.1 and E.2 also concentrate exclusively on native-born white women and African American women. As these tables indicate, the vast majority of women appearing before criminal and municipal courts for prostitution-related offenses were "American" (white, native-born) women and "Colored" women.
3. Unlike the brothel, sex workers did not reside in call flats but used them for appointments. Because call flats did not openly advertise themselves as houses of prostitution, they were generally more difficult for police to detect. Call flat prostitution offered sex workers a greater degree of independence than did working in a brothel. Prostitutes were not dependent on a madam for their clientele and could arrange their work schedules around family life or other employment. See Clement, *Love for Sale*, 199.
4. Ruth Rosen, *Lost Sisterhood*, 30–33; Gilfoyle, *City of Eros*, 306–15.
5. Erenberg, *Steppin' Out*; Peiss, *Cheap Amusements*, esp. 108–13; Stansell, *City of Women*; Meyerowitz, *Women Adrift*. On changes in marital sexuality, see D'Emilio and Freedman, *Intimate Matters*, 240–41, 265–70.
6. Mumford, *Interzones*, 94, 202n4.
7. Spear, *Black Chicago*, 12; Grossman, *Land of Hope*.
8. Grossman, *Land of Hope*, 181.
9. Scott, *Occupational Changes*, 232, 235, 236–49; Gareth Canaan, "'Part of the Loaf': Economic Conditions of Chicago's African-American Working Class during the 1920s," *Journal of Social History* 35, no. 1 (Fall 2001): 147–74; Chicago Commission on Race Relations, *The Negro in Chicago*, 367–69, 370–72, 378–85.

10. Jones, *Labor of Love, Labor of Sorrow*, 161; Chicago Commission on Race Relations, *The Negro in Chicago*, 378–85.
11. Chicago Commission on Race Relations, *The Negro in Chicago*, 347.
12. A black community eventually formed on the West Side. See Grossman, *Land of Hope*, 123, 127; Arnold R. Hirsch, *Making the Second Ghetto: Race and Housing in Chicago, 1940–1960* (New York: Cambridge University Press, 1983), 4.
13. Spear, *Black Chicago*, 201–22; Philpott, *The Slum and the Ghetto*, 147–202.
14. Hirsch, *Making the Second Ghetto*, 4.
15. Chicago Commission on Race Relations, *The Negro in Chicago*, 343–44.
16. Reckless, *Vice in Chicago*, 194.
17. Paul Kinzie, "Commercialized Prostitution," December 10, 1922, folder 92, Juvenile Protective Association Papers, Special Collections, Richard M. Daley Library, University of Illinois at Chicago; Landesco, *Organized Crime in Chicago*, 25–43; Reckless, *Vice in Chicago*, 137–63, 192. On black organized crime, see Lombardo, "Black Mafia."
18. Reckless, *Vice in Chicago*, 137.
19. "Schiller Cabaret, 318 East 35th Street," December 3, 1922, folder 93, Juvenile Protective Association Papers, Special Collections, Richard M. Daley Library, University of Illinois at Chicago.
20. "Cabaret, Dreamland, 3520 S. State St.," April 28, 1923, folder 92, ibid.
21. "Cabaret, Lorraine Cabaret, 4116 S. State Street," November 27, 1922, folder 93, ibid.
22. Chad Heap, *Slumming: Sexual and Racial Encounters in American Nightlife, 1885–1940* (Chicago: University of Chicago Press, 2009), 189–230.
23. "Furnished room in flat, 2920 S. State Street," April 28, 1923, folder 92, Juvenile Protective Association Papers, Special Collections, Richard M. Daley Library, University of Illinois at Chicago.
24. See Lauren Rabinovitz, *For the Love of Pleasure: Women, Movies, and Culture in Turn-of-the-Century Chicago* (New Brunswick, NJ: Rutgers University Press, 1998).
25. Lucille Bogan, "They Ain't Walking No More," March 1930, Chicago, Brunswick 7163. Later in the year, Bogan recorded "Tricks Ain't Walking No More," a slightly different version of the same song (December 1930, Chicago, Brunswick 7186).

Bibliography

Archives and Collections

Carter G. Woodson Regional Library, Chicago Public Library.
Vivian Harsh Collection, Illinois Writers' Project, "The Negro in Illinois."

Chicago Historical Society, Chicago. Clifford Barnes Papers; Irene McCoy Gaines Collection.

Circuit Court of Cook County Archives, Richard J. Daley Center, Chicago. Records of the Chicago Criminal Court (microfilm).

Illinois Regional Archives Depository, Ronald Williams Library, Northeastern Illinois University, Chicago. Chicago City Council Proceedings Files.

National Archives and Records Administration—Great Lakes Region (Chicago). District Courts of the United States. General Records. Record Group 21.

University of Chicago, Joseph Regenstein Library, Special Collections, Chicago. Chicago Committee of Fifteen Papers.

University of Illinois at Chicago, Richard M. Daley Library, Chicago. Juvenile Protective Association Papers; Sanborn Fire Insurance Maps of Chicago, 1910 (microfilm).

Government Documents

City of Chicago. *The Charter and Ordinances of the City of Chicago.* Chicago, 1856.

———. *The Municipal Code of Chicago, 1881.* Chicago: n.p., 1881.

———. *Police Department of the City of Chicago, Annual Report, 1906.* Chicago: n.p., 1906.

———. *Police Department of the City of Chicago, Annual Report, 1912.* Chicago: n.p., 1912.

————. *Police Department of the City of Chicago, Annual Report, 1914*. Chicago: n.p., 1914.

————. *Police Department of the City of Chicago, Annual Report, 1916*. Chicago: n.p., 1916.

————. *Police Department of the City of Chicago, Annual Report, 1920*. Chicago: n.p., 1920.

————. *Police Department of the City of Chicago, Annual Report, 1922*. Chicago: n.p., 1922.

————. *Police Department of the City of Chicago, Annual Report, 1924*. Chicago: n.p., 1924.

————. *Police Department of the City of Chicago, Annual Report, 1928*. Chicago: n.p., 1928.

————. *Police Department of the City of Chicago, Annual Report, 1930*. Chicago: n.p., 1930.

————. *Report of the General Superintendent of Police of the City of Chicago to the City Council, 1904*. Chicago: n.p., 1904.

————. *Report of the General Superintendent of Police of the City of Chicago to the City Council, 1906*. Chicago: n.p., 1906.

————. *Report of the General Superintendent of Police of the City of Chicago to the City Council, 1908*. Chicago: n.p., 1908.

————. *The Revised Municipal Code of Chicago of 1905*. Chicago: n.p., 1905.

Illinois General Assembly, Senate Vice Committee. *Report of the Senate Vice Committee*. Chicago: n.p., 1916.

U.S. Bureau of the Census. *Eighth Census of the United States, 1860. Compendium.*

————. *Eighth Census of the United States, 1860. Population.*

————. *Eleventh Census of the United States, 1890. Compendium*, pt. 1, *Population.*

————. *Eleventh Census of the United States, 1890.* Vol. 15, *Population*, pt. 1.

————. *Negro Population, 1790–1915*. Washington, DC: GPO, 1918.

————. *Ninth Census of the United States, 1870.* Vol. 1, *Population.*

————. *Seventh Census of the United States, 1850: Population.*

————. Tenth Census (1880). Chicago Manuscript Schedules (microfilm).

————. Thirteenth Census (1910). Chicago Manuscript Schedules (microfilm).

————. *Thirteenth Census of the United States, 1910.* Vol. 2, *Population*, pt. 1.

————. Twelfth Census (1900). Chicago Manuscript Schedules (microfilm).

————. *Twelfth Census of the United States, 1900.* Vol. 2, *Population*, pt. 1.

Newspapers and Periodicals

Chicago Broad Ax

Chicago Conservator

Chicago Daily Democratic Press

Chicago Daily Journal

Chicago Daily News

Chicago Defender
Chicago Evening Journal
Chicago Morning News
Chicago Record-Herald
Chicago Times
Chicago Tribune
Chicago Whip
Crisis
Indianapolis Freeman
Minneapolis Western Appeal
Portland (OR) Advocate
Record Changer

Recordings

Bogan, Lucille. "They Ain't Walking No More," March 1930, Chicago. Brunswick 7163.
———. "Tricks Ain't Walking No More," December 1930, Chicago. Brunswick
7186.
Hill, Bertha "Chippie." "Street Walker Blues," June 15, 1926, Chicago. Okeh
8437.

Books, Articles, and Unpublished Manuscripts

Abbott, Edith. *The Tenements of Chicago, 1908–1935*. Chicago: University of
Chicago Press, 1936.
Addams, Jane. *A New Conscience and an Ancient Evil*. New York: Macmillan Co.,
1912.
Albert, Alexa. *Brothel: Mustang Ranch and Its Women*. New York: Random House,
2001.
Albertson, Chris. *Bessie*. New York: Stein and Day, 1972.
Allen, Irving Lewis. *The City in Slang: New York Life and Popular Speech*. New York:
Oxford University Press, 1993.
Anderson, Eric. "Prostitution and Social Justice: Chicago, 1910–15." *Social Service
Review* 48, no. 2 (1974): 203–28.
Andreas, A. T. *History of Chicago*. Vol. 2. Chicago: A. T. Andreas Co., 1885.
Asbury, Herbert. *Gem of the Prairie: An Informal History of the Chicago Underworld*.
New York: Alfred A. Knopf, 1940. Reprint, Dekalb: Northern Illinois Univer-
sity Press, 1986.
Baldwin, Davarian L. *Chicago's New Negroes: Modernity, the Great Migration,
and Black Urban Life*. Chapel Hill: University of North Carolina Press,
2007.

Barber, E. Susan. "Depraved and Abandoned Women: Prostitution in Richmond, Virginia, across the Civil War." In *Neither Lady nor Slave: Working Women of the Old South*, edited by Susanna Delfino and Michele Gillespie, 155–73. Chapel Hill: University of North Carolina Press, 2002.

Barnes, Clifford W. "The Story of the Committee of Fifteen of Chicago." *Social Hygiene* 4, no. 2 (April 1918): 145–56.

Barth, Gunther. *City People: The Rise of Modern City Culture in Nineteenth-Century America*. New York: Oxford University Press, 1980.

Bederman, Gail. *Manliness and Civilization: A Cultural History of Gender and Race in the United States, 1880–1917*. Chicago: University of Chicago Press, 1995.

Bell, Ernest A. *Fighting the Traffic in Young Girls*. Chicago: n.p., 1910.

Bernheimer, Charles. *Figures of Ill Repute: Representing Prostitution in Nineteenth-Century France*. Cambridge, MA: Harvard University Press, 1989.

Bernstein, Laurie. *Sonia's Daughters: Prostitutes and Their Regulation in Imperial Russia*. Berkeley and Los Angeles: University of California Press, 1995.

Best, Wallace. *Passionately Human, No Less Divine: Religion and Culture in Black Chicago, 1915–1952*. Princeton, NJ: Princeton University Press, 2007.

Blackmar, Elizabeth. *Manhattan for Rent, 1785–1850*. Ithaca, NY: Cornell University Press, 1991.

Blight, David. "'For Something beyond the Battlefield': Frederick Douglass and the Struggle for the Memory of the Civil War." *Journal of American History* 75 (March 1989): 1156–78.

Borchert, James. *Alley Life in Washington: Family, Community, Religion and Folklife in the City, 1850–1970*. Urbana: University of Illinois Press, 1980.

Boris, Eileen. "Black Women and Paid Labor in the Home: Industrial Homework in Chicago in the 1920s." In *Homework: Historical and Contemporary Perspectives on Paid Labor at Home*, edited by Eileen Boris and Cynthia R. Daniels, 33–52. Urbana: University of Illinois Press, 1989.

Bowen, Louise De Koven. *The Colored People of Chicago: An Investigation Made for the Juvenile Protective Association*. Chicago: Juvenile Protective Association, 1913.

———. *The Public Dance Halls of Chicago*. Chicago: Juvenile Protective Association, 1917.

———. *The Road to Destruction Made Easy in Chicago*. Chicago: Juvenile Protective Association, 1916.

Boyer, Paul. *Urban Masses and Moral Order in America, 1820–1920*. Cambridge, MA: Harvard University Press, 1978.

Bradford, Perry. *Born with the Blues: Perry Bradford's Own Story*. New York: Oak Publications, 1965.

Brandt, Allan M. *No Magic Bullet: A Social History of Venereal Disease in the United States since 1880*. New York: Oxford University Press, 1985.

Branham, Charles. "Black Chicago: Accommodationist Politics before the Great Migration." In *Ethnic Chicago: A Multicultural Portrait*, edited by

Melvin G. Holli and Peter d'A. Jones, 211–62. Grand Rapids, MI: William B. Eerdmans Publishing Co., 1984.

Brantlinger, Patrick. "Victorians and Africans: The Genealogy of the Myth of the Dark Continent." In *"Race," Writing, and Difference*, edited by Henry Louis Gates Jr., 185–222. Chicago: University of Chicago Press, 1986.

Breckinridge, Sophonisba P., and Edith Abbott. "Chicago's Housing Problem: Families in Furnished Rooms." *American Journal of Sociology* 16, no. 3 (November 1910): 289–308.

Bricktop. *Bricktop*. With James Haskins. New York: Atheneum, 1983.

Brodie, Fawn M. *The Devil Drives: A Life of Sir Richard Burton*. New York: W. W. Norton and Co., 1967.

Brown, Elsa Barkley, and Gregg D. Kimball. "Mapping the Terrain of Black Richmond." In *The New African American Urban History*, edited by Kenneth W. Goings and Raymond A. Mohl, 66–115. Thousand Oaks, CA: Sage Publications, 1996.

Brown, Kathleen M. *Good Wives, Nasty Wenches, and Anxious Patriarchs: Gender, Race, and Power in Colonial Virginia*. Chapel Hill: University of North Carolina Press, 1996.

Burton, Jean. *Sir Richard Burton's Wife*. New York: Alfred A. Knopf, 1941.

Butler, Anne M. *Daughters of Joy, Sisters of Mercy: Prostitutes in the American West, 1865–90*. Urbana: University of Illinois Press, 1985.

Canaan, Gareth. "'Part of the Loaf': Economic Conditions of Chicago's African-American Working Class during the 1920s." *Journal of Social History* 35, no. 1 (Fall 2001): 147–74.

Carbine, Mary. "'The Finest Outside the Loop': Motion Picture Exhibition in Chicago's Black Metropolis, 1905–1928." *Camera Obscura* 23 (May 1990): 9–41.

Carby, Hazel. "Policing the Black Woman's Body in an Urban Context." *Critical Inquiry* 18 (Summer 1992): 738–55.

Castells, Manuel, and Alejandro Portes. "World Underneath: The Origins, Dynamics, and Effects of the Informal Economy." In *The Informal Economy: Studies in Advanced and Less Developed Countries*, edited by Alejandro Portes, Manuel Castells, and Lauren A. Benton, 11–37. Baltimore, MD: Johns Hopkins University Press, 1989.

Chamberlin, Everett. *Chicago and Its Suburbs*. Chicago: T. A. Hungerford and Co., 1874.

Chauncey, George. *Gay New York: Gender, Urban Culture, and the Making of the Gay Male World, 1890–1940*. New York: Basic Books, 1994.

Chicago Coalition for the Homeless. "Unlocking Options for Women: A Survey of Women in Cook County Jail." Chicago, 2002.

Chicago Commission on Race Relations. *The Negro in Chicago: A Study of Race Relations and a Race Riot*. Chicago: University of Chicago Press, 1922. Reprint, New York: Arno Press and the New York Times, 1968.

Chicago South Side Club. *Survey of the Conditions Demoralizing to Women and Girls in the Saloons of Chicago*. Chicago, 1913.

Clark-Lewis, Elizabeth. *Living In, Living Out: African American Domestics in Washington, D.C., 1910–1940*. New York: Kodansha International, 1996.

Clement, Elizabeth Alice. *Love for Sale: Courting, Treating, and Prostitution in New York City, 1900–1945*. Chapel Hill: University of North Carolina Press, 2006.

Clinton, Catherine. "'With a Whip in His Hand': Rape, Memory, and African American Women." In *History and Memory in African-American Culture*, edited by Genevieve Fabre and Robert O'Meally, 205–18. New York: Oxford University Press, 1994.

Cohen, Cathy J. *Boundaries of Blackness: AIDS and the Breakdown of Black Politics*. Chicago: University of Chicago Press, 1999.

Cohen, Lizabeth. *Making a New Deal: Industrial Workers in Chicago, 1919–1939*. Cambridge: Cambridge University Press, 1990.

Colbert, Elias, and Everett Chamberlin. *Chicago and the Great Conflagration*. New York: Viking Press, 1871.

Collins, Mary. *Oh, Didn't He Ramble: The Life Story of Lee Collins*. Urbana: University of Illinois Press, 1989.

Committee of Fifteen (New York City). *The Social Evil*. New York: Putnam, 1900.

Comstock, Alzada P. "Chicago Housing Conditions, VI: The Problem of the Negro." *American Journal of Sociology* 18, no. 2 (September 1912): 241–57.

Connelly, Mark Thomas. *The Response to Prostitution in the Progressive Era*. Chapel Hill: University of North Carolina Press, 1980.

Cook, Frederick Francis. *Bygone Days in Chicago: Recollections of the "Garden City" of the Sixties*. Chicago: A. C. McClurg and Co., 1910.

Curon, L. O. *Chicago, Satan's Sanctum*. Chicago: C. D. Phillips and Co., 1899.

Curry, Leonard P. *The Free Black in Urban America, 1800–1850: The Shadow of the Dream*. Chicago: University of Chicago Press, 1981.

Dance, Stanley. *The World of Earl Hines*. New York: Charles Scribner's Sons, 1977.

Davis, Angela. *Blues Legacies and Black Feminism: Gertrude "Ma" Rainey, Bessie Smith, and Billie Holiday*. New York: Vintage Books, 1998.

———. *Women, Race, and Class*. New York: Random House, 1981.

Davis, Elizabeth Lindsay. *Lifting as They Climb*. N.p.: National Association of Colored Women, n.d.

———. *The Story of the Illinois Federation of Colored Women's Clubs, 1900–1922*. N.p., 1922.

Davis, Ralph Nelson. "The Negro Newspaper in Chicago." MA thesis, University of Chicago, 1939.

de Certeau, Michel. *The Practice of Everyday Life*. Translated by Steven Rendall. Berkeley and Los Angeles: University of California Press, 1984.

Dedmon, Emmett. *Fabulous Chicago*. New York: Random House, 1953.

D'Emilio, John, and Estelle B. Freedman. *Intimate Matters: A History of Sexuality in America*. New York: Harper and Row, 1988.

Drake, St. Clair. *Churches and Voluntary Associations in the Chicago Negro Community*. Chicago: Illinois Works Projects Administration, 1940.

Drake, St. Clair, and Horace R. Cayton. *Black Metropolis: A Study of Negro Life in a Northern City*. New York: Harcourt, Brace and Co., 1945. Reprint, Chicago: University of Chicago Press, 1993.

DuBois, W. E. B. *The Philadelphia Negro: A Social Study*. Philadelphia: University of Pennsylvania Press, 1899. Reprint, Philadelphia: University of Pennsylvania Press, 1996.

———. *Some Efforts of American Negroes for Their Own Social Betterment*. Atlanta, GA: Atlanta University Press, 1898.

Duis, Perry R. *Challenging Chicago: Coping with Everyday Life, 1837–1920*. Urbana: University of Illinois Press, 1998.

———. *The Saloon: Public Drinking in Chicago and Boston, 1880–1920*. Urbana: University of Illinois Press, 1983.

Eastman, John C. "Village Life at the World's Fair." *The Chautauquan* 17, no. 5 (August 1893): 602–4.

Eaton, Isabel. "Special Report on Negro Domestic Service in the Seventh Ward." In *The Philadelphia Negro: A Social Study*, by W. E. B. DuBois, 426–509. Philadelphia: University of Pennsylvania Press, 1899. Reprint, Philadelphia: University of Pennsylvania Press, 1996.

Einhorn, Robin L. *Property Rules: Political Economy in Chicago, 1833–1872*. Chicago: University of Chicago Press, 1991.

Erenberg, Lewis A. "Ain't We Got Fun." *Chicago History* 14, no. 4 (Winter 1985–86): 4–21.

———. *Steppin' Out: New York Nightlife and the Transformation of American Culture, 1890–1930*. Chicago: University of Chicago Press, 1981.

Fabian, Ann. *Card Sharps, Dream Books, and Bucket Shops: Gambling in 19th-Century America*. Ithaca, NY: Cornell University Press, 1990.

Fisher, Miles Mark. "The History of Olivet Baptist Church of Chicago." MA thesis, Graduate Divinity School, University of Chicago, 1922.

Flinn, John J. *The Best Things to Be Seen at the World's Fair*. Chicago: Columbia Guide Co., 1893.

———. *Chicago: The Marvelous City of the West*. Chicago: National Book and Picture Co., 1893.

———. *History of the Chicago Police*. Chicago: Chicago Police Fund, 1887. Reprint, Montclair, NJ: Patterson Smith, 1973.

Gerber, David A. *Black Ohio and the Color Line, 1860–1915*. Urbana: University of Illinois Press, 1976.

Gibson, Mary. *Prostitution and the State in Italy, 1860–1915*. New Brunswick, NJ: Rutgers University Press, 1986.

Gilfoyle, Timothy J. *City of Eros: New York City, Prostitution, and the Commercialization of Sex, 1790–1920*. New York: W. W. Norton and Co., 1992.

———. "Prostitutes in History: From Parables of Pornography to Metaphors of Modernity." *American Historical Review* 104, no. 1 (February 1999): 117–41.

———. "Prostitutes in the Archives: Problems and Possibilities in Document-ing the History of Sexuality." *American Archivist* 57, no. 3 (Summer 1994): 514–27.

Gilmore, Al-Tony. "Jack Johnson and White Women: The National Impact, 1912–1913." *Journal of Negro History* 58, no. 1 (January 1973): 18–22.

Goldberg, David Theo. *Racist Culture: Philosophy and Politics of Meaning.* Cam-bridge, MA: Blackwell, 1994.

Goldman, Marion S. *Gold Diggers and Silver Miners: Prostitution and Social Life on the Comstock Lode.* Ann Arbor: University of Michigan Press, 1981.

Gosnell, Harold F. *Negro Politicians: The Rise of Negro Politics in Chicago.* Chicago: University of Chicago Press, 1935.

Gottlieb, Peter. *Making Their Own Way: Southern Blacks' Migration to Pittsburgh, 1916–30.* Urbana: University of Illinois Press, 1987.

Graham, Sandra Lauderdale. *House and Street: The Domestic World of Servant and Masters in Nineteenth-Century Rio de Janeiro.* Cambridge: Cambridge Univer-sity Press, 1988.

Greene, Lorenzo J., and Carter G. Woodson. *The Negro Wage Earner.* Washington, DC: Association for Negro Life and History, 1930.

Gross, Kali N. *Colored Amazons: Crime, Violence, and Black Women in the City of Brotherly Love, 1880–1910.* Durham, NC: Duke University Press, 2006.

Grossman, James R. *Land of Hope: Chicago, Black Southerners, and the Great Migra-tion.* Chicago: University of Chicago Press, 1989.

Groth, Paul. *Living Downtown: The History of Residential Hotels in the United States.* Berkeley and Los Angeles: University of California Press, 1994.

Guy, Donna J. *Sex and Danger in Buenos Aires: Prostitution, Family, and Nation in Argentina.* Lincoln: University of Nebraska Press, 1991.

Hall, Jacqueline Dowd. "'The Mind That Burns in Each Body': Women, Rape, and Racial Violence." In *Powers of Desire: The Politics of Sexuality,* edited by Ann Snitow, Christine Stansell, and Sharon Thompson, 328–49. New York: Monthly Review Press, 1983.

Haller, Mark H. "Illegal Enterprise: A Theoretical and Historical Interpretation." *Criminology* 28, no. 2 (1990): 207–35.

———. "Policy Gambling, Entertainment, and the Emergence of Black Politics: Chicago from 1900 to 1940." *Journal of Social History* 24, no. 4 (Summer 1991): 719–40.

Halpin, T. M., comp. *Halpin's Eighth Annual Edition of the Chicago City Directory, 1865–1866.* Chicago: T. M. Halpin, 1865.

Hammond, Dorothy, and Alta Jablow. *The Africa That Never Was: Four Centuries of British Writing about Africa.* New York: Twayne Publishers, 1970.

Hammonds, Evelynn M. "Toward a Genealogy of Black Female Sexuality: The Problematic of Silence." In *Feminist Genealogies, Colonial Legacies, Demo-cratic Futures,* edited by Chandra Talpade Mohanty and M. Jacqui Alexan-der, 170–82. New York: Routledge, 1997.

Harding, Philip, and Richard Jenkins. *The Myth of the Hidden Economy: Towards a New Understanding of Informal Economic Activity*. Philadelphia: Open University Press, 1989.

Harland, Robert O. *The Vice Bondage of a Great City, or The Wickedest City in the World*. Chicago: Young People's Civic League, 1912.

Harley, Sharon. "'Working for Nothing but for a Living': Black Women in the Underground Economy." In *Sister Circle: Black Women and Work*, edited by Sharon Harley and Black Women and Work Collective, 48–66. New Brunswick, NJ: Rutgers University Press, 2002.

Harris, I. C. *Colored Men's Professional and Business Directory of Chicago*. Chicago: I. C. Harris, 1885.

Harris, Michael. *The Rise of the Gospel Blues: The Music of Thomas Andrew Dorsey in the Urban Church*. New York: Oxford University Press, 1992.

Harrison, Carter H. *Stormy Years: The Autobiography of Carter H. Harrison, Five Times Mayor of Chicago*. New York: Bobbs-Merrill Co., 1935.

Harrison, Daphne Duval. *Black Pearls: Blues Queens of the 1920s*. New Brunswick, NJ: Rutgers University Press, 1988.

Hayden, Dolores. *The Power of Place: Urban Landscapes as Public History*. Cambridge, MA: MIT Press, 1995.

Hazzard-Gordon, Katrina. *Jookin': The Rise of Social Dance in African-American Culture*. Philadelphia: Temple University Press, 1990.

Heap, Chad. *Slumming: Sexual and Racial Encounters in American Nightlife, 1885–1940*. Chicago: University of Chicago Press, 2009.

Hendricks, Wanda Ann. "The Politics of Race: Black Women in Chicago, 1890–1920." PhD diss., Purdue University, 1990.

Hershatter, Gail. *Dangerous Pleasures: Prostitution and Modernity in Twentieth-Century Shanghai*. Berkeley and Los Angeles: University of California Press, 1997.

Higginbotham, Evelyn Brooks. "Rethinking Vernacular Culture: Black Religion and Race Records in the 1920s and 1930s." In *The House That Race Built: Black Americans, U.S. Terrain*, edited by Wahneema Lubiano, 157–77. New York: Pantheon Books, 1997.

———. *Righteous Discontent: The Women's Movement in the Black Baptist Church, 1880–1920*. Cambridge, MA: Harvard University Press, 1993.

Hill, Marilynn Wood. *Their Sisters' Keepers: Prostitution in New York City, 1830–1870*. Berkeley and Los Angeles: University of California Press, 1993.

Hine, Darlene Clark. "Black Migration to the Urban Midwest: The Gender Dimension, 1915–1945." In *The Great Migration in Historical Perspective: New Dimensions of Race, Class, and Gender*, edited by Joe William Trotter Jr., 127–46. Bloomington: Indiana University Press, 1991.

———. "Rape and the Inner Lives of Black Women in the Middle West: Preliminary Thoughts on the Culture of Dissemblance." *Signs: Journal of Women and Culture in Society* 14 (Summer 1989): 912–20.

Hirata, Lucie Cheng. "Free, Indentured, Enslaved: Chinese Prostitutes in Nineteenth-Century America." *Signs: Journal of Women and Culture in Society* 5 (Autumn 1979): 3–29.

Hirsch, Arnold R. *Making the Second Ghetto: Race and Housing in Chicago, 1940–1960.* New York: Cambridge University Press, 1983.

Hobson, Barbara Meil. *Uneasy Virtue: The Politics of Prostitution and the American Reform Tradition.* New York: Basic Books, 1987.

Hodes, Martha, ed. *Sex, Love, Race: Crossing Boundaries in North American History.* New York: New York University Press, 1999.

———. *White Women, Black Men: Illicit Sex in the Nineteenth-Century South.* New Haven, CT: Yale University Press, 1997.

Holli, Melvin G., and Peter d'A. Jones, eds. *Ethnic Chicago: A Multicultural Portrait.* Grand Rapids, MI: William B. Eerdmans Publishing Co., 1984.

Hoyt, Homer. *One Hundred Years of Land Values in Chicago: The Relationship of the Growth of Chicago to the Rise in Its Land Values, 1830–1933.* Chicago: University of Chicago Press, 1933.

Hunter, Jane Edna. *A Nickel and a Prayer.* Cleveland, OH: Elli Kani Publishing Co., 1940.

Hunter, Tera. *"To 'Joy My Freedom": Southern Black Women's Lives and Labors after the Civil War.* Cambridge, MA: Harvard University Press, 1997.

James, George Wharton. *Chicago's Dark Places.* Chicago: Craig Press and Women's Temperance Publishing Association, 1891.

Jiménez, José Blanes. "Cocaine, Informality, and the Urban Economy in La Paz, Bolivia." In *The Informal Economy: Studies in Advanced and Less Developed Countries,* edited by Alejandro Portes, Manuel Castells, and Lauren A. Benton, 135–49. Baltimore, MD: Johns Hopkins University Press, 1989.

Johnson, Claudia D. "That Guilty Third Tier: Prostitution in Nineteenth-Century Theaters." *American Quarterly* 27, no. 5 (December 1975): 575–584.

Johnson, Earl Shepard. "The Natural History of the Central Business District with Particular Reference to Chicago." PhD diss., University of Chicago, 1944.

Johnson, Jack. *The Autobiography of Jack Johnson: In the Ring and Out.* Chicago: National Sports Press, 1927.

Jones, Jacqueline. *Labor of Love, Labor of Sorrow: Black Women, Work and the Family from Slavery to the Present.* New York: Vintage Books, 1985.

Karras, Ruth Mazo. *Common Women: Prostitution and Sexuality in Medieval England.* New York: Oxford University Press, 1996.

Katzman, David M. *Before the Ghetto: Black Detroit in the Nineteenth Century.* Urbana: University of Illinois Press, 1975.

———. *Seven Days a Week: Women and Domestic Service in Industrializing America.* New York: Oxford University Press, 1978.

Keire, Mara L. "The Vice Trust: A Reinterpretation of the White Slavery Scare in the United States, 1907–1917." *Journal of Social History* 35, no. 1 (2001): 5–41.

Kellor, Frances. "Assisted Emigration from the South: The Women." *Charities* 15, no. 1 (October 7, 1905): 11–14.

———. "Southern Colored Girls in the North." *Charities* 13, no. 25 (March 18, 1905): 584–85.

Kenney, William Howland. *Chicago Jazz: A Cultural History, 1904–1930.* New York: Oxford University Press, 1993.

Kirkland, Joseph. "Among the Poor of Chicago." In *The Poor in Great Cities,* edited by Robert Woods et al., 195–239. New York: Charles Scribner's Sons, 1895. Reprint, New York: Arno Press, 1971.

———. *The Story of Chicago.* 2d ed. Chicago: Dibble Publishing Co., 1892.

Knupfer, Anne Meis. *Toward a Tenderer Humanity and a Nobler Womanhood: African American Women's Clubs in Turn-of-the-Century Chicago.* New York: New York University Press, 1996.

Kusmer, Kenneth L. *A Ghetto Takes Shape: Black Cleveland, 1870–1930.* Urbana: University of Illinois Press, 1976.

Lakeside Annual Directory of the City of Chicago. Chicago: Chicago Directory Co., 1879–1915.

Landesco, John. *Organized Crime in Chicago.* Pt. 3, *Illinois Crime Survey.* Chicago: Illinois Association for Criminal Justice, 1929.

Lane, Roger. *Roots of Violence in Black Philadelphia, 1860–1900.* Cambridge, MA: Harvard University Press, 1986.

Langum, David J. *Crossing of the Line: Legislating Morality and the Mann Act.* Chicago: University of Chicago Press, 1994.

Larson, T. A. *History of Wyoming.* 2d ed. Lincoln: University of Nebraska Press, 1978.

Leach, William. *Land of Desire: Merchants, Power, and the Rise of a New American Culture.* New York: Pantheon Books, 1993.

Lemann, Nicholas. *Promised Land: The Great Migration and How It Changed America.* New York: Vintage Books, 1991.

Lemke-Santangelo, Gretchen. *Abiding Courage: African American Migrant Women and the East Bay Community.* Chapel Hill: University of North Carolina Press, 1996.

Lewis, Earl. "Afro-American Adaptive Strategies: The Visiting Habits of Kith and Kin among Black Norfolkians." *Journal of Family History* 12, no. 4 (1987): 407–20.

———. "Connecting Memory, Self, and the Power of Place in African American History." In *The New African American Urban History,* edited by Kenneth W. Goings and Raymond A. Mohl, 116–41. Thousand Oaks, CA: Sage Publications, 1996.

———. *In Their Own Interests: Race, Class, and Power in Twentieth-Century Norfolk, Virginia.* Berkeley and Los Angeles: University of California Press, 1991.

Lewis, Lloyd, and Henry Justin Smith. *Chicago: The History of Its Reputation.* New York: Harcourt, Brace and Co., 1929.

Lindberg, Richard C. *To Serve and Collect: Chicago Politics and Police Corruption from the Lager Beer Riot to the Summerdale Scandal.* New York: Praeger, 1991.

Lofland, Lyn. *A World of Strangers: Order and Action in Urban Public Space.* Prospect Heights, IL: Waveland Press, 1973.

Lombardo, Robert M. "The Black Mafia: African-American Organized Crime in Chicago, 1890–1960." *Crime, Law, and Social Change* 38, no. 1 (July 2002): 33–65.

Long, Alecia P. *The Great Southern Babylon: Sex, Race, and Respectability in New Orleans, 1865–1920.* Baton Rouge: Louisiana State University Press, 2004.

Longstreet, Stephen. *Chicago: 1860–1919.* New York: David McKay Co., 1973.

Lott, Eric. *Love and Theft: Blackface Minstrelsy and the American Working Class.* New York: Oxford University Press, 1993.

Lubiano, Wahneema, ed. *The House That Race Built: Black Americans, U.S. Terrain.* New York: Pantheon Books, 1997.

Luzerne, Frank. *The Lost City! Drama and the Fire-Fiend.* New York: Wells and Co., 1872.

Mackey, Thomas C. *Red Lights Out: A Legal History of Prostitution, Disorderly Houses and Vice Districts, 1870–1917.* New York: Garland, 1987.

Maloka, Tshidiso. "*Khomo Lia Oela*: Canteens, Brothels and Labour Migrancy in Colonial Lesotho, 1900–40." *Journal of African History* 38 (1997): 101–22.

Mayer, Harold M., and Richard C. Wade. *Chicago: Growth of a Metropolis.* Chicago: University of Chicago Press, 1969.

McCarthy, Kathleen D. *Noblesse Oblige: Charity and Cultural Philanthropy in Chicago, 1849–1929.* Chicago: University of Chicago Press, 1982.

McDowell, Edward D. "The World's Fair Cosmopolis." *Frank Leslie's Popular Monthly* 36, no. 4 (October 1893): 415.

McKee, Margaret, and Fred Chisenhall. *Beale Black and Blue: Life and Music on Black America's Main Street.* Baton Rouge: Louisiana State University Press, 1981.

Melendy, Royal. "The Saloon in Chicago." *American Journal of Sociology* 6, no. 3 (November 1900): 289–306.

Meyerowitz, Joanne J. "Sexual Geography and Gender Economy: The Furnished Room Districts of Chicago, 1890–1930." In *Gender and American History since 1890*, edited by Barbara Melosh, 43–71. New York: Routledge, 1993.

———. *Women Adrift: Independent Wage Earners in Chicago, 1880–1930.* Chicago: University of Chicago Press, 1988.

Midway Types: A Book of Illustrated Lessons about the People of the Midway Plaisance. Chicago: Engraving Co., 1893.

Miller, Donald. *City of the Century: The Epic of Chicago and the Making of America.* New York: Simon and Schuster, 1996.

Miller, Kelly. "Surplus Negro Women." In *Race Adjustment: Essays on the Negro in America*, 168–78. New York: Neale Publishing Co., 1908.

Miller, P. E., and R. Venables, eds. *Esquire's 1946 Jazz Book.* New York: A. S. Barnes, 1946.

Mitchell, Michele. "Silences Broken, Silences Kept: Gender and Sexuality in African-American History." *Gender and History* 11, no. 3 (1999): 433–44.

Morton, Patricia. *Disfigured Images: The Historical Assault on Afro-American Women.* Westport, CT: Praeger, 1991.

Mumford, Kevin J. *Interzones: Black/White Sex Districts in Chicago and New York in the Early Twentieth Century.* New York: Columbia University Press, 1997.

Myrdal, Gunnar. *An American Dilemma: The Negro Problem and Modern Democracy.* New York: Harper and Bros., 1944.

Nasaw, David. *Going Out: The Rise and Fall of Public Amusements.* Cambridge, MA: Harvard University Press, 1993.

The New Grove Dictionary of Jazz. New York: Macmillan, 1988.

Nostwich, T. D., ed. *Theodore Dreiser: Journalism.* Vol. 1, *Newspaper Writing, 1892–1895.* Philadelphia: University of Pennsylvania Press, 1988.

Odem, Mary E. *Delinquent Daughters: Protecting and Policing Adolescent Female Sexuality in the United States, 1885–1920.* Chapel Hill: University of North Carolina Press, 1996.

Osofsky, Gilbert. *Harlem: The Making of a Ghetto.* New York: Harper and Row, 1966.

Peiss, Kathy. *Cheap Amusements: Working Women and Leisure in Turn-of-the-Century New York.* Philadelphia: Temple University Press, 1986.

———. *Hope in a Jar: The Making of America's Beauty Culture.* New York: Metropolitan Books, 1998.

Petrik, Paula. "Capitalists with Rooms: Prostitution in Helena, Montana, 1865–1900." *Montana: The Magazine of Western History* 21, no. 2 (Spring 1991): 28–40.

Philpott, Thomas Lee. *The Slum and the Ghetto: Immigrants, Blacks, and Reformers in Chicago, 1880–1930.* New York: Oxford University Press, 1978.

Pierce, Bessie Louise. *A History of Chicago.* Vol. 1, *The Beginning of a City, 1673–1848.* Chicago: University of Chicago Press, 1937.

———. *A History of Chicago.* Vol. 2, *From Town to City, 1848–1871.* New York: Alfred A. Knopf, 1940.

———. *A History of Chicago.* Vol. 3, *The Rise of the Modern City, 1871–1893.* New York: Alfred A. Knopf, 1957.

Portes, Alejandro, Manuel Castells, and Lauren A. Benton, eds. *The Informal Economy: Studies in Advanced and Less Developed Countries.* Baltimore, MD: Johns Hopkins University Press, 1989.

Rabinovitz, Lauren. *For the Love of Pleasure: Women, Movies, and Culture in Turn-of-the-Century Chicago.* New Brunswick, NJ: Rutgers University Press, 1998.

Ramsey, Frederick, Jr., and Charles Edward Smith, eds. *Jazzmen.* New York: Harcourt, Brace and Co., 1939.

Raphael, Jody. *Listening to Olivia: Violence, Poverty, and Prostitution.* Boston: Northeastern University Press, 2004.

Reckless, Walter. "The Natural History of Vice Areas in Chicago." PhD diss., University of Chicago, 1925.

———. *Vice in Chicago*. Chicago: University of Chicago Press, 1933.

Reed, Christopher Robert. *"All the World Is Here!": The Black Presence at White City*. Bloomington: Indiana University Press, 2000.

———. *Black Chicago's First Century: 1833–1900*. Columbia: University of Missouri Press, 2005.

Residents of Hull House. *Hull House Maps and Papers: A Presentation of Nationalities and Wages in a Congested District of Chicago*. New York: Thomas Y. Crowell and Co., 1895.

Rhea, H. W. *Rhea's New Citizens' Directory of Chicago, Ill.* Chicago: W. S. McCleland, 1908.

Rice, Edward. *Captain Sir Richard Burton: The Secret Agent Who Made the Pilgrimage to Mecca, Discovered the Kama Sutra, and Brought the Arabian Nights to the West*. New York: Scribner's, 1990.

Rice, Wallace, Paul Thomas, and Caroline Margaret McIlvaine. *Chicago and Its Makers*. Chicago: F. Mendelsohn, 1929.

Roberts, Bryan. "The Informal Sector in Comparative Perspective." In *Perspectives on the Informal Economy*, edited by M. Estellie Smith, 23–48. New York: University Press of America, 1990.

Roberts, Kimberly. "The Clothes Make the Woman: The Symbolics of Prostitution in Nella Larsen's *Quicksand* and Claude McKay's *Home to Harlem*." *Tulsa Studies in Women's Literature* 16, no. 1 (Spring 1997): 107–30.

Roberts, Randy. *Papa Jack: Jack Johnson and the Era of White Hopes*. New York: Free Press, 1983.

Rose, Al. *Storyville, New Orleans: Being an Authentic, Illustrated Account of the Notorious Red-Light District*. Tuscaloosa: University of Alabama Press, 1974.

Rosen, Christine Meisner. *The Limits of Power: Great Fires and the Process of City Growth in America*. Cambridge: Cambridge University Press, 1986.

Rosen, Hannah. "'Not That Sort of Women': Race, Gender, and Sexual Violence during the Memphis Riot of 1866." In *Sex, Love, Race: Crossing Boundaries in North American History*, edited by Martha Hodes, 267–93. New York: New York University Press, 1999.

Rosen, Ruth. *The Lost Sisterhood: Prostitution in America, 1900–1918*. Baltimore, MD: Johns Hopkins University Press, 1982.

Rosenzweig, Roy. *Eight Hours for What We Will: Workers and Leisure in an Industrial City, 1870–1920*. Cambridge: Cambridge University Press, 1983.

Rowe, Mike. *Chicago Blues: The City and the Music*. New York: Da Capo Press, 1975.

Russell, William. "Boogie Woogie." In *Jazzmen*, edited by Frederick Ramsey Jr. and Charles Edward Smith, 183–205. New York: Harcourt, Brace and Co., 1939.

Ryan, Mary P. *Cradle of the Middle Class: The Family in Oneida County, New York*. New York: Cambridge University Press, 1981.

———. *Women in Public: Between Banners and Ballots, 1825–1880*. Baltimore, MD: Johns Hopkins University Press, 1990.

Rydell, Robert W. "The World's Columbian Exposition of 1893: Racist Underpinnings of a Utopian Artifact." *Journal of American Culture* 1, no. 2 (Summer 1978): 253–75.

Salem, Dorothy. *To Better Our World: Black Women in Organized Reform, 1890–1920*. Brooklyn: Carlson, 1990.

Sampson, Henry T. *Blacks in Blackface: A Source Book on Early Black Musical Shows*. Metuchen, NJ: Scarecrow Press, 1980.

———. *The Ghost Walks: A Chronological History of Blacks in Show Business, 1865–1910*. Metuchen, NJ: Scarecrow Press, 1988.

Sawislak, Karen. *Smoldering City: Chicagoans and the Great Fire, 1871–1874*. Chicago: University of Chicago Press, 1995.

Schick, Louis. *Chicago and Its Environs*. Chicago: Louis Schick, 1893.

Schneider, John C. *Detroit and the Problem of Order, 1830–1880*. Lincoln: University of Nebraska Press, 1980.

Scott, Estelle Hill. *Occupational Changes among Negroes in Chicago*. Chicago: Works Progress Administration, 1939.

Shaw, Stephanie. *What a Woman Ought to Be and to Do: Black Professional Women Workers during the Jim Crow Era*. Chicago: University of Chicago Press, 1996.

Shumsky, Neil Larry. "Tacit Acceptance: Respectable Americans and Segregated Prostitution, 1870–1910." *Journal of Social History* 19, no. 4 (1986): 665–79.

Shumsky, Neil Larry, and Larry M. Springer. "San Francisco's Zone of Prostitution, 1880–1934." *Journal of Historical Geography* 7 (January 1981): 71–89.

Simmons, Alexy. *Red Light Ladies: Settlement Patterns and Material Culture on the Mining Frontier*. Anthropology Northwest, no. 4. Corvallis: Department of Anthropology, Oregon State University, 1989.

Smith, Alson J. *Chicago's Left Bank*. Chicago: Henry Regnery Co., 1953.

Smith, Carl. *Urban Disorder and the Shape of Belief: The Great Chicago Fire, the Haymarket Bomb, and the Model Town of Pullman*. Chicago: University of Chicago Press, 1995.

Smith, M. Estellie. "Introduction." In *Perspectives on the Informal Economy*. edited by M. Estellie Smith, 1–22. New York: University Press of America, 1990.

———, ed. *Perspectives on the Informal Economy*. New York: University Press of America, 1990.

Smith, Willie "the Lion." *Music on My Mind: The Memoirs of an American Pianist*. With George Hoefer. Garden City, NY: Doubleday and Co., 1964.

Smith-Rosenberg, Carroll. *Disorderly Conduct: Visions of Gender in Victorian America*. New York: Oxford University Press, 1985.

Snider, Denton J. *World's Fair Studies*. Chicago: Sigma Publishing Co., 1895.

Spear, Allan H. *Black Chicago: The Making of a Negro Ghetto, 1890–1920*. Chicago: University of Chicago Press, 1967.

The Sporting and Club House Directory. Chicago: Ross and St. Clair Publishing, 1889.

The Standard Guide to Chicago. Chicago: Standard Guide Co., 1893.

Stansell, Christine. *City of Women: Sex and Class in New York, 1789–1860.* Urbana: University of Illinois Press, 1987.

Stead, William T. *If Christ Came to Chicago.* Chicago: Laird and Lee, 1894. Reprint, Evanston, IL: Chicago Historical Society Bookworks, 1990.

Steiner, John, and Charles A. Sengstock. "A Survey of the Chicago *Defender* and the Chicago *Whip;* Covering the Years 1909 through 1930 with Respect to the Development of Jazz Music in Chicago." Chicago: n.p., 1966.

Stevenson, Brenda. *Life in Black and White: Family and Community in the Slave South.* New York: Oxford University Press, 1996.

Sugrue, Thomas J. *The Origins of the Urban Crisis: Race and Inequality in Postwar Detroit.* Princeton, NJ: Princeton University Press, 1996.

Symanski, Richard. *The Immoral Landscape: Female Prostitution in Western Societies.* Toronto: Butterworths, 1981.

Tan, P. L. "Belt Railroads of Chicago." MS thesis, University of Chicago, 1931.

Taylor, Frank C. *Alberta Hunter: A Celebration in Blues.* New York: McGraw-Hill, 1987.

Taylor, Graham. "The Story of the Chicago Vice Commission." *Survey* 6 (May 1911): 239–47.

Thomas, J. J. *Surviving in the City: The Urban Informal Sector in Latin America.* London: Pluto Press, 1995.

Tokman, Victor E., ed. *Beyond Regulation: The Informal Economy in Latin America.* Boulder, CO: Lynne Rienner Publishers, 1992.

———. "The Informal Sector in Latin America: From Underground to Legality." In *Beyond Regulation: The Informal Economy in Latin America,* edited by Victor E. Tokman, 3–20. Boulder, CO: Lynne Rienner Publishers, 1992.

Tong, Benson. *Unsubmissive Women: Chinese Prostitutes in Nineteenth-Century San Francisco.* Norman: University of Oklahoma Press, 1994.

Travis, Dempsey J. *An Autobiography of Black Chicago.* Chicago: Urban Research Institute, 1981.

———. *An Autobiography of Black Jazz.* Chicago: Urban Research Institute, 1983.

———. *An Autobiography of Black Politics.* Chicago: Urban Research Institute, 1987.

Trotter, Joe William, Jr. *Black Milwaukee: The Making of an Industrial Proletariat, 1915–1945.* Urbana: University of Illinois Press, 1985.

———, ed. *The Great Migration in Historical Perspective: New Dimensions of Race, Class, and Gender.* Bloomington: University of Indiana Press, 1991.

Turner, George Kibbe. "The City of Chicago: A Study of the Great Immoralities." *McClure's Magazine* 28, no. 6 (April 1907): 575–92.

Valverde, Mariana. "The Love of Finery: Fashion and the Fallen Woman in Nineteenth-Century Social Discourse." *Victorian Studies* 32 (Winter 1989): 169–88.

Venkatesh, Sudhir Alladi. *Off the Books: The Underground Economy of the Urban Poor.* Cambridge, MA: Harvard University Press, 2006.

Vice Commission of Chicago. *The Social Evil in Chicago: A Study of Existing Conditions with Recommendations*. Chicago: Gunthorp-Warren, 1911.

Voegeli, V. Jacque. *Free but Not Equal: The Midwest and the Negro during the Civil War*. Chicago: University of Chicago Press, 1967.

Vynne, Harold. *Chicago by Day and Night: The Pleasure Seeker's Guide to the Paris of America*. Chicago: Thomson and Zimmerman, 1892.

Walkowitz, Judith R. *City of Dreadful Delight: Narratives of Sexual Danger in Late-Victorian London*. Chicago: University of Chicago Press, 1992.

———. *Prostitution and Victorian Society: Women, Class and the State*. New York: Cambridge University Press, 1980.

Waller, Gregory. *Main Street Amusements: Movies and Commercial Entertainment in a Southern City, 1896–1930*. Washington, DC: Smithsonian Institution Press, 1995.

Warner, Sam Bass, Jr. *The Private City: Philadelphia in Three Periods of Its Growth*. Philadelphia: University of Pennsylvania Press, 1968.

———. *Streetcar Suburbs: The Process of Growth in Boston, 1870–1900*. Cambridge, MA: Harvard University Press and MIT Press, 1962.

Warren, James Francis. *Ah Ku and Karayuki-san: Prostitution in Singapore, 1870–1940*. Oxford: Oxford University Press, 1993.

Washburn, Charles. *Come into My Parlor: A Biography of the Aristocratic Everleigh Sisters of Chicago*. New York: National Library Press, 1936.

Washington Intercollegiate Club of Chicago. *Book of Negro Achievement Featuring the Negro in Chicago, 1779–1929*. Chicago, 1929.

Waters, Ethel. *His Eye Is on the Sparrow: An Autobiography*. With Charles Samuels. New York: Doubleday, 1951.

Wells, Ida B., et al. *The Reasons Why the Colored American Is Not in the World's Columbian Exposition*. Edited by Robert W. Rydell. Urbana: University of Illinois Press, 1999.

Wendt, Lloyd, and Herman Kogan. *Lords of the Levee: The Story of Bathhouse John and Hinky Dink*. Indianapolis: Bobbs-Merrill Co., 1943.

Wentworth, Harold, and Stuart Berg Flexner, eds. *Dictionary of American Slang*. New York: Crowell, 1960; 2d supp. ed., 1975.

White, Deborah Gray. *Ar'n't I a Woman? Female Slaves in the Plantation South*. New York: W. W. Norton and Co., 1985.

———. *Too Heavy a Load: Black Women in Defense of Themselves, 1894–1994*. New York: W. W. Norton and Co., 1999.

White, Luise. *The Comforts of Home: Prostitution in Colonial Nairobi*. Chicago: University of Chicago Press, 1990.

Wiebe, Robert H. *The Search for Order, 1877–1920*. New York: Hill and Wang, 1967.

Williams, Fannie Barrier. "The Need of Social Settlement Work for the City Negro." *Southern Workman* 33, no. 9 (September 1904): 501–6.

Willrich, Michael. *City of Courts: Socializing Justice in Progressive Era Chicago*. Cambridge: Cambridge University Press, 2003.

Wolcott, Victoria W. "Bible, Bath, and Broom: Nannie Helen Burroughs's National Training School and African-American Racial Uplift." *Journal of Women's History* 9, no. 1 (Spring): 88–110.

———. "The Culture of the Informal Economy: Numbers Runners in Inter-war Black Detroit." *Radical History Review*, no. 69 (Fall 1997): 46–75.

———. *Remaking Respectability: African American Women in Interwar Detroit*. Chapel Hill: University of North Carolina Press, 2001.

Wood, Junius B. *The Negro in Chicago*. Chicago: Chicago Daily News, 1916.

Woods, Robert, et al., eds. *The Poor in Great Cities*. New York: Charles Scribner's Sons, 1895. Reprint, New York: Arno Press, 1971.

Wooldridge, Clifton R. *Hands Up! In the World of Crime*. Chicago: Police Publishing Co., 1901.

———. *Hands Up! In the World of Crime*. Chicago: Thompson and Thomas, 1901.

———. *Hands Up! In the World of Crime*. Chicago: Stanton and Van Vliet Co., 1901.

Work, Monroe Nathan. "Negro Real Estate Holders of Chicago." MA thesis, University of Chicago, 1903.

Wright, Gwendolyn. *Moralism and the Model Home: Domestic Architecture and Cultural Conflict in Chicago, 1873–1913*. Chicago: University of Chicago Press, 1980.

Wright, Richard R., Jr. "The Industrial Condition of Negroes in Chicago." BD thesis, University of Chicago Divinity School, 1901.

———. "The Migration of Negroes to the North." *Annals of the Academy of Political and Social Science* 27 (January–June 1906): 559–78.

Writers' Program of the Works Projects Administration, Wyoming. *Wyoming: A Guide to Its History, Highways, and People*. Wyoming: Works Projects Administration, 1941. Reprint, Lincoln: University of Nebraska Press, 1981.

Young, Kimball. "A Sociological Study of a Disintegrated Neighborhood." PhD diss., University of Chicago, 1918.

Zorbaugh, Harvey Warren. *The Gold Coast and the Slum: A Sociological Study of Chicago's Near North Side*. Chicago: University of Chicago Press, 1929.

Index

Abbott, Robert, 210
Addams, Jane, 248n20
Adelphi variety theater, 111
Adler, Jake "Jakie," 137
after-hours clubs, 205; and commercialization of leisure, 11,
16, 160, 166–72, 175–77, 180,
185. *See also* cabarets; saloons;
taverns; *specific club name(s)*
African American men. *See* black
men
African American women. *See* black
women
ages, of brothel prostitutes, 35, 39
alcohol: bootleg, 176, 244n11; and
gender, 156–59; public drinking
in establishments, 167, 171–72,
178, 183; sale of, 24, 162, 176;
women and children deliver-
ing, 158. *See also* Prohibition;
saloons
Alexander, Edward, 200
Allen, Frankie, 207–8
Allen, Irving Lewis, 262n19
Allen, Lizzie, 82–83, 129, 249n22,
260n77
Amanda Smith Home, 203
Amazonian black women, 93,
94–106. *See also* Dahomeans
Annex, 130
Anti-Crime League, 174
anti-prostitution reform, 5–6,
208–9, 212, 220, 284n4; and
leisure culture, 165; and urban
sex economy, 136–37, 143, 147

anti-vice reform, 5–6, 8, 15–17,
233, 271n30, 284n4; and leisure
culture, 183; and spatial boundaries, 96; strategies, 187–222;
and urban sex economy, 131,
143–44, 146; and wage work, 36
Archer, Allie, 43
archives and collections, 291
Asbury, Herbert, 95, 137–38, 139,
264n48, 273n56, 273n59
assignation houses, 69–70, 114,
125, 129, 248n22, 269n16; and
anti-vice reform, 216, 219–20;
and commercialization of
leisure, 180, 181, 184
Atchison, Topeka, and Santa Fe
Railroad Company, 84

Bachelor Buffet, 170
backwardness, 87, 121, 188
Bad Lands, 73, 93, 96–97, 102, 105,
258n49. *See also* Levee
Baker, Adams, 44
Baker, Georgia, 183
Baker, Judge, 262–63n31
Barland, Napoleon, 75, 259n63
Barnett, Ferdinand L., 107, 118,
120–21, 267n83
Beasley, William, 115, 162
beauty parlors, 247n16. *See also*
hair salons and hairdressing
Belle Meade Club, 170
Bengal Tigress, 95–97, 99, 106
Benson, John F., 116
Bently, Anna, 144

179; rooming-house district, 287n58; vice district, 129

Odd Fellows, 110
Olivet Baptist Church, 108, 119, 274n1
Olson, Harry, Chief Justice, 220
Olympic Theatre, 110
O'Neill, Francis, Police Chief, 129
oppression: and defeat, 9–10; and power, 9; sexual, 242n20, 257n44
Owens, John, 75

Paine, Jennie "Ginger Heel," 76–77
Palace Sample Room, 116
Palace Theater, 164, 168
Panama Club, 171
pandering, 183, 279–80n57
panel houses, 52, 60–61, 73–79, 81, 85, 258n53
Parker, Bell, 73
Parker, Irene, 37
Parker, Mollie, 61
Park Theatre, 112–13
parlor houses, 50, 51–52, 57, 60–70, 79, 81–82, 232, 255n16, 255n19; and leisure culture, 161–62; and spatial boundaries, 91–93, 95, 106, 108; and urban sex economy, 130, 133, 135; and wage work, 43–46
patriarchy, 26, 211
Peiss, Kathy, 7–8, 174
Pekin Inn, 154
Pekin Temple of Music, 154
Pekin Theatre, 154–56, 162–64, 171–72, 276n11
People's Theatre, 112
periodicals and newspapers, 292–93. See also specific titles
Perry, Dora, 78
perverted sex behavior, 143
Philadelphia Negro, The (DuBois), 7, 243n6, 267n83
Phillips, Sally, 44
Phyllis Wheatley Home, 202–3
Phyllis Wheatley Women's Club, 203
pimps, 10, 55, 90, 165–66, 177, 183, 234, 279n47
Plymouth Place, 57, 61, 82, 84, 125
police graft, 137–38, 280n69
police harassment, 2, 48, 140, 144–46, 165, 231–33. See also unlawful invasions

politics, racial, 3
pool, 24, 44, 46, 57, 61, 68, 108, 116, 145, 173–74, 277n17, 277n19. See also billiards
popular culture, 276n7, 276n11. See also leisure culture
porters, 21, 43, 44, 53, 56, 66, 123, 161, 176
post-emancipation, 10–11, 14, 25
power, and oppression, 9
pregnancy, 48, 189, 191, 194, 200–201
Proctor, James, 44
Progressive Era reform, 6, 9, 15, 26
Prohibition, 138, 178, 281n85. See also alcohol
prostitutes and prostitution: ages of, 35, 39; causes of, 204–5; and commercialization of leisure, 149–86; criminalization of, 17, 223–27, 233, 284n4, 288n2; demographics of, 14, 28–32, 35; disorderly, 93; for economic independence, 26–39; as forced choice for black women, 10–11; independent, 16, 233; as label, 20; as means of capital accumulation for women, 239–40n4; nativity of, 8, 21, 28–32, 53, 55, 89, 128, 224–25, 253, 288n2; residential, 175–84, 185; silences about, 6–12, 56, 194, 210–11, 214, 220; as social evil, 6, 8, 15, 36, 90, 136, 146, 212, 219, 271n30; and spatial boundaries, 94–106; as symbolic issue, 3, 6, 16; trafficking of, 120; unregimented, 233–34; urban, 5–6, 9–10; as victimization, 3–4; voices of, 9, 12–14, 17, 236; as wage work, 43–45; working the economy, 50–85. See also black women; houses of prostitution; sex work; wage work; white women

Queen Solace, 174
Quinn Chapel African Methodist Episcopal (A.M.E.), 108, 274n1

race: and respectability, spatial boundaries of, 14–15, 86–122; and sex economy, 45–47; and sexuality, 9, 52; and urban sex economy, reconstruction of, 15, 123–48; and wage work, 45–47. See also nativity
Race Relations Commission. See Commission on Race Relations
racial equality, 218

racial lines. *See* color lines
racial order, 14, 86, 222. *See also* social order
racial politics, 3
racial purity, white, 121, 235
racial-sexual hierarchy, 47, 52, 92, 143, 236
racial subordination, 67
ragtime, 276n11
Ralston, Fannie, Mrs., 202
Ranier Buffet and Cabaret, 270n57
Rapp, A., 73
Reckless, Walter, 233, 268n6
Rector, T. S., 117
red-light districts, 1, 6, 13, 15, 65, 71,
    226–27, 250n35; and anti-vice reform,
    212–16; closing of, 6, 184–85, 212,
    271n66, 273–74n66; and commercial-
    ization of leisure, 151, 163–64, 172,
    177–79, 184–85; urban, 2–4; and urban
    sex economy, 124, 127, 129, 131–33,
    136, 138, 140, 146–47; and wage work,
    19, 33–34
Redmond, Susan, 135
reform. *See* anti-prostitution reform; anti-
    vice reform; moral reform; Progressive
    Era reform; social reform
residential prostitution, 175–84, 185. *See
    also* buffet flats
resorts, 16, 17, 50–52, 55–57, 60, 63, 65–68,
    70, 73–74, 77–81, 83–84, 228–29,
    232, 234, 260n80, 271n32, 273n59,
    288n71; advertisements for, 277n16;
    and anti-vice reform, 202, 204, 216–17;
    and commercialization of leisure, 151,
    153, 156, 159, 161–63, 165, 170–76,
    178, 180–81, 184, 186; gentlemen's,
    116–17; map, 231; and spatial boundar-
    ies, 90–94, 97, 106, 114–16; and urban
    sex economy, 127–30, 133–35, 137–38,
    140–41, 143–46; and wage work, 23–24.
    See also disorderly resorts; *specific resort
    name(s)*
respectability, 3, 7, 10–11, 13, 67–68; and
    employment of women, 205; middle-
    class discourses of, 187–88; and race,
    spatial boundaries of, 14–15, 86–122; of
    white men, 211–12
Richardson, Lillian, 42, 46, 62, 65–68,
    81–82
Ritchie, Emma, 60, 82–83, 129, 260n80
robbery. *See* theft and thievery
Robinson, C. E., 84, 261n85

rooming houses, 233–34, 248n22, 256n41,
    268–69n12, 283n103, 283n105,
    287n58; and anti-vice reform, 215; and
    commercialization of leisure, 157, 172,
    176, 177, 180–84, 185; and prostitution
    economy, 55, 70; and spatial bound-
    aries, 97; and wage work, 26, 38
Rosen, Ruth, 7–8, 165, 247n19
Ross, Minnie, 83
Rundell, William, 75
Russell, Sylvester, 175

saloons, 11, 70, 151, 232, 266n68, 277n17,
    277n19, 277n22; and anti-vice reform,
    215; and commercialization of leisure,
    156–59, 180, 184, 185; and gambling,
    159–66; and spatial boundaries, 115,
    117. *See also* after-hours clubs; cabarets;
    disorderly saloons; gambling; taverns;
    specific saloon name(s)
sample rooms, 115–16, 118, 156
Sampson, Henry, 276n11
Samuels, Allen, 183
Sanborn Fire Insurance Maps, 12
Sanders, D. W., 274
Sante Fe Railroad, 125
Sappho Club, 131, 137
Schick, Louis, 257–58n45
Schiller Cabaret, 233–34, 289n19
Schreiber, Belle, 193–94, 201
Scott, Andrew J., 117, 135–36
Scott, Daniel, 115–17, 266n81–82
Scott and Stanton's Pool Room and Billiard
    Hall, 174
segregation, 269n19; as insult, 111; and
    moral spaces, 107; racial, 5, 13, 52,
    107, 111, 113, 228–29; residential, 2–3,
    122; in vice districts, 53, 129, 182–83,
    212–15, 265n52
self-reliance, 11–12
self-respect, 3, 11, 48–49
self-sufficiency, 52
self-willed, 69
servants, 4, 243n5, 244n8, 251n46–47,
    256n37, 260n77, 264n50; and anti-
    vice reform, 196–97; and prostitution
    economy, 53, 55, 58, 66, 69; and wage
    work, 21–22, 38, 43–44
servitude, 38, 66, 209
sewing skills, 24, 246–47n15. *See also*
    dressmaking

Lightning Source UK Ltd.
Milton Keynes UK
UKHW011826100919
349541UK00003B/223/P

9 780226 597584